Management and higher education since 1940

Management and higher education since 1940

The influence of America and Japan on West Germany, Great Britain, and France

Robert R. Locke
European Institute for Advanced Studies in Management, Brussels
University of Hawaii, Manoa

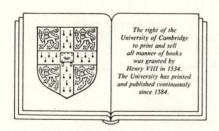

The right of the
University of Cambridge
to print and sell
all manner of books
was granted by
Henry VIII in 1534.
The University has printed
and published continuously
since 1584.

Cambridge University Press
Cambridge
New York   New Rochelle   Melbourne   Sydney

Published by the Press Syndicate of the University of Cambridge
The Pitt Building, Trumpington Street, Cambridge CB2 1RP
32 East 57th Street, New York, NY 10022, USA
10 Stamford Road, Oakleigh, Melbourne 3166, Australia

First published 1989

Printed in the United States of America

Library of Congress Cataloging-in-Publication Data

Locke, Robert R., 1932–

Management and higher education since 1940 : the influence of
America and Japan on West Germany, Great Britain, and France /
Robert R. Locke.

p.   cm.

Bibliography: p.

Includes index.

ISBN 0-521-34102-7 hard covers

1. Management – Study and teaching (Higher) – Germany (West)
2. Management – Study and teaching (Higher) – France.
3. Management – Study and teaching (Higher) – Great Britain.
4. Management – Study and teaching (Higher) – United States.
5. Management – Study and teaching (Higher) – Japan. I. Title.
HD30.42.G39L63 1989
658'.007'114 – dc19   88-37094
                                                                CIP

British Library Cataloguing in Publication Data

Locke, Robert R. 1932–

Management and higher education since 1940:
the influence of America and Japan on West
Germany, Great Britain, and France

1. Higher education institutions. Curriculum
subjects. Business studies, 1940–1988
I. Title
658'.007'11

ISBN 0-521-34102-7 hard covers

To my mother, Katharine Locke, who because of a terrible illness cannot understand what her son has done but would be proud of the doing

'Tis with our judgements as our watches, none
Go just alike, yet each believes his own.
 – Alexander Pope, *An Essay on Criticism*

Contents

Figures and tables

Figures

Tables

Preface

I should like to do two things in this Preface: (1) say a few words about the scope of the study, and (2) acknowledge my debt to those who have helped me in its preparation.

I have subtitled the book *The influence of America and Japan on West Germany, Great Britain, and France.* When I started work seven years ago no such thoughts were in my mind. I originally set out to write a book about West Germany, Great Britain, and France. This book is primarily about these three countries. Nonetheless, as the research proceeded it became impossible to overlook the Americans and the Japanese. Both have, at different times, set the pace in management thought and practice, and both have raised questions, important ones, about business studies and higher education since the Second World War.

This does not mean that the European experience is understood as some sort of reflection of foreign influence. The Alexander Pope quotation is apt: "None / Go just alike." If the American and Japanese influences have been great, they have had to be woven into the fabric of national traditions and the results in each case are unique. Still, I have incorporated so much of the American and Japanese experience into the book that I have ended up putting the two countries in the title.

Nobody writes a book, especially a scholarly one, without the help of numerous individuals and institutions. I am indebted especially to the European Institute for Advanced Studies in Management (E.I.A.S.M.) for appointing me (1982–84) to its Esso European Chair, created by a generous grant from that corporation. I had no idea when I accepted the appointment what a rich and rewarding experience those two years would be, for they permitted me to associate on a regular basis with nonhistorians. Everybody should spend some time with people in another field because it helps so much to understand his own. This book could not have been written without that stay. Therefore, I must thank two people in particular for making it possible: Professor Philippe Naert, then director of E.I.A.S.M. (currently Dean at the Institut Européen d'Administration des Affaires [I.N.S.E.A.D.]), and Professor Herman Daems, then deputy director of E.I.A.S.M. (currently at the Harvard Graduate School of Business Administration). The full support they gave me during my tenure, sometimes under very trying circumstances, is much appreciated.

Two people at the London School of Economics and Political Science must be thanked for the assistance rendered on research and publication: Professors Leslie Hannah of the Department of Economic History, and Anthony Hopwood of the Department of Accounting and Finance. During months spent in the Business History Unit, Professor Hannah and his colleagues, especially Dr. Jonathan Liebenau and Dr. Richard Davenport-Hines, made my stay both agreeable and intellectually profitable.

I should also like to express my appreciation to the Fulbright people for the financial assistance provided for a nine-month stay in 1986 and to The Spencer Foundation of Chicago for the remaining three months of the year. Their generous aid gave me the time to finish research and to write most of the manuscript. And the Department of History at the University of Hawaii has kindly granted the leave necessary to pursue all these tasks.

It is impossible, of course, to thank all the others who have given so generously of their time. The list would be quite long and the provider would risk committing injury to some inadvertently ignored. By way of exception, I would like, however, to express my thanks to two people for their constructive criticisms. One is Professor Leslie Hannah, whose comments have helped improve the sections on Great Britain; the other is Marc Meuleau, of the Banque Indo-Suez, whose critique has helped with the French. The reader will get some idea how many other people have had a hand in the making of the book by consulting footnotes and bibliography.

Finally, I need to thank those who have helped in the preparation of the manuscript. To Patricia Locke I owe a special debt. She has helped from beginning to end. To Vanessa Locke Sedighi and to Sally Hughes I am grateful for the sharp-eyed diligence with which every manuscript must be treated to be a success. And I am obliged to Susan Abe for typing diagrams and tables. I alone, of course, am responsible for the result.

ROBERT LOCKE

Honolulu
May 1988

1. The new paradigm

This chapter and the next introduce the subject of the book and, at the same time, constitute an important part of the subject. The subject matter is the new paradigm in business studies, the application of science to the solution of managerial problems, which became a focus of higher education after the Second World War.[1] That application, which is integral to the story of business education, is explained. The discussion of the new paradigm, however, also introduces the book because it clarifies and justifies the specific approach to management education taken here. Every scholar has an approach and usually it reflects the peculiarities of his or her training. I am no exception. As a historian I bring the special perspective and research methods of my craft to the task. Possession, however, does not in itself warrant use. For the historian's approach to be justified it must shed new light on business education. Indeed, the methodologies of the new paradigm were themselves touted for their superiority over those they replaced, including, of course, historical method.[2] The exposition, then, not only lays out the new paradigm in business studies, but, taking issue with the scientific view, shows why the methodologies that constitute the new science-based paradigm are themselves insufficient to explain its growth and why the historian's approach, followed in subsequent chapters, offers a promising form of explanation.

It is important, therefore, to stress at the outset that this essay, if historically based, is not an exercise in antiquarianism. The book does

1 Although an old Greek word which means pattern, model, example, exemplar – *paradigm* has come to signify a logical or conceptual structure serving as a form of scientific thought, within a given area of experience, that provides model problems and model solutions to a scientific community. In this book, however, the term loses such scientific rigor. It simply means the set of assumptions, which can and have changed, upon which people base their study of management.
2 See Richard Roehl, "French Industrialization: A Reconsideration," *Explorations in Economic History* 13:3 (July 1976): 233–81; Donald N. McCloskey, "The Achievements of the Cliometric School," *The Journal of Economic History* 38 (1978): 13–28.

address subjects in which historians have been and are deeply inter-ested. It in fact projects arguments about comparative economic perfor-mance developed for an earlier period in a previous work (*The End of the Practical Man: Entrepreneurship and Higher Education in Ger-many, France, and Great Britain, 1880 to 1940*) into the post–Second World War world.[3] Contemporary business management education need not have anything to do with what happened in 1900 or 1930. The business conditions could have, and have, changed considerably, thereby making solutions to past problems inapplicable to current problems. For those interested in present problems and for those try-ing to anticipate future ones, studying the recent history of business management education could be a waste of time.

If the historian is not necessarily preoccupied with explaining current problems uniquely as a product of the past, history is not irrelevant to today's problems. Problems have, or can have, cultural configurations that are deeply embedded in the history of each country. Historical methods can produce a book as much for those interested in the present and the future of management education as for those interested in the past, for its usefulness to the former is not in the way it elucidates past events but in the way it shows how contemporaries carry around in their heads ideas, values, and attitudes inherited from the past that shape the education of managers in various countries. The following analysis of the new paradigm in business studies, therefore, emphasizes to those whose interest in history is at best minimal (and who have dismissed it as largely irrelevant) the importance of a historical methodology precisely because of its relevance to comprehending contemporary problems.

The new paradigm

Figure 1.1, which is used throughout to explain the new paradigm in business studies, shows that the formal sciences are self-contained in that they do not have to refer to either social or physical reality for verification. Rather they are involved in the introspective process of establishing rules of behavior deductively. The diagram thus distin-guishes the formal from the empirical sciences which must deal with physical and social realities. The empirical sciences are themselves divided into theoretical (pure) and practical (applied) branches, the

3 Greenwich, Conn., 1984.

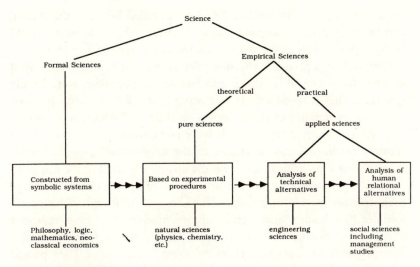

Figure 1.1. <u>Science schema</u>

Source: Adapted from a diagram in Peter Ulrich and Peter Hill, "Wissenschaftstheoretische Aspekte ausgewählter betriebswirtschaftlicher Konzeptionen," in *Wissenschaftstheoretische Grundfragen der Wirtschaftswissenschaften,* by Hans Raffée and Bodo Abel, 163; my translation.

latter being separated into technical and human relations subgroups. The arrows between the boxes indicate that the sciences to the left influence those to the right. The relationships indicated hardly describe all the relationships that actually exist between sciences. Arrows could be drawn to show movement to the left, formal sciences being influenced by natural sciences and natural sciences by applied. Or arrows could be drawn to show interrelationships between sciences within groups, for example, between logic and mathematics or chemical and electrical engineering. The diagram does not represent all relationships but simply illustrates the nature of the new paradigm in business studies.

If this is the new paradigm, then what was the old? Actually, that too can be shown with reference to the diagram, for its arrows are conditioned by time. If a chart were drawn for different dates, the arrows on each would diminish in number the farther the period represented receded into the past. The arrows of interest here, those between the sciences and management, would disappear first, followed by the arrows between the theoretical sciences and engineering, the epoch for disappearance depending on the kind of engineering involved (e.g., mechanical engineering sooner than civil). Finally, at a certain point, no relationship could be signaled between the formal and the pure and the applied sciences. There, where the chart would really be meaningless, we would find the old paradigm.

It was, then, a period without applied science. Still, people employed in what we now call technical and business occupations were hardly ignorant. They learned a craft that was a body of skills built up by the collective experience of practitioners on the job. But they were practical men and women whose skills were not informed by science. Such training traditions can be traced to the apprenticeship-journeyman-master craftsman educational process institutionalized in the old guild system. Nonetheless, practical training was not just a characteristic of preindustrial modes of production. The son of Joseph Whitworth, founder of a leading nineteenth-century machine tool firm, reported that in his company "all our engineers have come up from the ranks. They entered here about age fourteen on the average. They passed through all the workshops. They learned all the techniques with their own hands. As for their scientific instruction – nothing but what they could learn in night school."[4] Nor was this practicality just a phenomenon of the technical world, for the office apprentice was as much a fixture of the merchant house as the workshop apprentice was of the manufacturing firm.

On-the-job training did not exclude the possibility of some formal education. There were technical and commercial schools of varying quality in most industrializing countries under the old paradigm. But these schools, which taught mechanical and commercial skills currently in praxis, had very little to do with science. As educational institutions, moreover, they stood in marked contrast to the universities that traditionally had nothing but the greatest disdain for this vocationalism. The disdain obviously was somewhat hypocritical because priests, lawyers, and medical doctors had been trained in universities for centuries. Universities were always places where people prepared for an occupation. The strictures against vocationalism applied, then, to technical and commercially related forms of education. That is why Oxford University refused to admit accounting into its curriculum. Universities were, according to the conventional wisdom, motivated by a higher disinterested desire to seek the truth. They positively

4 Quoted in Max Leclerc, *La Formation des ingénieurs à l'étranger et en France* (Paris, 1917); my translation.

prided themselves on their lack of practicality. Pure science, not applied, was their raison d'être.

Consequently, a great gap existed between higher education and vocational training. The gap, moreover, was hard to fill, for it was not a question of finding an existing bridge between theory and practice, one that had been shrouded in a fog of haughty academic prejudice, but of building a bridge between the two. People who established business schools in institutions of higher education quickly learned this lesson for there was, at the outset, no discipline to teach. Science-based management had to be invented. At Wharton, the first business school (1880), Steven Sass notes "pioneer business professors . . . had found most of their curricular material in the business world, not in the universities (in science). Despite their energy and enthusiasm, their scholarship had essentially been an extended form of business journalism."[5] The heavy reliance on business for teaching material offended academic sensibilities. Sass observed of the neoclassical-oriented economists at Wharton, "As a group the school's economists of [the interwar] period had been cool to the practical descriptive thrust of Wharton's business programs and had had little interest in managerial arts and sciences that were taught in those parts of the school."[6] Traditionally academic subjects were included in the early business school curriculum (chemistry, physics, economics). But, inasmuch as they were not developed with the problems of business in mind, these subjects had no obvious relevance to the subject matter taught in the practical courses (accounting, finance, sales, etc.). The business school program itself, therefore, initially and for a long time, reflected the gap between science and vocationalism which characterized the old paradigm in business training.

All the complex connections cannot be colored into the diagram. But some of the significant arrows can be sketched in to show the development from the old paradigm in business studies to the new. The place to begin is with the formal sciences on the left of the diagram and in them with mathematics, for mathematics is the most significant and pervasive scientific tool of modern times.[7] Before it could achieve

---

5 Steven A. Sass, *The Pragmatic Imagination: A History of the Wharton School, 1881–1981* (Philadelphia, 1982), 268.
6 Ibid., 270–71.
7 What follows is extremely elementary for the mathematically informed. It is included in order to make clear to the generally educated but nonmathematically knowledgeable reader how mathematics shaped the new paradigm in management studies.

this utility, however, mathematics had to undergo significant transformation. The history of the discipline can, in fact, be divided into a premodern and a modern era. The early history runs from the ancient Egyptian and Babylonian civilizations up to the nineteenth century, the second, that of the so-called era of modern mathematics, from about 1800 to the present. "During the earlier epoch," W. W. Sawyer states, "men thought about mathematics exclusively in terms of the things with which it dealt; geometry was about shapes, arithmetic was about numbers and algebra was about the relations and properties of numbers in general (as expressed by arbitrary symbols, usually letters of the alphabet)."[8] Early in the last century two ideas introduced into mathematical reasoning brought about fundamental change.

First came a realization that mathematics was not concerned exclusively with numbers and shapes, the prenineteenth-century idea, but that it could "deal with anything (although anything often continued to be related in some way to numbers and shapes)."[9] Second, the idea emerged that mathematics need have no relationship to anything in particular, that "carrying the process of abstraction further, mathematics could be regarded essentially as 'logical procedures.' "[10] Sawyer, an algebraist, went on to point out how "scientists, as distinct from mathematicians, are attracted to the first idea; it suggests that mathematics may have a much wider sphere of application than had ever been imagined. The second idea appeals more to pure mathematicians, who have come to regard mathematics simply as the study of beautiful patterns."[11] The freedom that mathematicians achieved through this liberation of their subject from shapes and numbers, the variety introduced into mathematics by considering it to be beautiful patterns, proved to be particularly fruitful for the natural sciences because it provided a powerful set of tools for solving its problems.

Numerous examples can be given where the mathematician's work occurred before the scientific application, or indeed before any conscious realization that the mathematics involved would prove to be useful (they were playing with beautiful patterns). Probably the most famous is Albert Einstein's use of Grassman's tensor calculus to ex-

---

8 "Albegra," in *Mathematics in the Modern World: Readings from Scientific American,* ed. Morris Kline (San Francisco, 1968), 102.
9 Ibid.
10 Ibid.
11 Ibid.

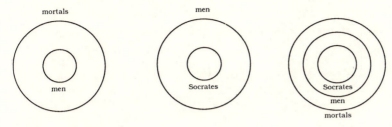

Figure 1.2 . Boolean logic 1

Source: Laurie Buxton, *Mathematics for Everyone* (New York, 1984), 153.

plain his (Einstein's) perception of space and time. It could only have happened because mathematics had been undergoing its own evolution. But mathematics' relationship with another formal science, logic, because of its special implications for management science, is worth discussing in some detail. The mathematization of logic was to a very large extent the achievement of the Englishman George Boole (1815–64), for he, in *The Laws of Thought* (1854), used mathematics to analyze the logic of language. His work demonstrates the new abstract character of modern mathematics in two ways. First, he utilized set theory in order to describe logical relationships. Set theory obviously applies to numbers: the cardinal numbers and the ordinal numbers are examples of sets. When a standard numerical set is generated in an orderly fashion by adding one unit repeatedly, each set can be matched (placed in a one-to-one correspondence) with a part or proper subset of its immediate successor. For instance, three points (...) can be matched with part of a seven-point series (.......), i.e., since three is less than seven one would say that the relationship established is a proper subset of, or gives some structure to, the collection of standard sets by arranging them in an order. In numerical parlance, structure is provided by sets of numbers based on a radix – 10, 8, 5, 2, or whatever. Set theory also applies to shapes as well as to numbers, where the sets and subsets are compared by shapes (teacups or triangles, or whatever dimension or form is involved). So far we are in the realm of premodern mathematics. Since, however, set theory deals with relationships it easily frees itself from constraints of numbers and shapes. That is what Boole understood when he used set theory in logic. The syllogism "All men are mortal, Socrates is a man, Socrates is mortal" illustrates what this means. It can be diagramed as shown in Figure 1.2. Obviously these diagrams show that mortals are a set, that men

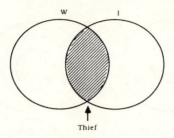

Figure 1.3. Boolean logic 2

Source: Laurie Buxton, *Mathematics for Everyone* (New York, 1984), 150.

are a subset, and that Socrates is a subset of men. Hence the visual display compels us to reach the appropriate conclusion.

Similarly, set theory enables us to disentangle more ambiguous statements. Suppose you walk out of a shop carrying something you have not paid for. In Figure 1.3, this act, the walking out of the store, is enclosed in the space labeled W. In law the question is whether a person is a thief. It is possible, in a fit of absentmindedness, to walk out of the store with an item intending to pay. Such a person is not a thief. Only those (1) who intend to deprive the store of a good and walk out with it are thieves. The diagram permits the act to be clarified logically, for mathematics abstracts the relationship that exists; it ignores the issue of what we are talking about to concentrate on one idea lying within another, overlapping it, or being entirely distinct.[12] Set theory, then, proved particularly useful in clarifying thought, for the fundamental laws of Boolean algebra were abstracted from the behavior of subsets of a universal set.

The second example of where Boole's use of mathematics escaped the constraints of number and shape was in the application of algebra to thought. Boole invented a system of symbols in which the propositions of Aristotelian logic were reduced to equations that were analogous to those in elementary algebra.[13] Accordingly, many of the rules of ordinary arithmetic (i.e., the commutative, the associative, and the distributive) were applied to logic.[14] The principle of application is

12 Laurie Buxton, *Mathematics for Everyone* (New York, 1984), 150.
13 Sawyer, "Algebra," 10.
14 Ibid., 11. To refresh memories: "The commutative rule states that whatever objects a and b might stand for and however complicated the operation of combining them might be, we are always entitled to expect that a + b will mean the same as b + a.
"Another important property of addition and multiplication in ordinary arithme-

Decimal Number	Binary Equivalent of Decimal Number	Electrical Signal for Binary Number	
0	000	○○○	(off, off, off)
1	001	○○●	(off, off, on)
2	010	○●○	(off, on, off)
3	011	○●●	(off, on, on)

Figure 1.4. Binary-electrical conversions

Source: Edna E. Kramer, *The Nature and Growth of Modern Mathematics* (Princeton, N. J., 1981), 7.

called isomorphism, "an exceedingly important concept in modern mathematics since reasoning in a single system establishes corresponding facets in all systems that are isomorphic to it."[15] George Boole perceived that logical processes could be clarified by the precision of mathematical reasoning because algebraic and logical systems were isomorphic. If, as Joseph Gerard Brennan notes, "all sciences tend toward the condition of mathematics," it could be added that mathematics itself aspires to the condition of logic.[16] George Boole's work demonstrated the functional relationship between the two formal sciences depicted on the diagram.

The principle of isomorphism also explains how mathematics and symbolic logic could be tied through physics to management science. Because Boolean algebra, which is based on a binary radix, turned out to be isomorphic with electrical circuits, it could be used to design the most efficient forms of electronic circuitry in computers. The reason why this binary base worked so well, with 1 and 0 representing "on" and "off," can be seen in Figure 1.4. It was Claude E. Shannon who, in

tic is that these operations are associative. In other words, if one has to work out 3 + 4 + 5, it does not matter whether one obtains the answer by considering 3 + 9 or by considering 7 + 5" (Sawyer, "Algebra," 109).

"A third basic property of ordinary arithmetic is expressed by the distributive rule, which in symbols states that $a(b + c) = ab + ac$. The distributive property has a way of turning up in unexpected situations. For instance, the boundary of the area covered by California and Illinois is the boundary of California added to the boundary of Illinois. It is not difficult to see a connection between this statement and the equation $b (C + I) = bC + bI$, in which b stands for 'the boundary of' and C and I are the initials of the states involved" (Sawyer, "Algebra," 109).

The commutative, the associative, and the distributive rules are thus applied to logic.

15 Edna E. Kramer, *The Nature and Growth of Modern Mathematics* (Princeton, N.J., 1981), 7. An *isomorph* is something identical with or similar to something else in form or structure. In mathematics, a one-to-one correspondence between two mathematical sets or, as in the case just cited, an identity in form and structure between logical and arithmetic systems.

16 Eugene Montes, seminar paper (in author's possession).

a 1938 research paper, observed the analogy between "the truth values of Boolean propositions and the states of switches and relays in an electrical circuit." Shannon showed that "switching algebra" is a concrete application of the abstract binary Boolean algebra and hence is isomorphic to the truth-table algebra of propositions.[17] From this observation it was a short step to the modern electronic computer which programmed Boolean algebra into its logical system. Without symbolic logic the development of the computer would have been impossible. Without the computer scientific management would have been deprived of a powerful aid. No more impressive example can be given, therefore, of the impact of modern mathematics on management than that of its influence on symbolic logic.[18]

Economics is another example of a formal science that affected business studies. But like mathematics economics had itself to experience considerable change, often brought about through contact with other sciences (e.g., engineering and mathematics), before it could exert any influence on business studies. The first step occurred with the transformation of the subject into a formal science. In the late nineteenth century the historical-institutional school of economics was still very powerful. Empirical and nontheoretical in orientation, it stressed detailed inductive research into specific socioeconomic contexts. People wrote exhaustive regional and national studies about the growth of industries and economic institutions. The neoclassical school adopted a radically different approach to economics. It accepted a liberal conception of the individual which separated him from family, class, clan, or country and made him self-determinate, capable of judging his own actions in terms of economic utility. With this economic man detached from the world of art, law, and morality, neoclassical economic theory, like classical economic theory before it, presented the idea of utility maximization as

17 Kramer, *Modern Mathematics,* 129.
18 "Electronic digital computers are in fact made up of two basic kinds of components: logic elements (often called switching elements) and memory elements. In virtually all modern computers these elements are binary, that is, the logic elements have two alternative pathways and the memory elements have two states. Accordingly, all the information handled by such computers is coded in binary form.... To make a digital computer it is necessary to have memory elements and a set of logic elements that are functionally complete.... For each symbolic circuit one can construct a 'truth-table,' in which are listed all possible input states and the corresponding output states. Each truth-table, in turn, can be represented by a Boolean statement that expresses the output of the circuit as a function of the input" (David C. Evans, "Computer Logic and Memory," in *Mathematics in the Modern World,* ed. Kline, 349). See this article for a good, short summary of how a computer is constructed.

the motivational foundation for individual action. The neoclassical economists turned the discipline into a formal science. The German economist Erich Schneider described this approach:

Theoretical propositions are always conditional propositions of the form: If A, then B. If this or that assumption is fulfilled, then this or that relationship is valid. The theoretical proposition always has the character of logical necessity and is according to the assumptions made either right or wrong. A theoretical proposition, like a dogma, cannot be denied. The most that can be said is that a theoretically correct proposition is not relevant because its assumptions do not apply to the present situation. That does not mean the proposition is wrong. It only means that the proposition does not apply to present circumstances [*ist nicht aktuell*].[19]

These neoclassical economists were not interested in the origins of economic events. The most exact knowledge about an economic event (say, the price of a good) might be of interest to the historical-institutional economist but it would not answer the question that neoclassical economists asked, how price is determined by markets. The answer to such a question could not be found in any historical or nonhistorical form of empirical investigation, for, as Schneider explained, "One forgets that the sea of facts is dumb and can only be forced to reveal interconnections when properly queried. Intelligent [*sinnvoll*] questions can only be derived from theoretical (formal) analysis."[20] Because the neoclassical economists, like the mathematicians, argued from assumptions which were not intended to be empirically examined, their great debate with the historical-institutionalists (the famous *Methodenstreit* of the late nineteenth century) was largely a dialogue of the deaf. But it was a dialogue the neoclassical economists clearly won.

Thus the neoclassical economists formulated a view of the economy as a self-contained system of economic exchange "in which an understanding of economic activities could be derived from the postulates of the system." The chief postulates, the economic man and utility maximization, were transformed into the analytical device of marginalism. Philip Wicksteed described marginalism in the following manner:

[B]y increasing our supply of anything we reduce its marginal significance and lower the price of an extra unit on our scale of preferences; and suitable

19 Winfried Vogt, "Erich Schneider und die Wirtschaftstheorie," in *Erich Schneider, 1900–1970: Gedenkband und Bibliographie*, ed. Gottfried Bombach and Michael Tacke (Kiel, 1980), 13–48, 37; my translation.
20 Ibid.

additions to our supply will bring it down to any value you please. Thus, whatever the price of any commodity that the housewife finds in the market may be, so long as its marginal significance to her is higher than that price, she will buy; but the very act of putting herself in possession of an increased stock reduces its marginal significance and the more she buys the lower [the significance] becomes. The amount that brings it into coincidence with market price is the amount she will buy.[21]

The assumption that the utility of a good declines as the stock increases means that the process described by Wicksteed is an equilibrating one, for as the stock of a good changes, the value of additional units change, thus creating a situation where the marginal value is just equal to the price.

Marginal utility theory, then, made relative price and relative scarcity the fulcrum of economic analysis, for, if the total utility of one commodity (water) is greater than another (diamonds), the marginal utility of one (diamonds) is higher because of scarcity. In the crisscrossing of buyers and sellers a rational sorting out occurs which not only satisfies all those concerned but, by allocating given quantities of scarce resources among competing claims most efficiently, serves the general welfare. The neoclassical economics, armed with marginal utility theory, described the economic system as an enormous conglomeration of interdependent markets which, through the price mechanism, tended towards equilibrium – where marginal value (utility) of commodities equals price.

But what implications did neoclassical microeconomic theory have for management? There are two. First, by an emphasis on individualism, the neoclassical view of the firm isolates the entrepreneur from his or her institutional and organizational environment. He or she operates alone, acts rationally, and makes decisions, like the housewife, in terms of utility maximization, defined in the entrepreneur's case in terms of profit maximization. Secondly, since the firm operates in an economic system, the entrepreneur's decisions are subject to the same system rules as the decisions of all other people, rules that have been revealed by theoretical economic analysis. Since, according to the postulates of neoclassical economics, each firm seeks to maximize profits (the entrepreneur's individualistic egoism, the economic man) and to do so has to operate according to the rules of the system, the entrepre-

---

21 Daniel Bell, "Models and Reality in Economic Discourse," in *The Crisis in Economic Theory,* ed. Daniel Bell and Irving Kristol (New York, 1981), 50.

neur has to act to bring marginal costs (the addition to total cost which the entrepreneur expects would be caused by adding production) into line with marginal revenue (that revenue caused by added production, i.e., sales). The entrepreneur desires added costs to be at the point of added revenue, not to exceed it, of course, because marginal cost exceeding marginal revenues would reduce profit, but also not to fall under it, because if the increased cost and greater output would add more revenue than cost, to stop at that point would be to stop before profit maximization.

These marginal cost–marginal revenue concerns are about the firm's outputs. Managerial decisions about the firm's inputs are based in neoclassical microeconomics on the same sort of rational profit-maximization, entrepreneurial decision-making model. Like marginal cost and marginal revenue, in the case of output, marginal factor cost (e.g., what supplies cost marginally, i.e., what the additional supplied unit, needed to increase output by one unit, costs) determines input. In fact, since the firm operates as part of a market-determined economic system, the entrepreneur calculates the inputs (factor costs) and outputs (production costs and sales revenues) simultaneously and all calculations are made in terms of marginal utility.[22] Neoclassical economists, then, seek to explain the rational basis of entrepreneurial decision making within the contexts of microeconomic equilibrium theory.

The attempt to introduce scientific rigor into economics depended on techniques borrowed from the sciences. Marginal analysis resulted from what is now called (and what was widespread practice in natural science) model building, for the economists knew equilibrium theory was a model of, not a mirror of, reality. They only claimed that it was sufficiently general in its conception to include all the essential variables (and their interdependencies) necessary to explain a broad spectrum of economic behavior (that of housewife, wage earner, fishmonger, entrepreneur, an industry, an entire economy, etc.). Because they converted economics into model building, moreover, the neoclassical economists could concentrate on the abstracted variables. This emphasis led them to shift from problems of causation, which stressed temporal events, to problems of functionalism (inherent in the complex, simultaneously mutual, conditioning relations of economic factors) and, consequently, to drop literary forms of analysis (whose ordinary

22 Fritz Machlup, "Marginal Analysis and Empirical Research," *American Economic Review* 36:2 (1946): 519–54, 538.

logic permitted only a partial and successive exposé of phenomena) in favor of mathematical analysis, whose equations could state how the variables in the equilibrium model simultaneously and mutually affected each other.

It is hardly a coincidence, therefore, that the rise of mathematical economics accompanied the development of marginalism. Stanley Jevons, cofounder with Karl Menger of the marginal utility school, used mathematics. He was the first consciously to seek, according to Léon Walras, "to apply mathematics to economic theory."[23] Walras's own *Eléments d'économie pure,* which "presented the ensemble of economic theory as essentially a mathematical theory, where all the important propositions could be stated in equations," was published in 1874.[24] His achievement, a system of simultaneous equations which expressed general equilibrium theory, has been hailed as the great accomplishment of modern economics.[25] He, Alfredo Pareto, and a handful of others were the pioneers because literary economics faded into the background.

Neoclassical economics, however, was still of marginal interest to those concerned with business studies. This was true, for one reason, because of its formal character. To the empirically based practical man its theoretical orientation was managerially fuzzy. Neither the theory nor the analytical tools employed were of much use to decision makers. The marginal utility theory of the firm stated that the entrepreneur, to maximize profit, tried to bring marginal costs into line with marginal revenues. But what are costs (or revenues)? They are not given entities but the results of multiple activities that occur in the firm. All technologically feasible combinations of the activities involved in production constitute what is referred to as the production function. The entrepreneur, if he wants to optimize, has to select the most profitable point in the production function, the optimal combination of factors and activities. That is his job, and the neoclassical theory of the firm had little to say about it. Terms like marginal costs and revenues could not give the entrepreneur guidance in his task. Their marginal character was determined primarily by the pricing

23 Bertrand Nogaro, "Questions théoriques: Les Mathématiques considerées comme logique formelle et la mise en équation des problèmes économiques," *Revue d'économie politique* 54 (1940): 467–84; my translation.
24 Ibid. Also, see Richard Stone, "Un siècle d'économétrie," in "Problèmes Economiques," *Documentation française* 1.72 (July 15, 1981): 26–32, 26.
25 See Erich Schneider's comments for a typical example of this admiration, i.e., *Volkswirtschaft und Betriebswirtschaft – ausgewählte Aufsätze* (Tübingen, 1964).

mechanism of the market, over which the entrepreneur had little control, or by a combination of factors, inputs over which the entrepreneur might have some control but about which the marginal costs themselves said nothing. In short, the marginalist theory of the firm is outward-looking, the entrepreneur's viewpoint inward-looking, for the theory of the firm treats the operations within the firm as a black box, an unknown, a problem that has already been solved. Because it assumes that the entrepreneur knows how to run his firm efficiently, it stops at the point where the entrepreneur wants analysis really to begin.[26]

Not surprisingly, perhaps, the mathematics neoclassical economics employed also proved to be inappropriate to the entrepreneur's problems. Neoclassical economics, G. Morton points out, "derived equilibrium conditions in an elegant and general fashion by means of the differential calculus."[27] And the same mathematics was used by marginal utility economists when dealing with the firm. But the entrepreneur had to decide about the right combination of factor inputs in order to optimize the production function. For this he needed technical data that referred to a number of alternative production processes, each requiring definite factors of production stated in fixed proportions. He needed to use fixed technical coefficients and production possibility curves composed of a number of straight-parts (because of limits in factor substitution) rather than a continuous smooth curve (which assumed perfect factor substitution). "Whether one believed that production indifference curves," Morton continued,

as commonly used, should be broken down into a series of linear segments or into curvilinear segments it seems clear that some breakdown is necessary. If we are ever to obtain realistic production functions empirically we shall have to distinguish between different processes of production and to denominate our factors in terms more homogeneous than "land," "labour," and "capital."[28]

---

26 "Once it is admitted that markets do not uniquely determine a firm's production function, price movements, and resource allocation patterns, so that firms cannot simply be seen as the intersection of cost and revenue curves, the 'black box' of firms' decision processes and their implementation needs to be explored to understand patterns of economic change." It was the neoclassical economists' failure to admit this problem or acknowledge it that made their analysis so useless to the entrepreneur. Quote from Richard Whitley, Alan Thomas, and Jane Marceau, *Masters of Business?* (London, 1981), 14.

27 "Notes on Linear Programming," *Economica*, NS, 18:72 (Nov. 1951): 397–411, 398.

28 Ibid.

Because calculus could not deal realistically with the firm's production possibilities (i.e., with a "number of alternative production processes, each requiring factors of production in fixed proportions"), "the allocation problem," Erich Schneider, that great admirer of the neoclassical mathematical economists, eventually admitted, "is not to be solved with the method of infinitesimal calculus."[29] Consequently, John von Neumann and Oskar Morgenstern could observe in their famous book *Theory of Games and Economic Behavior* (1944), "the concepts of economics are fuzzy but even in those parts of economics where the descriptive problem has been handled more satisfactorily, mathematical tools have seldom been used appropriately. Mathematical economics has not achieved very much."[30] Since this came from a great twentieth-century mathematician, it was a serious rebuff. Neoclassical economics was not, from a business decision-making perspective, relevant.

Additional bridges had to be built before science and economics could become more managerially useful. One particularly helpful bridge, with respect to the problem of practical applicability, was built with statistics. Statistical science was not created by economists. Natural scientists, for example, the mathematician Adolphe Quételet (1796–1874), the geneticist Francis Galton (1822–1911), and the mathematician-geneticist Karl Pearson (1857–1936), had much more to do with its initial development. But statistics appealed to economists who, like everybody in the soft sciences, could not adopt the scientific method in their investigations. Sir Francis Bacon had defined that method in the seventeenth century: experimentation, the drawing of tentative conclusions from the observations done (making hypotheses), and determining whether the conclusions squared with the known facts. Stafford Beer notes that traditionally the scientific method could only work in the laboratory: "only there could all variables be held constant except two that were varied in order to obtain precise results."[31] Since social sciences could not be pursued in laboratories, such controlled experiments were impossible. Mathematical statistics evolved as a substitute for laboratory experimentation.

Statistics consists of a general body of methods and procedures used

29 "Der Weg der Betriebswirtschaftslehre in den letzten 25 Jahren," in *Volkswirtschaft und Betriebswirtschaft*, by Erich Schneider, 452–57, 454; my translation.
30 *Theory of Games and Economic Behavior* (Princeton, N.J., 1944), 8.
31 *Decision and Control: The Meaning of Operational Research and Management Cybernetics* (London, 1966), 12.

to assemble, describe, and infer something from numerical data. It replaced the controlled experiment within the laboratory with a theory of the proper design of experiments; it substituted conclusions based on laboratory experimentation with statistical inferences based on the mathematics of probabilities, i.e., the degrees of uncertainty aroused in the observer when generalizing from a limited number of observations.[32] When economics adopted statistics as a substitute for the experimental method available to the physical sciences, the result was econometrics.[33]

The econometric movement sought, therefore, to make economics more reality conscious by combining the mathematized deductive reasoning of neoclassical economics with the rigorous scientific methods of statistical inference. Statistical inference is not concerned with general hypotheses like "cancer is caused by a virus." Its assumptions are about "the frequency functions of a random variable." It wants to know, for instance, what the probability is that heads will appear after so many flips of a coin, or, of more interest to the manager, if information available on three factories (or three machines) reflects conditions in an entire industry (or factory). During the years 1928–33, Jerzy Neyman and Egon S. Pearson, Karl Pearson's son, developed a theory for testing these kinds of hypotheses which, along with other advances in statistical testing, enabled economists to assume a more realistic attitude towards the decision-making process within the firm. Since the neoclassical view of the firm assumed that the entrepreneur had perfect knowledge, it had been of limited interest to the businessman. Probability-based mathematical statistics permitted him to make more informed decisions under conditions of uncertainty. This wedding proved to be useful when dealing with the problems of the firm.

Inasmuch as statistics is about numerical data and the inferences that can be made from them, its tests and procedures could not repair shortcomings in praxis arising from economic theory. To do that, short of abandoning neoclassical economic theory (which, of course, is a formal, not an empirical, science), algorithms based on that theory but which had operational significance had to be found. "Algorithm,"

32 Kramer, *Modern Mathematics,* 317.
33 Mary S. Morgan, "The History of Econometric Thought: Analysis of the Main Problems of Relating Economic Theory to Data in the First Half of the Twentieth Century," 9. A Thesis for the Degree of Doctor, London School of Economics and Political Science, University of London, 1984.

the shorter Oxford Dictionary tells us, "derives from 'Al-Kuwarizmi' which means 'the man of Kuwarizmi.' " This was the surname of the Arab mathematician Abu Ja'far Muhammad ibn Musa whose writings introduced the Arabic system of numeration to Europe. The word *algorithm* became attached originally to this system and to the arithmetical processes that it made possible. Eventually algorithm detached itself from a specific system to become a word that meant *routine* in general. It did not have to be arithmetic or even a mathematical routine. It could be any set of rules by which something is done. A computer is unable to think, so it needs somebody to devise a set of rules appropriate to its inner workings. It needs an algorithm. (Boole provided it).[34] Similarly, the working manager needed algorithms that would help him solve the complex problems he had to confront. Marginal utility theory sought to provide the entrepreneur with such routine guidelines in decision making (i.e., to maximize profits, marginal costs are brought into line with marginal revenues) and with the mathematical tools to accomplish a task. Inasmuch as the cost and revenue component in the equations did not constitute the significant variables with which the managers had to contend, nor was calculus the appropriate mathematical tool, the economists required an algorithm that could make their theories practice relevant.

They found it after the war principally in linear programming. George B. Dantzig and his Rand Corporation associates developed the simplex linear programming algorithm for the United States Air Force in 1947. The procedure, which provided for comparisons of sets of ratios existing among sets of consumption of various inputs and rates of production of various outputs, utilized modern mathematical (vector algebra, matrix theory, symbolic logic) and statistical techniques. The algorithm was based on the following assumptions:

1. Objectives can be stated mathematically.
2. Resources can be stated mathematically.
3. Alternative courses of action are too numerous for discussion by older methods.
4. Variables had to be related linearly, i.e., "when two variables are linearly related this means that a change in one causes exactly proportionate change in the other."[35]

34 Buxton, *Mathematics for Everyone*, 184.
35 Richard L. Levin and Rudolph P. Lamone, *Linear Programming for Management Decisions* (Homewood, Ill., 1969), 216.

Even though linear programming required more information than the cost and revenue approach of the economists, it provided more information, information that permitted the entrepreneur not only to define goals (optimal quantities of inputs and outputs) but to obtain specific directions about how to achieve these goals, stated in terms of the various activities available to the firm.[36]

This algorithm was also not created by economists. Economists readily acknowledge that linear programming approached management from the viewpoint of engineering not economics.[37] The mathematics it required, moreover, was, if not new to mathematicians, natural scientists, and engineers, so unfamiliar to economists that when explaining the new algorithm to their colleagues, economists included special sections on vectors and matrices in the book.[38] But the economists were drawn to linear programming as much for psychological reasons as for practical, because whereas it was helpful to management, it did not undermine the body of economic theory which had been built up so painfully during the twentieth century. Linear programming was, the economists insisted, just a special case of marginal analysis and, hence, quite compatible with neoclassical economic theory.[39]

Although the most important algorithm, linear programming was but one of the new activity analysis algorithms to which economists were attracted. Léontief's input–output algorithm, first formulated in 1938 but not given a full exposition until 1941, provided an analytic framework for determining the effect in the economy of altering production goals, or the feasibility of a production program given available resources and possible methods of production. The Léontief model, which dealt with national economics and with industrial sectors, was of limited use at the level of the firm. Moreover, it did not allow for alternative production mixes to be taken into consideration, as did linear programming. But it did provide economists with an operationally oriented system. Even more important in this respect was the development of game theory. The mathematician Emile Borel introduced it in 1921 in order to make predictions about games of

36 Robert Dorfman, Paul A. Samuelson, and Robert M. Solow, *Linear Programming and Economic Analysis* (New York, 1958), 141.
37 Ibid., 133.
38 Ibid.
39 Schneider, "Der Weg," 454; and Dorfman, Samuelson, and Solow, *Linear Programming and Economic Analysis*.

chance. Although von Neumann developed further the modern approach to problems of competition and cooperation in the "Theory of Parlor Games" ("Zur Theorie der Gesellschaftsspiele," *Mathematische Annalen* 100 [1928]:295–320), the economic implications of game theory were not spelled out until von Neumann and the economist Oskar Morgenstern published *Theory of Games and Economic Behavior* in 1944. Game theory drew a straight line from modern mathematics (because von Neumann used algebra, matrix theory, and probability theory in his calculations),[40] through economics, to management to show how entrepreneurs, in conflict situations, could, under certain assumptions, act so as to be guaranteed at least a certain minimum gain (or maximum loss) by following the algorithm.[41]

Thus, to return to Figure 1.1, neoclassical economics' entry into the new paradigm of management studies was contingent upon relationships established with statistics and mathematics. Linear algebra, topology,[42] and probability theory replaced the diagrams of the distant past and the calculus of more recent times to give scientific status to economic knowledge and make it more operationally understandable to management. It did not matter in all these algorithms if the inputs were monetary or material, if the capacities involved were for a factory, a machine, or an advertising department, or what goals were sought – the lowest costs or the highest profits. What distinguished the algorithms from each other was the functional flexibility they offered management in its activity analysis.

The same was true of econometrics. It began separately from both economics and mathematics, for the studies done in the nineteenth century (*A History of Prices and of the State of Circulation,* during the years 1793–1856 by Thomas Tooke and William Newmarch; *History of Agriculture and Prices in England,* 1866–1902 by James E. T. Rogers; *Wages in the United Kingdom in the Nineteenth Century* by Sir Arthur Lyon Bowley; and the studies of *Life and Labour of the People in London,* 1886 to 1902, by Charles Booth) were not informed by either. Irving Fischer was the first to understand the necessity to form an international movement to promote this fusion between statistics,

---

40 Kramer, *Modern Mathematics,* 246.
41 Dorfman, Samuelson, and Solow, *Linear Programming and Economic Analysis,* 2.
42 Topology is a branch of mathematics that investigates the properties of a geometric configuration that are unaltered if the configuration is subject to any one-to-one continuous transformation.

mathematics, and neoclassical economics. Joined by Wesley C. Mitchell, Henry L. Moore, and a handful of others, including Ragnar Frisch and Charles F. Roos, he founded the Econometric Society (1930). Fischer was its first president. By 1978 there were 2,158 members in the Econometric Society and 3,143 institutional subscribers. The growth of econometrics, that is, its usefulness as a science, was promoted during this period by economists and mathematicians.

The line in Figure 1.1 between formal and management sciences was sometimes also drawn between theoretical natural science and management. Stafford Beer, in *Decision and Control,* shows how physics, through the second law of thermodynamics, helps management to understand information networks. In any system, he explains, which distributes heat and in which one zone is hotter than another, we know, according to the second law of thermodynamics, that the concentrated heat will spread through the system until the heat is uniform throughout. Because such a system is isomorphic with organizational information networks ("It is easiest to think of information as being news about the states of energy in the different zones of the system – news that is carried about by the energy shifts themselves"[43]), managers preoccupied, for example, with research and development (R and D) within an organization can be helped by physics. If the R and D unit is sealed off from the organization, then R and D remains "hot" but the organization itself is "dead." If the system has access to R and D, it will absorb R and D energy until that energy is dissipated throughout the system, unless there is an outside source of R and D energy piped into the organization. These considerations are important for designing R and D within a firm, particularly a high-tech firm, for Beer maintains, "the connection (between 'high information levels' and 'high differentials in internal energies') is not fanciful or literary; the mathematical equations describing these two aspects of a self-contained system (which can be developed independently) turn out to be the same as each other."[44] Beer's example of mapping between isomorphic systems is not exceptional. That existing between Boolean logic and electronic circuits has already been cited. And analogies between physical sciences and management systems are easily multiplied.

So too – moving to the practical applied sciences on the right of the

43 Beer, *Decision and Control,* 23.
44 Ibid.

diagram – were examples of contacts established between engineering and managerial studies. Of course, the physical sciences influenced engineering and this influence significantly affected management. The development of the computer, without which the new paradigm would have been impossible, illustrates this process. But the computer could not be developed without the proper physics. The vacuum tube, made possible by Lee de Forest's invention of the diode in 1922, was suited to the binary system of Boole's algebra. Claude E. Shannon's article (1938) relating the on-off feature of electronic circuitry to the circuitry of Boolean logic came after this discovery in physics. The first computers, containing 17,000 vacuum tubes, occupied two buildings and required teams working full-time to replace blown-out bulbs. The transistor brought computers without vacuum tubes, the integrated circuits, a miniaturization that had already been advanced dramatically with transistors. These inventions, however, depended on chemistry. The use of silicon, whose valences were changed to make it an appropriate conductor or inhibitor of electron impulses, permitted the microchip circuitry which revolutionized information technology.[45] Heinrich Welker's "3–5" compounds promise computers with even faster circuitry than those made of silicon. Although Charles Babbage's work on the computer was contemporary with Boole's on symbolic logic, engineers could not build the machine that fused the two until the physics and chemistry of the twentieth century were at their disposal.

The engineers themselves, moreover, directly influenced management studies. The management science movement at the turn of the century (e.g., Frederick Winslow Taylor in America, Henri Fayol in France, and Georg Schlesinger in Germany) was largely their creation. The break-even chart and standard cost accounting (where standards had to be set by engineers because of technical qualifications) were earlier management tools of engineers' invention. Linear programming when it handles production problems (e.g., optional location of machines on the factory floor, stock management, or the order followed in manufacture) and software when it involves computer-aided design or manufacture provide more recent examples of the engineers' involvement in management concerns. That engineering had this managerial dimension was not noteworthy. It became so when the engineering concerns spilled over in less obvious ways into other branches of

45 James Miller, of E. F. Hutton and Co., Honolulu, Hawaii. Interview, Oct. 12, 1985.

management. Thus in the 1950s the linear programming techniques that engineers had applied exclusively initially to production processes were borrowed and improved upon for purposes of marketing and financial analysis.

Finally, to shift to the human applied sciences on the diagram, traditional fields of business study found themselves not only affected by engineering and other sciences but influencing each other. This happened less perhaps to accounting which, if the old ledgers gave way to computer printouts, was still regulated by accounting conventions and law. But the uses to which accounting information was put changed. Accounting became just one source of information for management as special sorts of nonaccounting-based information gathering took place in order to enlighten management about a firm's operations. Marketing developed from a discipline uniquely concerned with describing institutions and distribution networks into one preoccupied with measuring consumer responses (combining empirical field research with mathematical statistics and psychology) and/or with constructing optimization marketing models (based on nonlinear computer programming). Finance evolved from a similar institution-oriented subject into one that, using linear program models, integrated finance, production, and investment planning, or which, relying on marginal utility neoclassical economics, based financial analysis on market theory.[46]

Finally, science's impact on management studies was also expressed through the behavioral sciences. Engineers had never been very subtle in their treatment of the labor force. Frederick W. Taylor, for example, had a crude psychology of work: workers had to be controlled because they were shirkers by nature. Not much attention then was paid from managerial as opposed to humanitarian perspectives to the personnel as social beings with psychological needs. But the sociologist Emil Durkheim noted that the breakdown of social groups during industrialization had serious consequences for work organization. His and similar ideas led to the series of studies done by Elton Mayo, Fritz Roethlisberger, and William Dickson at the Hawthorne Plant of the Western Electric Company (done between 1927 and 1932) which revealed irrational factors in the plant that interacted with the strongly controlled

46 See Al Mercer, "Operational Marketing Research," *Journal of Industrial Economics*, 18:1 (Nov. 1969): 15–32; Reinhard H. Schmidt, "Zur Entwicklung der Finanztheorie," in *Paradigmawechsel in der Betriebswirtschaftslehre?*, ed. Wolf F. Fischer-Winkelmann (Spardorf, 1983), 465–500; Sass, *Pragmatic Imagination*.

factors within the organization. A new view emerged, "that of the organization as a social system encompassing individuals, informal group and intergroup relationships, as well as formal structure. The existence of such informal grouping illustrated that humans require more than satisfaction of just economic needs."[47] This standpoint developed increasingly into a scientific investigation that sought to generalize about man's behavior in the office and the workplace. Such investigation leaned heavily on psychology and sociology. Much of it contradicted the assumptions about human behavior that underlay neoclassical economics. But that did not make it less scientific. This is true not just because the behavioral sciences claimed a scientific status but because they, like neoclassical economics, in order to strengthen the scientific rigor of their work, borrowed heavily from statistics and applied mathematics.

The new paradigm in management studies, whose emergence this discussion elucidates, was really a matrix of interlocking, mutually conditioning scientific relationships in which no one science or discipline predominated, unless it was the instrumentality of mathematics. But it was not a question of disciplines. The German business economist Eugen Schmalenbach observed:

Economics and business economics handle, to a large extent, the same materials [Stoffe] but they do not have the same spirit [Geist]. Economics is a philosophical science with philosophical characteristics. Business economics is, on the other hand, an applied science. Chemistry and mechanical technology are closer in spirit to business economics than is economics. Business economics is purposeful. It must think purposefully.[48]

Schmalenbach wrote this in 1919, so the economics he had in mind had not developed into the policy science it became after the Second World War. But his point is valid. It is not the specific science but the purpose for which it is being used that matters, or it is the utilization of the sciences to create a science or sciences of management that constitute the new paradigm.

Nothing illustrates this practical purposiveness better than the operational research movement which did so much to advance the new paradigm. The British team of scientists and engineers at Air Ministry, Bawdsey, who worked on "the operational use of radar information" could hardly have guessed how their efforts to solve this operational

47 Frank Drechsler and John Bateson, *Management, Information, and Expert Systems* (Dublin, 1986), 14.
48 "Selbstkostenrechnung," *ZfhF* 13 (1919): 257–99, 259; my translation.

problem would have such managerial consequences. Their success spawned operational research groups throughout the military on both sides of the Atlantic. "Never before," C. H. Waddington, who was involved along with two Nobel-prize winners and four other fellows of the Royal Society in antisubmarine operations, wrote, "has science been used by responsible executive authorities for such a thorough and such an unrestricted analysis of practical affairs as it was by the Royal Air Force from 1941 onward."[49]

The reference is to science, not to scientists, because it was not just a question of intelligent men helping out but of the methods used in science being, in the isomorphic sense, particularly valuable for solving operational problems.[50]

It was this faith in science, moreover, which was transferred to the operations research groups in business and industry after the war. Their aims were fixed to the masthead of the British review *Operational Research Quarterly:*

Operational Research is the application of the methods of science to complex problems arising in the direction and management of large systems of men, machines, materials and money, in industry, business and defence. The distinctive approach is to develop a scientific model of the system, incorporating measurements of the factors such as choice and risk, with which to predict and compare the outcomes of alternate decision strategies or controls. The purpose is to help management determine its policy and actions scientifically.[51]

Operations research itself was not a science; it simply utilized science in order to help management solve problems. That was why O.R. experts insisted that the success of an O.R. team depended on its being composed of people from a broad spectrum of sciences. Precisely because O.R. is not a science but a technique that uses science, it has to have recourse to as many scientific methods as possible. It has to be done by a team.

This scientific eclecticism reflected the increasing complexity of the management process itself. O.R. began by developing or borrowing a number of techniques – queue theory to optimize the handling of people and products in lines, transportation theory to minimize the cost of distributing a product from several points of supply (source) to a

---

49 OR in World War II: Operational Research against the U-Boat (London, 1973).
50 M. R. Dando and R. G. Sharp, "Operational Research in the U.K. in 1977: The Causes and Consequences of a Myth?," Journal of the Operational Research Society, 32 (1978): 936–59, 943. Also see Beer, Decision and Control.
51 See any copy of the journal.

number of points of demand (destinations), etc. – to master production and distribution problems.[52] These and similar, mathematically based techniques were then used in other fields of management (finance, marketing). But the problem with studying parts is that they involve wholes. Firms did not just make products; they had to sell them and to produce the raw materials to make and sell them. Consequently, "writers and researchers . . . increased their emphasis on the firm as a whole, i.e., an integrated unit where each decision made takes into effect the total operational environment instead of concentrating on a specific functional field, and the increased development of mathematical tools to aid management decision making."[53]

With this shift from the individual manager's decision problem to the process of decision making in an organization, the studies of different procedures, like operation procedures and internal information systems, fell together into a general systems analysis founded on mathematic decision modeling. The situation was made even more complicated by strategic considerations, i.e., management's preoccupation not only with the question of how best to produce and sell products A, B, and C, but what product or service the firm should be involved with in the future. As the nature of management evolved, the new paradigm developed from one applying scientific methods to traditional managerial functions to one integrating scientific method into the managerial decision process itself.

By the 1960s management had become the focus of science and science the focus of management as they had never been before. There was an excitement in academia after the war because of this utilitarianism. The Cowles Commission in Chicago, which had been developing tools of economic analysis since the 1930s, "inspired by Haavelmo's methodological blueprint (use of probability theory) for econometrics, . . . saw themselves as armed with very powerful precision engineered tools which they believed would solve a host of economic problems – in comparison with the previous economic tools fashioned in the bronze age [of economical analysis]."[54] Postwar economists, for the first time in the history of their discipline, could talk about actually managing an entire economy instead of just aspiring to understand the principles of eco-

52 On transportation problems, see Koopmans, *Econometrica* 15, supplement (July 1949): 136–45.
53 Report on annual meeting of German professors of business economics in *Der Volkswirt* 17:23 (1963): 131; my translation.
54 Mary Morgan, "History of Econometric Thought," 302.

nomic behavior. With the same tools, the same ambitions were extended from the macroeconomic policy sciences to the level of the firm. And the confidence exuded in America spread into Europe. German economists and business economists, for instance, voiced the general optimism at a two-day joint meeting, June 16, 1963:

In the last three decades a transformation in the work methods of the economic sciences is clearly recognizable. An analysis of the economic structure and the behavior of its components, which can be characterized accurately as natural science, has replaced the old backward looking descriptive and intellectually [*geistvoll*] conceived perspectives. In all branches the theory of economic circulation [*Wirtschaftskreislauf*] has led to important insights. A complete and purposefully oriented statistical science and the adoption of mathematical methods from engineering have afforded us new possibilities to verify our working hypotheses.[55]

A similar optimism shone forth from the organizational theorists in the new management schools. Herbert Simon, the leading theorist (at the Carnegie Institute of Technology), "declared himself positively exhilarated by the progress we have made . . . towards creating a viable science of management and an art based on that science."[56] And the creation of a Nobel Prize in Economics (1969) exalted the new business and economic managerial sciences.

Like economics, business studies began to attract top students in universities because of its intellectuality and economics, like business studies, started to draw numbers because of its greater utility. Utility and intellectuality in fact became the hallmark of both microeconomic and macroeconomic studies. "You cannot ask the Americans what influences consumption," the English economist J. R. Sargent mused,

you must inquire about characteristics of the consumption function. . . . No American economist ever thinks. He uses his analytical tools to arrive at meaningful theories. While these pomposities can be funny, I believe that they indicate a fundamentally right approach to the subject. This approach requires that definition be exact, and that terms should be distinctively named to avoid confusion. It requires that theory should be rigorous, and directed towards the possibility of comparison with the facts. In this respect it is difficult not to be impressed with the lack of a distinction between theoretical and applied economics in the United States.[57]

55 *Der Volkswirt*, 17:23 (1963): 131–32; my translation.
56 Quoted in Sass, *Pragmatic Imagination*, 304.
57 "Are American Economists Better?" *Oxford Economic Papers* 15:1 (March 1963): 1–7, 2.

Such a fusion of theory and practice enhanced the general attractiveness of the new policy sciences within the university community.

One casualty of this transformation of social studies was history; economic historians in particular fell under the scientists' spell. The consequences for the subject of this book have been particularly grave. Traditionally, historians perceived the British to have been the great entrepreneurs of the first industrial revolution, the Germans and Americans of the second (c. 1870–1940), and the French to have lagged behind in both. Higher education in France and Great Britain about 1900 was held at least partially responsible for these disappointing economic results. This view has been reinterpreted (i.e., the British and French entrepreneurial performance was not inferior and, consequently, their educational systems have not perpetrated entrepreneurial ineptitude) primarily because of the methodological effect that neoclassical economics and econometrics have had on economic history.

The work of two prominent revisionists, Donald N. McCloskey and Lars G. Sandberg, shows the methodological origins of this historical reinterpretation. "The various measures used," they explained in an influential revisionist article,

> are essentially identical. Higher profits can be achieved if more output can be produced with the same input, that is, if productivity can be raised. The measuring rod for entrepreneurial failure, then, can be expressed indifferently as the money amount of profit forgone, as the proportion by which foreign exceeded British productivity, as the distance between foreign and British production functions, or as the difference in cost between foreign and British techniques. All of these gave the same result and each can be translated exactly into any one or the other.[58]

All, it could be added, are drawn from neoclassical categories of microeconomic analysis. They are therefore not historical categories but functional categories peculiar to that formal science. Accordingly, these revisionists utilized productivity indices for individual firms (e.g., Floud's study of the machine tool firm of Greenwood and Batley) and entire industries (e.g., McCloskey's productivity comparisons of British and American steel) and studies of relative costs involved in factor substitution (e.g., Harlay's study of the shift from sail to steam) to push their cause. Already in 1970 McCloskey had announced, "There is little left of the dismal picture of British failure painted by historians.

58 "From Damnation to Redemption: Judgements on the Late Victorian Entrepreneur," *Explorations in Economic History* 7 (1971): 89–108, 103.

The alternative is a picture of an economy not stagnating but growing as rapidly as permitted by the growth of its resources."[59] In 1978, in a hymn to the achievements of "the Cliometric School," he concluded that, of the reinterpretations it had occasioned, "the most finished is the denial of entrepreneurial failure in Victorian Britain."[60]

The economic historians' acceptance of these analytical techniques is ironic, considering, on the one hand, the disdain that neoclassical economists had for historical explanations and, on the other, their admission that their methods were not well suited for historical analysis.[61] That historians would accept them indicates the extent to which the triumph of the new paradigm in economics and business studies was complete. It was difficult in the din of success to hear the voices of any doubting Thomases.

59 "Did Victorian Britain Fail?" *The Economic History Review* 33 (1970): 459.
60 "Achievements of the Cliometric School," 13–28.
61 See footnote 19 above.

2. The new paradigm revisited

Yet there were critics, right from the very beginning. Among them were the institutionalists from the old descriptive school who were distrustful of the mathematicians. Fearful that their models did not mirror reality, sure, in any event, that mathematics would make business studies incomprehensible to businessmen and hence separate them even more from academia, they often put up a spirited resistance.[1] But it was difficult to argue from the point of view of the old paradigm. Since the victory of the new men would make nonmathematically schooled business economists professionally passé, the mathematically ignorants' protests seemed self-serving. Besides, the powerful technical arguments of the self-confident purveyors of the new paradigm had to have their day. Until more numerate as well as nonnumerate people had experience with the new techniques, a telling body of criticism could not appear. But when they did, the doubters began to assemble.

The doubts, moreover, were not just expressed by knowledgeable outsiders. They crept up among those whose very occupational raison d'être arose from the creation of the new paradigm in management studies. This happened, for example, within the ranks of operations research scientists. It is easy to find maverick critics cavorting outside the citadel of a new discipline while the victory bells are still ringing inside. Quoting them is never a completely convincing form of argument. But there are good reasons for thinking that, as the 1960s turned into the 1970s, the opposition even within O.R. was neither excep-

---

1 See Richard Mattessich, "Zu Ischboldins Kritik der mathematischen Methode," *ZfbF* 12 (1960): 550–56; A. G. Howson, "Change in Mathematics Education, since the Late 1950s Ideas and Realisation, Great Britain," *Educational Studies in Mathematics* 9 (1978): 183–223; E. Koch, "Mathematik – pro und kontra," *Der Volkswirt* 14:24 (1960): 1176–78; M. Larsfeld, "Mathématique et sciences sociales," *Revue de l'enseignement sociale* 3 (1959): 142–43; Jean Marchal, "Dangers de la méthode mathématique," *Revue d'économie politique* 54 (1940): 245–61; A. Piettre, "Economie et mathématique," *Economie et humanisme* 20:131 (1961): 3–16.

tional nor inconsequential. One reason is that attacks on the new methods, which were particularly intensive in the late 1970s, were not sudden or unexpected. In 1981 Dando and Sharp evaluated the mood of operations research as reflected in the pages of the *Journal of the Operational Research Society* by looking at the issues published in 1963, 1968, 1973, and 1978.[2] Up to 1968 when "optimism about the future of OR" reigned, there was "almost a total lack of criticism and debate in the journal." In 1973 the papers reflected considerable doubt about the practical effectiveness of O.R., a doubt which by 1978 was being voiced in about one quarter of the major papers appearing in the journal.[3] The essays of the late 1970s were, therefore, a culmination of a decade of ever-increasing and deepening criticism at the very center of the new paradigm.[4]

Not only was the controversy long-standing, but as time progressed the defenders of operational science became increasingly pessimistic. The pessimism was especially pronounced when the subject of long-term predictions arose. The comments of Roger Collcutt, who was involved in planning studies for a third London airport, illustrate this pessimism. He observed that "alternative sites [for the airport] cannot be reliably distinguished by OR or any other method other than political." About all that O.R. studies could do was "suggest the feasibility of various futures which in certain circumstances may look desirable."[5] With all these "mays" and "mights" such a defense of O.R.

2 "A Kuhnian Crisis in Management Science?" *JORS* 32 (1981): 91–103, 93.
3 Ibid., 92.
4 For 1978 in the *JORS* see, for example, Sadler's article on "OR and the Transition to a Post-Industrial Society," Bevan and Byer's "On Measuring the Contribution of O.R.," Dando and Sharp's on "O.R. in the U.K. in 1977," Radford's "Decision-making in a Turbulent Environment," Harris's "Corporate Planning and OR," Rosenhead's "An Education in Robustness," Heggie's "Putting Behaviour into Behavioural Models of Travel Choice," and Sharrock's "Some Key Problems in Controlling Component Stocks." Examples of earlier papers or criticism in the *JORS* are, for 1973, "The State of Research in O.R.," a report by the Research Committee, and Professor Cook's review of his period as the journal's editor. For similar articles in other journals, see Samuel Eilon, "How Scientific Is O.R.?" *OMEGA* 3:1 (1975): 1–8; Roger H. Collcutt, "O.R. Changes," *JORS* 32 (1981): 361–69; Patrick Rivett, "Perspective for Operational Research," *OMEGA* 2:2 (1974): 225–33; Samuel Eilon, "Ackoff's Fables," *OMEGA* 7:2 (1979): 89–99; N. R. Tobin, K. Rapley, and W. Teather, "The Changing Role of O.R.," *JORS* 31 (1980): 279–88; Russell Ackoff, "Resurrecting the Future of Operational Research," *JORS* (1979): 189–99; W. G. McClelland, "Mathematics in Management – How It Looks to the Manager," *OMEGA* 3:2 (1975): 147–55; B. C. Bishop, "A Contribution to the Discussion on the Methodology of Operational Research," *ORO* 23:3 (1972): 251–60; M. G. Simpson, "Those Who Can't?" *JORS* 29:3 (1978): 517–22B.
5 "O.R. Changes," 368.

Table 2.1. *Membership in O.R. societies*

Country	O.R. Society Founded	No. of Members Per Million Inhabitants		Number of Qualified Members	
		1974/76	1980	1974/76	1980
France	1956	11	10	570	555
Germany	1961 (1957)	11	12	701	749
UK	1953	51	60	2,898	3,371
USA	1952	51*	47*	7,848	6,800
				(11,000)	(10,000)*

*There are two O.R. groups involved in the United States, the Operations Research Society of America and The Institute of Management Studies. Only 50% of T.I.M.S. members, however, could be considered to be O.R. people. The estimates in parentheses include T.I.M.S. memberships, those without exclude them. The members per million inhabitants include the T.I.M.S. members.
Source: H. J. Zimmermann, "Trends and New Approaches in European Operational Research," *Journal of the Operational Research Society* 33 (1982): 597-603, 598.

obviously conceded much to the opposition. The old belief in its ability to manage scientifically had certainly disappeared. A decline in membership in the Operational Research Society also indicates that all was not well. Whereas membership had grown between 1964 and 1974 at an annual rate of 20 percent, subsequently growth rates dramatically fell.[6]

A third reason for taking critiques seriously has to do with the nature of the movement. Table 2.1 provides relative comparative data on O.R. society membership in France, Germany, the United Kingdom, and the United States. The O.R. groups in these four countries are, in terms of numbers of qualified members, the four largest in the world. Among these four, however, two, the British and American, are by far the largest, judged both in terms of members per million inhabitants and total members in absolute numbers. Of the two leaders, moreover, the British are slightly ahead of the Americans in membership per million inhabitants. These two countries dominated the operations research movement; indeed, whereas in 1980 O.R. societies in the United Kingdom and the United States had 13,371 total members, those in all of Europe had only 4,720.[7] The doubts that had cropped up primarily in Great Britain and America had occurred in the countries where O.R. had the greatest experience and following.

6 See Rivett, "Perspective for Operational Research," 225.
7 Fourteen countries: Austria, Belgium, Denmark, Finland, France, Germany, Greece, Ireland, Italy, Netherlands, Norway, Spain, Sweden, Switzerland. In 1980 Israel had 214 members and Turkey 173. Other than Japan, the number of members in the rest of the noncommunist world would have been insignificant.

Since operations research and management science are generic terms, doubts about their efficacy actually cover a variety of managerial activities. They pertained, of course, to O.R. work in firms but, as the examples cited indicate, O.R. people also got heavily involved in local and regional government. Wilbur A. Steger points out that during the 1960s there was "a virtual avalanche of urban/regional models about new planning, program analysis, budgeting and other 'futuristic' decision-making and policy-related decision-making 'using' urban/regional models."[8] But he notes, too, how unsuccessful O.R. techniques were. "When reviewing this era (the 1960s) it is difficult not to wonder at the relative unsophistication. . . . [T]he assessment techniques . . . proved not to be very useful and often caused more damage than good in dozens of overly literal applications."[9] There were, moreover, criticisms of the new management techniques adopted in the national bureaucracy. The most famous P.P.B.S. (Planning Programming Budgeting System) was installed first in the Department of Defense by "Rand Corporation economists," after Robert McNamara left the Ford Motor Company for Defense in 1961, and extended, after 1965, to other government agencies.[10] It called for the application of O.R. techniques to government decision making (statement of a project's objectives mathematically, optimization of the means, through a systems analysis, for the attainment of goals or a statement as to why available means could not achieve goals as stated). The procedure was designed to make decisions scientifically, i.e., to optimize the means by which tasks are decided and realized.[11] But, Wadavesky observed, "P.P.B.S. has failed everywhere and at all times. Nowhere has [it] been established and influenced governmental decisions according to its own principles. The program structures did not make sense to anyone. They are not, in fact, used to make decisions of any importance."[12]

This judgment is just. No groups of men so fundamentally misread reality as those who implemented and used P.P.B.S. in the Pentagon during the Vietnam War. The complaint, moreover, is more than political. It is technical, for P.P.B.S. did not fail just because the Americans

8 "Assessment of Fifteen Years of Urban Modeling," *OMEGA* 7:6 (1979): 545–51, 548.
9 Ibid.
10 Pierre Lequéret, *Le Budget de l'état* (Paris, 1982), 113–14.
11 Ibid., 116.
12 Quoted in Geert H. Hofstede, "The Poverty of Management Control Philosophy," *Academy of Management Review* 3 (1978): 450–61.

who implemented it were discredited by the Vietnamese defeat; they lost the war because they did not understand the limitations of managerial methods like P.P.B.S. The relative failure of scientific management techniques used in other government bureaucracies supported this conclusion. President Carter's attempt to implement a sibling of P.P.B.S., the Zero Base Budgeting Procedure, in the federal administration was abandoned because of its inadequacies. The introduction in French state administration after 1965 of a scientific management process similar to P.P.B.S. (R.C.B., *Rationalisation des Choix Budgétaires*) also suffered, people later discovered, from "excessive hope."[13] O.R. models can never be a "perfect representation of a problem," Russell Ackoff observed. They leave out the human dimension, the motivational one; indeed Ackoff complained that the successful treatment of managerial problems deserves "the application not only of science with a capital S but also all the arts and humanities we can command."[14]

Finally, disappointing O.R. results have been obtained from macroeconomic analysis. Anybody familiar with the popular as well as the semischolarly and scholarly press knows about the lost credibility of the economists. "Twenty-five years ago," Robert Kuttner observed in 1985, "the age old problem of boom and bust seemed to have been solved. [But, s]ince 1970 an outpouring of serious and ideologically diverse articles and books has pronounced that economics is in a state of severe, perhaps terminal, crisis."[15] Kuttner was not just talking about the inability of the givens of neoclassical economics (the economic man, the omnipotent entrepreneur, etc.) to explain operational realities; he was also concerned with the failure of mathematicized econometric models to provide fruitful policy guidance. The era of macroeconomic prognostication got under way in the mid-1950s. The models were relatively successful as long as the future resembled the past, but such a requirement for success hardly inspires confidence. It means that models are useful when they are not of any particular interest, as long as things remain the same. But when the future does not resemble the past, spectacular failure to predict rates of economic growth, business profitability, inflation rates, private consumption

---

13 Lequéret, *Le Budget de l'état*, 121–27, and J.-C. Milleron, R. Guesnerie, and M. Crémieux, *Calcul économique et décisions publiques* (Paris, 1979), 16–18; my translation.
14 "The Future of Operational Research Is Past," *JORS* 30 (1979): 93–104, 102.
15 "The Poverty of Economics," *Atlantic Monthly* 255 (Feb. 1985): 74–80, 75.

levels, employment, etc., can and have resulted. Even if models did predict successfully, they were not very instructive because the few that did coexisted with many that did not and there was no way to know in advance which prognosis would be correct. The conclusions of W. Frederichs and K. Kübler about the reliability of German econometric models seem to apply to the entire macroeconomic exercise in model building: "Neither the econometric, nor the naive prognosis, nor the judgmental forecasts could satisfactorily predict future economic development."[16]

The solutions that the new mathematics provided, to replace those produced by the insufficiencies of the mathematics employed by neoclassical economists, have proved themselves, from the macroeconomic managerial perspective, to be inadequate. Indeed, a well-known economist, Kenneth Boulding, has called the whole mathematical enterprise in economics a mistake. "Perhaps the real villain," he wrote, "is the discovery of seventeenth century mathematics some two hundred years later by Cournot, Jevons, and most of all Walras, whose influence and brilliance set economics on a path that increasingly has become a dead end."[17]

This criticism of the new science-based management could prompt people to counsel retention of older business methods. This happened, for example, in financial management. Whereas businessmen had customarily used asset accounting instruments when dealing with acquisition, divestment, and merger valuations (i.e., the traditional balance sheet), the new policy scientists, thinking that cash flow or earnings better reflected company reality, had developed in its place valuation techniques based on "a multiple of past reported or projected earnings."[18] Experience taught, however, that the "properly audited balance sheet is . . . a surer basis and for that reason figures more prominently in many deals than [the new methods]." Better to chance one's money on the visible, permanent assets reported in the balance sheet than the intangible, transient reported earnings. "One could argue the case for adding a balance sheet (and an auditor) to the British National

16 "Die Leistungsfähigkeit ökonometrischer Prognose-Systeme," *Operations Research Verfahren* 26 (1977): 814–26, 814; my translation. Paper read at a symposium on O.R. at Heidelberg University, Sept. 1–3, 1976.
17 "What Went Wrong with Economics?," *The American Economist* 30:1 (Spring 1986): 5–12.
18 Mark F. Cantley, "Attitudes, Accounts, and Operational Realities: Thoughts and Illustrations on Inter-Disciplinary Development," *JORS* 30:5 (1979): 401–03, 403.

(Incomes and Expenditures) Accounts because of the fickleness of valuations based on cash flow or earnings."[19] Actually the idea of abandoning the balance sheet for new forms of evaluation had occurred to German business economists immediately after the First World War (during the great inflation). They had had to renounce the idea because current values were not, like historical ones, verifiable in the accounts. Whatever the standard adopted, whatever the scientific method or mathematical model applied, it seemed to be unsuccessful. Somebody had to "determine" what the current value would be, and when this happened the results were subject to miscalculation if not outright fraud.[20] Because the new policy science could not overcome this shakiness in company valuations, the advice was to stay with the historical values stated in the traditional balance sheet.

Why all these doubts? Actually, the most telling intellectual reasons for them can be found in the root and branch denial of the scientific precepts on which the new paradigm in management studies is based. Professor Donald N. McCloskey presents a list of these precepts:

1. Prediction and control is the goal of science.
2. Only the observable implications (or predictions) of a theory matter to its truth.
3. Observability entails objective, reproducible experiments.
4. If (and only if) an experimental implication of a theory proves false is the theory proved false.
5. Objectivity is to be treasured: subjective "observation" (introspection) is not scientific knowledge.
6. Kelvin's Dictum: "When you cannot express it in numbers, your knowledge is of a meagre and unsatisfactory kind."
7. Introspection, metaphysical belief, aesthetics, and the like may well figure in the discovery of an hypothesis but cannot figure in its justification.
8. It is the business of methodology to demarcate scientific reasoning from non-scientific, positive from normative.
9. A scientific explanation of an event brings the event under a covering law.
10. Scientists, for instance economic scientists, have nothing to say as scientists about values, whether of morality or art.
11. Hume's Fork: "When we run over libraries, persuaded of these principles, what havoc must we make? If we take in our hand any volume – of divinity, of school metaphysics, for instance – let us ask, Does it contain any abstract reasoning concerning quantity or number? No. Does it contain any experimental reasoning concerning matter of fact and existence?

19 Ibid.
20 Locke, *The End of The Practical Man*, 164.

No. *Commit it then to the flames, for it can contain nothing but sophistry and illusion.*" (italics his, 1748).[21]

It is pointless (since the subject has been fully debated in recent times) if not presumptuous (since the debate has been among philosophers of note) to pursue the broad issue of scientific epistemology here. Suffice it to say only that the new paradigm in management studies operated under these principles of "modernism" and that they are open to question. To quote McCloskey again: "Few in philosophy now believe as many as half of these propositions. A substantial, respectable, and growing minority believes none of them. But a large majority in economics believes them all."[22]

Still, whether philosophers accept or reject the propositions of modernism is of no great practical moment. Most people do not worry about the epistemology of modern science; they just accept the truth of the scientific method as an article of faith. Among most people, moreover, can be counted the scientists themselves. Those in the formal sciences are not technically even concerned with empirical verification. The pure mathematicians in particular are motivated by intellectual curiosity to construct their beautiful patterns, and the neoclassical economists can, in terms of self-justification, claim that they are involved in the same sort of logical game. Even their staunchest critics acknowledge that. Professor A. G. Papandreou stated, for instance:

It should be obvious that, . . . if economics is structured as a pure science while the other social sciences are structured as empirical sciences, the very question of a relationship between them becomes irrelevant. Pure sciences are tautological in character. Theories derived from postulates, though entailing a logical implication, are necessarily true, if the postulates are true. . . . Theorems of axiomatised deductive systems, therefore, can never come into contact with reality.[23]

What pure mathematicians or theoretical economists can claim, however, empirical scientists and practicing managers cannot, for their

---

21 "The Rhetoric of Economics," *Journal of Economic Literature* 21 (1983): 481–517, 485.
22 Ibid., 485. McCloskey's general attack on modernism was meant especially for neoclassical economics, but it amounted as well to a theoretical indictment of all the sciences that made up the new paradigm in management studies. His view is itself a fine example of how doubts have seized those who were once strong advocates of the new paradigm.
23 "Economics and the Social Sciences," *The Economic Journal* 60 (1950): 715–23, 715–16.

work has to stand the test of relevance. When the applied natural and behavioral sciences utilize formal science methods in their work, moreover, they cannot escape the question of practical relevance too. And on these grounds the new paradigm in management studies was found wanting.

Part of the problem is purely one of data, of facts. Management facts, compared to those of natural science and engineering, are not precise. The problem varies according to the type of data involved. Scientists often distinguish between hard and soft data, that is, between reliable or unreliable data. Generally, the hard data are found in the natural and the soft in the social sciences, although the relative degree of hardness and softness varies within each science group as well. Peter Ulrich and Peter Hill have observed that the reliability of models depends on the relative narrowness of the problem identification and that data reliability even affects problem definition.[24] Professor Erich Gutenberg's production model, for instance, includes costs, investment, and financial information but excludes data on the factory culture (i.e., personnel, information systems, etc.). The excluded data, in this case, are soft, uncertain, because of their subjectivity (it is always difficult to be precise about human motivation and social relations). Compared to the hard data on costs, investment, etc., the soft are not suited for mathematical expression, i.e., the prerequisite for linear programming, that the parameters and goals must be stated mathematically, cannot be met. What fruitfulness the Gutenberg production model gained from the reliability of its data, therefore, was lost by leaving out soft data, for the model did not contain all the variables pertinent to the decision problem entrepreneurs faced.[25]

The contrast between hard and soft data mirrors that frequently drawn between natural and social science. The nineteenth-century mathematician Henri Poincaré, greeting the new subject of sociology, commented that it has the most method and least results of any science.[26] The efforts to apply the tools of formal and natural science, including statistics, in the behavioral sciences were noted in the last chapter. But the attempt to make the social sciences part of the new paradigm in management studies has been the most problematic, for

24 "Wissenschaftstheoretische Aspekte ausgewählter betriebswirtschaftlicher Konzeptionen," in *Wissenschaftstheoretische Grundfragen der Wirtschaftswissenschaften*, by Hans Raffée and Bodo Abel, 161–90; my translation.
25 Ibid., 171.
26 *Revue d'économie politique* 62 (1952): 1970.

efforts to improve the scientific methods have not enhanced confidence in reliability very much. Professor Hubert Blalock, Jr., concluded after decades of statistical work that "the social sciences, lodged as they are between the natural sciences and humanities, have almost inevitably become a battleground over the suitability of natural science models and approaches to the study of human behavior and social processes."[27]

These attacks on the social sciences are important because of their significance for management science. If a scientific model is to inform us, we have to have confidence in its having all pertinent relations contained within it. If in management these pertinent relations are social-psychological ones, then they must be contained within the model; otherwise it is impossible to know what the consequence would be if a variable changed. In other words, you are damned if you exclude social-psychological variables from business management problems because of the damage their exclusion would do to the integrity of the decision model, damned if you include them because they cannot be stated mathematically.

Consequently, such operations research techniques as stock and inventory control seem useful, only "if," as one expert stated, "your input data is good enough and mostly it isn't."[28] More importantly, because of the data problem, even doubts about the appropriateness of applying a scientific method exist. Russell Ackoff, the O.R. pioneer who turned O.R. critic, states the case rather crudely. He accused O.R. people of engaging in "mathematic masturbation without substantive knowledge of organizations, institutions or their management."[29] M. G. Simpson, in a presidential address to the British Operational Research Society (1978) expressed a similar, if less trenchantly stated view:

Standard mathematical techniques or their immediate extension are rarely applicable. . . . This is borne out by surveys among past students, the majority of whom even several years after graduation, have never used queuing theory, linear programming or the rest. . . . The techniques themselves reflect and embody the underlying structures of commonly occurring processes. Thus in queuing situations while the arrival and service distributions, the queue discipline and of course the context may vary very substantially from one situation to another, they all have a basic form which is reflected in the mathematical methods used and in the resultant models emerging. The ability to draw and to exploit such analogies is clearly one of our strengths, though I fear there are

27 *Basic Dilemmas in the Social Sciences* (Beverly Hills, 1984).
28 Collcutt, "O.R. Changes," 367.
29 "The Future of Operational Research," 97.

still too many instances of Operational Researchers striving to re-invent the wheel. Quite apart from being aware both of the potential and the limitations of formal mathematical ways of handling problems of a given structure, I believe that a thorough appreciation of the techniques enables one much better to understand (or even to recognize) the existence of the underlying form. . . . [W]hile the techniques as such may never really be applicable, they can often be used in the initial stages of a study to give valuable "back of envelope" estimates of the likely effects of system change.[30]

Simpson's comments about mathematics are more encouraging than Ackoff's because he (Simpson) appreciates the intellectual schooling that mathematical modeling imparts. But it is a strange idiom that if it purports to be scientific, only offers "back of envelope" estimates to the users. Neither of these men, then, really had great confidence in the ability of applied mathematics to solve management problems. The mathematics was not wrong, only the application, and the difficulties arose there, at least in part, because of an insufficiency which is conditioned, if in part, by the data problem.

Yet the difficulties encountered in the new management studies paradigm do not crop up just because of the facts. Problems arise, as the McCloskey critique of scientism indicates, because of certain scientific assumptions about the nature of management man. A relevance problem arose for one reason because the scientists misunderstood the managerial function. The classic definition of what managers do is that they "plan, organize, co-ordinate, and control," in order to optimize. These are rational, analytical actions, which seem to be well suited to the techniques used in scientific management. But as Ian Glover noted, the manager's job is actually "of an unprogrammed character: [he or she] . . . is not much concerned with the flow and rational use of 'hard' information, his information is distorted, incomplete, his job is ambiguous."[31] He is not "primarily a decision-maker, a planner but an 'inspirer,' a fire fighter, and a rationalizer after the fact."[32] Professor Philippe Nemo has, in France, expressed similar sentiments. "The problem," he writes, "of social practice can be formulated in the following way: to adapt man's actions not to the facts that he knows (that deductive reason can take care of) but to facts that he does not know. Or, how to act best [*bien*] in a given circumstance in

30 "Those Who Can't," 518.
31 "Professionalism and Manufacturing Industry," in *Manufacturing and Management* by Michael Fores and Ian Glover (London, 1978), 115–31, 121.
32 Ibid.

which one cannot, in principle, know all the conditions and prospects."[33] Glover's and Nemo's views limit the connections possible between science and business studies. They suggest that to the extent that the studies conform to the guidelines of science, their usefulness to the practicing manager diminishes. As Glover phrased it, "attempts to 'study' decision making are overly academic, attempts at 'programming' it all seem to be like the search for fool's gold, confusing the academic ballgame of analysis with the executive task of synthesis."[34] Nemo, although he employs the word *science* (he is interested in the adoption of a "science of action" in business studies), really is not thinking of a discipline that is subject to the just outlined precepts of modernism. He complains about the sterility of instruction, "les techniques comptables, statistiques, informatiques."[35] Man acts adaptively not according to formal and theoretical scientific knowledge. This view of the manager, therefore, downgrades the knowledge as opposed to the skill component in his armory. He is like an artisan who acquires capability by absorbing the wisdom distilled in the traditions of his craft and he does so primarily on the job.

But if an inherent talent, coupled with skill acquired through experience, is essential to the manager, then, what about the knowledge coming from science? The answer to that question depends on how much knowledge, as opposed to skills, is needed in the manager's job. The German Engineering Association (V.D.I.) estimated some years ago that in engineering the knowledge-skill ratio was about fifty-fifty, that is, engineers need to learn their craft through practical experience and to acquire knowledge through a formal study of science in equal proportions. Nobody seems to have attempted to establish a similar knowledge-skill ratio for the manager's job. But it is clear that the ratio would be much less favorable to knowledge than it is in engineering. A manager in a large high-tech German firm, who is a business economist by education, explains why. He notes that firms rarely if ever ask management school academics for advice on how to solve a management matter but they often request the advice, if not the outright help, of engineering professors on a technical problem.

Academic research in business studies, in sum, differs almost com-

33 "Les Enseignements nontechniques dans les grandes écoles de gestion," *Revue française de gestion* (Nov.–Dec. 1984): 16–27, 21; my translation.
34 "Professionalism and Manufacturing Industry," 118.
35 "Les Enseignements nontechniques," 17.

pletely from that in engineering because it is based on a different premise. The business academic is an outsider who is trying to find out what is going on inside the firm. That is why so much business school research takes the form of case studies, participative projects, and surveys. In an engineering school scientific experimentation in the Baconian sense of laboratory work is important. Knowledge can be acquired, through these experiments, that people in praxis do not possess (and know they do not possess) and would like to have. Because of the difference in research purpose, cooperation between business schools and business is much more problematic than between engineering faculty and factory. Surely it is less conceivable that an engineer in a high-tech firm would be as dismissive of a top engineering school as James Glanvill, a partner at Lazard Frères, was of a leading business institution. "There have got to be some people," he said, "who go to the Harvard Business School and are not ruined by the experience."[36] (And the suggestion is that he has not found one.) Only because the knowledge component of management is so uncertain could such distrust of academia persist.

These problems can be perceived most easily in neoclassical economics. "Marginalism," Professor Erich Schneider explained, "is thinking in terms of changes in economic variables and in the relationship between such changes." Economic theory at heart is "a theory of adjustment to change. The concept of the equilibrium is a tool in this theory of change; the marginal calculus is its dominating principle."[37] From a practical viewpoint, marginalism, however, is based on a highly questionable sociology of man (i.e., the economic man), questionable not just because it does not describe the reality of human existence but because it does not accurately describe the economic part of that reality. In effect, if the marginalist principle assumes that the entrepreneur tries to bring marginal cost into line with marginal price (this is the calcul), and the concept of equilibrium assumes that, with every individual entrepreneur so acting in society, marginal price and cost tend towards equilibrium within the entire economy, both ideas are predicated on the assumption that the economy is made up of a lot of autonomous individual producers competing for supplies and cus-

---

36 "The Money Chase," *Time*, May 4, 1981, 36–42, 41.
37 "Der Realismus der Marginalanalyse in der Preistheorie," in *Volkswirtschaft und Betriebswirtschaft*, by Erich Schneider (Tübingen, 1964), 413–32, 415–16; my translation.

tomers who behave as profit maximizers. P. W. S. Andrews's studies of the actual behavior of entrepreneurs, which began before the Second World War, revealed, however, that entrepreneurs do not behave as profit maximizers.[38] More recent studies by W. J. Baumol, E. P. Penrose, Herbert Simon, R. M. Cyert and J. G. March make businessmen "satisficers" not "optimizers." They also take "non-pecuniary sources of satisfaction, including security, status, power, prestige, social service, moral behavior, leisure, and so on" into consideration when evaluating the entrepreneurs' behavior.[39] People do optimize; they do desire profit; but they also do not, and economic theory is incapable of determining when they do and when they do not. Hence, it is not able to say when a theory based on optimization is applicable, and not to know that is to know very little. The given (i.e., economic man) is not very useful.

Moreover, another given in neoclassical economic theory does not deal with the complexity of the managerial process within the firm. Probably the first step towards scholarly realization of the complexity came with the recognition of the managerial revolution. A second and important step, however, happened with the development of the strategy and structures argument. In 1961 Professor Alfred D. Chandler, Jr., and Fritz Redlich published an article in *The Business History Review* in which they discussed the development of managerial hierarchies, in particular, that transformation in the twentieth century from the U form single-product, multifunctional firm to the M form divisionalized multiproduct, multifunctional firm.[40] Whereas in U form corporations a head office executive committee, composed primarily of the firm's functional vice-presidents (i.e., one for sales, for production, etc.), runs the company, in the new M form organization a headquarters staff presides over decentralized (e.g., by product or geographical region) divisions which direct their operations with their own functional staffs. The M form, therefore, created a new layer of management in the firm, the headquarters staff, while pushing the functional managers (sales, production, etc.) down to the divisions. The manager's job changed with the structure; specifically, while divi-

---

38 *Manufacturing Business* (London, 1949); and "A Reconsideration of the Theory of the Individual Business," *Oxford Economic Papers,* NS 1 (1949): 54–89.
39 H. B. Malmgren, "What Conclusions Are to Be Drawn from Empirical Cost Data," *Journal of Industrial Economics* 7 (Mar. 1959): 136–44, 37.
40 "Recent Developments in American Business Administration and Their Conceptualization," *Business History Review* 35:1 (1961): 1–27.

sional managers operated their businesses, central headquarters concentrated on strategic decision making.

Chandler asserts that new technologies and the strategies they imposed fashioned the changes in managerial structures. Industries, he writes,

such as apparel, textiles from natural fiber, lumber, furniture, painting and publishing did not make a large sharp reduction of unit costs as the volume of materials through the plant increased. In these industries large mills, factories, or work had no striking cost advantages over small ones. In . . . the more capital intensive industries [however] . . . new processes of production were invented or vastly improved. . . . In [these] industries the throughput needed to maintain minimum efficient scale requires not only careful coordination of flow through the processes of production but also of the flows of inputs from the suppliers and the flow of output to the retailers and final consumers. Such coordination cannot happen automatically. It demanded the constant attention of a managerial team, or hierarchy.[41]

Chandler lists the refining and distilling industry (sugar, petroleum, animal and vegetable oil, whiskey, etc.), smelting (iron, copper, steel, aluminum, etc.), mechanical processing and packaging of agricultural products (grains, tobacco, etc.), the manufacturing of sophisticated light machinery (typewriters, adding machines, milk separators, etc.), the production of high-technology industrial machinery (high-speed turret lathes, etc.) and chemicals (dyes) among the complex of industries which achieved the economies of scale and hence required the managerial-organizational changes.

The growth of the managerial hierarchies did not necessarily destroy the free will of the entrepreneur. Chandler's point is that the differentiation of management according to operational and strategic-planning functions restored the ability of each management level, in the large firm, to do its job effectively and hence efficiently. Yet the view that the firm was run by some omniscient entrepreneur could not survive. The necessity to rely on subordinates for information required to formulate and execute plans restricted the executive manager's power to decide, or rather made the decision process systemic. The tendency, moreover, for organizations to develop informal information networks – a realization that gained scientific currency in the Hawthorne Studies but one that any practicing manager knows – further complicated the manage-

41 Ibid., 10–11.

rial process, for it introduced the "irrational" element into organization theory.[42]

If this critique of neoclassical economics prompts one to erase the arrows drawn between economics and business studies in Figure 1.1, it does not necessarily prompt one to go further. The very people responsible for the development of the new paradigm in management studies, the engineers, mathematicians, social and natural scientists involved in mathematical model building, often little respected economic theory. They too questioned its relevance and would gladly themselves erase the arrows from the chart between neoclassical economics and business studies, while, it might be added, drawing in those between other sciences and management studies in india ink. Everybody attacks the economists nowadays, even the historians. Professor Leslie Hannah, for instance, cites how historical analysis inspired by neoclassical economics has led his colleagues astray:

[T]he attempts to rescue late Victorian and Edwardian entrepreneurs in Britain from the accusation of failure, attempts most vigorously prosecuted by the American scholars McCloskey and Sandberg, fail dismally, since the assumption of their theory gives them their answer. If an entrepreneur is merely a neoclassical firm, responding automatically to external signals, rather than an economic actor, who might himself formulate new production functions, or develop new markets, thus fundamentally changing the signal in the economy, then it is easy to give him a clean bill of health, as McCloskey and Sandberg proceeded to do. . . . The fact remains, however, that between the 1880s and the mid-1920s, Britain was experiencing the slowest rate of growth of GDP per head of the past hundred years. . . . Once we cease to see entrepreneurs simply as optimisers subject to given constraints, but as actors with the potential to remove or change those constraints by developing new technologies or new organisations by moving into new industries – as actually happens in history – the case for the defence of the Edwardian entrepreneur collapses irremediably.[43]

The assumptions of neoclassical economics are just as unrealistic, then, when used to explain managerial behavior in the past as they are when used for the purpose in the present.

Yet the other sciences involved in the new management studies para-

42 See F. J. Roethlisberger and W. J. Dickson, *Management and the Worker* (Cambridge, Mass., 1939); Elton Mayo, *The Human Problems of an Industrial Civilisation* (New York, 1933); H. Landsberger, *Hawthorne Revisited* (Ithaca, N.Y., 1958); and J. H. Smith, "Elton Mayo Revisited," *British Journal of Industrial Relations* 13:2 (1972): 282–91.
43 *Entrepreneurs and the Social Science,* an inaugural lecture (The London School of Economics and Political Science, 1983), 12–13.

digm rest on hardly more solid ground than neoclassical economics. Of course, when a young engineer needs to establish inventory levels or a salesman needs to optimize coverage of his or her territory, he or she is just as grateful for the mathematical tools that O.R. research has provided as the historian who is trying to establish past productivity indices for a firm. Techniques used in operational analysis that have been provided by engineers or applied mathematicians are more pragmatically efficacious than anything neoclassical economics has provided managers. But their scientific assumptions are open to doubt, even from pragmatic points of view. We in fact operate in all sciences with certain truths, on certain assumptions about life, thought, and knowledge, which divorce man from social-economic reality.

Nothing illustrates this better than the dispute which went on for a generation among organizational theorists about the relative merits of a convergence as opposed to a contingency view of organizations. "The convergence thesis expresses a belief in the working of the 'invisible hand' applied to the diffusion of knowledge. Sooner or later knowledge gets codified, after which diffusion and hence, convergence, becomes inevitable."[44] Convergence, then, is predicated on the assumption that "where problems and the technical means available for solving them are similar, social groups which may differ widely in cultural outlook will find similar ways of tackling them."[45] This means, since organizations are converging, that the organizational environment is, in things that matter, culture-free. Contingency theory asserts the opposite: the structure and process within an organization are conditioned by its environment. Ostensibly supporters of a contingency viewpoint would seem, therefore, to be more sensitive, when discussing organizations, to uniqueness than advocates of convergence. But contingency people have generally refused to wander into the thicket of cultural relativity. Environment has been defined in noncultural terms, i.e., the nature of the technology, the size of the firm, and so on are the determinants, the contingents of structure and managerial functions. A most obvious example of this sort of contingency approach is Chandler's explanation of the rise of managerial hierarchies. American capitalists in a changing technical world, with new marketing strategies to match new technolo-

44 Max Boisot, "Convergence Revisited: The Codification and Diffusion of Knowledge in a British and Japanese Firm," *Journal of Management Studies* 20:2 (Apr. 1983): 159–90, 188.
45 Ibid., 159.

gies and products, set out to create and created the corporate and managerial structure necessary to their strategy. Derek Channon, in his study of British enterprise, pointed out that "the widespread adoption of a strategy of diversification and a multi-divisional organization highlighted the need for a large number of general managers without which the potential advantages offered by strategic and structural changes would be lost."[46] Although Channon makes management training contingent on Chandler's insight into the relationship between strategy and structure in the large firm, nothing about culture is necessary to these arguments. They are culture-free.

The triumph of the culture-free approach in operations research, in organizational theory, or in any other social science, resembles, then, its triumph in neoclassical economic theory. This can be seen if the idea of profit maximization or cost minimization is taken into consideration. It is not only a basic given in the neoclassical economists' analysis of entrepreneurial activity, it is the assumption underlying most mathematical models used in operations research. When this profit maximization or cost minimization motive is dropped, other sorts of universal explanations (i.e., stemming from human nature) are possible (e.g., desire for power, man as a "satisfier," etc.). But so are normative motives, based on contingencies. This is what the contingency theorists argue, but this argument shares the universalist outlook of the neoclassical economists in that it is also interested in generalizing (about organization behavior without regard to specific historical-cultural contexts). Supporters of the new paradigm would approve of this ambition: The wedding of managerial studies to science, freeing it from specific cultural contexts, marks in their opinion an important step towards an understanding of management process and with it towards the improvement of management performance. But is this true? There are reasons for thinking it is not, since the new paradigm in management cannot properly explain the single most important event in recent economic history: the rise of Japan to world eminence in business and industry.

Few people today think that the Japanese advantages can be attributed to knowledge, in the scientific or strict technological sense. Management in Japanese firms does not know something that Western firms do not know, either in the sense of engineering or managerial science.

46 *The Strategy and Structure of British Enterprise* (London, 1973).

On the contrary, the knowledge flow has been from an inventive West to an emulative Japan in both technology and management techniques. Rather the Japanese strength has resided in an ability to assimilate borrowed technology and managerial know-how and to improve incrementally upon it. The problem is that this Japanese management behavior cannot be clarified with the tools and ideas developed in the new paradigm. Several quotations about their management behavior will indicate why.

Thomas P. Rohlen, in "Managerial Philosophy in a Confucian Setting," has observed:

Japanese feel that cynicism regarding such visions (corporate philosophies) is misplaced and indeed destructive, something it took me (Rohlen) many months to fully understand and accept. I came to see a strong analogy between the Japanese approach and organizations like scouting in the West. The conscious intent to build a strong idealistic organization culture, the explicit management of that culture by its leaders and the compliance of the membership are among the notable similarities between the Japanese companies and organizations like the Boy Scouts. . . .

To our Western eyes such things as songs, creeds and company rituals may seem childish or fanatical or both, but they are neither and our impressions only serve to highlight the character of our own culture's approach to business organization, one that sees beliefs as properly private and would abhor the attempt of any employing organization to "dictate" moral values to us.[47]

Professor Nakagawa Keiichiro of the University of Tokyo in "Japanese Management in Its Historical Perspective," writes: "The present author once found it difficult to convince some American students that nothing special is promised to Japanese employees who are going to work for life in particular firms and that in fact no real contract is involved for such long term employments."[48] Professor Keiichiro observes further in the same article:

The German industrial firms also seem to borrow aggressively from banks, but it is said that the German banks do not get into such "community of interest" relations with industrial firms. Although German banks aggressively loan to industrial firms, they decisively write off the frozen credit once they find it hopeless to collect the credit. However, Japanese banks usually continue to

---

47 "Managerial Philosophy in a Confucian Setting: The Japanese Case and Its Implications for Western Management," typewritten manuscript, Business History Unit, LSE.
48 Nakagawa Keiichiro, "Japanese Management in Its Historical Perspective – Informal, Integrative, Democratic and Long-term-focus System," paper presented at the Anglo-Japanese Conference, Business History Unit, LSE, Aug. 20, 1986, 2.

support their staggering clients even by further loaning to the clients additional resources until the industrial firms recover from the crisis of bankruptcy.[49]

And, finally, he notes at the end of the essay:

[O]ne may ask why the business and industrial organizations in Japan have not turned out to be so individualistic, contractual, formal and short-term focused as in the case of American organizations. Here, in addition to the cultural homogeneity and easy communications in Japan, the role of Japanese "corporate familism" and the Confucian doctrine of "dezhi" (government by virtue or moral excellence) have to be pointed out as the bases of the Japanese informal social integrity. According to the Chinese philosophy that has deep roots in the mentality of modern Japanese businessmen, the "wangdao" (royal road) of rule or government should be based on the "de" (moral excellence) of the governor and it is only the "badao" (military government) that can be based on rights and authorities.[50]

Confucianism explains why workers do not need written contracts: They are needed only when the leader is morally suspect, not to be trusted because he does not possess "de." The sense of obligation and community explains why money is lent to a firm when it has become a bad risk in Western eyes. The behavior these quotations highlight is held to be primarily responsible for superior Japanese economic performance.

That superiority, moreover, is not expressed just in the acts of trust and confidence essential to the existence of close-knit organization. It arose from the way culture spilled over into technical organization. Japanese factories have been praised for their excellent quality control; they have been extolled for their inventory control, or rather, for their ability to operate without inventory (Just in Time, i.e., delivery of supply just in time for its use at the manufacturing point). These are highly impressive complex technical feats whose execution has cultural roots. In the West operations research has produced very complex control systems to assure coordination of such complex processes. The control is imposed from without. The Japanese, by contrast, rely not on O.R. control systems as much as on the capacities of a highly qualified but also highly motivated labor force to operate without surveillance; for, if people are highly qualified and motivated, an elaborate system of personnel control is not needed. Just let the people go; they will find the

49 Ibid., 15.
50 Ibid., 26.

most efficient way to work on their own. Professor Christer Karlsson stresses that in the Honda assembly plants he visited there are no elaborate systems of external control. Each worker has a button at the work place that can be pushed to stop the line when things go wrong. But the workers are so well qualified and highly motivated that they seldom use the buttons, and when they do co-workers rush to the trouble spot to solve the difficulty and then cooperate, subsequently, in order to see to it that this problem does not arise again. The Honda workers operate in teams, moving along the line, every worker qualified to do any of the team-assigned tasks, completing the specific job that needs to be done in order to accomplish the collective job as carefully and quickly as possible. The control is not external; it comes from within the worker. The technical and managerial systems are cultural systems, i.e., they are contingent on the existence of historically conditioned cultural traits embedded in the organization.[51]

Japan did not experience the Enlightenment. The Japanese society that underwent self-induced industrialization in the nineteenth and twentieth century did so with feudal values that expressed a Confucian ethic. Its morality was social rather than individual, or rather, the content of socially determined relations (i.e., husband with wife, father with son, brother with brother, older person with younger, friend with friend, emperor with subject) differed. The sets of mutual rights and obligations constitute, ideally, a moral order, one that, in fact, once external brute force has to be employed (by police or army) is dissolved. The truly moral society in this Confucian setting is one where the conscience of the individual makes him police himself.

These concerns extend from the outside world into the business and industrial firm. Because it is a community based on a Confucian ethic, the older worker takes charge of the younger, watching out after him, just as the company watches out after its new workers, for the heavy investment Japanese firms make in education is justified economically

51 Personal conversation. Professor Tsunehiko Yui argues, for the same reason, against the culture-free explanation of corporate structural evolution. He observes that Japanese corporations have not conformed (smaller headquarters staff, less diversification, etc.) to the American growth patterns, outlined by Chandler, because the culture on the ground prompted variants. This implies that the structural evolution of American corporations was itself a response to the peculiarities of American culture. See Tsunehiko Yui, "Development, Organization, and Business Strategy of Industrial Enterprise in Japan," *Yearbook of Japanese Business History* 5 (1988), and Johannes Hirschmeier and Tsunehiko Yui, *The Development of Japanese Business,* 2d ed. (London, 1981).

because the employees, for cultural reasons, are not ready to move. That ethic, moreover, serves the internal cohesion of the factory organization. Pay differential between top management and unskilled workers is not very great; the amount people earn is determined by length of service in the firm not by the talent of the individual. Studies of Japanese firms show that the workers' commitment to them is based on more than a desire for money or on fear of losing a job.[52] Boisot points out, for example, in a comparative study of Hitachi and English Electric, that employees, sitting in similar organizational structures, look outward into society (e.g., at other job possibilities in other firms) in one company (English Electric) and up the hierarchy in the other, i.e., they remain psychologically inside the organization and loyal to it.[53] The Japanese worker does not think of himself as engaged in an economic function (being an electrical engineer, a production engineer, lathe operator, accountant, etc.) which is divorced from the firm, an occupational function that can be done anywhere. He is a Hitachi man, a Honda man, and so on, a member of a community. It is a profoundly different way of looking at work.

Just how different it is can be illustrated by a story. An American manufacturer, Abraham Katz, who has business installations in America, England, and Japan, relates that when visiting his facilities, he lets his people know only generally about his arrival.[54] He wants to drop in at a time of his choice to observe normal work. On a visit to Japan recently he arrived half an hour before work, unannounced, as usual, to find his employees all gathered in a semicircle, having a pep rally before his photograph on the wall. Approaching unseen behind the group, he witnessed what appeared to be testimonials to past accomplishments and exhortations to even greater ones ("Last week I sold ten units; next week I'll sell fifteen!") by the workers. When somebody turned to find the living reality of the photograph standing there and drew everybody's attention to this fact, there was joy. The local general manager, a Japanese, advised Katz to present a flower personally to each employee, a small but significant act to honor them and to express his appreciation for their efforts. When Katz returned to New

52 See, for example, Arthur M. Whitehill, Jr., and Schin-Ichi Takezawa, *The Other Worker: A Comparative Study of Industrial Relations in the United States and Japan* (Honolulu, Hawaii, 1968).
53 Boisot, "Convergence Revisited," 188.
54 Personal conversation.

York he told his sons that he felt sorry for them – because they had to compete with the Japanese. What Katz meant has to do with motivation not knowledge, or, as Katz himself expressed it, "If I hung up my photograph in the New York plant, people would throw things at it."

Since the evidence that managers, indeed management, operate according to cultural norms is so convincing, it is hard to believe that people ignore the cultural factor. And yet Kuttner tells us that economists, despite all the proof to the contrary, continue to act as if the givens of neoclassical economics are true. And the economists are not alone, for all scientists involved in the new management studies paradigm are leery of historically shaped cultural explanations when dealing with managerial behavior and economic activity. They prefer science to culture. But what good is a science if it cannot, as in the Japanese example, cope with what it purports to explain? And how can people insist that it does provide the answers when the evidence clearly shows that it is inadequate to the task? To insist on science under such conditions is really to assume an ideological, not a scientific, attitude (when a science cannot explain something but is clung to as the proper way to explain it, that science, as in the case of scientific Marxism, or neoclassical capitalism, becomes ideology). There is ample evidence that the new management studies paradigm is itself as much a cultural as a scientific expression. We in the West are used to drawing certain historical conclusions about what was necessary for the industrial revolution to take place. The John Lockean (individual psychology and individual rights), Adam Smithian (economic man, the marketplace), Karl Marxian (emergence of the capitalistic ethic) view has become such a powerful motivating force in our societies that people think the Enlightenment conception of man is necessary to a thriving industrial society. Evidence now suggests that a feudal ethic, a sense of community instead of individualism, is a much superior basis on which to organize an advanced industrial society.[55]

Almost all criticisms of scientific methodology have within them the view that modernist principles of scholarly procedure simply do not apply to human activities. P. A. Sorokin recognized this insight in 1948 when he wrote:

---

55 The view is not just held in Japan. Traditional right-wing elements in the West had similar ideas. See, for instance, the ideology of French Legitimists in the nineteenth century in Robert R. Locke, *French Legitimists and the Politics of Moral Order in the Early Third Republic* (Princeton, N.J., 1974), chap. 2–4.

[M]ost of the defects of modern psycho-social science are due to a clumsy imitation of physical sciences. They seem to forget the cardinal fact that none of the established natural sciences has reached its maturity by merely imitating another science, especially when it is quite different. Each of them has built itself – in its basic concepts, uniformities, methods and techniques – by following its own path corresponding to the nature of the phenomena studied. The basic concepts, laws, methods, and techniques of physics are different from those of chemistry or biology, and vice versa. . . . There is no reason to expect that by plunging the conceptual network of physics into the basically different psycho-social ocean one can catch big psycho-social fish, and can learn the uniformities of their behavior.[56]

Sorokin's view certainly calls much of the new management studies paradigm into question. But even he is still thinking in terms of science, in terms of the development of a psycho-social discipline that seeks to generalize from specifics.

The Japanese case, however, is troublesome because it seems to deny the possibility of such an approach. The economic man, that abstraction which the eighteenth century bequeathed us, stands condemned by the feudal ethic of Japan, and more significantly, so does the management science on which it is based, for it incorporates the norms and values of the society that gave it birth – primarily America – and builds them into the heart of its scientific analysis. It is not just a question of adding a cultural dimension to the scientific study of management, it is one of showing how culture affects science itself. The elaborate operations research techniques and management control systems characteristic of the new paradigm turn out to be, to a large extent, not scientific but cultural developments, i.e., the sort of techniques that our culture, which has developed the economic man and the communityless abstract labor, needs, in order to operate an advanced economy, but the sort that is not called for, to anywhere near the same degree, within the very different cultural context of Japan. Because we assume that our values are necessary to an industrial society, we also assume that the Japanese will have to become, in time, like us. But this blinds us to understanding how an advanced industrial society, that is not like ours, prospers.

What then do all these ruminations about culture and the new paradigm in management studies have to do with this book on higher management education? Just this. When man acts adaptively, not ac-

---

56 "Fads and Foibles in Modern Sociology and Related Science," quoted in Dando and Sharp, "Operational Research in the U.K.," 948.

cording to formal and theoretical scientific knowledge, but, as F. A. Hayek tells us, "according to some acquired schema or rules (or norms or values) which predispose him to act in this or that sense, he does so because the type of component in question has been accepted [*valorisé*] by the group, i.e., adopted and memorized by it [*selectioné et mémorisé*]."[57] Since these norms are not universals but highly diverse specific manifestations of culture and civilization, their existence and acquisition are historically determined. And since historians deal with these specificities, they are particularly well qualified to explore their meaning. The didactic benefits to be derived from their investigations, as every historian knows, must be handled carefully. Cultural contexts are not only historically determined but unique. That is why in cultural matters it is so hard to know. But comparative studies are not a waste of time. As Professor H. Siedentopf notes: "A comparison should and must not lead to hasty importation of foreign models. It should lead us to understand the weaknesses and strengths of our own educational condition. [Foreign] models are not prototypes, to be emulated, but screens with which to test our own reality."[58]

Two conclusions, therefore, are in order. First, neither the Americans nor the Japanese are unique in their cultural distinctness. Although the most obvious cultural differences exist between this Asian and this Western country, highlighting the cultural aspects of their comparative business and industrial behavior, every country's culture is quite specific. The European countries, therefore, are quite different from the Japanese and the Americans in their cultural life and, within Europe, the Germans, the English, and the French (as well as others) are quite different from each other. This hardly means that their business studies have nothing in common. The scientific techniques, the tools used in financial analysis, in marketing, in inventorying, in production layout, and so on, are part of a common managerial science, one which the Americans largely, if not exclusively, invented, and one everybody borrowed. But the personnel and organization aspects of management, the skills and motivation, indeed, even the way the scientific techniques were borrowed and integrated in research and in praxis were and are culture-specific.

57 Quoted in Nemo, "Les Enseignements nontechniques," 21–22; my translation.
58 "Vergleichende Anmerkungen zur Ausbildung des Führungsnachwuchses der Verwaltung," *Die öffentliche Verwaltung* (1984): 530.

Secondly, the subject of business studies is itself a cultural phenomenon. This means that the acceptance of business studies in each country depended on the ability of that country's culture to foster and to assimilate it. And it also means that the form and the effectiveness of business studies will be, because cultures vary, different in each country. Therefore, the historians who can deal with the specificity of this educational evolution can shed light, more light perhaps than scientists who ignore culture, on the relationship between business studies and economic performance. The following chapters are, in fact, an attempt, through an historical analysis of the evolution of business studies in Europe, to do just that.

3. The heritage

Since traditionally people who ran commerce and industry were not trained in the universities, the university faculties limited themselves to teaching the arts, science, and the professions (theology, law, medicine). Of the three, only the professions were and are technologies in that their study involves cultivating the art of arriving at some end (heaven, justice, and health). But technology in a modern sense (the art of increasing business and industrial efficiency) had no place in higher education. This was true because it operated at a low level of sophistication, i.e., innovation could be carried on without science by artisans and merchants. Business organizations were also relatively uncomplicated. In a world where manufacturers did not integrate forward (market their products) or backward (supply their own raw and semi-finished materials), managerial hierarchies were not greatly needed.[1] Business and industry had to be different before the nature of higher education and its relationship with the business and industrial world could change and a new paradigm in business studies prosper.

It might seem appropriate, therefore, to leave the old paradigm and hurry to a point in time where connections between higher education and economic activities have been established. But the argument presented here is that culture is significant and if this is so then heritages in higher education formed during the old paradigm, which are an important part of culture, must influence eventual developments. The analytical principle involved is one of discontinuities in economics (in the sense that economies make different demands on educational systems at different times) and continuities in educational cultures (in the sense that educational traditions of noneconomic origins, those of the nineteenth century, have economic consequences when the conditions of entrepreneurship change as they did in the twentieth century). Un-

[1] See Chandler and Redlich, "Recent Developments."

derstanding the educational heritages is important, therefore, to comprehending how countries adjusted to managerial demands.

Because the university traditions of Germany, Britain, and France are diverse, it is best to describe essential differences first. The nineteenth-century German university was unique in one crucial way: It stressed scientific research. We owe to the German university the injunction that exists everywhere today to do research and publish or perish. This research imperative entails a specific conception about the nature of knowledge: In every field there is an accepted body of truth, but this body of truth is only a stage in our knowledge about the world. Science is an investigative process through which our knowledge is tested, deepened and perfected, which means that the process, scientific research itself, is integral to the transfer of knowledge through the teaching function. These ideas about the nature of knowledge were not peculiarly German. What made the Germans different was that they had managed by midcentury to formalize them educationally. In the Germanic world of middle Europe the Ph.D. was a research degree as was the *Habilitation*. Few who aspired to a professorship in a German university attained their goal unless they had proven their research capabilities by the completion of a doctoral thesis and a *Habilitationsschrift*.[2] Indeed research projects were undertaken on the undergraduate level.

Germans did not neglect the sciences in the nineteenth century. The term science (*Wissenschaft*) applied in the German-speaking world to all fields of knowledge because knowledge in most fields was subject to systematic, disciplined research. The universities pursued natural science (*Naturwissenschaften*) and turned history, art, and language into *Geisteswissenschaften*. The footnote, the article, the thesis, the book took over as the humanities ceased to be a medium primarily for the inculcation of *culture générale* (although there were still pretensions in that direction), and professional knowledge, the exclusive, on-the-job-learned, jealously guarded possession of private groups (the doctors, the lawyers in their associations), became an object of scholarly inquiry.[3]

2 Although the German doctorate is a necessary step for those who subsequently do the *Habilitation,* the two degrees are of a different order. The *Habilitation* is essentially a degree for someone who wishes to be a professor in a *Hochschule*. Few people in business or industry, therefore, have the *Habilitation*. Many people in business and industry, on the other hand, have doctorates.
3 See George Haines IV, *Essays on German Influence upon English Education and Science, 1850–1919* (New London, Conn., 1969).

From our perspective the system had its flaws. One was that no education was offered in the business sciences, and there were others. There were, for example, no graduate programs in the American sense, where students acquired a knowledge of research tools and methods in formalized study programs. Rather a student just did a thesis under a professor to obtain the higher degree. What research skills he learned depended on his own research initiative, on the demands made on him and by the skills of his professor. In some fields requirements were greater; for example, high standards prevailed in the natural sciences, not very demanding ones in law. Despite these variances, measured in contemporary terms German universities had become centers for serious science and research, to which students from England and America flocked in order to complete their advanced education and from which the Americans in particular borrowed heavily when developing their own graduate education during the last quarter of the nineteenth century.

English universities about 1850, which meant – aside from the recently (1839) founded University of London – Oxford and Cambridge, were not yet beset by C. P. Snow's two cultures, for not much study of natural science took place. Rather public schools and Oxbridge based their education on the humanities, the study of which was supposed to school the mind. Consequently, public school–university education was blamed for the deplorable state of science during the nineteenth century and the resulting unbridgeable gulf between the two cultures, because of the indifference, if not outright hostility, of those educated in the classics. Moreover, as cultivated in the public schools and at Oxbridge, even arts and humanities instruction amounted to a poor education in the German academic sense, because knowledge was incidental to educational purpose. School and college tried to develop the "leadership qualities" of an elite by bringing teacher and taught together in a fellowship of "leisure and confidence."[4] They sought to impart "effortless grace, casual assurance" and "light touch in command," qualities of a primarily landholding elite's cultured way of life. Although the arts and humanities provided the educational content of the system, the goal was an awakening of the "Gentleman-Ideal."[5] This is why so much emphasis was also, as the century advanced, placed on games: Play was to form the character of young gentlemen destined for higher service.

4 Claudius Gellert, *Vergleich des Studiums an englischen und deutschen Universitäten* (Munich, 1983), 4; my translation.
5 Ibid.

Whereas, therefore, universities in Germany became centers "for scholarship and knowledge," at Oxbridge they functioned "as a nursery for gentlemen, statesmen, and administrators." History, art, and languages were not, therefore, subjected in England to the constraints of *Wissenschaft*. There were no graduate studies. Neither were the liberal professions objects of *Wissenschaft*. Universities did not have professional schools; the liberal professions in England, with the exception of medicine, evidenced no great interest in scholarship and science, in "knowledge" as a systematic search for truth. Their knowledge was a rather esoteric body of received customs and practices which were acquired by the newcomer on the job and through independent study for professional qualifying examinations. It had, moreover, very little to do with the practical purposiveness of the industrial society of modern Britain. Ian Glover, tracing the historical evolution of English professions, explains:

Britain's economy turned industrial too early and too slowly to get rid of essentially aristocratic attitudes towards occupations and the rise of knowledge for practical ends. Knowledge was to be conspicuously consumed, not used as an input to the development of skill. Hard work was for the lesser breeds. None were keener to make such attitudes their own than the middle-class *arrivistes,* among whom the new professional occupations must be counted.[6]

Glover's point is that the London-based merchants and overseas traders, who were close to the court and government, had sought to adopt aristocratic values and that they did so, educationally, at public schools, by embracing the Gentleman Ideal. British higher education, therefore, not only, like the Germans, ignored the technical and commercial courses, it did not provide scholarly or scientific instruction in the humanities, the professions, or the natural sciences.

French universities were, like those in England and Germany, old institutions whose origins stretched back to the Middle Ages. The modern French university system, however, also like the German (e.g., the University of Berlin), dated from the Revolutionary-Napoleonic period. The French universities differed in two ways, however, from the German. First, like the English universities, those in France were not interested in *Wissenschaft*. Nor were they like the English concerned with educating gentlemen. French universities had been re-

6 "Professionalism and Manufacturing Industry," 125.

formed for different purposes – Napoleon Bonaparte had made it quite clear –

Teaching is a function of the state, because this is a need of the nation. In consequence, schools should be state establishments and not establishments in the state. They depend on the state and have no resort but it; they exist by it and for it. They hold their right to exist and their very substance from it; they ought to receive from it their task and their rule.[7]

One task Napoleon gave French universities: train public servants rather than scientists. Since research was neglected, so were research facilities. The *cours magistrale*, the "systematic exposés of a subject by a professor before a large audience of passive students," was the hallmark of French university education.[8] It also meant that French universities were much more under the hand of a central educational authority than the German and, of course, the English which were completely autonomous. The state-appointed rectors served as an extension of the ministerial administration; the faculty deans who, unlike the Germans, served long terms, acted less as representatives of the professoriat (as in Germany) than as intermediaries between ministry and faculty; professors' chairs were not institutionalized. In short, deprived of the strong research ethos of the German professor and subject to the authority of the state, the typical French professor had mediocre authority and prestige, as compared to the German, within the university and international scientific community.

The university did not conceive of its educational service in a narrow technical fashion. Since law was considered to be the proper preparation for careers in administration as well as the magistracy, the nineteenth-century faculties of law flourished. So did the faculties of medicine and pharmacy which provided the much needed expertise in health care. And, of course, the university, through the *agrégation,* trained the corps of secondary school instructors and university professors. That was its major function. But – and this is its second chief neglect as an educational institution – the French university did not serve trade and industry. French higher education did not ignore engineering education. A system of so-called *grandes écoles,* so-called because there is no official school system designated as *grandes écoles,*

7 Quoted in Margaret S. Archer, *Social Origins of Educational Systems* (London, 1979), 35.
8 Van de Graff, in *Reorganizing Education: Management and Participation for Change,* ed. Edmund J. King (London, 1977), 195.

assumed this function independent of the universities, thus creating at the university level a dual system of higher education.

A commitment to *grandes écoles* of engineering came early. The first of these schools, the School of Bridges and Roads, which started a distinguished tradition in French construction engineering, was founded in 1715. It was followed by two military schools, the Artillery School (1720) and the Military Engineering School (1748), and another civil engineering school, the School of Mines (1783). There were, in addition, two other schools of lesser importance, the Naval Engineering School and the Hydrographic School, which rounded out an imposing eighteenth-century system of higher education. Nonetheless, the most significant reform period began in 1793 when France set up the Polytechnic School (founded in 1794) to train the engineers so vitally needed for national defense. This school became the most famous engineering school of modern times. Reform, however, did not stop there. Since the Polytechnic School produced military and state service engineers, several prominent men in 1829 started a school of civil engineering, the Central School, to train engineers for private industry.[9]

It was, then, the Polytechnic School, the School of Roads and Bridges and of Mines, and the Central School that, in France, constituted by the midnineteenth century a justly renowned system of higher education in engineering. These *grandes écoles* acquired an enormous prestige. Foremost stood the Polytechnic School. Its first professors were among the more famous scientists of the day. Gaspard Monge, the mathematician, was a cofounder and a director, and Louis Joseph Gay-Lussac, Jean-Baptiste Biot, Sadi Carnot, François Arago, and Henri Poincaré – chemists, mathematicians, physicists, and engineers of the very highest achievement – were its students. The Polytechnic School became the glory of French engineering and state administration. Its students composed the engineering corps in the French army and navy. Its graduates became the chief administrators of all the state's technical services. Indeed, one of them, Sadi Carnot, was president of the Republic from 1887 to 1894. In no other country at the time (except perhaps America) could an engineer have become chief of state. *Polytechniciens,* moreover, dominated the upper echelons of the technical services in certain sectors of private industry. All the heads of French railroads and many

9 Gaston Rouvier, *l'Enseignement public en France au début du XXe siècle* (Stockholm, 1905), 88.

top men in the metallurgical and mining industry were graduates of the school. *Centraliens* were, besides, even more in evidence in the private sector. Contrast this situation with that in Britain, where men without formal engineering education headed the largest firms, and it becomes quite clear that the graduates of engineering schools held an honored place in midnineteenth-century French society.

Thus in Germany *Wissenschaft*, in England the Gentleman Ideal, and in France state service were the very different forms of higher education. But to these important dissimilarities must be added similarities. All schools everywhere were elitist. Only a very small part of the population in each country received any higher education. The secondary schools that fed students into higher education were the same. They could not in fact have educated much of the population because of the education they gave. In Germany the humanistic *Gymnasium* provided a no less classical education than the English public school to the point that the German language, in this most famous system of German secondary education, was originally neglected. The curriculum also included mathematics but no technical subjects; even natural science was considered to be of lesser importance. The classics and mathematics also predominated in the French state *lycées* and the municipal *collèges*. There were differences. The English public schoolboy did not study as much mathematics as the French or German secondary pupil. In England, moreover, emphasis on character building had led to stressing sports in public schools, especially during the cricket season.[10] Nothing of this sort occurred on the Continent, but in all three countries the emphasis was on "useless" classical subjects. Indeed in England science, mathematics, and modern languages "were often excluded from a public school education" because of their "usefulness."[11]

There are two exceptions, one real and one more apparent than real, to this statement. The real exception was German university chemists. They led the world in the application of chemistry in agriculture and industry. Peter Borscheid's study of the organic chemical industry shows that it was actually more scientifically than industrially induced.[12] Although bankers and merchants frequently put up capital,

10 Philip Stanworth, "Trade, Gentility, and Upper-Class Education in Victorian Britain," *International Studies of Management and Organization* 10:1–2 (1980): 46–70, 54.
11 Ibid.
12 *Naturwissenschaft, Staat und Industrie in Baden (1848–1914)* (Stuttgart, 1976).

university-educated research chemists (Heinrich Caro at Badische-Anilin-Soda Fabrik [B.A.S.F.], Carl A. Martinus at Agfa, Wilhelm Meister at Hoechst, etc.) – men who had learned their discipline from Justus von Liebig or one of his students (e.g., Hoffman) – promoted the companies. Only by knowing modern chemistry could its industrial and commercial potential be fully appreciated. And the German Ph.D. chemists startled the world with their demonstration of industrial usefulness. Yet such practicality was exceptional. Only a small percentage of the German university population even studied science (in 1841, 290, 13.6 percent of the students, majored in mathematics and natural sciences in German universities).[13] The scientists, moreover, persevered in making a distinction between pure and applied work. Insistent on the university maintaining itself as a preserve for the pursuit of disinterested knowledge, disdainful of vocationalism, the German university was in fact and in ideology predisposed to have nothing to do with commerce and industry.

The exception which is more apparent than real was the French *grandes écoles* of engineering. These famous schools really had quite tenuous relationships with industry. The Polytechnic School was a military school. The School of Bridges and Roads and the School of Mines trained engineers primarily for state service. This emphasis was not new. For thousands of years, depending on the civilization, states needed construction engineers for large public works projects. Graduates from these French *grandes écoles* were working in an old tradition. The great change for the engineering profession came with the application of science to manufacturing, for construction engineers sufficed only when manufacturers were artisans. With the industrial revolution manufacturers required specialized engineers to plan and run the new factories (various kinds of electrical, chemical, and mechanical, as well as construction, engineers). The French *grandes écoles* of engineering did not provide this education.

This occurred even in the Central School. The school's founders believed, as one prominent engineer phrased it, that "the engineer must not only know pure science, which is particularly useful in his career, and the principal industrial sciences, but have at least summary ideas about all the specific applications while avoiding specializa-

13 Donald S. L. Cardwell, *The Organisation of Science in England* (London, 1957), 134.

tion."[14] The French called this kind of engineering education encyclopedic. They believed it produced a superior engineer "who could move easily from job to job and change his career with facility" because he had learned about "all matters which are confronted in a career."[15] And they persisted in this belief throughout the century. After "a very thorough study" of the relative merits of encyclopedic and specialized education undertaken at the Central School from 1901 to 1910, the school officials concluded that their school, "destined above all to produce leaders in industry," could not change its traditional methods of instruction.[16] The stress on encyclopedic knowledge determined the manner of classroom presentation. Laboratory work was downgraded in favor of the lecture hall. Students at the Central School found themselves sitting in lectures from 550 to 600 hours a year taking copious notes on an increasing number of subjects.

Ironically, therefore, instruction at the Central School denied students the broad spectrum education in engineering which encyclopedic implied. It was possible to learn a lot about construction and mechanical engineering in lecture and design courses. Students could also imbibe inorganic chemistry rather well because in ninety-nine out of a hundred cases reactions in inorganic chemistry were, being mathematically predictable, easily presented in lecture. But the gulf in scientific methodology which "separated inorganic and organic chemistry" prevented the two subjects from being taught in the same way. Organic chemistry, not being "subject to mathematical reasoning," was a laboratory experimental science.[17] Like much of applied electrical and mechanical science, it had to be learned in the laboratory. By sticking to traditional teaching formats, the Central School denied its students good instruction in fields of rising industrial importance. And by remaining an undergraduate institution exclusively, the school prevented professors and students from developing any research-oriented conception of education. Because of the stress on encyclopedic education, professors did not specialize; indeed, professors were, because of it, not even engi-

---

14 A. Blondel, "Considérations générales sur les techniciens et l'enseignement technique," *Revue scientifique* (1916), cited in Leclerc, *La Formation des ingénieurs,* 85.
15 A. Blondel, "Quelques remarques complémentaires sur l'enseignement des ingénieurs," *Revue de métallurgie* (1917): 402–31, 415; my translation.
16 Léon Guillet, "Etude comparative de l'enseignement technique supérieure en France et à l'étranger," *Revue de métallurgie* 12 (1915): 396–420, 412; my translation.
17 Eugène Grandmougin, *L'Enseignement de la chimie industrielle en France* (Paris, 1917), 124; my translation.

neers, but physicists and chemists, often imported from a university where they held a chair in science. These university professors had no experience in industry. Applied research in engineering at the Central School was, under these conditions, out of the question.

Encyclopedic education, moreover, isolated the Central School from industry. Neither the professors nor the students worked regularly with industry in any extended period. *Centraliens* did undertake a tour of industrial establishments, as an obligatory part of their education, but factory tours cannot be compared with work-periods. Their purpose was really quite different, for, while *Centraliens* visited a large number of factories briefly in order to complete their encyclopedic education, the student who specialized deepened his particular knowledge through practical work on the job. As for the professors in the Central School, they were forbidden right up to the First World War, in order to prevent conflicts of interest, to work as industrial consultants. Yet without the goal of specialization, neither the professors nor the students in the Central School had any pedagogic reason to develop systematic working contacts with industry. On the contrary, encyclopedic education found such contacts to be useless if not outright disadvantageous. The encyclopedic education, moreover, produced a different employee from the specialist. Every position at entry level requires specialized skills. The encyclopedically educated, without this specialized knowledge, was unemployable at entry level. More like members of an *état major,* graduates of the *grandes écoles* of engineering followed career paths that avoided the specialized low-level engineering functions.

If the Central School, which was established for the manufacturing industry, did so poorly, what could be expected from the Polytechnic School, whose foundation preceded, and whose original purpose had little to do with, manufacturing? In 1911, a professor at the School of Bridges and Roads observed that the education of French construction engineers was quite satisfactory, their superior talents being internationally recognized.[18] Since graduates from the Polytechnic School, who studied in the School of Bridges and Roads, were among the nation's most illustrious construction engineers, the Polytechnic School had reasons to be satisfied. Nonetheless, the school retained a premanufacturing educational orientation which limited its value for an industrial

18 Blondel, "Quelques remarques complémentaires," 415.

economy. *Polytechniciens,* like *Centraliens,* spent far too much time in the lecture hall, were taught by professors who had no regular relationships with industry, learned mechanical and construction engineering (again laboratory equipment was very poor), and failed to learn about the factory firsthand by working as student engineers. Instruction was encyclopedic and the students were isolated in a boarding school under military discipline.

To these remarks about the education received in engineering schools can be added one about the characteristics of all *grandes écoles.* The prospective student for the Polytechnic School, the School of Mines, the School of Mines at Saint-Etienne, the School of Bridges and Roads, the Central School, and the nonengineering *grandes écoles* (like the Superior Normal School which educated *lycée* instructors) needed besides the *baccalauréat* (the French equivalent of the German *Abitur* and the present day British A levels) to pass the dreaded *concours.* It was the *concours* which separated *grandes écoles* from university faculties, for entry into the university required only the secondary school *baccalauréat.* Although ostensibly each *grande école* of engineering established its own *concours,* that of the Polytechnic School set a standard. And since the Polytechnic School was highly selective, the examinations, which stressed mathematics, were extremely difficult. After receiving a *baccalauréat,* therefore, candidates for admission into the *grandes écoles* enrolled in a special course in mathematics, primarily in order to prepare the *concours.* Few were able to succeed after a year. In fact, in 1900, 74 percent of the successful candidates for the Polytechnic School had spent three years in *spéciales,* that is, they had had to do the same course three years running before they could score enough points in the *concours* to gain admission into the school.[19] A graduate from the Polytechnic School, then, could have studied five years after the *baccalauréat* (three years *spéciales,* two in the Polytechnic School), without having encountered any engineering specialty.

The *concours* resulted in the French engineer's superiority in mathematics. But that to some contemporaries was a problem. Why should an engineer spend so much time on mathematics, and so little on engineering? Instead of using mathematics as a tool in engineering, the *concours* made it an end in itself, thereby diverting the engineering student from his chief occupational goal. The director of the Central

19 *Mémoires – Ingénieurs civils de France,* no. 4 (1917): 203.

School, Paul Buquet, complained in 1899 about the bad effects that mathematics had on his students. Long years of intense mathematical preparation developed such a penchant for abstract analysis in the students (those without this interest or capacity would have been eliminated because of the mathematics requirement) that, Buquet noted, when they had "a course on bridges, roads, railroads, architecture, they say – 'that is meant for masons and workers' – and we have to propagandize them for months in order to make them understand that they cannot make a living on algebra."[20]

Critics of this mathematics emphasis believed that it harmed the training of engineers. "It must not be forgotten," Eugène Grandmougin wrote,

that mathematics is only a means and not an end. We can sum it up by saying that it, after all, is only literature. It assumes an ideal situation which has never in fact existed. Mathematical deduction starts with often arbitrary givens in order to arrive at an exact theoretical result. But the only way to move from theory to practice is by experimentation.[21]

The issue was the same, then, as that which divided encyclopedists from specialists. Whereas mathematics fit well into the curriculum of those who emphasized general education in engineering, it seemed, to those stressing the need for specialization, "to detach people from industrial and economic realities. If it formed encyclopedists of great knowledge, it did not, on the other hand, provide enough specialists."[22]

The *concours*, too, harmed nineteenth-century French engineering because of its social selectivity. This selectivity can be demonstrated statistically. The number of students who attended the Polytechnic School and the Central School was quite small. In 1892, for example, the Polytechnic School admitted only 152 students, the Central School 136, the School of Mines 28, and the School of Bridges and Roads 3.[23] Entrance statistics also reveal a geographical recruitment bias. Paris examinees in 1892 constituted 143 of the 155 candidates admitted to the Polytechnic School and 134 of the 136 taken into the Central School.[24] People in the provinces were not incompetent, but the prepa-

---

20 Buquet was testifying before the Ribot committee on higher education. Cited in Leclerc, *La Formation des ingénieurs*, 76; my translation.
21 "L'Enseignement de la chimie industrielle," 4.
22 Ibid.
23 Archives nationales, *Ministère de l'Instruction publique*, F17, fol. 6927.
24 Ibid.

ratory schools essential to successful candidacy were located primarily in Paris. And it signified that only the rich, who could afford the prolonged financial outlay of Parisian boarding schools, could enter and stay in *grandes écoles*.

Statistical compilations for the nineteenth century, moreover, corroborate this information. They show that sons of the upper classes and middle classes predominated in the Polytechnic School and the Central School. Sixty-six percent of the *Polytechniciens* (1815 to 1880) were from privileged families (27 percent *rentiers* and landlords; 13 percent liberal professions; 14 percent higher civil servants and superior army officers; 12 percent industrialists and large merchant families). Less than 13 percent were from the *classes populaires*, about 2 percent from families of artisans and shopkeepers. In the nineteenth century 77.7 percent of *Centraliens* were from the privileged classes too (landlords, 26.5 percent; liberal professions, 9.7 percent; civil servants, 13.5 percent; industrialists and large merchant families, 28 percent).[25] The elitist education of the schools combined with the social origins of the students to create career possibilities that fostered a gulf between the engineers of the *grandes écoles* and people in the everyday world of commerce and industry. The fact that the Polytechnic School gave special entrance points to candidates with a classics *baccalauréat* shows a social bias rather than a utilitarian bent in these gentlemen engineers. They formed more of a caste within the traditional *grande bourgeoisie* of nineteenth-century French society than a group of scientifically inspired industrial entrepreneurs.

In 1981, Martin Wiener finished a book, *English Culture and the Decline of the Industrial Spirit, 1880–1980,* that drew and continues to draw considerable attention.[26] Wiener argues that the dominant culture in Great Britain is antiindustrial because it expresses aristocratic values, emanating from a rural way of life that was inimical to a town-based manufacturing middle class. The public school and Oxbridge, which exuded the ethos of this dominant culture, absorbed the sons of the entrepreneurs into their midst, thereby, through a process of gentrification, stifling the entrepreneurial spirit in the country. He attributes Britain's economic problems to this culture. The book has been strongly criticized: it does not deal with the industrial managers

25 Terry Shinn, *L'Ecole Polytechnique, 1794–1913* (Paris, 1980), Tableau 1, 185, and Tableau 4, 220.
26 Cambridge University Press.

of Britain (it is a literary study); it makes comparative statements without doing comparative analysis; it ignores the development of a utilitarian higher education in industrial Britain; and it overlooks the fact that the British culture was not unique in its antiindustrialism.

The comparative aspect of the criticism is pertinent here. The middle classes' avid desire to emulate the bureaucratic-aristocratic military elite in Prussia and the cautious *rentier* spirit of the French upper middle class are classic examples of the predominance of antiindustrial attitudes among elites elsewhere in Europe. So is the fact that the educational systems just described, with the exceptions mentioned, had little to do with training technologists and managers. The university in midnineteenth-century Europe, if it served a rising middle class, did it for noneconomic reasons; the middle-class German or Frenchman used education primarily to gain entry into the bureaucracy and the liberal professions. The dissimilarities in German, English, and French higher education are not significant in the midnineteenth century in this regard; they show no system closely linked to industry and commerce. Still they are of interest because, despite their common dissociation from industry and commerce, they were different educational cultures. If Wiener, therefore, is clearly wrong in that the British were not much worse than the French or the Germans in the nineteenth century when it came to serving a commercial-industrial state educationally, he is not necessarily wrong in that the British preindustrial forms of education, unlike the German and French, could be inherently less capable of accommodating commercially and industrially useful forms of education.

The halfway house (c. 1880–1940)

This educational heritage began to affect the industrial history of these three countries, when, between 1880 and 1940, for the first time, higher education became important to economic performance. This period can be characterized as a halfway house on the way to the new paradigm in management studies. It was a halfway house because the impact of science on management study was, compared to the subsequent period, quite incomplete: Management per se was not the object of scientific inquiry. None of the highly mathematized decision models developed after the Second World War was used; no attempts to establish isomorphic mapping between natural science or technical systems and management problems were made. On the other hand, some auxiliary management functions, like accounting, sales, and finance, which had previously been learned exclusively on the job, became objects of rational study in colleges and universities. These auxiliaries were not necessarily studied with the aid of science. Much of what people learned was normative (i.e., best practice), but academics employed scientific conceptions, drawn especially from economics and statistics, in their research and teaching in order to make these functional auxiliaries more managerially coherent and useful.[27]

Two things had to happen in order to move from the old paradigm into the halfway house. First, business and industry had to ask for people with qualifications that could best be satisfied through formal as opposed to on-the-job education. The new high-tech industries (organic chemistry, pharmaceuticals, sophisticated mechanical manufactures, i.e, automobiles and electricals, etc.) and the mass-produced consumer industries (packaged brand foods, household appliances, etc.) of the second industrial revolution, whose appearance and managerial needs Professor Chandler's work so skillfully describes, met this demand. Secondly, scientific knowledge had to satisfy the needs of praxis. It obviously did in science-induced industries (e.g., aniline dyes or pharmaceuticals). Without scientific discoveries, these industries could not have even existed. And it is also true in less obvious industries like computers, which, despite the potential demand and the presence of the right mathematics (Boolean algebra) in the nineteenth century, could not develop until science produced the electronics and the chemical-metallurgical products essential for success in the twentieth.

It must not be forgotten, however, that the development of useful science was not just a result of rational response to self-interest in both praxis and in academia. When "science" is being applied to managerial as opposed to technical problems this is particularly the case. Most of what we now perceive as obvious was not so obvious to people before it happened. Since the issues involved the ability to predict the future, and

27 German business economists distinguish between the study of management (*Lehre von der Führung*) and the study for management (*Lehre für die Führung*). "The study for management," Walter Trux and Werner Kirsch explain, "consists of specific elements of knowledge taken from neighboring disciplines that the study of management considers relevant for its tasks." If the study of management was not a subject of scientific inquiry before the war, the study for management was. Walter Trux and Werner Kirsch, "Strategisches Management oder die Möglichkeit einer 'wissenschaftlichen' Unternehmensführung," *Die Betriebswirtschaft* 39 (1979): 215–35, 217; my translation.

the people had no better idea of what the future would require in the nineteenth century than they do today, what the business and industrial community desired from higher education or what the educators themselves were ready to provide was not determined uniquely or even principally by accurate, rational economic calculation. What, then, people in business and industry and in education called their self-interest was as much culturally determined as determined by any rational knowledge about what self-interest really required. Efforts to found a commercial college in Cologne at the end of the last century illustrate what this means. When the banker Gustav Mevissen bequeathed a million marks for its creation, he had neither economic nor scientific goals in mind.[28] Concerned about the low status of businessmen, he thought, because of the near mania for academic titles that existed in Imperial Germany, to raise the businessman's social status by conferring college degrees on members of the business estate. Had he been in Britain or in France, where academic titles were not particularly prestigious, he would not have thought of an educational solution to his problem. Certainly he would not have thought of founding the school in order to teach a business science that would improve performance, if for no other reason than that there was, in fact, no subject matter of a scientific nature to teach in a commercial school when Mevissen made his bequest; it still had to be created. Accordingly, inherited status attitudes about education had as much to do with the development of business studies in Germany, Great Britain, and France during the period of transition to the new paradigm as any clear appreciation of how useful these studies would prove to be scientifically. Since the heritages were so diverse, so were the educational responses. This can be shown by examining changes or the lack of them first in technical and then in commercial education.

Since German achievement is to be used as a gauge with which to measure English and French, the way the German heritage shaped the introduction of the first economically utilitarian subject, engineering education, will be handled initially. German university professors were professional snobs in that they thought they served a high-status professional education (the law or medicine) that was not dominated by crass commercial consideration like engineering or commerce, or that

28 Fritz Schmidt, ed., *Die Handelshochschule, Lehrbuch der Wirtschaftswissenschaften* (Berlin, 1927), 17–18; and Balduin Penndorf, *Wie studiert man auf der Handels-Hochschule?* 2d edition (Stuttgart, 1919), 35.

they were engaged in a higher calling, in the nonpractical [*zweckfrei*] search for truth in a value-free environment, unlike engineering and commerce. Because useful knowledge, knowledge that supposedly served special interests, had no place in the professions or in *Wissenschaft,* the professors successfully opposed the introduction of engineering education into universities.[29] Higher education in engineering, therefore, grew up in the nineteenth century outside the universities in special technical *Hochschulen.* Still, because of the prestige of university *Wissenschaft,* no self-respecting discipline in institutions of higher education could hope in Imperial Germany to find acceptance academically unless it conformed to the university *Wissenschaft* model. And the engineers and industrialists sought acceptance. Consequently, the sponsors of the technical *Hochschulen,* attempting to make more of them than glorified trade schools, tried to counter effectively the oft repeated accusation, emanating from the universities, that engineering was somehow not scientifically respectable. They did so by making engineering part of applied natural science, science which demanded research based on the most exacting methodology.

In their educational forms, therefore, the new technical institutes copied the universities. Since the university research tradition was objectified in academic degrees, gaining the right to grant them became an avid preoccupation of the newcomers. In engineering, where economically related higher education developed first, it was a long climb; but by 1900, students in the technical institutes were officially authorized, in the best traditions of *Wissenschaft,* to acquire doctorates (*Dr.-Ing.*), the first engineering doctorate in the world. Indeed, in that year, in Prussia, the King-Emperor William II, an admirer of scientific technology, granted the engineering schools the right to issue the two degrees (*Dipl.-Ing.* and *Dr.-Ing.*) that placed them, formally, on the same level as the universities.[30] Research facilities, moreover, expanded impressively, particularly during the two decades before the First World War. The Royal Institute of Physics, created at Charlottenburg, aroused the admiration of the international scientific com-

29 Karl-Heinz Manegold, *Universität, Technische Hochschule und Industrie* (Göttingen, 1971); and Wilhelm Lexis, ed., *Das Unterrichtswesen im deutschen Reich,* vol. 4 (Berlin, 1904).
30 For a reaction of contemporary engineers to the reforms see "Reform der höheren Schulen," *Zeitschrift des Vereins deutscher Ingenieure* (ZVDI) 34:50 (Dec. 15, 1900): 651; and the memoir cited in D. Blumenthal, "Erinnerungen an Slaby," *ZVDI* 47:9 (May 1, 1913): 204–06.

Table 3.1. *Attendance at technical institutes*

	Number of Students		
School	1890	1900	1910
Charlottenburg	1,640	4,343	2,943
Munich	882	2,476	3,062
Darmstadt	318	1,674	1,768
Karlsruhe	571	1,538	1,343
Hannover	580	1,458	1,770
Dresden	403	1,161	1,447
Stuttgart	496	1,034	1,224
Aachen	198	567	916
Brunswick	273	483	663
Danzig	---	---	1,315
Breslau	---	---	117
Total	5,361	14,734	16,568

Source: Deutscher Ausschuss für technisches Schulwesen, *Berichte aus dem Gebiete des technischen Hochschulwesens,* IV (Berlin, 1912), Anlage 2:b.

munity. It was, however, only the most spectacular example of the numerous electrical, chemical, mechanical, and metallurgical laboratories established in German technical institutes for students as well as professors. Detailed descriptive articles with accompanying photographs, which the German engineering journal frequently published, testify to the elaborate and thoughtful care with which these teaching-research laboratories were installed.[31]

Thus the German engineering schools, the technical institutes, had, by the turn of the century, managed to integrate themselves into the *Wissenschaft* tradition. At the same time that they improved their scientific stature, moreover, they also multiplied in number and increased in size. By 1900 schools existed throughout the Empire: in Charlottenburg (Berlin), Brunswick, Danzig, Hannover, Munich, Dresden, Stuttgart, Aachen, Darmstadt, Karlsruhe, and Breslau. These eleven technical institutes and the three mining schools (Berlin, Freiberg, and Claustal) formed the already renowned German system of higher education engineering. The two sets of statistics in Tables 3.1 and 3.2 illustrate these schools' growth. The first shows the phenomenal increase in their student population during the last decade of the nineteenth century. Whereas the German population increased in this period by 10 percent, the number of students increased by 171 percent, from 5,361 to 14,734.[32] Table 3.2 shows the rapid increase in the

31 See *ZVDI.*
32 "Rundschau," *ZVDI* 35:8 (Feb. 23, 1901): 280.

Table 3.2. *V.D.I. membership*

Year	Number of Members
1856	172
1866	1,215
1876	3,212
1886	5,630
1895	10,995
1905	19,581

Source: L'Association des ingénieurs allemands, *Mémoires et comptes rendus des travaux de la société des ingénieurs civils de France*, no. 1 (December 22, 1906), 886.

membership of the German engineering fraternity (V.D.I.). The V.D.I. was more than a powerful supporter of the technical institutes. Its leadership was recruited largely from their graduates. Indeed, the director of the V.D.I. during these critical growth years (1856–90) was Franz Grasshof, professor in the technical institute of Karlsruhe.

So much, then, for how the development of German engineering education reflected the *Wissenschaft.* Since good engineering is as much a result of practical skill as scientific knowledge, the *Wissenschaft* tradition could not, as important as it was and is, serve alone the educational needs of engineering. All the reformers emphasized science in order to add this essential element to traditionally craft-based technical activities, but the craftsmanship was not forgotten. Realizing that engineers were scientists, i.e., knowledge seekers and technologists (purveyors of purposefulness), the Germans managed to create a homeostatis between *Wissenschaft* and practical purposiveness in their system of engineering education.

In the technical institutes, this ability to keep their feet on the ground was acquired through a continuously close cooperation between educational establishments and industry. Men in praxis paid attention to the technical institutes when they were being developed during the nineteenth century. As one engineer wrote in 1913:

While the state scarcely uses the technical institutes, except for the education of its construction engineers, German industry fully understands how to make the technical institute serve its purpose by extracting practical profit from its scientific activity. Industry not only gets its technical personnel from the graduates of the technical institutes but also top people for industrial administration. Consequently, industry follows the development of the technical institute very carefully. It tries, and quite successfully because of industry's representation on the German Commission for Technical Education, to influence the form and content of instruction in technical institutes and makes sure the institute laboratories undertake research of practical interest by providing the industrial machines and equipment and the wherewithal for the school laboratories to carry out these industrially desirable tasks.[33]

The needs of industry were, in fact, incorporated into the curricula of the technical *Hochschulen*. Each school offered instruction in architecture and in construction, mechanical, electrical, and chemical engineering. Moreover, some schools added a specialty which served regional needs – Aachen, metallurgy; Charlottenburg, marine engineering; Danzig, naval construction; Karlsruhe, hydraulics and forestry – to their programs. Engineering students studied four years, with the last two devoted to a specialty. In 1900 at Karlsruhe, for example, the students could major in construction, mechanical, electrical, chemical, electrochemical, physical-chemical, and forest-hydraulic engineering plus architecture and pharmacy.[34] And the range of specialties at Karlsruhe was not exceptional. Upon specializing, however, the student did not cut himself off from engineering developments outside his field. He was able, because of course availability, to learn not only about other fields but about how their technological development bore upon his own. Thus the student in architecture learned about electric motors, heat engineering, and mechanical construction, as well as design and other subjects common to architecture in order to include the latest technology in his buildings; students in metallurgy absorbed chemical and electrical engineering because of their importance. Specialization occurred even in the older industries. The mining school in Berlin, for example, offered four diplomas to its students – mining exploration, mining topography, iron metallurgy, and nonferrous metallurgy – which incorporated newer specialties like chemical engineering into its programs.

Flexibility in instruction, moreover, matched that in curriculum. German students could study where they wanted and what they wanted (except for a standard set of basic courses the first two years). A student could take a course in any technical institute and have it automatically accredited in another. He could, therefore, select courses from the full

33 Quoted in Martin W. Neufeld, "Die technischen Hochschulen Preussens bei der Beratung des Staatshaushaltsetats für das Etatsjahr 1913," *Zeitschrift des Vereins Deutscher Diplom-Ingenieur (ZVDDI)* 4 (July 1, 1913): 321–325, 323; my translation.
34 M. Vogt, "L'Enseignement technique," *Revue de métallurgie, Mémoires* 4 (1906), 471–75.

panoply of national offerings, from the full teaching faculty of the technical institutes, according to the special claims of his particular study program, future job, or engineering interest. Lecture courses, moreover, only provided background information for practical work in laboratories. For the average engineering student laboratory experiments consumed 38 percent of work time the first, 67 percent the second, and 80 percent the third year of school.[35] Modern industrial engineering demanded this concentration. What a contrast with non-laboratory straight-lecture methods of instruction in the French *grandes écoles* of engineering!

A proviso that every student (except those in construction engineering, chemical engineering, and architecture) spend at least twelve months working as a student engineer in workshop or factory (six months of which had to be in consecutive service) intensified the practical bent of German engineering studies. During this work period (*Praktikum*) the student engineer was supposed to work under the direct supervision of an engineer who submitted performance reports to the student's technical institute. Considerable complaint was heard about this work period just before the First World War. Many firms, instead of moving a student around the factory to acquaint him with a variety of engineering tasks, gave him some menial job, off in a factory corner, thereby foiling the program's educational purpose. Often students did not gain maximum benefits from this experience because it was spent in firms with outmoded equipment or business methods. Yet none of the critics, whether industrialists or engineers, sought to eliminate the work period. A number of large firms (Lud. Loewe, Siemens, M.A.N., etc.), in fact, had excellent programs. In 1914 the Association of German Graduate Engineers systematically sounded out its members on the work period.[36] Despite many criticisms, which varied and were sometimes contradictory, the vast majority of the respondents to a questionnaire supported one year of work experience for students. Indeed they all said that their own had been most helpful to their careers. If the practice could be improved, German industrialists and engineers thought the combination of formal engineering education

35 Charles Lauth, *Rapport général sur l'historique et le fonctionnement de l'Ecole Municipale de physique et de chimie industrielles* (Paris 1900), 61.
36 Ernst Werner, *Die praktische Werkstattausbildung der Studierenden an technischen Hochschulen unter besonderer Berücksichtigung der Diplom-Ingenieure* (Berlin 1914).

with on-the-job training to be a particular strong point of German engineering education.

This cooperation, moreover, was not just expressed in study programs and *Praktikum*. The technical institutes were careful to recruit engineering professors from praxis. To do so, the technical institutes had to deviate from normal university practice. Although a university professor was required to have a *Habilitation* to qualify scientifically for his chair, in engineering this proviso was ignored. Professors of engineering frequently had only doctorates (Dr.-Ing.) and sometimes no doctorates at all, for what was stipulated as a qualification requirement for a professorship was a *Habilitation* or its equivalent, which came to mean, for engineering, proof that while working in industry, the professor-candidate had made a contribution through publications and/or the acquisition of patents to the advancement of engineering science.

Members of a common culture, engineering professors and engineers in industry closely cooperated with each other. Working engineers frequently came to professors with their problems, which were often given to students as doctoral projects. Undergraduates, who were required to do industry-related work projects and to spend some months in industry (the *Praktikum*) during their studies, were also given a practically oriented scientific instruction. The cooperation between industry and technical institutes, which stretched back into the nineteenth century, became as much a part of engineering education as *Wissenschaft*.

Left to fend for themselves in their own special *Hochschulen* because of university prejudices, but incorporated, nonetheless, by force of will and law into the university-influenced system of higher education, German engineers developed a third science, or *Technik* to use the untranslatable word German engineers employ to define that unique combination of scientific knowledge and craftsmanship which characterizes their subject. If the first science was the arts and humanities, and the second the natural sciences, *Technik* was indeed a reflection of neither. That is obvious as far as the humanities are concerned although there is a humanistic element within engineering; but if less obvious it is also true as far as natural science is concerned, for *Technik* is not applied science – a subordinate of pure science with all the connotations of intellectual inferiority that the idea implies – but the particular combination of knowledge (*Wissen*) and skill (*Können*) that makes it something else. As such, *Technik* represents a singular blend of German university and industrial tradition.

What about the effects of English and French traditions on the development of engineering education? As they were traditions as different from each other as they were from the German, the results were quite different, too. In England, where people saw industrial hegemony disappear during the second industrial revolution, alarmed reformers, especially those who had emigrated from the Continent or those who had studied there, blamed the decline on educational deficiencies. And their complaints drew people's attention. Consequently, during the second half of the nineteenth century, when the now famous redbricks came into existence, English universities grew considerably in size and number. At the same time C. P. Snow's second culture, natural science, attained maturity. Many of the great names of British science – J. J. Thompson, Lord Kelvin, Osborne Reynolds, Charles Wheatstone, Ambrose Fleming – were professors in the English civic and the Scottish universities. "For all the prestige of Chemnitz, Stuttgart, Freiburg, and Charlottenburg," Michael Sanderson wrote, "when it came to scientific content it was evident that Leeds, Manchester, Birmingham, and Imperial College were not a jot behind."[37] The distinguished record of British science is directly traceable to these times and universities, which, with the resurgence of scientific studies at Oxbridge, made British science among the most fruitful in Europe. The number of Nobel Prizes won by the British before the Second World War alone amply testifies to this achievement.

At the same time engineering studies took root in universities. Although a chair in engineering was not founded at Oxford until 1907, Cambridge had an engineering department as early as 1875. By the end of the First World War (1922) there were 527 engineering students there, a number which remained relatively stable, but nonetheless important, since it represented about 10 percent of total Cambridge enrollment throughout the interwar years (1928, 475 students; 1932, 500; 1938, 555).[38] Even more students in the new civic universities read engineering. There were 1,129 students of engineering in English and Welsh universities by 1913; between the wars the total output of graduate engineers in Great Britain was 9,997. The Cambridge engineers

37 *The Universities and Industry* (London, 1972), 240.
38 T. J. N. Hilken, *Engineers at Cambridge University, 1783–1965* (Cambridge, 1967), 256.

were associated particularly with the development of the electrical and aeronautical industries. C. A. Niblett's study of the relationship between Metropolitan-Vickers and Cambridge engineering shows, for example, that recruitment by 1922 was regular and systematic; not only did the company employ Cambridge engineers in its research department, an even greater percentage of the qualified engineers in mechanical engineering were from Cambridge.[39] It was in fact the policy of the Education Department, the other half of the government's composite Research and Education Department, to draw Cambridge engineers into jobs other than research in British industry.

Nonetheless, England did not follow the German path in higher education. German *Wissenschaft,* as explained in the first section of this chapter, embodied both the natural sciences and the human (*Geistes*) sciences; in England science meant natural science. Its development in the last part of the nineteenth century did not bring into existence an English equivalent of *Technik.* People who needed skilled qualifications for their jobs continued to acquire them on the job; those admitted into the officially sanctioned engineering associations were trained in this way, i.e., they were apprenticed in a factory or workshop for the time needed to qualify for membership. Not until the late nineteenth century did these professional engineering bodies even recognize the importance of any formal written entry examination.[40] The qualification tests, moreover, were, when they came, quite practical in character in that they were drafted by working professionals in order to ascertain a candidate's knowledge of current practice. The science content was not very great. Members of the engineering associations were admitted without university education. In fact, as late as 1950, 90 percent of those who became mechanical engineers in England were nonuniversity educated, that is, they had studied part-time at night while working and gained their admittance into the association through the qualification examination.[41] Not only were the rank and file of the engineering associations nonuniversity educated (a large percentage of the membership of the German V.D.I., too, was not university educated) but, unlike the Germans, so was the leadership in

39 "Images of Progress: Three Episodes in the Development of Research Policy in the U.K. Electrical Engineering Industry," 110. Ph.D. diss., Department of Liberal Studies in Science, University of Manchester, 1980.
40 Locke, *The End of the Practical Man,* 58.
41 Ibid.

the English engineering societies. A 1930 editorial in a leading periodical, *Mechanical World and Engineering Record,* typifies the leadership's attitude toward the scientific education of engineers:

In these days of organised college courses it is well to remember that in the last analysis the leaders in our industry are produced from one source – they are the products of workshops or factories. . . . It may be said that they are scientific without being scientists. A list of past presidents of our senior engineering institutions would include many names of distinguished leaders whose unique merit consisted in a highly developed mechanical instinct which was sufficient to guide them to the right point of view on any problem connected with their work. Without anything more than this valuable intuition many of our great engineers of the past would continue to be eminent to these days. A perusal of the correspondance and inquiry columns of engineering journals and the proceedings of institution meetings makes manifest the fact that the real difficulties of engineers are principally those of a practical character.[42]

These professional engineers did not realize that the knowledge essential to engineering could no longer be acquired on the job any more than, as they correctly observed, the skills necessary to the engineer could be learned in a classroom.

Niblett's illustration of industrial receptivity to university-educated engineers was clearly, therefore, an exception. As he himself notes:

in that the firm appeared anxious to recruit from Cambridge [it was] not following the conventional wisdom of the day, in which industry was still very wary of graduates, especially those from Cambridge. Even in a modern technical industry, such as aircraft manufacture, there was a strongly held belief that Cambridge graduates were of no use and inefficient Cambridge men had blazed a trail of opposition . . . such that one man took it as a compliment to be referred to as being "not so bad for a Cambridge man."[43]

The disdain with which English engineering societies and people in praxis treated the university-acquired scientific content of their subject was returned by the British universities in the way they treated the practical skill component. English higher education, retaining the two-culture concept of higher education, tended to ignore the German idea of engineering as a third science. Although the English universities classified engineering under the science part of the arts and science

42 84 (Nov. 22, 1929): 2238.
43 "Images of Progress," 116. The same opinion, that Metropolitan-Vickers was far from typical when hiring university-educated engineers, can be found in Michael Sanderson, "Research and the Firm in British Industry," *Science Studies* 2 (1972): 107–51.

dichotomy, they accorded it, as Peter Lawrence has observed, "a junior, dependent and subordinate status under the aegis of science."[44] It was applied and inferior because what the German called *Können,* the practical purposiveness of the third science, the craftsmanship considered by Germans to be, along with *Wissen,* integral to engineering studies, made it in the British eyes inferior to pure science.

Because engineering could not attain the status of a third science in Great Britain, it received poor treatment in English education. The student numbers involved were ludicrously small. In Oxbridge before the First World War even the natural sciences were neglected. Between 1880 and 1900 only 56 students at both universities received Bachelor of Science (B. Sc.) honors degrees.[45] In 1913 there were ten times as many engineering students in the German technical institutes as in the universities of England and Wales.[46] Between the wars the total output of graduate engineers in Great Britain was comparatively small. German technical institutes alone in 1923 had twice as many students as British universities had graduates in engineering between 1925 and 1939. And this excludes the large number of students, particularly in chemistry, who had after 1900 begun to study technological subjects in German universities. Because the British engineering fraternities stressed practical skills and because the universities emphasized scientific knowledge, the gulf between them was not easily bridged.

Overshadowed by the Germans after the 1870 defeat, French engineering education unavoidably underwent a critical reevaluation in the late nineteenth century. Charles Lauth, one of the French reformers, observed in a report inspired by a study of the German chemical industry that the French chemical industry suffered from a lack of chemists. He observed:

There are no professors charged with teaching applied chemistry, with doing research on the transformation of a scientific fact into a practical result, with the creation of a new industry. In our educational establishment there is not even a school where a professor who wished to implement such a program could get a job. Neither the *Conservatoire des arts et métiers,* nor the Central School, nor the mechanic schools comply with this desideratum.[47]

44 *Managers and Management in West Germany* (London, 1980), 97.
45 Cardwell, *Organisation of Science in England,* 97.
46 Ibid.
47 Charles Lauth, *Rapport sur les produits chimiques et pharmaceutiques* (Paris, 1881), 132–33; my translation.

Lauth was not alone. Jean Roulin, professor of chemistry in the Lyons Faculty of Science, alarmed at the number of Swiss and German chemical engineers employed by French firms in his region, began a course in applied chemistry. In Nancy, a Professor Hall, conscious of the necessity for Frenchmen to study chemical and electrical engineering in Germany and Switzerland (he had himself studied in Germany), organized several technical institutes in the University of Nancy. In Grenoble Professor Paul Janet had so much success with his lectures on applied physics that he started a regular course in electrical engineering at the university. These stories, which can easily be multiplied, are indicative of the great concern about the inability of *grandes écoles* of engineering to serve the needs of the new high-tech and science-based industries and the great push that took place around 1900 for new engineering schools and university engineering institutes.

The earliest and certainly one of the more important of these institutions, the Paris Advanced School for Chemistry and Physics, was founded in 1882 and financed exclusively by the city of Paris.[48] Placed under the department of technical instruction rather than the department of higher education, it was not officially an institution of higher learning. Most of the new institutions, however, were university affiliated. A law of 1897 permitted French universities to issue diplomas distinct from those given by the state. And some faculties wanted to increase their incomes by attracting large numbers of students into industry-related programs. Consequently, faculties of science created diplomas in electrical and chemical engineering and established institutes of engineering and applied science. Much work was done in the decade before the First World War: In Nancy a number of technical institutes, the most important of which was an institute of electrotechnology, were started; in Grenoble the Polytechnic Institute, which stressed electrical engineering, was established in 1911; in Lyons, the School of Industrial Chemistry and in Toulouse the institutes of chemical and electro-engineering were founded in 1907.[49]

Belatedly, then, French engineering education began to respond to industry's special needs, for the new institutes exhibited many of the features which had been missing in the *grandes écoles* of engineering. Admission was based on the presentation of a *baccalauréat* or, in lieu

48 Lauth, *Rapport général sur l'historique.*
49 Leclerc discusses these schools in *La Formation des ingénieurs.*

of that, on proof of competency by examination. In other words, there were admission standards but no competitive entrance examination (*concours*) and no absolute requirement that the student have a *baccalauréat*. Moreover, mathematics did not figure prominently in entrance requirements or in curricula. It was considered to be an auxiliary of engineering science. Instruction, by definition specialized, was directed toward industrial careers, and work in laboratories was emphasized. Graduation requirements did not, as in Germany, include a work period in industry, but students were encouraged to do such a *stage* which an institute frequently arranged. Great efforts were made to bring engineers from neighboring industries into institutes to teach on either a full-/ or part-time basis. These new schools and institutes amounted to a separate system of engineering education in France, one created not by the *grandes écoles* but by, to a large extent, university science professors working with industry.[50]

Since the new specialized education so obviously fulfilled industrial requirements, it might be asked why the reformers did not introduce specialized education into the existing *grandes écoles* in order to make them more responsive to industry's need and to unify the system. The answer can be discerned by comparing the educational heritages that produced what were very different engineering educational systems in Germany with those that produced the *grandes écoles* in France. Actually, educational distinctions in both countries were, as they were in England, social distinctions. Whereas, in England, the upper classes shunned engineering as low-status working-class vocational education, in France the classically educated upper bourgeoisie let its sons be educated as engineers in the *grandes écoles,* from which they moved into positions of influence and power in the French state and economy.[51] In Germany, the attitude of the "directing classes" toward engineering resembled the English more than the French. They left the engineering profession to the middle classes. Although the *Wissenschaft* tradition in higher education, unlike in Britain where a different educational tradition blocked the development of engineering schools, created the fusion between science and craft expressed in the technical

50 Ibid.
51 At Cambridge the brightest students disdained engineering as an inferior subject, despite the fact that Cambridge engineering education, to avoid this stigma, tended to be much more abstract than industry appreciated. There was more *Wissen* (knowledge) acquired than *Können* (skill) in Cambridge.

Hochschulen, nonetheless, through this transitional period, the German upper class denigrated the engineering profession. In 1879, a prominent German engineer noted that a "Prestigedifferenz" existed between "higher civil servants, judges, professors, medical doctors, and theologians, on the one side, and the technicians-engineers on the other."[52] A quarter of a century later, the German engineering association (V.D.I.) still lamented this *Prestigedifferenz,* despite the profound impact that technology had had on Germany. "A technical question has existed in Germany for a long time," one economist wrote in 1904.

Technology has been praised in Germany and its progress has been astonishing. Nonetheless, by some incomprehensible logic the technician is put in an inferior social position. The engineer's work is not recognized as intellectual (*geistestätig*), the difficult academic studies of the engineer are not appreciated, and the engineers who come out of the technical institutes are not considered equals by the "learned" professions, i.e., lawyers, medical doctors, etc.[53]

From an educational perspective this *Prestigedifferenz* reflected the deep-seated prejudices the classically educated *Gymnasium* students had against the practically oriented engineer. The same prejudice existed in France, but it was not exercised against students enrolled in the *grandes écoles* of engineering, who were recruited from the same pool of classically educated *lycée* students as those attending university faculties.

German engineers, in fact, never held or attained the standing in state service achieved by the graduates of the Polytechnic School. The German state continued during the late nineteenth century to recruit its higher civil servants from the university law faculties where the upper bourgeoisie educated its sons. A lawyer monopoly (*Juristenmonopol*) in civil service even persisted in the German state technical service bureaucracy where graduate engineers (Dipl.-Ing.) held only subordinate positions that did not entitle them to be career civil servants (*Beamte*). Moreover, German engineers did not acquire places of great importance in industry. Some of the captains of German industry, like Emil Rathenau, founder of Allgemeine Elektrizitäts-Gesellschaft (A.E.G.),

52 Jürgen Kocka, *Unternehmensverwaltung und Angestelltenschaft am Beispiel Siemens, 1847–1914* (Stuttgart, 1969), 526; my translation.
53 Ludwig Bernhard, "Die Stellung der Ingenieure in der heutigen Staatswirtschaft," *Schmollers Jahrbuch für Gesetzgebung, Verwaltung und Volkswirtschaft* 28:1 (1904): 117–31, 127; my translation.

were graduates of technical institutes. But he was an exception. While *Polytechniciens* and *Centraliens* were running large-scale French corporate enterprises in the late nineteenth century, German engineers were complaining about the lawyer monopoly in the corporate as well as state directorates. And the complaint was just.[54] In Prussia, for example, only two of the heads of twenty-three railroads were engineers. All the others were trained as jurists. Because German engineering schools were not, like the French *grandes écoles*, a stepping-stone into higher positions, they provided the specialized middle-range technical education suited to the career ambitions of the middle not the upper class.[55]

In France, the *grandes écoles* of engineering and the new specialized schools, which were inspired by the German technical *Hochschulen*, did not therefore just present different views about how to train engineers. They constituted different and opposed political worlds, work worlds, and social worlds, based on contrasting methods of training. Charles Lauth, commenting on the social origins of students in the Paris School for Chemistry and Physics, "the prototype of all the new university affiliated engineering institutions," noted that "a large part of our students were born into poor families. They are generally sons of workers, of artisans, of small manufacturers."[56] He also remarked, "In 1899 of thirty-seven students admitted, twenty-nine came from the upper primary schools (*écoles primaires supérieures*) and the communal secondary schools (*collèges*), seven from the *lycées* of Paris or the departments and one from a private institution." These statements clarify the social composition of the new engineering schools. They were rooted in a lower middle class which sought, through education, to improve its position in society and in the economy. As Lauth himself put it: "These sons of workers and artisans have the ardent desire to become heads of industrial firms. They realize that it is through [school] that they can reach their goal."[57]

People talked at the turn of the century about the need for the universities to assimilate the *grandes écoles*, for the new specialized engineering schools in the university faculties seemed to fulfill industry's needs much better than did the *grandes écoles*.[58] If the new schools were

54 Leclerc, *La formation des ingénieurs*, 112.
55 Locke, *The End of the Practical Man*, 26.
56 Lauth, *Rapport général sur l'historique*, 21.
57 Ibid., 22.
58 Locke, *The End of the Practical Man*, chap. 2.

popular, the position of the *grandes écoles* remained unaffected. Two kinds of institutions of higher education in engineering, therefore, came into existence in France, at the turn of the century, which served different social clientele, gave different educations, and funneled graduates into different careers. Sons of the upper middle and upper classes went to the *lycées,* crammed mathematics in Parisian preparatory schools, and then entered the *grandes écoles* (first choice usually the Polytechnic School, second, the Central School); those from the lower middle and artisan classes, who came through "inferior" secondary and primary schools, only found the newer institutions of engineering within their grasp. In the *grandes écoles,* the students received an encyclopedic education; in the new schools, a specialist one. On graduation from the *grandes écoles,* students entered the state technical services (the *grandes corps*) or the army, or climbed onto the fast track for advancement into top management in industry. On graduation from the new schools, the students went to specialist middle management positions, principally in private enterprises.

By creating a dual system, the French managed to have higher education in engineering that cut across class lines. In France, therefore, the upper classes got involved in engineering education in the *grandes écoles;* in Germany they did not. The sons of German middle-class manufacturers flocked to German technical *Hochschulen;* the upper-class elite continued to study the nontechnical prestige subjects (law, medicine, etc.) at universities. German engineering education consequently differed fundamentally from French because top German civil servants (*Beamte*), even in the technical services, and a great percentage of top corporation executives in industry were educated in law.[59] The German elite unlike the French was not, therefore, drawn from engineering and hence drawn to engineering studies. However, the Germans had a more homogeneous form of engineering education, for it did not matter where one studied, since career patterns were similar for all engineering graduates (specialist entry in industrial and transportation middle-management careers, no civil service jobs of importance). In France, the school mattered because it determined the nature of subsequent careers in the bureaucracy as well as in industry.

Consequently, the French possessed, compared to the Germans, a

59 W. Franz, "Ingenieurstudium und Verwaltungsreform," *ZVDDI* (June 1, 1910): 223–31.

fragmented form of engineering education. It was fragmented because there was very little movement between the two systems. The French upper class did not, since it spurned the new schools, recruit engineers from them into their midst. In the long run, the *grandes écoles,* because of their power and prestige, thwarted the will of turn-of-the-century educational reformers. Seeking to distance themselves from the universities, in order to escape the stigma of being second-class institutions, the specialized schools copied the *grandes écoles* by adopting the elitist entry requirements that they had on their founding purposefully avoided, i.e., the *concours.* The effort was quite successful, for, by the Second World War, twenty former science faculty institutes had been recognized by the French state as *écoles nationales supérieures.*[60] Educational tradition in the shape of the *grandes écoles* took hold of the engineering educational reform movement and remade it in its own image. The effect was to perpetuate the differences between the *grandes écoles* of engineering (now expanded by these additions) and universities, which remained estranged from industry and commerce. Engineering education, moreover, was not homogenized, for the older, primarily Parisian *grandes écoles* remained apart from the new specialized *petites grandes écoles* of engineering, despite efforts at emulation.

Even after the turn-of-the-century reforms, then, the educational dichotomy between the *grandes écoles* of engineering and the universities remained a principal feature of French higher education. Since the *grandes écoles* did not have graduate research degrees of their own and since the universities themselves did not recognize the degrees from the *grandes écoles* (as a qualification to do graduate research in a university), the students from the engineering *grandes écoles* continued in their education to ignore scientific research. The most brilliant students in France (measured in terms of competitive entrance examinations) were not directed by the system into scientific research. A more research-oriented system of *grandes écoles* was, it is true, taking shape in the new engineering schools and institutes, for the applied science research faculties out of which they grew were much closer to industry. But the old *grandes écoles* of engineering, convinced that their encyclopedic education produced the best engineers in the world, as-

60 See Alfred Landucci, "Note sur les écoles nationales supérieures," *Revue de l'enseignement supérieur* 1 (1957): 17–21. Also see, for the development of a regionally based engineering school, Culbert Mayer, "L'Université de Nancy et la vie économique en Lorraine," ibid. 4 (1956), 43–45.

sured, moreover, that their engineers were destined for elite positions, saw no reason to emulate the specialized training of the newer schools. Accordingly, before the Second World War no research doctorates could be attained in French *grandes écoles* of engineering. The form and content of French engineering education during the second industrial revolution clearly reflected the absence in France of the *Wissenschaft* tradition.

Inasmuch as engineering education is not management education, the history of higher technical education is of interest only insofar as it delineates educational patterns that pertain to the subject matter of the book. In the German case, the pattern followed in engineering education was repeated a generation later in business education. This happened institutionally with the founding of schools of business economics, the *Handelschochschulen,* just as was done and for the same reason (disdain in universities towards vocationalism) with the technical *Hochschulen,* outside the universities. The first *Handelshochschule* began at Leipzig in 1898.[61] Cologne got a school in 1901 as did Frankfort on the Main. Thereafter a number of new schools were organized in quick succession (Aachen, 1903; Berlin, 1906; Mannheim, 1907; Munich, 1910; Königsberg, 1915; Nuremberg, 1919). Like the engineers, too, and again for the same reason, the men involved in the *Handelshochschulen* followed the *Wissenschaft* tradition. Before the proper research study programs could be established, the professors were needed to run them; but before the professors could be recruited, a scientific business economics had to exist in which the professors could be trained. Since the discipline did not exist in 1900, the first professors of business economics were, academically speaking, i.e., from the university's perspective, not properly qualified. They were either secondary commercial school teachers, men drawn from business or industry, or, if academics, men trained in other fields (economics, political science, law, etc.).

Nonetheless, this first generation of professors rapidly repaired these scientific deficiencies. By 1920 it was possible to acquire the full range of undergraduate and graduate degrees in business economics, and the possession of such research degrees became increasingly important for appointment to professorships in business schools. Indeed it was exceedingly difficult for people without them to get a chair. In just

---

61 Locke, *The End of the Practical Man,* chap. 5.

one generation the German professoriat in business economics became a serious group of researchers who provisioned themselves with all the scholarly appurtenances deemed necessary for this essential professorial task. The oldest periodicals in business economics, Schmalenbach's *Zeitschrift für betriebswissenschaftliche Forschung,* known today as *Schmalenbachs Zeitschrift für handelswissenschaftliche Forschung,* and Heinrich Nicklisch's *Zeitschrift für Handelswissenschaft und Handelspraxis* were founded, respectively, in 1906 and 1908. They were research organs from the first which not only published articles on numerous topics but reviewed critically current books and articles, foreign and domestic. To this periodical literature, which expanded significantly after the First World War, must be added publications in book form. By 1938 the ninety-nine business economists listed on the membership rolls of the Association of German Teachers of Economic and Social Sciences had authored 465 and coauthored or edited 565 works, amounting to 10.40 per person.[62] Among these volumes were the elaborate bibliographical and research references characteristic of every scientific discipline. Professor Erich Schäfer's *Das Schrifttum über betriebswirtschaftliche Marktforschung* and Kurt Schmaltz's *Betriebswirtschaftlicher Literaturführer* were books of this kind. But the really impressive achievement came with the five-volume *Handwörterbuch der Betriebswirtschaftslehre (Concise Dictionary of Business Economics)* published under the general editorship of Heinrich Nicklisch. First printed in 1926 and kept up-to-date in subsequent editions, this 1,520-page reference work was a monument to business economics in Germany. It placed before professors and students a complete bibliography of both foreign and domestic publications on most aspects of the subject.[63]

As a corpus, the writings show, therefore, that business economics had become the discipline of the research-oriented faculties of the new commercial schools. The professors were fully conscious of what they were doing and what it signified in German education. All the scholarly accoutrements of academic business economics served to create a sophisticated social science in the best tradition of German *Wissenschaft.* The professors, in their research seminars and in their research projects, and the graduate students, engaged in thesis work under the

---

62 Ibid., 115.
63 Schäfer's book was published in Berlin, 1925; Schmaltz's in Berlin, 1936.

guidance of these professors, who replenished their ranks from the academically most successful research students, developed the discipline. The knowledge generated was taught to students primarily on the undergraduate level. Since a thorough theoretical education was necessary to complete the scientific instruction considered to be essential for any qualified degree holder (*Diplom-Kaufmann*), the teaching function was no mean task. It made demands on students and teachers alike that increased as the discipline was developed.

In 1900, students could complete the comprehensive undergraduate education in two years. In 1924, the length of the study period was increased to three years. At the same time the numbers enrolled, despite the First World War and the financial crisis of the Weimar Republic, increased impressively. By 1928, total enrollment reached 3,119 students, 516 auditors (*Hospitanten*), and 1,330 attendants at public lectures. In that year over 16,000 had received degrees from a business school (*Dipl.-Kaufmann* or *Diplom-Handelslehrer*).[64] The number continued to increase, especially during the period of National Socialism.

The stress on *Wissenschaft*, then, mirrors engineering education. What about the concept of craftsmanship, the second and necessary ingredient of the engineer's conception of *Technik?* From the very beginning people in business economics were quite conscious of the need to base their study on praxis. Eugen Schmalenbach, the pioneering figure of the first generation of academic business economists, called the discipline a *Kunstlehre* instead of a science, by which he meant that the business economist's first duty was, like the engineer's, to serve the businessman in praxis.[65] The Schmalenbach view was opposed by those who thought that the academic business economist aimed to develop the science. This difference of opinion which arose before the First World War expresses the irritation that the scientific outlook always engenders when it confronts practical men. Through cultivating a healthy relationship between *Hochschule* and industry, the engineers solved this problem by creating the "third science." Schmalenbach sought to do the same but with much less success.

The failure to establish homeostasis between science and praxis in German *Betriebswirtschaftslehre* (B.W.L.) can be attributed to the imbalance that existed between science and craftsmanship. Because of

64 Locke, *The End of the Practical Man,* 200.
65 Eugene Schmalenbach, "Selbstkostenrechnung," *ZfhF* 13 (1919): 257–99, 321–56, 259.

the stronghold physical science occupies in engineering, even the most practical men could not deny its necessity. Because such a scientific component was inherently weak in business and management the craft outlook prevailed among businessmen. This was particularly true during the transitional period of the new paradigm. The development of prewar B.W.L. was affected in two ways. First, the subject was not fully accepted by the universities. Even after the Second World War people in universities complained about the inadequate scientific content of business economics. It was viewed as an intellectually weak subject, attuned to vocational studies, that is, a subject which deals with business conventions rather than scientific truth. Secondly, and as a consequence of their need to acquire a scientific respectability, a need shared by all social sciences, academic business economists tended to cling to university norms more than did engineers. Whereas the engineers, in order to recruit professors from praxis, did not insist on their having the *Habilitation,* the business economists did insist on this universally acknowledged proof of a professor's scientific qualification. Since few people in praxis had a *Habilitation,* the requirement made it difficult to recruit people from praxis into the professoriat of the *Handelshochschulen.* The close relationship established between *Hochschule* and praxis did not materialize in B.W.L. to the extent that it did in engineering.

Nonetheless, between the two world wars B.W.L., if looked at askance by many, improved its status in the academic community. The statistics in Table 3.3 show the number of business economists hired in German universities before the Second World War and the extent to which they had been trained in the *Handelshochschulen.* Considering that the universities had refused to accept business economics, thereby forcing the subject into special institutes – the *Handelshochschulen* – the fact that university faculties had begun to teach the subject in their economics departments and that they had hired men educated in these originally spurned schools to teach it indicates that the university economists were on the road to accepting the new discipline before the outbreak of the Second World War. If a halfway house, German business economics had become, with American, the most highly developed in the world. It used sophisticated economic conceptions to advance the understanding of cost values and of prices. It developed managerial control instruments to guide businessmen to improved performance and profitability. German B.W.L. conquered a great follow-

Table 3.3. *Business economists in German universities in 1938 (excluding Frankfort and Cologne)*

Individual	University	Undergraduate Education Business School	Graduate Educ. in Business School	Year Appointed Instr.	Year Appointed Prof.
Rössle	Bonn	Yes, Dipl.-Kaufm.	Yes	1928	1937
Obst	Breslau	No	No		1919
Hintner	Erlangen	Yes, Dipl.-Kaufm.	No	1930	1932
Hasenack	Freiburg	Yes, Dipl.-Kaufm.	Yes		1935
Auler	Giessen	Yes, Dipl.-Kaufm.	Yes		1925
Kruse	Giessen	Yes, Dipl.-Handelslehr.	No		1933
Weigmann	Göttingen	Yes, Dipl.-Kaufm.	Yes	1936	
Hauck	Greifswald	Yes, Dipl.-Handelslehr.	Yes	1935	
Schmaltz	Halle	Yes, Studied in HHS	Yes	1929	1935
Eisfeld	Hamburg	Yes, Dipl.-Kaufm.	Yes		1922
Sewering	Hamburg	Yes, Dipl.-Handelslehr.	No		1934
Fleege-Althoff	Heidelberg	Yes, Dipl.-Handelslehr.	Yes		1933
Gerstner	Heidelberg	Yes, Dipl.-Handelslehr.	No	1924	
Lysinski	Heidelberg	No	Yes		1934
Malteur	Heidelberg	Yes, Studied in HHS	Yes		1934
Sandig	Heidelberg	Yes, Dipl.-Kaufm.	Yes	1934	
Sommerfeld	Heidelberg	Yes, Dipl.-Handelslehr.	No		1933
Thoms	Heidelberg	Yes, Studied in HHS	Yes		1936
Lampe	Jena	Yes, Dipl.-Kaufm.	Unknown	1925	
Pape	Jena	Yes, Leipzig	Yes		1923
Lohmann	Kiel	Yes, Dipl.-Kaufm.	Yes		1925
Hoffmann	Leipzig	Trained in Business	No		Unknown
Fischer, G.	Munich	Yes, Dipl. (BWL)	Yes		1934
Hertlein	Munich	Yes, Dipl.-Handelslehr.	Yes		1934
Gutenberg	Münster	Yes, Dipl.-Kaufm.	No		1936
Lindhardt	Münster	Yes, Dipl.-Kaufm.	No	1936	
Preiser	Rostock	Yes, Dipl.-Handelslehr.	Yes	1931	
Rieger	Tübingen	No. Economics/Strassburg	Yes		1928

Source: Robert R. Locke, *The End of the Practical Man* (Greenwich, Conn., 1984), 230.

ing in Scandinavia, in Eastern Europe, in Turkey, in Italy, in Spain, and in Japan. When in 1953 Kobe University in Japan awarded its first honorary doctorate in business economics, it went to Professor Schmalenbach, with whom many of the Japanese professors of business economics had studied; this prewar generation had assimilated the precepts of German B.W.L. into their own discipline.[66]

Concurrently, the German business economists cultivated praxis. Two examples, which are taken from the efficiency movement, one in which academic engineers had a most prominent part, can be used to illustrate the academic business economists' involvement in praxis. The first concerns the Frankfort Society, a private organization, founded in

66 In the *ZfbF* (1953): 436, announcement is made about the honorary doctorate by Prof. Dr. Yasutaro Hirai, Prof. Dr. Yoshimoto Kobayashi, and Prof. Dr. Katsuji Yamashita. On Schmalenbach's eightieth birthday, a festschrift for him was published in Japan (1953). It had numerous articles on a wide variety of topics handled in German business economics and shows just how thoroughly familiar the Japanese business economists were with German accomplishments. See notice of the festschrift in *ZfbF* 6 (1954): 548.

1903, which brought leading professors of engineering, economics, business economics, and administration together with industrialists and businessmen to promote performance "where the question of good administration, in the broadest sense of the word, plays a role."[67] Since this Society began before business economics had developed fully, professors of engineering and economics were much more important participants in its earliest activities than professors of business economics. But as the B.W.L. discipline ripened, the participation of business economists grew. They arranged for all members of the Society to receive free subscriptions to two B.W.L. journals, Schmalenbach's *Zeitschrift für handelswissenschaftliche Forschung* and Nicklisch's *Zeitschrift für Handelswissenschaft und Handelspraxis*. The Society also published a monograph series, *Current Questions in Business Economics (Betriebswirtschaftliche Zeitfragen)*, which treated subjects like the measurement of production intensity (a technical subject) and the influence of volume on production costs (an economic one).[68] The Frankfort Society sponsored the annual meetings, begun in 1907, of professors teaching economics in technical institutes, which sought to tailor economic education to the needs of engineers. In 1908, it directed industry's attention to cost accounting by conducting an essay competition on that subject. The best essays, which described actual costs systems and were written by accountants and engineers, were published in Schmalenbach's journal.[69] The Society sponsored ad hoc conferences, too, which alerted businessmen and industrialists to problems in business economics. In October 1913, it co-sponsored a conference in Cologne on the organization of business and economic archives. In 1921, the Society organized a special gathering of businessmen in Cologne on the problems currency devaluation raised in business administration. At that meeting Schmalenbach spoke on the tax problems created by inflated profits and Professor Prion on the effects of inflation on business finance.[70]

The second example is the Reichskuratorium für Wirtschaftlichkeit (R.K.W.) which functioned much like the Frankfort Society. Both were

---

67 Gesellschaft für wirtschaftliche Ausbildung, e. V. zu Frankfurt am Main, *Bericht über das achte Geschäftsjahr 1910* (Frankfort, 1911); my translation.
68 W. Steinthal, *Intensitätsmessungen in der Industrie* (Berlin, 1924); and Herbert Peiser, *Der Einflluss des Beschäftigungsgrades auf die industrielle Kostenentwicklung* (Frankfort, 1924).
69 *ZfhF*.
70 "Mitteilungen," *ZfhF* 16 (Sept. 1, 1922): 84.

coordinating agencies, bringing diverse organizations together in a common cause, and educational agencies, seeking to instruct an interested public about the best way to accomplish economic efficiency. Nonetheless, the two organizations differed. Although a private association, the R.K.W., after 1925, received financial support from the German state. Between 1925 and 1933, the government gave RM 6,716,000 to the trust.[71] The number of people involved in its activities grew proportionately. "Just ten years after [its] foundation," one of the members wrote, "there were about 4,000 honorary co-workers from employer and employee, industrial and commercial circles, from various branches of science and government who, with fifty regular employees bore the principal burden of its 150 committees and work groups, scattered all over Germany."[72] Money and numbers, therefore, allowed the R.K.W. to operate on a much larger scale postwar than had the prewar Frankfort group.

Between 1922 and 1926 engineers and technicians monopolized R.K.W. councils. The business director of the Committee for Efficient Production (Ausschuss für wirtschaftliche Fertigung) was a graduate engineer named Kreide. Under his leadership Professor Georg Schlesinger supervised a work group that studied the application of power to machinery and Professor Aumund one that investigated efficient conveyer systems. Their presence reflected the strong influence engineers exercised in the early stages of the German Scientific Management Movement. Since that movement had been concerned with the factory (*Betriebswissenschaft*), i.e., scientific management essentially as F. W. Taylor conceived of it, the R.K.W.'s work was "cultivated by engineers and technicians who [had] dealt with technical problems of production from the standpoint of the factory manager."[73] Sometimes R.K.W. committees were composed only of engineers. The Committee for Machines and Forges (Maschinenarbeit und Schmieden), for example, had originally been set up by the German Engineering Association (V.D.I.). It was transferred to the jurisdiction of the R.K.W. after its creation in order to avoid duplication of efforts. The Committee for Efficient Production, too, was a V.D.I. creation taken over by the

71 Reichskuratorium für Wirtschaftlichkeit, *Jahresbericht, 1932/33*, RKW-Veröffentlichungen, 95, 14.
72 Hans W. Büttner, *Das Rationalisierungskuratorium der Deutschen Wirtschaft* (Düsseldorf, 1973), 11; my translation.
73 A. Schranz, "Recent Tendencies in German Business Economics," *The Accounting Review* 12 (1937): 278–85, 80.

R.K.W. The work these committees did showed this technical bent. A committee on time and motion studies (*Zeitstudien*), for example, emphasized the engineering tasks. Other committees, whose jurisdictions were ostensibly broader, were in practice just as restrictive in their work. In the Committee for Efficient Production, instead of handling cost accounting in general, the members worked exclusively on costing systems for the mechanical engineering industry.

In 1925, the *Journal of the Association of German Business School Graduates* complained about the R.K.W.'s penchant to ignore the subject of business administration and marketing. And the editor blamed this oversight on the engineers. "This impression is confirmed," he explained,

especially if one looks at the men on the central committee of the R.K.W. Among these 119 only a few businessmen can be found; the others are technicians or civil servants or men whose names have a certain resonance [*Klang*] in public or political life. Representatives of business economics cannot be found at all. The problems in distribution and administration will certainly not be solved in this way.[74]

Six months later, however, Professor Fritz Schmidt of the Frankfort Faculty of Business Economics considered these complaints to be groundless. What had happened?

Schmidt had not just interpreted the same fact differently. When, in December 1925, the journal attacked the R.K.W., it was in the process of changing its composition through the creation of a Committee on Administrative Efficiency. Eleven of this committee's members were professors of business economics (Tibertius, Seyffert, Schmidt, Schmalenbach, Rossle, Nicklisch, Mahlberg, Kalveram, Hummel, Geldmacher, and Bucerius). In addition, business economists with academic connections (Botheme, Muser, and Klinger of the Association of German Business School Graduates; Eicke and Schluter, assistant professors in business schools) were on the panel. The committee's work encompassed all aspects of business administration, including accounting, general administration, sales and distribution, finance, and office management. The transformation it brought to the R.K.W. can be appreciated by looking at one subject, cost accounting. Its study was shifted from the engineer-dominated Committee of Efficient Production to a special ac-

74 *Zeitschrift des Verbandes Deutscher Diplom-Kaufleute* 6:1 (1926): 17; my translation.

counting subcommittee (*Fachausschuss*) under the new Committee on Administrative Efficiency. The subcommittee, chaired by Schmalenbach, investigated commercial and business as well as industrial cost accounting. In addition, the subcommittee took up bookkeeping techniques, budgeting, financial accounting, and business statistics. Subsequently the R.K.W. added other committees to handle commercial and monetary aspects of the efficiency movement (e.g., on banking and distribution), and it also made formerly independent business research institutions part of its purview (e.g., the Research Center for Commerce in Berlin, the Institute for Research on Consumer Goods in Cologne, and the Institute for Research on Marketing of Finished Products in Nuremberg). Prominent business economists were no less involved in the work of these committees.

The point about the Frankfort Society and the R.K.W., whose work covered decades, is that they illustrate how academia cooperated with praxis. Academics were not the only people involved in these groups; otherwise there could have been no contact with praxis. Nor were the people from praxis on committees necessarily themselves graduates. Plenty of nongraduates were involved in both productivity groups just as they were in other economic organizations (e.g., the German Engineering Fraternity, V.D.I.). But the presence of nonuniversity people in the councils does not belittle the influence of academia so much as confirm it, for the graduates usually dominated the committee leadership, thereby exercising the greater authority. The fact that business economists as well as engineers were present demonstrates the extent to which in the years before the Second World War the development of a practical purposiveness in German higher education embraced business as well as technical faculties.

The commercial-business education movements in France and Great Britain were shaped by the same educational heritages that affected technical educational reform in each country. Because the accomplishments were quite meager in Great Britain, events there will be treated first. In Britain, engineering education suffered because neither the engineers nor the institutions of higher education perceived a need for it. A lack of coordination between university and praxis produced even worse results in business education than in engineering. The accounting profession can be used to illustrate this reluctance among businessmen. British accounting associations, like British engineering societies, regulated admittance into the profession. As with the engineers, too, professional preparation involved apprenticeship programs and accountant-society-administered qualification examinations. The accounting groups resented and resisted any incursions into their territory and they did not take kindly to those who suggested that accountancy could be learned in universities. A Mr. Paterson expressed this general prejudice before an assembly of incorporated accountants in 1911:

I find, and I think it is the experience of all who have carefully examined the cases that came under their notice, that a student who has been in a good office, and who has the natural ability to assimilate what he sees and reads, makes a better accountant than the man who starts off with the halo of a university education (Applause). I think that our method of examination, subject to certain qualifications, is a far better test than even a degree in economics in the Berlin University (Hear, hear!). We get far better results from a practical examination than from one in mere theory.[75]

This sort of resistance continued right up through the Second World War. In 1950, "the vast majority" of accounting students in the British Isles prepared with the aid of correspondence schools for their examinations while working as articled clerks in an accountant's office.[76] And English accountants continued to utter the old clichés about the superiority of apprenticeship and to honor it in practice.

It was, then, an article of faith among British businessmen and industrialists that managers were born not made. This amounted less to a belief in individual talent as in social qualification, for the "natural authority" to which so many referred was not some innate individual quality but one acquired in public schools. When British managers proclaimed management was an art not a science to be learned in school, they were really protecting the leadership prerogatives of privileged classes against the threat of the upstart individual who based his claim to advancement on an "abstracted, formalized" knowledge, the kind embodied in "a formal qualification, such as a university degree." "Formal education of any kind," Thomas remarked about the traditional British manager, "beyond a certain minimum of general education, . . . tended to be severely downgraded."[77]

75 C. Hewetson Nelson, "Professional Education," *The Incorporated Accountants' Journal* 23 (Oct. 1911): 20. Paterson was speaking after the session on Nelson's talk.
76 N. H. Stacey, *English Accountancy: A Study in Social and Economic History, 1800–1954* (London, 1954), 248.
77 Alan B. Thomas, "Management and Education: Rationalization and Reproduction in British Business," *International Studies of Management and Organization* 10:1–2 (1980): 71–109, 72.

Among academics commercial and/or business studies fared no better. At Oxford and Cambridge the subjects were not developed, including accounting, the core of German business economics. A commerce degree was introduced in the University of Birmingham in 1902, in the University of Manchester in 1904, and in London University in 1920. During the 1920s only 647 people took commerce degrees in the three universities.[78] During the 1930s just 781 graduated and in the 1950s the program atrophied. The result from a scientific viewpoint was just as discouraging as from a numeric, for the will to build a thriving discipline in management study failed. There was one flicker of hope. The London School of Economics moved in the right direction in the 1930s. During a reorganization of the school in 1932, a graduate section on commercial education was added, which was charged with the research goal of finding and perfecting "the methods of economic analysis that were susceptible of being used on practical business problems." The right idea, it came too late and in too limited an institutional scope to alter the insignificant nature of British commercial studies before the war. With such feeble results, Dr. Shirley Keeble's recent effort to make a doctoral thesis out of the evidence must have been a frustrating experience, as it always is when writing about what did not happen. At every point along the way there was scarcely more than a negative report, no response, indifference at best, if not outright hostility from business and industry toward the graduates, and, as a consequence, no hope of attracting students into the program.

It might seem odd that, in Britain, the mecca of economics, so little attention would be paid to business. But the two subjects were intellectually and educationally quite distinct in the English mind. In 1902, the newly appointed economist in London, Edward Cannan, "argued that the practical usefulness of economic theory was not in private business but in politics."[79] At Cambridge, where mathematics had become an entrenched discipline, analysis and the search for the fundamental economic tenets, not the interpretation of facts, fascinated

---

78 Shirley Keeble, "University Education and Business Management from the 1890s to the 1950s: A Reluctant Relationship," Ph.D. diss., London School of Economics and Political Science, 1984, 56.
79 Edward Cannan, "The Practical Usefulness of Economic Theory," presidential address to Section F of the British Association for the Advancement of Science, Belfast, Sept. 1902, in *Essays in Economic Method*, ed. R. L. Smith (London, 1962), 188.

economists. In Germany academic business economists before the Second World War had borrowed heavily from economic theory in order to develop a management accounting useful to the firm.[80] In Britain, although marginal analysis was cultivated in economics, the will to apply it to business-related problems was absent. Products of a public school educational process that was divorced from industrial life, isolated in idyllic Cambridge from the commercial life of the country, the economists considered business management problems, as one scholar wrote in 1937, "to be the domain of second rate minds, incapable of aspiring to the scholarly economist's highest level of activity: the development and perfection of the classic theory and the theory of distribution."[81] If engineering education suffered in Britain because of its subordination to the arrogant pure scientist, business education suffered more because the social scientist did not recognize its scientific respectability as much as the natural scientist did engineering's. There was very little hope in these circles for the development of a third science in business studies.

Neither, despite the presence of John Maynard Keynes, was there much hope that government would afford Cambridge economists much voice in policy or operational decision making. It is true that a council of economic advisors was set up during the 1930s to serve the government.[82] But the number of advisors was never very great; indeed, the number of economists working temporarily or full-time in Whitehall was never very great. Alfred Coats puts their number as late as 1950 at a paltry seventeen.[83] This failure to develop a close cooperation between government and university economists is the same as the failure to develop one between business and university economists: the economics graduates were not much appreciated in praxis. There are two reasons why this was true. One has little to do with the study of economics per se; rather it stems from a general prejudice within the British civil service about the nature of leadership and the education proper to its execution. The Northcote-Trevelyan Report of 1854,

80 Locke, *The End of the Practical Man*, chap. 4.
81 John Jewkes, "L'Université de Manchester," in *Cinquantenaire de la revue d'économie politique*, special issue (1937): 111–17, 112–13; my translation.
82 Susan Howson and Donald Winch, *The Economic Advisory Council, 1930–1939: A Study in Economic Advice during Depression and Recovery* (Cambridge, 1977).
83 A. W. Coats, "Britain: The Rise of the Specialists," in *Economists in Government: An International Comparative Study*, ed. A. W. Coats (Durham, N.C.: 1981), 27–66, 33.

which shaped the British civil service at the moment of its inception, "recommended the establishment of a unified permanent civil service recruited by competitive examination." The examination was meant to select men with the leadership qualities of the generalist not the skills of the specialist. Accordingly, the perfect civil service officer needed character more than knowledge, the qualities inculcated at public school and Oxbridge. The arts and humanities – and at Cambridge mathematics – provided the "gentleman ideal" educational content considered to be necessary for a successful "administrator" in the new civil service. The British civil service, therefore, was, from the specialist point of view, a know-nothing organization, or rather, it was an organization in which the sort of knowledge acquired was useless in a technical-expert sense, for the general class of administrative officer out of which the leadership was recruited had no specific professional or technical qualifications. Classics scholars were preferred by the Treasury. Inasmuch as after 1921 the permanent head of the Treasury was the head of the civil service, this preference set the tone for other services. The top civil servants were generalists who appreciated the dialectical skills aroused by the study of classics and mathematics, not the technical knowledge imbibed in the study of economics. Method of selection and promotion, therefore, discouraged the entry of economists into the government.

The second reason for people in government shunning economists was the way the subject was actually taught. British economists played a leading role in the marginalist revolution of the late nineteenth century which gave birth to neoclassical microeconomics. In the 1920s they (Sraffa, Robinson, Chamberlin) made major contributions to what Donald Winch describes as a "radically new theory of the firm acting under market conditions that varied from perfect competition at one extreme . . . to monopoly at the other."[84] The dethronement of perfect competition microeconomics was followed by Keynes's achievements in macroeconomics which denied, in part, the application of the logic of individual market behavior to an aggregate market. "If these were major theoretical achievements," Winch further explained,

their significance for policy-making . . . was negligible, or at most indirect. It can best be thought of as the result of a process of regeneration which was internal to the academic community, rather than as a response to demands

84 *Economics and Policy: A Historical Study* (New York: 1969), 324.

made by external circumstances; it was a successful extension of neo-classical marginalism to deal with theoretical anomalies that had long been recognized. . . . The only criticism one might make . . . in this period is that the effort put into theoretical refinement was not matched by attempts to test theory against empirical evidence.[85]

If the gentlemen generalists in Whitehall had seen no reason to demand sophisticated skills, the gentlemen economists in the universities had, because of their educational heritage, also seen no reason to provide them. Consequently the homeostasis between the demands of praxis and those of science which spurred the development of a policy science in some other countries did not occur in Great Britain.

French business education, too, moved along the familiar path trod by that country's technical education. Commercial education was not developed in the university faculties but in the *grandes écoles*. Comparison between engineering and commercial education in the *grandes écoles* must be made carefully. Since the state had no interest in commerce graduates, the prestige which state sponsorship brought to engineering schools did not accrue to *grandes écoles* of commerce. Nonetheless, the Paris Chamber of Commerce and Industry began to sponsor higher education in commercial studies in the nineteenth century. Accordingly, *écoles supérieures de commerce* were founded in various French cities at various times. By 1900 two existed in Paris and eleven in the provinces (Algiers, Bordeaux, Dijon, le Havre, Lyons, Marseilles, Nancy, Nantes, Rouen, and Toulouse). The schools gained a certain international renown, enough for American visitors to inspect them when setting about organizing their business schools. One French admirer of the schools, the accountant Maurice Ravisse, claimed in 1909, after "a personal inquiry," that "the education given [in them] is perfect. An elite of professors has warmheartedly taken up the task of shaping enlightened employees."[86]

Because of the *Wissenschaft* tradition, German business economics sacrificed contact with practice to develop a scientific discipline; because of the absence of a *Wissenschaft* tradition, the French schools emphasized the necessity to have close relationships with praxis. French *grandes écoles,* in effect, strove to produce an elite that would find its way to the top in banking and commerce like the graduates of

85 Ibid.
86 Maurice Ravisse, "De l'enseignement des méthodes pratiques dans les écoles supérieures de commerce," *Mon Bureau* 1:5 (Nov. 1909): 90–95, 91; my translation.

the *grandes écoles* of engineering did in manufacturing. Of all the schools which set themselves this task, the most important was H.E.C., the School for Advanced Commercial Studies (Ecole des Hautes Etudes Commerciales). A school historian wrote, "As a result of the more theoretical character of its studies, by the necessary extent of their abstract form, the student from H.E.C. is destined to occupy the highest commercial position in public administration as well as in private enterprise."[87] The claim was somewhat exaggerated because graduates from H.E.C. did not attain the highest positions in public administration. But even before the war they moved up the management hierarchy in private enterprise. A list of H.E.C. graduates at the end of the Second World War reads like a Who's Who of French commerce (François Peugeot, several Hottinguers, a Neuflize, a Viallet, a Guerlaine, a Hersieck counted among them). It successfully cultivated a national clientele.

Marc Meuleau's studies of H.E.C. between the two wars charts this transformation. In 1912 89 percent of the H.E.C. students succeeded their fathers in a family business; in 1939 only 45 percent did.[88] Clearly H.E.C. graduates, as the structure of the firm evolved, found themselves more and more absorbed into the professional managerial hierarchies of the large firm. Some of these changes were rather dramatic. When Saint-Gobain reformed its management system in the 1930s, for instance, it hired seven H.E.C. graduates into its new financial and accounting departments. In the automobile sector the number of H.E.C. graduates in management functions grew from sixteen in 1912 to ninety-nine in 1939, of which eighty-one were in the big three (Renault, Peugeot, and Citroën). Generally, H.E.C. people did not rise to the top positions in these firms during the interwar period, but when they did it obviously benefited the school. Thus, during the time (1917–39) that Samuel Guillelmon was Louis Renault's right-hand man, forty-one H.E.C. graduates entered the firm; while Alfred Pose was director of the Banque Nationale pour le Commerce et l'Industrie (B.N.C.I.), the number of H.E.C. graduates employed rose from eleven (1932) to fifty (1950). H.E.C. men were responsible for managerial

87 L. Ricard, "L'Enseignement commercial en France et les écoles supérieures pratiques de commerce et d'industrie," *Mon Bureau* 2:11 (Nov. 1910): 273–77, 275; my translation.

88 "Les HEC: d'un diplôme marginal à la célébrité scolaire et professionnelle (1881–1980)," paper delivered at the Colloquium on the History of Management, Paris, March 11–12, 1988.

innovation in these large enterprises. Léon Caillet introduced management accounting in the chemical sector at Saint-Gobain in the 1930s; Jean-Jacques Vignault reformed the export services of the perfume manufacturer, la Maison Coty; Jacques Daum and Jacques Guédan helped develop a new form of commerce when they created the popular retail chain stores, Prisunic, for the department store Le Printemps. Daum installed a system of budgetary control for the firm. This interest in managerial rationalization, moreover, prompted H.E.C. graduates to join the French equivalent of the R.K.W., le Comité National de l'Organisation Française (C.N.O.F.). Forty entered the association between 1927 and 1938 where they proselytized new merchandising, accounting, and organizational methods.

Concurrently the educational program at H.E.C. underwent reform. In 1922 the school, following the example of the *grandes écoles* of engineering, adopted the competitive entrance examination (*concours*) which led to greater selectivity. Less stress was placed at the school on course work in law, more on commerce, management accounting, modern merchandising, and finance. A course, "Gouvernement des entreprises," made popular by the French management pioneer Henri Fayol and taught in the school by one of his disciples, Jean Carlioz, was introduced into the curriculum. And in 1931 the Paris Chamber of Commerce started a Centre de Préparation aux Affaires (C.P.A.) which, utilizing the Harvard case method of instruction, offered postexperience management education. The Center did not cater uniquely to H.E.C. students but with its founding more H.E.C. graduates stopped doing a *licence* in law, concurrently with their diploma at H.E.C., completing their education with a certificate from the Center instead. The H.E.C.-C.P.A. educational experience constituted, then, a shift from a juridical approach to commercial studies to one that emphasized more managerial know-how.

Still, it must not be thought that between the wars higher business education in France resembled German. This was true because of the numbers involved. The enrollment in the *grandes écoles* of commerce was a fraction of the enrollment in German *Betriebswirtschaftslehre*. Moreover, the development of sophisticated study programs did not occur everywhere. Provincial *grandes écoles* of commerce remained hardly better than secondary schools that taught commercial skills rather than business. Even H.E.C., the most advanced of the French *grandes écoles,* did not measure up to German schools when it came to scientific standards.[89] Whereas the Germans had a three-year undergraduate program by the 1920s, H.E.C. did not change from a two- to a three-year course until the 1940s. But the length of study was not the important difference. To develop modern business studies a discipline has to be created. That discipline – a unified study, one that borrows, perhaps, for its purposes from other disciplines but one that is more than the sum of its parts, one that needs a corpus of experts, like those assembled in the *Handelshochschulen* to accomplish its task – did not appear. At H.E.C. there was no permanent teaching faculty: The teaching was handled on a part-time basis by university professors, politicians, members of the Chamber of Deputies, civil servants, businessmen – men whose work at H.E.C. was just a job among many, and not their principal one. Since each man had a specialty, the teaching of which would scarcely differ at H.E.C. from the way it was taught elsewhere (in the economics or political science department of a university faculty, for instance), and since there was at H.E.C. no graduate study and no research program (and how could there be without a permanent teaching staff), no discipline could be created.

Therefore, even though a close contact existed between H.E.C. and its graduates, this relationship did not unite science with praxis. The one essential element to the union, science, was missing. In 1910, an observer at the Vienna Congress for Commercial Education reported: "One could clearly see how the business faculties in the German speaking regions had begun to develop into teaching and research institutions in economics and how the Latin countries, with their very different academic [*Hochschule*] goals, tried more and more to copy and to hold fast tenaciously to routine business practice."[90] H.E.C. and the other French commercial schools fit this Latin pattern. The contacts established with praxis were meant primarily to serve as a network for the placement of school graduates, less a pipeline through which to develop the science of business economics in praxis. H.E.C., like all *grandes écoles,* sought to enhance its academic reputation not by the excellence of its science but by the selectivity of its entry requirements, i.e., by adopting the *concours*.

89 Unfortunately we do not have studies of the other Parisian schools. Hence we do not know the extent to which they sought to follow H.E.C.
90 Felix Werner, "Die Betriebswirtschaftslehre und die Handelshochschulen," quoted in Locke, *The End of the Practical Man,* 152.

Table 3.4. *Business economists in German technical institutes in 1938*

Individual	Institute	Undergraduate Education in Business School	Graduate Educ. in Business School	Year Appointed Instr.	Prof.
Maedge	Aachen	No, business practice	No		1920
Münstermann	Aachen	Yes, Dipl.-Handelslehr.	Yes	1932	
Eich	Berlin	Yes, Dipl.-Kaufm.	No	1935	
Funke	Berlin	No, Dipl.-Ing.	No, in THS	1935	
Hardach	Berlin	Yes, Dipl.-Kaufm.	Yes	1938	
Kühn	Berlin	Practical Experience	No, in THS	1937	
Lorenz	Berlin	No	No, in THS	1937	
Moede	Berlin	No. Univ.-Leipzig	No, in THS		1921
Prion	Berlin	Yes, Dipl.-Kaufm.	Yes		1925
Schnutenhaus	Brunswick	Yes, Dipl.-Kaufm.	No, in THS		1936
Lembke	Danzig	No	No, in THS	1935	
Ziegler	Darmstadt	Yes, Dipl.-Handelslehr.	Yes		Unknown
Beste	Dresden	Yes, Dipl.-Kaufm.	Yes		1927
Hennig	Hannover	Yes, Studied in HHS	No, in THS		1923
Bucerius	Karlsruhe	Practical Experience	No, in THS	1927	
Fricke	Karlsruhe	Yes, Dipl.-Kaufm.	No	1936	
Krüger	Munich	Yes, Dipl.-Kaufm.	Yes	1935	
Reuther	Munich	Yes, Dipl.-Kaufm.	Yes	1926	
Weinreich	Munich	Yes, Dipl.-Kaufm.	Yes	1935	

Source: Robert R. Locke, *The End of the Practical Man* (Greenwich, Conn., 1984), 235.

Thus different heritages in higher education brought forth in each country different patterns of educational response, first in engineering and then in commerce. Commercial/business education, which came last and was shaped by precedent, then in turn affected, through its development, the way engineering institutions provided management education. Since engineers had to work efficiently economically as well as technically, even before the First World War in Imperial Germany, professors, practicing engineers, and government bureaucrats began to talk about a need to introduce economic subjects into the engineering curriculum. The need could not be met easily because the economics in the university available in 1900 did not discuss the sort of problems engineers faced – the expertise of economics was, therefore, not pertinent. Hence, as the *Handelshochschulen* developed, the engineers began to look to the new business economists. Evidence of cooperation has been given, for engineers and business economists worked together in the Frankfort Society and in the R.K.W. Instances of this cooperation in schools can also be cited. Table 3.4 shows, for instance, the number of business economists hired in German technical institutes before the Second World War and the extent to which their education had been received in business economics at *Handelshochschulen* or in the business faculties at universities which had begun as *Handelshoch-*

schulen. Their presence shows that engineers were being taught management science by business economists.

Since the demands of technical education were so great, engineers were not willing to concede much of the student engineers' time to business economics, so special programs of industrial administration were established in some engineering schools. The first program, that of the *Wirtschafts-Ingenieur* (Economics-Engineer), was established in 1921 at the technical institute in Berlin (Charlottenburg).[91] Some other engineering schools followed. The *Wirtschafts-Ingenieur* program, composed half of subjects in engineering and half in business economics, explicitly recognized the economic dimension as just as important to the manufacturing business as the purely technical one. Both should be studied together scientifically.

It was Willy Prion, a business economist (no engineering degrees), who organized the *Wirtschafts-Ingenieur* program and ran it in Berlin between the wars. Indeed, because the business economists worked in engineering schools and because their publications could be found in the scientific literature, the *Wissenschaft* that the business economists formulated in the *Handelshochschulen* could be fused with engineer-created industrial administration into the *Wirtschafts-Ingenieur* program. The point is, then, that events in the engineering schools were affected by the creation of a business economics in the *Handelshochschulen*. And the corollary to this point is that the same development did not occur in England or in France because similar educational institutions in business economics had not developed.

Especially negative results ensued for the management education of engineers in England. The engineering associations, against which educational reformers had fought so hard in the interests of a scientific technical education, resisted the call for university-level management studies in engineering even more than they did technical studies. In 1930, an engineering professor, F. W. Burstall, proposed that business and management courses be added to the engineering curricula at universities. But *The Engineer*, which published Burstall's appeal, opposed it. "We have always held," the editor of this leading professional journal said,

that apprenticeship or pupilage is an absolutely essential element in the education of an engineer. Indeed, if we had to choose between an extension of the

91 Willi Prion, *Ingenieur und Wirtschaft: Der Wirtschafts-Ingenieur* (Berlin, 1930), 608.

college course and workshop training, we should unhesitatingly select the latter. . . . Possibly technical schools and universities might be made more useful to young engineers by the introduction of the subjects Professor Burstall . . . suggests but we do not believe that any amount of college education in them can ever take the place of the day-to-day touch which is given by a few years as an apprentice or pupil.[92]

University-level management education in English engineering, therefore, lagged even further behind that in German technical *Hochschulen,* for, if German accomplishments in this respect were modest, the English were nonexistent.

The failure of the French schools of commerce to establish permanent faculties to engage in research and to create a scientific discipline meant that the French *grandes écoles* of engineering, like engineering departments in British universities, were left to their own devices when developing management education for engineers. French engineers were the managerial elite in French industry; in this regard they differed fundamentally from English engineers. French engineers, because of their managerial leadership were, again unlike British engineers, among the most illustrious advocates of scientific management in Europe. In this capacity, a few worked on educational projects during the 1920s and 1930s. But French management education was, to the extent that it existed at all between the wars, postexperience education taught by practicing managers to practicing managers in evening courses. The regular academic program in the *grandes écoles* of engineering was hardly touched by it. No equivalent *Wirtschafts-Ingenieur* program appeared in French engineering schools.

Indeed the economics taught, since no business economics discipline had been created in French commercial schools, had very little to do with business problems. It was macroeconomics and, oddly enough, even at the Polytechnic School, economics had a low mathematics content, for "[i]n order to avoid the reproach, so often directed at *Polytechniciens,* that they cultivated mathematics too much," the school introduced mathematics into economics "very slowly [*très tendrement*], rather in the form of allusions which haunted the lecture presentations, where the theory of Walras was scarcely touched on and then only partially."[93] The course on "politi-

92 *The Engineer* 149:3884 (June 20, 1930): 689–90.
93 Francois Divisia, "Les Ecoles techniques," in *Cinquantenaire de la revue d'économie politique,* 45; my translation.

cal economy" at the School of Bridges and Roads did not even discuss Walras's theories. In it only a little mathematics, taken from Cournot, Dupuit, and Colson, was used, but it was "insufficiently advanced to be able to lead to important developments."[94] Economics was handled the same way in other technical schools where "mathematical economics" was either "scarcely taught or nonexistent." As for the courses in statistics in the School of Bridges and Roads and the Conservatoire des Arts et Métiers, they were too elementary to assist people in econometrics.

Pioneers are by definition unique. Those who were responsible for the development of management studies before the First World War can be counted among the exceptional people of their generation. But exceptional individuals do not work in a vacuum. Their creativity depends on the environmental possibilities. Had industry not developed new technologies and organizational structure to demand and accommodate university-educated business graduates, the work of pioneers in higher education would have been fruitless. But opportunity had more to do with environment than economic demand. The ability to perceive, respond to demand, indeed, even the arousal of demand in industry and business themselves, required an interplay of social-psychological factors of which institutionalized, expressed, educationally inherited ones were most important. If, therefore, everybody everywhere did not reach the halfway house in management studies in the same way, to the same extent, at the same time, educational traditions are an important cause.

Innovation in management studies created strange bedfellows. This was especially true during and after the Second World War when all sorts of scientists got involved in management problems. But the same sort of unaccustomed behavior was needed to advance prewar management studies into the halfway house. Engineers had to think about economics, economists about engineering, and both about how their separate disciplines could help create a new problem-solving approach to the management of business and industrial firms. The contention here is that, because German educational traditions provided a more fruitful environment for this cross-fertilization, Germans made it into the halfway house of management studies earlier and more completely than did the French or the British. This happened both in the qualita-

94 Ibid.

tive sense – in terms of the sophistication of the business economics developed – and the quantitative – in terms of the degree to which the knowledge and skill developed were proselytized.

Episodes from the lives of three pioneer German management scientists indicate how the German educational heritage promoted innovation in management science. The relationship between the education and the work of Professor Erich Schneider, Germany's leading economist about 1945, is one example.[95] Schneider admired the marginal-utility, general-equilibrium mathematical economists, a group to which he belonged. But Schneider was an expert in the engineering aspects of industrial administration as well as in business economics. His first chair was in business economics (1936) at Aarhus University, Denmark. His publications, his teaching, and his research required a fusion of knowledge drawn from mathematics, economics, industrial engineering, and business economics. How did he manage it? He did it, of course, because he was an intensely curious man. But he also succeeded because the German educational system fostered that curiosity. Schneider earned his doctorate in business economics under Fritz Schmidt, a leading German business economist of the interwar period, in 1922 at Frankfort University. Afterward he studied mathematics and physics before completing a *Habilitationsschrift* in economics. (He worked with Josef Schumpeter at Bonn University when Schumpeter, after leaving Vienna, spent a few years there before going to Harvard.) During these years Schneider also worked with engineers, writing several studies for the periodical, published by the German Engineering Society, *Technik und Wirtschaft*.[96] At Frankfort, under Schmidt, then, Schneider learned about business economics (no doubt this Frankfort doctorate qualified him for his chair in business economics in Denmark).

95 See Bombach and Tacke, *Erich Schneider, 1900–1970*.
96 Erich Schneider, "Mathematische Betrachtungen über den nationalen Gütertransport," *Technik und Wirtschaft, Monatsschrift des Vereines Deutscher Ingenieur* 17 (1924): 204–08; "Uber den Einfluss veränderlichen Geldwertes auf die Handelsbeziehungen zwischen In- und Ausland," ibid. 17 (1924): 299–304; "Uber die Reziprozität zwischen Geldwert und Warenpreis," *Zeitschrift für angewandte Mathematik und Mechanik* 4 (1924): 254–60; "Die Forschungen auf dem Gebiete der mathematischen Sozialökonomik," *Technik und Wirtschaft* 18 (1924): 104–10; "Ist die technisch beste auch die jeweils wirtschaftlichste Lösung?" ibid. 18 (1925): 226–30. Hans Kroner and Erich Schneider, "Die Rentabilität einer Produktion als Funktion der Nachfrage," *Technik und Wirtschaft* 19 (1926): 135–38; Hans Kroner and Erich Schneider, "Zur Rentabilität der Unternehmung. Verkaufspreis – Umsatz – Gewinn," ibid. 19 (1927): 245–48.

These diverse contacts shaped Schneider's scientific work. He observed that, with Schumpeter, the discussions in Bonn ranged over

Moore's "Synthetic Economics," Schultz' "Statistical Demand and Supply Curves" and Frisch's "Measurement of Marginal Utility" i.e., all attempts to build a statistical base for mathematical theoretical analysis. Other subjects discussed were Mayer's "Critique of Functional Price Theory," Divisia's "Loi Circulatoire," Cournot's "Kapital ueber das Sozialeinkommen . . . ," Léontief's "Statistische Methode zur Ermittlung von Angebots- und Nachfragenkurven usw."[97]

Schneider became known after the war as a Keynesian in West Germany but it is clear, from this citation alone, that in Bonn he had prepared for postwar developments in econometrics as well as in macroeconomic theory. Macroeconomic concerns did not stop him from dealing with business economics; indeed, they spurred him to apply economic theory to questions that, from his education and his teaching (the chair in Denmark), were very much on his mind. In the late 1930s Schneider published many articles on business economics, concentrating especially on cost accounting problems. Because of his work with engineers, moreover, he was able to draw upon their knowledge, as well as upon economic theory, when dealing with business economics.[98]

Careers are unique; nobody's exactly followed Schneider's. Moreover, since Schneider was an exceptional man, such diversity is exceptional. But patterns of cross-fertilization educationally and hence intellectually do not seem to have been all that rare in prewar Germany. Otto Bredt, the second example, who as editor of *Technik und Wirtschaft* had worked with Schneider in the 1920s, had studied engineering under Professor Georg Schlesinger in Berlin. No doubt Schlesinger, who was once called the German Frederick Winslow Taylor, aroused Bredt's interest in management questions, for Bredt be-

---

97 "Schumpeter – wie ich ihn kannte," in *Volkswirtschaft und Betriebswirtschaft*, 461–67; my translation.
98 Schneider was especially interested in the problem of fixed costs, which he felt German business economists (Schmalenbach, etc.) had not covered very well. He believed that the engineers' work on the subject was much better. See Schneider's "Die Problematik der Lehre von den festen Kosten," in *Volkswirtschaft und Betriebswirtschaft*, 369–99, 370 (originally published in 1944). Works by engineers he especially liked were K. Rummel, "Proportionale Abschreibung," in *Archiv für das Eisenhüttenwesen* 11 (1937): 629; Otto Bredt, "Sinn und Bedeutung der betriebsbedingt festen Kosten," *Nordisk Tidsskrift for Teknisk Økonomie* (Aug. 9, 1943): 122; F. Henzel, *Kostenanalyse*, "Praktische Untersuchungen über die Abhängigkeit der Kosten" (Buehl/Baden, 1937), among others.

came a management consultant. In fact, he became an auditor (*Wirt-schaftsprüfer*), thereby associating more with business economists than with engineers. Bredt, like Schneider, worked with the R.K.W. in the 1920s. Indeed, after the Second World War he headed this organization during the rebuilding of the German economy. In Bredt's career, therefore, the managerial and technical are fused in education and on the job. The same thing happened, to cite a final example, with Erich Gutenberg, the most important figure in German business economics, as Erich Schneider was in economics, during the immediate postwar period. He started studying physics in Hannover before the First World War, switched to economics and philosophy in Halle after the war, then studied business economics with Fritz Schmidt and Wilhelm Kalveram in Frankfort, before completing his *Habilitationsschrift* in economics at the University of Münster. Although Gutenberg was in business economics and Schneider in economics, their educations permitted the former to incorporate economics into his work and the latter business economics into his, i.e., to engage in the cross-fertilization necessary to the advancement of management studies. Both men in fact leaned on each other's work just as they did, if to a lesser extent, on the work of the engineer Bredt.

These three career patterns did not just happen; the educational system produced a broad-based scientific culture. This scientific culture, the *Wissenschaft* tradition, is the key to understanding the German universities; to those who conformed to its canons came respectability and acceptability into the German system of higher education. Scientific recognition was gained first by the technical *Hochschulen* and then by the business institutes. With *Wissenschaft* as a common denominator an educational leveling between institutions took place. Professors and students moved around from university to university, from technical institute to technical institute, without any stigma being attached to the changes. The flexibility permitted students to stress the subject studied instead of the place where the studying was done. It also, since all subjects were equally valid from a *Wissenschaft* viewpoint in all *Hochschulen*, allowed people to change majors at various stages in their education without losing face. The business economist could study engineering, the engineer economics, the economist business economics. That is what the three men described in the text, Schneider (the economist), Gutenberg (the business economist), and Bredt (the engineer) did and in the process they promoted the cross-fertilization of ideas necessary to the growth of management studies in their country. To accomplish so much individually took a long time. Schneider got his Ph.D. in 1922; he completed his *Habilitationsschrift* ten years later.

British and French heritages in higher education had less salutary effects on academic management studies. Where would the Oxford economics student learn engineering or business subjects before the Second World War? Could or would he take a commerce degree in Birmingham? No, the prestige of Oxbridge in English education meant that he would not consider studying in another place; the fact that Oxford, if not so much Cambridge, downgraded engineering studies and ignored business economics meant that, since they could be studied only in the redbricks, they would not be learned at all, not by Oxbridge students. Besides, the absence of graduate research programs signified that one would not move around in Great Britain from place to place and from field to field over the years in a quest for scientific education. The prejudices of the arts people against science and the science people against applied science prevented the growth of engineering and commercial studies in a way that would lead to the wedding of science to management studies. The same thing was true, if to a lesser extent, in France. Few French engineers would study in a university at the graduate level. Graduate degrees in engineering were rarely pursued; there were no doctorates in engineering. Business subjects could not be studied in university faculties and the commercial schools were without graduate programs. The engineer who wanted to learn about management could take some postexperience courses in nonacademic institutions. But the traditional bifurcation of French higher education into universities with graduate research programs, without studies in engineering and business economics, and *grandes écoles* of engineering and commerce, without graduate research programs, stymied the development of academic management studies and business economics in the country right up to the war.[99]

99 Robert Locke and Marc Meuleau, "France et Allemagne: Deux approches de l'enseignement de la gestion," *Revue française de gestion* 70 (Sept.–Oct. 1988): 186–202. Special number: "Les Racines de l'entreprise."

4. Continuities and discontinuities, 1940–1960

The image of a halfway house suggests a smooth transition along the road to the final destination. But that destination is a new paradigm in business studies and a paradigm connotes discontinuities, in the Kuhnian sense that one paradigm does not evolve out of another but constitutes a radical break from the previous one in terms of presuppositions about the nature of truth and its method of derivation. Since under the old paradigm business and industrial praxis were the source of managerial knowledge and under the new, scientific method, if not exclusively, replaced it, the new paradigm did amount to a radical break. Because much of the old paradigm was still present in business studies at the halfway house, the adoption of the new represented a discontinuity in that business professors and business systems of study extant about 1940, if a great improvement over the old paradigm, could not and did not themselves produce the new paradigm after the war. Innovation is not the same thing as emulation, nor does it require the same conditions for success. Neither does emulation happen automatically once innovation occurs. Neoclassical economic theory notwithstanding, there is no free, uninhibited flow of information across frontiers. It is a premise of this study that cultural and institutional factors are and were just as important for successful emulation of a new paradigm in business studies coming mainly out of postwar America as they were for the creation of the paradigm in America itself.

But why innovation in America? There was nothing about the intellectual achievement that went into the new paradigm that was essentially American. Modern mathematics, without which little could have been done, was not the work of Americans, not the new algebra, which was principally English in origin, nor symbolic logic, topology, graph theory, or matrix algebra. Europeans from Russia to Ireland did this work generations before the new paradigm in management studies came into existence. The theoretical work in economics was also mostly European. Alfred Marshall and Stanley Jevons, the Englishmen, and Karl Menger, the Austrian, were the seminal thinkers in marginal utility theory; Jules Dupuit, Léon Walras, and C. Colson, Frenchmen, Knut Wicksell, a Swede, and Vilfredo Pareto, an Italian, in mathematized general equilibrium theory. Nor were the pioneer statisticians – Francis Galton, R. A. Fischer, and Karl Pearson were all Englishmen – Americans. Americans could be found among the scientists in each field but the body of theory out of which the science developed was certainly not theirs.

Even the work done in America to fashion the new paradigm could not be said to have been American. The commission, founded in 1932 by the Chicago businessman Alfred Cowles, which made such important contributions to the mathematization of economics, was composed, to a large extent, of immigrants. Jacob Marschak and Tjalling Koopmans, who directed the commission, were, respectively, a Russian and a Dutchman; Abraham Wald, the gifted statistician who had a strong influence on the commission's work, was Rumanian by birth and partly by education (he was also educated in Vienna). Trygve Haavelmo, who studied with Ragnar Frisch in Oslo and worked in America during the war, was a Norwegian. Both Oskar Morgenstern and John von Neumann, who developed game theory (von Neumann also contributed to the development of computers and worked with the Cowles Commission on mathematical statistics), were Austrians. Like the scientists who made the atomic bomb, among whom, incidentally, von Neumann could be counted, those formulating new management sciences literally brought intellectual distinction and practical prowess to the United States from abroad. The fact that they and their illustrious predecessors did not develop the new paradigm in business studies in Europe demonstrates the causal limitations of intellectual history in such matters.

There are at least three reasons why America was the innovator and Europe the emulator in the final breakthrough to the new paradigm in business studies. The first has to do with American business structure. Alfred Chandler's description of corporate structural change pertained to America; for although the simpler single-product, single-function firm and the larger single-product, multi-functional U form corporation existed on both sides of the Atlantic in 1940, the large multi-product, multi-function divisionalized firm was, with rare exceptions,

American.[1] The demand, therefore, for a well-trained headquarters managerial elite was more pronounced in America; in fact, even the functional skills necessary to run the multidivisional American corporation were more in demand there. European corporations were less involved with marketing and finance problems than the American multinational. Perhaps this explains why German business school professors before the war neglected marketing questions much longer than American professors.[2] This happened, above all, after the Third Reich abandoned the market for the planned economy. German business economists really did not concern themselves with marketing per se, with studies of consumer psychology and behavior for the purpose of expanding market share; rather, assuming rational consumer behavior, they concentrated on the traditional sales and distribution problems encountered by the firm. Nor did the Germans, like the Americans, integrate financial and production planning as thoroughly into their theoretical work.[3] The differences in German and American business economics between the wars may have reflected the greater importance of the large multidivisional firm in the American economy.

Different corelationships between educational and capitalistic institutions outside the firm (but with which the firm interrelated) also called forth new management skills in prewar America. This was the case especially in stockbroking. Although the wealthy individual investor predominated before 1940, the institutional investors (insurance companies, union pension funds) came to constitute an important clientele on both sides of the Atlantic.[4] And change in investment clientele was important because of the different demands made on stockbroker skills. Technical knowledge (financial theory, actuarial mathematics) is required to handle the investment portfolios of the institutional investors to a much greater extent than those of the individual. With the latter, the broker's social skills are more useful than a technical knowledge which the individual investor would have difficulty understanding (the person investing the money for an institution, on the other hand, might be quite sophisticated in technical matters).

1 See Channon, *Strategy and Structures of British Enterprise,* and Gareth P. Dyas and Heinz T. Thanheiser, *The Emerging European Enterprise: Strategy and Structure in French and German Industry* (London, 1976).
2 Locke, *The End of the Practical Man,* chap. 4.
3 Ibid.
4 William J. Reader, talk on "Philip and Drew: Making a Modern Stockbroking Firm," Senate House, University of London, Mar. 14, 1986.

This meant, in London, that the stockbrokers traditionally had had to gain the confidence of their clientele, to resemble them, to be or give the appearance of being gentlemen, regular chaps with the proper public school ties, men who had not necessarily attended Oxbridge but, if they had, would have read useless art subjects. Poorly trained in finance theory, they could not talk to the new corporate investment technician, but they could tell a good story at lunch or at scotch-and-soda time in the club. Social skills, not knowledge, were needed to sell stocks to this clientele and these skills the English stockbrokers possessed. The institutional investor appeared in the two major finance centers, London and New York, about the same time, but the American stockbrokers, with business school ties, acquired the technical skills first, thereby exploiting the new institutional investment market earlier and more skillfully than the British.[5] Accordingly, the demand for more sophisticated forms of finance education developed earlier in the United States.

War is the second factor which promoted innovation in America. During the First World War the American productive capacity had not been used optimally. Determined to avoid such mismanagement in the future, Congress passed a National Defense Act in 1920 which provided for wartime economic mobilization. The various services (Quartermaster Corps, Ordnance, Air Corps, Corps of Engineers, etc.) were composed of military men, officer technicians, but, as Charles de Gaulle pointed out in 1934,

and this is the originality of the American organization, each one of [the service corps] is assisted by a permanent study committee formed from the business world which directly aids it (the service corps) in its work. . . . The Americans have taken steps to assure that both sides have the right personnel. The Army Industrial College has been established to give the military officers in the technical services the desired training. Some of them have even been sent to take courses in the Harvard School of Business Administration.[6]

De Gaulle clearly perceived how corporate America had been able to call into being a managerial form of economic warfare.

Yet the Second World War, despite early organizational efforts, created unprecedented managerial problems for which unprecedented solutions were needed. John von Neumann described one which, if the

5 Ibid.
6 "Mobilisation économique à l'étranger," reprinted in *Trois études* (Paris, 1973), 125–36, 131.

most important and epoch-making of all, still illustrates the nature of the demand. While working on atomic bomb computations he said, "Probably in its solution we shall have to perform more elementary arithmetical steps than the total in all the computation performed by the human race heretofore."[7] Von Neumann and his colleagues, since they had no computer, had to simplify the calculations for the atomic bomb so that they could be done with pencil and paper and the adding machine. This problem and others spurred a search for solutions. It is no surprise that F. L. Hitchcock formulated his transportation theory, when, in 1941, the United States had to face the most complicated problems of moving vast amounts of men and matériel, as efficiently as possible, on a limited number of ships, trains, and aircraft. Nor is it astonishing, considering von Neumann's concerns, that research on the development of computers proceeded apace. In 1944, the electrical engineer J. P. Eckert, Jr., and the physicist John Mauchly created ENIAC, the Electronic Numerical Integrator and Computer which was designed to compute artillery firing tables for the U.S. Army. Von Neumann himself worked on the logical designs for this computer. Later he and his associates at the Institute for Advanced Studies, Princeton, built one of the first computers, MANIAC I (Mathematical Analyzer Numerical Integrator and Computer). Although completed in 1952, MANIAC I was a direct result of the war-inspired work.

The use of science to solve management problems was not a peculiarly American wartime achievement. The British team of scientists and engineers at Air Ministry Research, Bawdsey, which began work in 1936 on the "operational use of radar information" were the pioneers, for radar was not just a technical problem that the military men could handle by themselves.[8] The experts working for the Royal Air Force

7 Stanislaw M. Ulam, "Computers," in *Mathematics in the Modern World,* ed. Kline, 337–46, 338.
8 On wartime Britain, see tributes in the *ORQ (Operational Research Quarterly)* which became *JORS (Journal of the Operational Research Society)* in 1978 to P. M. S. Blackett, and others. P. M. S. Blackett, "Operational Research," *ORQ* 1:1 (1950): 3–6; Solly Zuckermann, "In the Beginning – and Later," *ORQ* 15:4 (1964): 287–92; E. C. Williams, "The Origin of the Term 'Operational Research' and the Early development of the Military Work," and Charles Goodeve, "The Growth of Operational Research in the Civil Sector in the United Kingdom," *ORQ* 19:2 (1968): 111–16; C. H. Waddington, "Appreciation: Lord Blackett," *ORQ* 25:4 (1974): i–vi; Charles Goodeve and Rolfe Tomlinson, "Lord Blackett – A Mémoire," *ORQ* 25:4 (1975): vi–vii; "Eric Charles Williams (1915–1980)," *JORS* 31:7 (1980): 559–61; "Sir Charles Frederick Goodeve," *JORS* 31:11 (1980): 961–64; Ronald G. Stansfield, "Harold Lardner, Founder of Operational Research," *JORS* 34:1 (1983): 1–7; B. H. P. Rivett, "K. D. Tocher," *JORS* 34:4 (1983): 267–70.

realized that they "needed unbiased scientific assessment of the efficacy of radar" and "how to implement the system in service." So scientists were brought to the task.[9] Their success generated operational research groups in Britain and through Britain in America. Scientists in the American antisubmarine-warfare operations-research group, for example, who collaborated with O.R. groups in Coastal Command, undoubtedly learned a great deal from the more experienced British.[10] The British, moreover, did a lot of early work on computers. But the Americans, with their greater material resources, with the strengths gained from powerful business organizations and private management know-how gone to war, and with a distinguished group of scientists available, could make the greater effort.

The emigrant scientists worked in this context. Jean Monnet, the father of postwar French planning, acknowledged his debt to the Americans, incurred while in Washington, D. C., from 1943 to 1954. He "earnestly cultivated contacts in higher political, military, legal, banking, academic, and business circles in the United States. He learned much from the economists Stacy May and Robert Nathan who applied their statistical and analytical skills to United States war production programs. . . . The success of American war production efforts impressed the French mission who perceived . . . wartime mobilization techniques."[11] Monnet's story typified that of scores of distinguished mathematicians and scientists who joined with native Americans to apply science to war-engendered management problems.

A third factor that pushed America into the forefront in the development of the new paradigm was the cold war. After the First World War, the world returned to normalcy, in the sense that the government stopped managing huge amounts of business and industrial resources for military purposes. The cold war, reversing postwar demobilization, led America into a sustained defense effort which required efficient management of resources on a scale almost as great as during the Second World War. The management teams put together for the duration in 1941 now had to be reconstituted and to operate on a permanent basis. The most significant scientific management applications

9 C. H. Waddington, *Science in War* (London, 1940), 2. Also see Ronald G. Stansfield, "Harold Lardner," *JORS* 34 (1983): 1–7, 4.
10 Waddington, *Science in War*, 18.
11 Richard F. Kuisel, *Capitalism and the State in Modern France: Renovation and Economic Management in the Twentieth Century* (Cambridge, 1981), 219.

developed out of the cold war defense establishment. Among them the most famous management tool was probably linear programming. George B. Dantzig and his associates (Marshall Wood and Alex Orden) developed it at the Rand Corporation in 1947 on U.S. Air Force contracts, applying it first to military operations – aircraft utilization in the Berlin airlift, troop deployment problems, and analysis of bombing patterns. Because it was a defense secret, the simplex method was not even published until 1951.[12] The computer is another example of cold war stimulation. The first big commercially built computer, UNIVAC I, was not delivered to the first industrial user, the General Electric Company, until 1954. Before that date (except for a UNIVAC I delivered to the Bureau of the Census in 1951), computers were used on military problems and atomic research.[13]

The military also instigated cooperative scientific management research in higher education and industry. The Case Institute of Technology in Cleveland was the first academic institution to start an operations research department. It did so partly at the urging of industry (financial support from the Chesapeake and Ohio Railroad Co.), partly in response to the Air Force (funded research on airplane design).[14] This institute organized the first national conference (November 1951) on operations research in business and industry to which 150 people came from all over America. Military officers and Department of Defense civilians in operations research attended the conferences at home and abroad, for the Americans in NATO propagated operations research techniques among allied military circles. American military O.R. people participated in the many international meetings of O.R. societies when O.R. came to European institutions of higher education and to European business and industry in the late 1950s. (Sometimes American associations – Operations Research Society [O.R.S], The Institute of Management Studies [T.I.M.S.] – met in a European city; sometimes the international association of O.R. societies held its meetings in Europe.)[15] The American military, moreover, indirectly advanced the new

---

12 Levin and Lamone, *Linear Programming for Management Decisions,* 215.
13 Ulam, "Computers," 338. Bertold Gamer, "Planung und Einsatz elektronischer Datenverarbeitungsanlagen in einer chemischen Grossunternehmung," *ZfbF* 13 (1961): 353–67.13.
14 H. P. Künzi, "Operations Research – Rückblick und Ausblick." Speech given at the TU Munich on the seventieth birthday of Prof. Dr. Joseph Heinhold, July 5, 1982, *ZfOR* 26 (1982): B217–B228, 219.
15 These meetings were well publicized in the periodicals.

management sciences through the support it gave to American computer firms. IBM, the obvious example, an important defense contractor, taught the new computer-based techniques – game theory, linear programming, queue theory, search theory, information theory – assiduously on both the military and the civilian sides of the managerial fence.

These three factors, then, combined to make America the center of the new paradigm. To them a fourth explanation should be appended: the exceptional condition in which the non-American world found itself during and immediately after the Second World War. Many Americans today talk about the relative decline of American prowess as if it were a result of some betrayal (of labor unions, of liberals, of our allies). They forget that the overwhelming American preeminence was completely abnormal. In 1945 Europe was devastated. England, which had been in economic decline for three generations, faced grim years after its prolonged effort to fight a terrible enemy. The Soviet Union had suffered incredible destruction. Japan, the rising force in Asia, had been undone by its unequal struggle with the United States. All that was left relatively unscathed was the third world and America. The third world offered (and still offers) no great threat to American superiority. No wonder the Americans dominated.

Aside from the general effects of the war, very particular events temporarily furthered the imbalance between America and other industrially advanced countries. One was the politically stupid and morally depraved Nazi persecutions that sent to America, and deprived Germany of, a rich crop of scientists and mathematicians. Moreover, Germans and Japanese, looking up after winning the desperate immediate postwar struggle for survival, found that they did not have control over their own destinies. Their institutions were dismantled, their countries occupied and ruled by foreign powers. The universities, the scientific periodicals were closed down. Thousands of men, still in captivity, had not returned from the war. Several years elapsed before the defeated regained control over their resources. Even then they encountered problems. An engineer, Herr Gamer (from the Hoechst Corporation), who visited the United States with mathematicians, economists, and accountants in 1954, in order to study the computer, observed: "As we sought to get direct experience with electronic computers, we found to our surprise that we Germans at the time still stood at a halfway point between an old opponent and a new ally. For then,

American firms which produced such equipment [computers] were not directly forbidden to export them to Germany but, in practice, they were not available."[16] Not only were computers inaccessible, the kinds of activities in which they had been used almost exclusively, and which, consequently, were responsible for the computer's initial development, were forbidden to Germans, namely, military and atomic research. In 1955, only a few computers were used commercially in America, but, Gamer remarked, "an avalanche of preparations by almost all firms had been made for the adoption of such equipment. There was a singular belief in the future of these machines."[17] Without accessibility, Germany and Japan had to postpone the adoption of the new computer-reliant management techniques.

But once Japan, Europe, and the Soviet Union recovered, American hegemony had to disappear. Americans themselves promoted the process when they encouraged European and Japanese recovery. The Europeans who had gone to America during the war to play their important role in American developments were natural facilitators in the transfer of management technology from the new world to the old. If they did not return to governmental or university positions in Europe, they frequently attended the many conferences and symposiums which accompanied European recovery programs. In the immediate post war period, too, the expansion of American business abroad brought the transfer of American management methods. This occurred, for example, in France where the head of the French branch of Colgate-Palmolive, François Gautier, and the head of Cal-Tex, Henry Ballande, borrowed management methods from parent firms. Since American firms were eager to locate in Europe and they hired Europeans to manage operations (i.e., Gillette-France, Proctor and Gamble, and International Harvester were, for instance, invaded by graduates from H.E.C.), and since these people frequently left these American branch firms to work in native companies, the American influence spread in the private sector. Private French firms were also instigators of this interchange. Thus Louis Devaux, of the jewelry firm Cartier, after spending three years in America (1946–49) as chairman of the board of Cartier Incorporated, New York, and learning firsthand about American management methods, applied them to the firm in France

16 Gamer, "Planung und Einsatz," 390.
17 Ibid.

Table 4.1. *Foreign affiliates of U.S., U.K., and West German multinationals*

Home Country	1 Country	2-9 Countries	10-19 Countries	Over 20 Countries	Total
United States	1,228	949	216	75	2,468
United Kingdom	725	805	108	50	1,692
West Germany	448	452	43	11	954

Source: Karl P. Sauvant and Bernard Mennis, "Corporate Internationalization and German Enterprise," University of Pennsylvania, The Wharton School, 1974, 21.

upon his return.[18] Many of the demand factors that had stimulated innovations in America also appeared in Europe. Of course the war had created the demand for operations research in Britain even before it did in America. Postwar reconstruction in huge nationalized basic industries gave birth immediately to operations research teams in British and French coal, electricity, and transportation industries. The rearmament of Europe, moreover, reproduced, if on a modest scale, operations research teams in the European military services, and changes along American lines in the organizational structure of European-based firms also created a need for managerial talent and know-how.

A study by Karl P. Sauvant and Bernard Mennis illustrates the last development most graphically. The authors noted in 1973 that "relatively recent and accurate data are available on the distribution of MNC (multi-national corporation) headquarters. In 1968–69, 7,276 corporations in the United States and 14 West European countries had affiliates in one or more foreign countries. The United States alone is the home country of 2,468 or 34 percent of all MNCs."[19] Table 4.1, which is taken from this study, gives the relative number of American, British, and German M.N.C.s for 1968–69, and it states the number of affiliates firms headquartered in one country have in others.

A company's organizational structure is not revealed by the fact that it is a multinational. But inasmuch as the M.N.C. is partial to the M form and that in 1945 there were so few (about a dozen) M form corporations in Europe, the statistics imply that considerable growth in divisionalized forms, with their managerial hierarchies, took place in Europe after the war. Besides, the American multinational firms

18 Meuleau, "Les HEC."
19 "Corporate Internationalization and German Enterprise: A Social Profile of German Managers and Their Attitudes regarding the European Community and Future Strategies." University of Pennsylvania, The Wharton School, 1974, 21.

were themselves often in European countries where they could set the corporate management example for European-based firms.

A potential demand for science-based management education existed in Europe, then, shortly after the war. But the ability of Europeans to respond to the demand, indeed their ability to create as well as to fulfill it, was influenced by educational cultures. People had to have the technical competence, primarily skills in modern mathematics, in order to be able to apply science to managerial problems. Where there was a will but not a way, the development of science was delayed until the technical competence could be reached. This was not easy, for the person who does not learn mathematics as a young student has great difficulty subsequently making up for the omission. In fact, it is really necessary to send a new generation through the entire educational process in which the mathematical skills necessary to the new paradigm in business studies are steadily acquired. Where there was a way but no will, the development of managerial science was also delayed. This happened when people with the necessary mathematics did not wish to apply their skills to management problems. What was needed to emulate American developments quickly was for both the will, the interest in management study, and the way, the technical competency to pursue it, to coincide. Only two specific educational heritages engendered immediate adoption, and even they did not do so to the same extent. Otherwise, for one reason or another, educational heritages delayed emulation.

The most favorable was the French engineering educational heritage. It is ironic perhaps that the graduates from the *grandes écoles* of engineering benefited so much from their education, inasmuch as this education had been so severely criticized before the war. That criticism had, moreover, been just, for it had not trained students very well for the new high-tech engineering specialties emerging in the late nineteenth century. The defenders of the French system argued that this had not been its purpose: The *grandes écoles* educated an elite of generalist managers. But even in this respect the education had been deficient, for it had taught the students nothing about management. What it had taught them, both in preparing for, and after, entry into a *grande école,* however, was the one skill which, if it proved rather useless to people located in the previous halfway house of management studies, was the sine qua non for full participation in management studies under the new paradigm – mathematics.

Mathematics, however, was not the only advantage. Indeed, it was not an obvious advantage since modern mathematics was not taught in the *lycée,* the preparatory class, or the *grandes écoles* immediately after the war.[20] Something had to prompt the engineer initially to learn the new technical languages on his own and that something was the motivation that graduates of the *grandes écoles* encountered at work. Because they were a managerial elite who ran the state *grands corps* and large-scale industries, French engineers had grappled constantly with economic as well as technical problems, long before the creation of the new paradigm had made such application evident. This does not mean that French engineers, as a group, had cultivated management science for a long time. As a recent thesis stressed, the French engineers who did think about economics were isolated individuals; no school of *ingénieurs-économistes* existed before the Second World War.[21] Nonetheless, the fact that individual engineers did make significant contributions early to the creation and the propagation of the new management paradigm in France suggests that by education and professional duties, French engineers were predisposed – and this predilection increased as the paradigm took shape – to think along management science lines.

One man in particular, Jules Dupuit, had worked on marginal cost pricing in the 1840s, work of a practical nature, for he sought solutions to transportation problems encountered on the job. Educated as a scientist, he formulated solutions in mathematical-economic terms. The results were published for working managers to consult in a civil engineering journal, the *Annales des Ponts et Chaussées.*[22] This publication, however, hid this and subsequent articles from economists who did not read technical journals. Their discovery of Dupuit was delayed until the 1930s when five of his articles were published in a book (1933) edited by an Italian economist, and when Harold Hotelling's

20 France, like other countries, underwent the new math campaign primarily in the 1960s.
21 François Etner, *Les Ingénieurs-Economistes français (1841–1950).* Thèse pour l'obtention du titre de docteur "sciences économiques," option: économie appliquée, Doctorat d'Etat, U.E.R. Sciences des Organisations, Université de Paris (Paris IX-Dauphine), 1978. Etner observes that courses in economics were considered to be secondary for the students in engineering schools. "The view that an *ingénieurs-économistes* tradition fought against another tradition [literary economics] in order to impose a "scientific" approach to economics . . . is false up to 1930"; ibid., 146; my translation.
22 Jules Dupuit, *De l'Utilité et sa mesure* (Paris, 1844).

article appeared (1938) in *Econometrics*.[23] Hotelling's piece finally provoked international debate among economists about marginal pricing, a debate from which French economists were cut off, however, by defeat in 1940. But French *ignénieurs-économistes* continued to think about economics during the occupation. Maurice Allais's book, *A la recherche d'une discipline économique* (1943), especially, gave new impetus to marginal utility analysis; it presented a modern and complete explanation of Pareto's theory of the optimum (under the nomenclature theory of social return) which relied particularly on marginal cost analysis.[24]

Shortly after the war, recently nationalized basic industries (numerous small concerns – electricity, gas, railroads – were combined into single monopolistic state enterprises) demanded sophisticated managerial expertise. At Electricité de France, an O.R. group under Jacques Massé, a *Polytechnicien,* applied economic theory to managerial problems.[25] None of the E.D.F. group had degrees in economics, but marginal utility theory guided their investment and pricing policy studies. For this to occur the mathematics the marginal utility economists employed at the turn of the century had to be discarded in favor of mathematical statistics and linear programming. It was relatively easy to do because the *Polytechniciens'* greater mathematical culture permitted them to assimilate and apply these new techniques rapidly. As Allais noted, "the statistical and mathematical techniques which the engineer-economists need are not techniques specific to economics; their application is general and these techniques apply to all natural sciences."[26] The engineers' rather useless cultivation of mathematics, then, proved to be very valuable in the new managerial context.

The team that Massé assembled at Electricité de France embarked on the most far-reaching analyses. Studies were done on tariff construction and price policy, on consumption, on operating policy, and on

23 J. R. Nelson, ed., *Marginal Cost Pricing in Practice* (Englewood Cliffs, N. J., 1964), vi.
24 Reprinted as *Traité de'économie politique,* no. 2 (Paris, 1952).
25 See Pierre Massé and R. Gibrat, "Application of Linear Programming to Investments in the Electric Power Industry," *Management Science* 3:2 (1957): 149–66; Pierre Massé, *Application des probabilités en chaîne à l'hydrologie statistique et au jeu des réservoirs* (Paris, 1944); Pierre Massé, "La Notion d'ésperance marginale, la théorie générale de J. M. Keynes et le problème de l'intérêt," *Revue d'économie politique* 1 (1948): 88–132; Pierre Massé, "Les Investissements électriques," *Revue de Statistique appliquée* 1:3–4 (1953): 119–29.
26 Maurice Allais, *Traité d'économie pure* (Paris, 1952), 267; my translation.

investment policy, which applied marginal utility economic theories to problems whose solution required quite sophisticated mathematical statistics. In December 1953, a two-volume study published by the Director of Equipment in Electricité de France showed that Jacques Massé's group was a first-class team whose work bore practical fruit.[27] Electricité de France adopted its famous Green Tariff in 1956, which was nothing less than a rate structure inspired by marginal cost theory. Here is a splendid example of the triumph of the new paradigm in management studies in France: a major decision in a major industry was based on a scientific rationale.[28] One principle, marginal cost analysis, was at play. Although it proved to be of limited value, its early use demonstrated the *ingénieurs-économistes'* ability – to employ Professor Allais's phraseology once again – to apply a general knowledge of economic sciences to the study of the particular problems posed by the management of firms and to do that by calling upon the most elaborate techniques currently at our disposal."[29]

The Electricité de France group sparked emulation in other nationalized industries. The Coal Board (Charbonnages de France) commissioned Professor Maurice Allais to do a study on the economics of coal mining.[30] The study concluded strongly in favor of marginal cost pricing. The same board also commissioned J. Audibert and A. Terra to analyze short- and long-term investment policies in the same industry. At the Gas Board (Gaz de France) the definition and the calculation of marginal costs were done by F. Gardent and his colleagues; at the national railroad, the S.N.C.F., Roger Hutter evaluated marketing problems and rates schedules on marginal principles.[31] When in 1959 Jacques Massé was appointed Chief French Planner (*commissaire gén-*

27 See J. R. Nelson, "Practical Applications of Marginal Cost Pricing in the Public Utility Field," The *American Economic Review* 53:2 (1963): 474–81. Also Jacques H. Drèze, "Some Postwar Contributions of French Economists to Theory and Public Policy," *The American Economic Review* 54:4.2 (June 1964): 1–64.
28 Pierre Massé, "Quelques incidences économiques du tarif vert," *Revue français de l'énergie* 9:97 (May 1958): 392–95.
29 Jacques Lesourne, *Technique économique et gestion industrielle*, 2d ed. (Paris, 1960), xvi; my translation. The introduction is by Allais, Lesourne's mentor.
30 Maurice Allais, *La Gestion des houillères nationalisées et la théorie économique* (Paris, 1953).
31 Lesourne, *Techinque economique*, xxxix; Marcel Boiteux, "Le tarif vert d'Electricité de France," *Revue française de l'énergie* (Jan. 1957), and Jacques Massé and R. Gibrat, "Application of Linear Programming"; Guy Sitruk, "A Constantly Evolving OR Team," *JORS* 34:3 (1983): 183–91; R. Hutter, "La Théorie économique et la gestion commerciale des chemins de fer," *Revue génerale des chemins de fer* 69 (1950): 318–32, 443–60.

éral de plan d'équipement et de la productivité) for the Third Plan, the influence of the engineer-economist spread: Jean Mothes moved from Gaz de France (1952–57) to S.N.C.F. (Société Nationale des Chemins de Fer Français) (1957–60) to S.E.M.A. (Société de mathématiques et d'economie appliquées), a consultancy; Jacques Lesourne from the Coal Board (1954–57) to S.E.M.A.; Pierre Maillet from being *chef des travaux* at the Polytechnic School (1950–53) to a study group preparing the Third and Fourth Plans for the modernization and equipment of France.

With few exceptions, and the exceptions are mostly mathematicians, these men were engineers from one *grande école,* the Polytechnic School. Many of them had also studied under Professor Maurice Allais at the Ecole Nationale Supérieure des Mines de Paris or at the Institut de Statistique of the University of Paris where he was also a professor (1947–68).[32] Allais pointed out that many of the biggest names among the engineer-economists had been his students.[33] No doubt Allais had much to do with directing these young men into applied economics, for he had held the chair of applied economics at the School of Mines since 1944. But the engineers could not have followed, indeed Maurice Allais could not have led, had they not been *Polytechniciens,* i.e., mathematicians.

Beneficiaries of this educational heritage, the engineer-economists also became its benefactors. A cycle of studies, created by M. Guilbaud, R. Henon, E. Morice, and J. Mothes at the Institut de Statistique in Paris, repaired deficiencies in statistics. All the problems current in industry, which this educational elite often knew by direct experience, were discussed in Allais's seminar at the School of Mines, in R. Roys's seminar on econometrics, and in the first seminar on operations research, founded by the director of the Institut de Statistique, M. Guilbaud. The creation of the Société Française de Recherche Opérationelle in 1956 and the publication of its journal fostered the educational effort beyond the confines of industry and classroom. And a new periodical (*Revue de statistique appliquée*), organized by the same close-knit group, proselytized the new methods. Since it was an engineering tradition, especially for *Polytechniciens* in the *grands corps,* to

---

32 The Institute de Statistique de l'Université de Paris was founded in 1952 to train engineers and managers in the industrial applications of statistics. See George Darmois, "La Statistique," *Revue de l'enseignement supérieur,* no. 1 (1960): 31–42.
33 See Nelson, "Practical Applications," and Drèze, "Some Postwar Contributions."

maintain a liaison with the *grandes écoles,* many of Allais's disciples interrupted their working careers to become researchers and teachers. Among them, Jacques Lesourne, after his studies at the Coal Board, taught economics and statistics at the School of Mines in St.-Etienne (1956–59) before moving to the Institut National de la Statistique et des Etudes Economiques (1959–61) and then to the Conservatoire National des Arts et Métiers (C.N.A.M.); Jean Mothes worked at the Institut National de la Statistique et des Etudes Economiques (1943–60) with Marcel Boiteux, who lectured at the Ecoles de Ponts et Chaussées (1964–67), Edmond Malinvaud, who became director of the Ecole Nationale de la Statistique, and Pierre Maillet, who became a professor of economics at Lille.

Much of the educational literature, especially at the beginning, was American. Not until 1958, when Jacques Lesourne's book *Technique économique et gestion industrielle* appeared, did the engineers have in French "for the first time, a complete exposé of the economics of the firm that was based on a solid foundation in economics and on a full awareness of mathematical and statistical techniques."[34] A perusal of bibliographies shows how deep the debt was to the Americans. But these bibliographies also testify to the serious work done by the French themselves. Because the publications (if they were publications, for much of the earlier work consisted of study papers done in a ministry or industry) appeared in engineering journals (*Annales des Ponts et Chaussées, Bulletin des Ponts et Chaussées et des Mines; Revue de l'industrie minérale; Revue française de l'énergie; Revue française de recherche opérationnelle*), American economists were surprised to find such work had been going on in France. J. R. Nelson, who discovered the French engineer-economists, noted, "Delay [of knowledge of their work] is especially likely if the good news happens to appear first in a journal for highway engineers; and delay is yet more likely, as far as English-speaking economists are concerned, if the engineering journal happens to be the *Annales des Ponts et Chaussées.*"[35] But perhaps the fault lay not with the French engineers as much as with American economists who remained isolated from the technical world. When Ragnar Frisch gave a lecture series on econometric modeling in Paris in 1955, he did it at the School of Bridges and Roads.

The French engineer-economists thought highly of themselves and

34 Lesourne, *Technique économique,* ix.
35 Nelson, *Marginal Cost Pricing,* vi.

of their work, for, in Professor Allais's opinion (1958), **"the work done by French engineer-economists in the last fifteen years ... lifts France into the first rank, very far ahead, in my view, of Great Britain and the United States in the domain of the economy of the firm."**[36] **The** claim is assuredly true in regard to Great Britain, probably false with respect to the United States. But French accomplishments were very substantial.

Nonetheless, it is important to consider the limitations of the achievement. There are two. First, only a very small number of people were involved. The French believe in the prowess of elites, and an elite carried out the studies and the plans. The average French engineer and businessman were not involved. Secondly, the science involved was limited in scope. In America, the management science revolution and the behavioral science revolution occurred almost simultaneously; in France they did not. Since the French engineer-economists were so deeply engaged in the management science revolution, they really ignored the behavioral dimension. They were technocrats, mathematical system builders and planners, not managers of people.

The second educational heritage that promoted the new paradigm was in German business economics (B.W.L.). How it embraced the new paradigm is best explained with reference to the work of the most influential academic business economist of postwar Germany: Erich Gutenberg. Professor Horst Albach asserts that Gutenberg has the distinction of having transformed German business economics into "a scientific discipline [*eine wissenschaftliche Disziplin*]."[37] For this to be entirely true, the work of the great pioneers in German business economics has to be ignored. And that cannot be done. Eugen Schmalenbach, Wilhelm Rieger, Fritz Schmidt, and their colleagues utilized economic science when they analyzed business problems. Schmalenbach, in particular, borrowed heavily from marginal utility theory in order to develop a pricing and product-costing management-decision model.[38] Discussions among prewar German business economists about valuation, moreover, took them beyond the conventional accounting practice, which equated value with money, to the economist's concept of differ-

36 Lesourne, *Technique économique*, xxxix.
37 Horst Albach, "Die Betriebswirtschaftslehre: Eine Wissenschaft, zum Gedenken an Erich Gutenberg," memorial lecture given at Cologne University, Dec. 11, 1985; my translation.
38 Locke, *The End of the Practical Man*, 170–75.

ent values standards for different purposes.[39] It was their work that moved German business economists into the halfway house of *Wissenschaft*. The translators of the English edition of Schmalenbach's *Dynamic Accounting* make the point: "This book [which was written in 1919] does not set out to be a technical handbook of book-keeping and accounts, but it is an attempt to present the subject in its proper perspective, as a branch of economics. Few men have been better qualified to bridge the gap between economics and accountancy than was Professor Schmalenbach."[40]

Yet Albach's comment about Gutenberg's achievement is still quite apt. Schmalenbach maintained that B.W.L. is a *Kunstlehre*, a skill, and many of his colleagues agreed. Professor Willi Prion of the Munich Business School described how business was taught shortly before the First World War:

All who have anything to do with the faculties of commerce know that all . . . of them, in Cologne, as in Munich, Berlin, Leipzig, or Mannheim attempt in exactly the same way to promote one end: to make the businessman effective in business, to show him how a business is set up and conducted, how the organization of the accounts, of the business or of the plant is done, how financing is achieved in commercial life, what role the balance sheet plays for business and for the general public, how purchases, sales, and calculations are made in various businesses, what role bills of exchange, checks, stocks, play in commercial and economic life, how the conditions of existence of individual firms, their legal constitutions, their effect on economic life in general, etc., etc., take place. All the business schools teach that to their students and all teach it, in principle, the same way.[41]

This program smacked more of commercial than of scientific studies. Indeed, research was especially pragmatic. Professor Alfred Isaac, of the Nuremberg Business School, estimated that 50 percent of the articles published between 1906 and 1914 in Schmalenbach's *Zeitschrift für handelswissenschaftliche Forschung* were case studies on book-keeping and administrative methods in specific firms.[42] They were written by engineers or accountants or academics with practical experience who often, having worked in the plants described, knew the systems well. Although Schmalenbach and the others brought economic

39 Ibid., 162–68.
40 Eugen Schmalenbach, *Dynamic Accounting*, tr. G. W. Murphy and K. S. Most (London, 1959), 5.
41 Letter from Prion to Schmalenbach, in *ZfhF* 7 (1912–13): 231–42; my translation.
42 Alfred Isaac, "Gegenwärtiger Stand betriebswirtschaftlicher Forschung und Lehre," *ZVDDK* 7:5 (May, 1927): 138.

thought into their work in remarkable ways between the wars, business economics before 1940 never abandoned its vocational outlook.

Consequently, it contrasted markedly with university-level neoclassical economics. Most university economists, if they considered business economics at all, took it to be an inferior part of their subject. Karl Diehl of Leipzig University expressed this opinion:

Economists are never interested in individual commercial, industrial, and agricultural businesses just for themselves but only to understand the complex in which they (the firms) exist. [Economists] look at the firm as part of a greater economic organism, whose structure and form are being researched. The detailed inner organization of individual firms is of interest only insofar as it is necessary for an understanding of the economic system.[43]

Microeconomics, then, was invented by economists quite independently of business studies, for the economists wanted to use it to help explain economic processes. Gutenberg ended this methodological split between business economics and economics (V.W.L).

Although Gutenberg's opponents often accused him of being an economist instead of a business economist, this was not true. In his 1927 doctoral dissertation, *Die Unternehmung als Gegenstand der Wissenschaft (The Enterprise as Object of Science)*, he insisted that he, like Schmalenbach, concentrated on the firm. He sought, by isolating it from the general economy, to study its inner economic workings. Moreover, he agreed that the study of the firm had a practical purpose: to assist the entrepreneur in decision making in order to improve management. To fault Gutenberg's loyalty to his discipline is, therefore, incorrect.

But if business economics' object is the firm, it is, Gutenberg insisted, nonetheless a science, a *Wissenschaft,* not a *Kunstlehre.* To build this science, he borrowed heavily from economics, considering it, to use Erich Schneider's formulation, a *Denktechnik,* a "think technology" (which people employ, like language, in order to describe relationships), and from higher mathematics, viewing it as a *Denkform,* "form of thought," which best clarifies the logic of interrelated variables. These views were more implicit than explicit in his doctoral thesis. Indeed, because of career delays brought on by the war (he served in both world wars) and defeat (German academia was shut

---

43 "Privatwirtschaftslehre, Volkswirtschaftslehre, Weltwirtschaftslehre," *Jahrbücher für Nationalökonomie und Statistik* 43 (1912): 94–112; my translation.

down for some time), not until 1951, when the first volume of his three-volume *Foundations of Business Economics* appeared, were his views stated and presented fully to the scientific community.[44] The book is easily the most influential postwar work in German business economics.

Erich Schneider, the economist, who was Gutenberg's intellectual twin, commented in a favorable book review:

Whoever works his way through this book receives a mental [*gedankliches*] training that enables him to see and understand in its essential lines how what occurs in business is interrelated. Precisely for this reason to do business economics in this way is highly practical. An intellectual mastery of the economic processes of the firm cannot be acquired just by an intensive study of facts and practical rules. "There is only one possibility [says Schmalenbach]: a theoretical schooling of thought [*Denkschulung*] which permits one, through reflection and application, to master the countless practical tasks of economics, also in cases never encountered before." Gutenberg's book provides this theoretical *Denkschulung*.[45]

This book review is as much propaganda as objective analysis. To enlist the support of the respected master – Schmalenbach – for Gutenberg's work makes curious reading, for Gutenberg broke from Schmalenbach as he did from many, if not most, prewar academic business economists. To say that Gutenberg trod Schmalenbach's path, therefore, must have been meant less to tell the truth than to entice reluctant members of academia to follow Gutenberg on a scientific path that the reviewer knew differed from Schmalenbach's in at least one important way.

The difference can be explained by a look at accounting, the most important subject studied in prewar German business economics. Nineteenth-century business and manufacturing firms used certain accounting instruments. Financial accounting was concerned with the documentation of a firm's outside relationships. It encompassed the preparation of the balance sheet and the profit-and-loss statements, which dealt with the outside in the sense that they reported the results of operations to the stockholders and the general public. Cost accounting, to cite a second instance, was preoccupied, since it embraced the cost of producing and marketing a product, with the firm's interior relations. Because these inherited accounting instruments were poor informational systems, Schmalenbach and his colleagues had sought to

44 See review by Schneider in *Volkswirtschaft und Betriebswirtschaft*, 400–14.
45 Ibid., 402, my translation.

make them into more effective managerial aids.[46] Schmalenbach introduced the dynamic balance sheet; Fritz Schmidt, the organic balance sheet. Schmalenbach argued in favor of marginal cost pricing and developed uniform charts of accounts; his colleagues elaborated standard cost accounting and budgeting. If, however, economic concepts were used to reform accounting theory and practice, economics did not replace inherited accounting methods as the principal focus of their work.

Gutenberg shifted the discussion among German business economists to a different plane. For him the central scientific problem was not the effectiveness of accounting instruments (the nature of costs or the elimination of false profits from the balance sheet) but the interdependence of input–output functions within the firm. Erich Schneider identified factor interrelationships as the chief concern of neoclassical economics, so Gutenberg was, in effect, applying these economic concepts to the firm. Although he eventually discussed three major functions – production, sales, and finance – all of which are critical in the life of the firm, the first volume of *Foundation of Business Economics,* which sparked the "Gutenberg revolution" in 1951, discussed production. In it Gutenberg noted that there are three basic factors involved in production: labor, capital (*Betriebsmittel*), and material (*Werkstoff*). It is the manager's job to see that these production factors are combined efficiently, and it is the job of business economics to clarify the nature of the factor combination. Gutenberg wrote two hundred pages, borrowing heavily from economic theory, which described the functional relationships of labor, capital, and material in production. Since he was interested in simultaneous factor combination he also borrowed from mathematical economics, for, as Schneider said of Gutenberg's book, "it is in the nature of things that this *Denkschulung*. . . entails the capacity to deal with quantitative interrelationships. Gutenberg knows that an exact knowledge of quantitative interrelationships is a condition sine qua non of every business disposition."[47]

Whereas the interwar generation of business economists wrote books and articles on subjects like balance sheet accounting, cost ac-

---

46 Eugen Schmalenbach, *Selbstkostenrechnung und Preispolitik* (Berlin: 1931), 4.
47 See Schneider's review of Gutenberg's *Foundation of Business Economics,* in *Volkswirtschaft und Betriebswirtschaft,* 402. Also see Erich Schneider, "Preistheorie oder Parametertheorie," for comments on *Denkschulung,* originally published in *Weltwirtschaftliches Archiv* 76:1 (1956), reprinted in *Volkswirtschaft und Betriebswirtschaft.*

counting, short-term profit, and inflation accounting, Gutenberg and his postwar followers wrote about factor combinations involved in productivity and input–output relationships.[48] Accounting was not neglected; it was one source of information about input–output flows. But it was only one source. Management had to make special data surveys for information needed in decision making. Accounting, moreover, was in itself unable to explain how the factor combination could be accomplished most efficiently. That is why Gutenberg turned to microeconomic theory.

Gutenberg's revolution, then, completed the development of the new paradigm in German business economics. It was an affirmation, a triumph of the *Wissenschaft* tradition, for a belief in the efficacy of science permeated the movement. University instructors did not seek to teach students actual business techniques, although that was still done. They taught *Denktechnik*, which scientific study showed to be the basis of economic activity. Nor did the university researcher aim to solve real business problems. Praxis-related research was desired but it could not be allowed to get in the way of the theoretical endeavor: to formulate, through the hypothetical deductive methods of neoclassical economics and mathematics, a business science. Since the science allegedly helped the businessman and the industrialist, its cultivation was pragmatically justified.

The point is not just that Gutenberg's work produced the analytical framework of the new paradigm but that this result was, despite the pervasive influence of the Americans after the war, so very much a product of German education. Gutenberg's achievement was, if not caused by it, nonetheless made possible by the *Wissenschaft* tradition. This was true in the inspirational sense. No discipline in a German university could have any ambition other than a scientific status. Gutenberg was pleased to have, as Professor Albach phrased it, "assured for business economics a secure place among the sciences of the university."[49] But it was also true because the German educational system provided the wherewithal to fuse science and business studies.

Gutenberg himself described how this tradition stimulated his scien-

48 Professor Klaus Chmielewicz notes that the difference between Schmalenbach and Gutenberg-influenced accounting can still be discerned in German B.W.L. publications, the Gutenberg-influenced books appearing with titles like *Production and Cost Theory*, the Schmalenbach with titles like *Cost Accounting* (in a personal conversation).
49 Albach, "Die Betriebswirtschaftslehre," 1.

tific intellectual growth. He had extensive practical experience during the long years of graduate education. Between 1922 and 1924 he worked for Maschinenbau AG in Hirschberg. In 1930, he worked, after losing an assistantship at Münster University, for a German auditing firm in Berlin (Deutsche Genossenschaft Revisions – und Treuhand GmbH) before moving to another auditing firm in Essen (Deutsche Wirtschaftsprüfung AG) where, after he passed his auditor's examination (*Wirtschaftsprüfer*) in 1934, he joined its board of directors. During this period of practical experience he became interested especially in price policy. He relates how a discussion about the pricing of ties in a client's firm made him realize that the price theory in the economic literature could not explain practice. This realization prompted him to formulate a theory of *"doppelt geknickte Preisabsatzfunktion"* to replace pricing based, according to Schmalenbach, on *"U-förmig gedachte Grenzkostenkurve."*[50] The reflections which practice induced would not, however, have occurred without prior theoretical knowledge. Gutenberg describes how he acquired the necessary theoretical knowledge:

In the mid-1920s I became acquainted with Erich Schneider in Münster [where Gutenberg studied economics] who directed me toward microeconomic theory, about which I, at the time, knew nothing at all. I fell under the spell, above all of Pareto and Cournot, the more so because then, in the last half of the 1920s [when Gutenberg was a graduate assistant in economics], German business economics had practically ignored the price problem.[51]

He complained justly about inadequacies of German business economics. But the point made in the last chapter, that the educational system in which he, Erich Schneider, and others grew up helped them to develop the *Wissenschaft* paradigm in German business economics, is nonetheless true.

The educational tradition, too, facilitated the quick acceptance and absorption into German business economics of the Gutenberg view. Gutenberg borrowed extensively from economics. The fact that business economics was being incorporated as a discipline into the university community, even before Gutenberg's revolution, guaranteed that ideas drawn from both disciplines were readily exchanged. It led to a blending of economic studies in Germany. In some universities the dis-

50 Ibid., 4.
51 Ibid., 7.

tinction between business economics and economics disappeared; generally, however, it remains. Nonetheless, the two subjects now rest on a common core of studies, a *Grundstudium* of two years that all students in these subjects take before specializing in either business economics or economics during the *Hauptstudium*. Students in economics are required to learn business economics; those in business economics, economics. This blending reflects the *Denkschulung* that Gutenberg borrowed from economics primarily in the 1940s and 1950s. It constituted the earliest expression of the new paradigm in management studies in West Germany. There was opposition, e.g., Professor Mellerowicz in Berlin objected to the application of economic and mathematical sciences in business economics. But Gutenberg, appointed to the most prestigious chair in business economics, Schmalenbach's chair in Cologne, could use the *Wissenschaft* institutionalized in German graduate education (i.e., training Ph.D. and *Habilitation* students, who then took chairs in German universities) to push his view. It rapidly became orthodoxy in German business economics faculties.

What were the pioneers' limitations? One was modern mathematics. Gutenberg was no mathematician; he was not sufficiently skilled technically to introduce game theory or linear programming into research. The new paradigm in Gutenberg's hands amounted more to the incorporation of marginal economics than mathematical and statistical science into B.W.L. In this respect his work fell short of the *Polytechniciens*. The second limitation German business economists shared with the *Polytechniciens*. One of Erich Schneider's admirers observed that, at bottom, for him, the successful application of microeconomic tools did not depend on noneconomic or, above all, political factors.[52] Schneider paid little attention to political or cultural facts; he did not pay much attention to facts. He emphasized deductive science. Erich Gutenberg also ignored the social sciences. In his *Grundlage der Betriebswirtschaftslehre* (4 vols., 1951–69) and in his *Einführung in die allgemeine Betriebswirtschaftslehre*, although the latter contains a chapter on the "special tasks of management," he ignored personnel matters in the firm. The failing is shared by other big names in postwar German business economics who touched but slightly on personnel.[53]

52 Harald Sherf, "Erich Schneiders Keynes-Rezeption," in *Erich Schneider, 1900–1970*, ed. Bombach and Tacke, 49–67, 59.52.
53 Erich Kosiol, *Einführung in die Privatwirtschaftslehre* (Wiesbaden, 1978); Wilhelm Rieger, *Einführung in die Privatwirtschaftslehre* (Erlangen, 1959), e.g. Only a few

Table 4.2. *German students of economics-related subjects*

Year	Total Students in Higher Educ.	Economics (VWL)	%of Total	Business Econ. (BWL)	% of Total	W-I	%of Total
1950	107,444	3,138	(3.7)	4,879	(5.9)	64	(.01)
1958	143,708	5,568	(3.8)	10,027	(7.0)	789	(.08)
1965	237,633	10,620	(4.5)	19,294	(9.1)	2,619	(1.1)

Source: *Statistische Jahrbücher* (Wiesbaden), 1950–66.

"The development of business economics in the German speaking world," Werner Kirsch observed,

occurred . . . in isolation from the behavioral sciences. The long years of struggle to clarify the scientific objectives of business economics marked its development and strongly influenced its content. Because of these efforts, which could be attributed not least to the endeavor of business researchers to justify their existence as scientists, a gulf opened up between [German] business economics and behavioral science, which especially after the last war was widened in particular by Gutenberg and Schneider. They propagated a very narrow cooperation – if not a union – between business economics and economics on the basis of a common macro-micro economic theory.[54]

Although detracting from German business economics, the two shortcomings did not significantly reduce the discipline's capacity to break through to the new paradigm immediately after the war. Intellectual innovation, moreover, was reinforced by quantitative growth in B.W.L. studies. Table 4.2 charts the number of German students (foreigners excluded) in economics (V.W.L.), business economics (B.W.L.), and economic engineering (*Wirtschafts-Ingenieur*) in West German *Hochschulen* at three intervals during the fifteen-year postwar period. It also registers (the numbers in parentheses) the percentage of total university enrollment that these figures represent. The table shows that a significant number of university students studied economic subjects; that within the general field of economics, business economics, that is, the study that prepares people specifically for careers in business, was important; and that the technical institutes, in addition to management

manuals treated the subject of social science in B.W.L., e.g., Karl Hax and B. Belanger, "Das Personalwesen," in *Handbuch der Wirtschaftswissenschaften* (Cologne, 1958); and H. Seischab and K. Schwantag, "Personalwesen" in *Handwörterbuch der Betriebswirtschaftslehre* (Stuttgart, 1960).
54 "Die verhaltenswissenschaftliche Fundierung der Betriebswirtschaftslehre," in *Wissenschaftstheoretische Grundfragen*, by Raffée and Abel, 105–37, 107–08.

courses given to all engineering students, offered a well-established, if small, program in industrial administration. Growth was modest in the first year of recovery but, building on a solid tradition in business studies, accelerated quickly thereafter.

If French traditions in engineering education and German in B.W.L. favored a quick postwar propagation of the new paradigm in business studies, other educational heritages did not. Those which hindered the development of a new management studies paradigm will be examined in terms of education (1) in engineering and natural sciences, (2) in economics, and (3) in business and/or commercial studies.

Engineering and natural sciences

The mathematical culture *Polytechniciens* possessed gave them an advantage when approaching the new paradigm in business studies. Engineers and natural scientists in other countries enjoyed this advantage to a lesser degree probably than the high-powered French, for the former were not as precocious or highly educated in mathematics as the latter. Nonetheless, university-educated engineers and natural scientists everywhere knew enough mathematics to master the techniques of applied economics and operations research. The fact that engineers and natural scientists outside France did not adopt the new management paradigm as rapidly as the *ingénieurs-économistes* has to be attributed, therefore, to motivation rather than capability.

For Germany, there are at least two explanations for the delays. First, there was the problem, not to be discounted lightly, of being a defeated nation. Not only did Germans have to pick themselves up out of the rubble and organize their scientific and educational communities, they had the restrictions placed on them by the victorious allies. Delay was inevitable. Second, whereas in France *Polytechniciens* held key positions in the *grands corps* and in the state planning ministries, in Germany the engineers did not. Even today, despite efforts to introduce engineers and business economists into top bureaucratic jobs, a *Juristenmonopol* persists.[55] A recent survey of the top civil servants in Bonn shows that 80.8 percent studied law.[56] "One can still speak,"

55 Siedentopf.
56 Christiane Dreher, letter to author, Jan. 20, 1987. Frau Dreher is preparing a thesis on Bonn *Beamte*.

Christiane Dreher observes, "of the dominance of legal-trained civil servants in the top positions." Perhaps as a result, the German civil service, unlike the French, does not permit its people to take long-term leave in order to work in business or industrial management. Since German administrative law makes promotion in the civil service dependent on continuous administrative service, movement into industry and banking is discouraged. Results of a recent questionnaire reveal that "only 5% of the queried civil servants believed that it is desirable to take temporary positions in the economy." Dr. Dreher, who conducted the survey, concludes: "It seems that the firms, too, are not particularly interested in hiring those with top civil servant qualifications. . . . One cannot speak, therefore, of a systematic exchange between top civil service and business-industrial management."[57]

Because top German civil servants were ignorant of the new techniques and did not work with engineers or natural scientists, because they worked almost exclusively in private industry and the new paradigm in management studies started in the military and in nationalized industries, German engineers and natural scientists were not challenged to develop a new management science as early as the French. Consequently, the first O.R. chair was not founded in the German cultural area until 1956 (in Switzerland). The technical university in Munich established an Institute for Applied Mathematics and Operations Research in 1957; the technical university in Zurich set one up in 1958.[58] If, thereafter, O.R. chairs multiplied quickly in West German technical *Hochschulen* and universities, the new management techniques did not enter German industry or higher education until the end of the 1950s, a time when they were already commonplace in France.

Inasmuch as engineers and natural scientists could assimilate the new analytical techniques more quickly than social scientists, the delay in Germany prevented them from teaching the techniques to the business economists at technical *Hochschulen,* who, in turn, could have transferred the techniques to their colleagues in business economics at German universities. There Gutenberg-trained or inspired people were predisposed intellectually to use them. In 1960, Gutenberg himself noted that the next task of German business economics would be linear programming, investment planning under uncertainty, game theory, and decision theory, all of which relied on mathematical

57 Ibid.
58 Künzi, "Operations Research."

skills.[59] His conception of business economics, input–output analysis, easily accommodated these techniques; it made their absorption into German postwar business economics normal.

As a system, German higher education, moreover, could have facilitated the transfer. Since various departments existed in the universities which had permanent interests in managerial matters, the potential for a response was there. The *Wissenschaft* ideal welded older departments with new (i.e., applied mathematics or cybernetics) in a common scientific endeavor. Subsequent attendance at O.R. meetings and contributions to O.R. journals confirm this broad academic participation potential. At a 1959 meeting of the German O.R. society, for example, papers were presented by people from departments of business economics, applied mathematics, agricultural economics, econometrics, and mechanical engineering which were located in both technical universities and universities without engineering faculties. Mathematicians and engineers predominated at the session but economists and business economists attended (Paul Samuelson's attendance testifies to the sort of interchange that existed between American economists and mathematicians). Gutenberg's son-in-law, Professor Albach, was present. He was, in fact, one of the business economists who pushed operations research techniques in German business economics. It is clear, then, that because of the *Wissenschaft* tradition German business economists could have learned about these techniques sooner had German engineers and natural scientists earlier led the way.

The educational delays which the engineers and natural scientists encountered in Great Britain were of a different order. Whereas operations research penetrated German industry late, Britain was the pioneering country in its techniques. The war work was the most dramatic, but in peacetime O.R. teams were also especially active in Britain, as in France, in the postwar nationalized industries. Yet English educational traditions hobbled O.R. studies at universities. Roger H. Collcutt, who lived through the pioneering period of operations research on both sides of the Atlantic, observed, "It is interesting to remember the different ways in which education in O.R. developed in the U.K. and the U.S.A."[60] In the United States "many of the staff [in wartime jobs] were university professors, prominent among them Professor Morse, from

59 Erich Gutenberg, 'Die gegenwärtige Situation der Betriebswirtschaftslehre," *ZfbF* 12 (1960): 118–29.
60 "O.R. Changes," 362.

MIT." After the war, when the professors were demobilized and returned to university duties, they brought O.R. into their institutions. "At MIT," Collcutt noted, "a United States Navy O.R. evaluation group was set up to work with Professor Morse, and at George Washington University in Washington, D.C., a similar [university] group worked for the army."[61] University connections were also established in the United States when O.R. got into the private industrial corporation. H. P. Künzi recalled, for example, that the Chesapeake and Ohio Railroad sponsored the first O.R. group at the Case Institute of Technology, under Professor C. W. Churchman. It endowed a chair in operations research, with the stipulation that the occupant do research on the railroad's managerial problems.[62] That university connection was missing in Britain.

In fact, the first university-based course, inspired by Sir Charles Goodeve of the Operational Research Club and Professor Egon Pearson, the eminent statistician, only came in 1949. Then it was presented, in typical British fashion, as a one-time, three-months evening course. A British university did not offer another short-term course for five years. During this interval several leading American academic institutions created operations research programs (Carnegie Tech, Case, U.C.L.A., University of Chicago, Johns Hopkins, Cornell University, University of Pennsylvania). Of these, Ohio State University and Case were by the mid-1950s especially active in industrial consultancy. There were, moreover, private consultancy firms (Booz, Allen, and Hamilton alone had fifty-two offices which counseled clients on operations research methods) which worked with universities. And the American Management Association, in frequent symposiums, included academics in its education effort.[63] American universities and colleges by the mid-1950s had gotten very deeply involved in the development and propagation of O.R. In contrast, a regular university course, a one-year master's at Lancaster University, did not start in Britain until the early 1960s. That was over twenty years after O.R. had begun in the country.

There was a conflict in Britain between academic and working O.R. people and, because of the lateness and sluggishness of O.R.'s academi-

61 Ibid.
62 Künzi, "Operations Research."
63 American Management Association, eds., *Operations Research: Mittel moderner Unternehmensführung* (Essen, 1958), 20.

zation, a great imbalance between the two. It was as if the academic version of O.R. did not take root in the United Kingdom as it had in the United States. That version was dominated by abstract, complex, highly theoretical mathematical models which, because of academic career conventions – publish or perish – captured the scientific O.R. journals. Even the British *Journal of the Operational Research Society (JORS)* reflected the greater academization of American as opposed to British O.R., for, increasingly, the scientific articles in it came from academics employed in American educational institutions. Patrick Rivett in an analysis of the articles published during one twelve-month period observed that "of 103 papers..., 81 were by academics of whom only 31 were British. The *Journal* has over half of the papers in the form of theoretical material from overseas academics."[64] Considering the size of British O.R. society membership, the vast majority of working O.R. people, that is, the vast majority, since the academic operational research group was so small, of O.R. people, did not publish. Rivett claimed that "80% of OR people go through life without publishing anything."[65]

There was hardly any complaint in *The Operational Research Quarterly* about this reluctance to study O.R. in British universities. On the contrary, articles primarily criticized the O.R. that was taught there. Practical O.R. people even denied the relevance of the mathematical models proffered by academics, arguing that they were a poor yardstick with which to judge the health of O.R. in Britain. N. R. Tobin, K. Rapley, and W. Teather, in an article entitled "The Changing Role of OR," observed:

In the Third International Research Conference on O.R. and Management Science at Bowness in April 1979, more than one attender was left with an impression of a widening gap between the university-based O.R. man and the in-house O.R. man, the former full of gloom and despondency because O.R. is not being used in any important areas, the latter are often carrying out useful O.R. in quite important areas.[66]

The implication is that a dichotomy existed in British O.R. between the academics and the practical men who still gave useful advice to British management because they ignored the work of the academics.

64 Patrick Rivett, "In Praise of Unicorns," *JORS* 32 (1981): 1051–59, 1057.
65 Ibid.
66 Page 283.

The split involves more than the usual skepticism of practical men toward theoreticians. Apparently, large numbers of O.R. scientists in Britain – who had to believe, inasmuch as that was O.R.'s purpose, in the efficacy of applying science to management problems – shared the traditionally deep-seated English suspicion of academics. Neither the O.R. Society nor its journal had been created by them. Like all British professional associations, it was started by practitioners. Academization came later.

The reverse happened in West Germany. O.R. had difficulties getting established in German industry, for German businessmen had doubts about using methods that were not, because of their complexity, understood. Not until the mid-1960s did O.R. really achieve a breakthrough in German industry; not until the 1970s was this breakthrough consolidated into a mature management science. At least one German professor, H. J. Zimmermann of Aachen Technical University, blames the delay on the nature of O.R. education in German universities. He stated that O.R. was sufficiently complicated and self-contained to constitute a study in its own right. The fact that German O.R. education took place "in the framework of business, engineering or mathematics programmes, with very little time devoted to OR" hampered the progress of these studies in the German Federal Republic.[67] It simply could not be taught properly as part of other study programs. But nobody in Germany suggested that it could not be taught in the university. Nobody claimed in the German journal of operations research (*Zeitschrift für OR*) that the academic's theoretical work harmed operations research. Germans knew that theory did not necessarily work in praxis but they did not conclude that academic-centered work was worthless. They thought the discrepancies between theory and practice should motivate people to get the theory right because a proper theory would help praxis.[68] Because the British practitioners thought practice proved the academic theorists wrong, they had no faith in their ability to instruct practice. Both the German and the British were as much an expression

67 H. J. Zimmermann, "Trends and New Approaches in European Operational Research," *JORS* 33 (1982): 597–603, 600–01.
68 Professor Zimmermann, after registering the complaint that there is "too much theory and too little practice," in Germany, observed that "there is a lack of good mathematical theory (including algorithms) for quite a number of problem structures . . . [and] . . . a lack of non-mathematical theory: theory of the type that engineers need and use in their day-to-day practice" ibid., 602. He did not question theory but bad theory, the remedy for which is not practical experience in lieu of theory but good theory combined with or based on practical experience.

of educational cultures as scientific outlooks, for while Germans had great faith in the efficacy of university research, the British did not. This is one reason why the implementation of O.R. was done in Germany with the full cooperation and participation of university professors and why in Britain its penetration into academia was, despite its presence in practice, delayed.

Economics

Postwar German business economists and French engineer-economists readily applied economic theory to management studies. But what about the economists themselves? What role did they play in the application of economic theory to business studies? The answer for West Germany has already been given. The economists had, through the business economists with whom they associated (the Erich Schneider and Erich Gutenberg examples), considerable impact on *Betriebswirtschaftslehre*. In Great Britain and in France, on the other hand, educational traditions in economics shackled the development of a new management-study paradigm.

The British story is all the more frustrating, indeed paradoxical, because of their achievements in economics. The fame that British academics had achieved before the war cast a brilliant light, because of John Maynard Keynes, across academia. British achievements did not stop there, for, as Professor J. R. Sargent noted, two of the most important postwar theoretical developments, "the doctrine of imperfect competition and concept of equilibrium growth," were made by Britishers, although the ideas were simultaneously arrived at in America.[69] There was no reason for the British in the era of Keynes to think they were behind anybody.[70] But the educational inheritance sketched in the last chapter hampered the creation of the communication network, within educational establishments and between them and praxis, upon which the application of economic theory depended.

Alfred Coats gives the following numbers for postwar employment of economists in the British civil service: 1950, 17; 1964, 21.5; 1970, 208.5; 1975, 365; 1980, 379.[71] Obviously the figures indicate that something happened when after 1964 economists in Whitehall in-

---

69 "Are American Economists Better?" 5.
70 Ibid.
71 Coats, "Britain: The Rise of the Specialists," 33.

creased dramatically (by 1970 a 1,226 percent change since 1950). But that was two decades after the war. During this period British employment of economists followed the prewar pattern (between 1950 and 1964 only a 20 percent increase), contrasting sharply with government employment of economists in other countries. R. L. Marris noted (1954) how the Netherlands with one-tenth the British national income had many more government economists. "The United Kingdom," he observed, "has one of the lowest proportions of economists to other officials [in the world]."[72] Donald Winch also pointed out that in America "any one of several [governmental] agencies could sport more than the total number of economists in government service in Great Britain. . . . Battles for the recognition of professional economic expertise that would be inconceivable in America were still being fought in Britain until recently."[73] This sort of governmental expertise was necessary to evoke great awareness of management science in the firm.

Indeed, it seems that economists were not employed directly by business and industry immediately after the war either. Unfortunately, it is difficult to make very accurate comments about the extent to which this is true. "The business community is so large and heterogeneous," A. E. Booth and A. W. Coats remarked, "that there is little hope of obtaining precise data on the number of economists."[74] The available surveys, if not very good, do indicate that, as with economists in government service, in business and industry" a period of limited recruitment [of economists] in the mid-1950s was followed by a sustained expansion in job opportunities up to the early 1970s."[75]

The failure to employ economists means that their expertise was not much appreciated in praxis. Classics scholars were preferred in Whitehall after, as well as before, the war. Next to classics scholars the historians were in favor. In the early 1960s, for instance, a third of the recruits in the general administrative class of civil servants were historians. Of these entrants half came from Oxford, six out of seven from

72 R. L. Marris, "The Position of Economics and Economists in the Government Machine: A Comparative Critique of the United Kingdom and the Netherlands," *The Economic Journal* (Dec. 1954): 759–83.
73 *Economics and Policy*, 335.
74 "The Market for Economists in Britain, 1945–1975: A Preliminary Survey," *The Economic Journal*, 88 (Sept. 1978): 445.
75 Ibid.

Oxbridge.[76] If these people had special knowledge, therefore, it was of history, mathematics, and the classics – nothing that was technically useful for solving management problems. R. L. Marris (1954), comparing Dutch with British experience, noted that in the Treasury's economic section people used

a mixture of qualitative and quantitative analysis, such as involves only the more elementary theoretical concepts and the most elementary statistical methods – inspection, simple derived statistics, index numbers and other weighted averages, national income arithmetic. . . . The difference between the Hague and Whitehall is that whereas in Whitehall these are, as far as is known, the only methods allowed, in the Hague there is a consistent attempt to exploit in addition the "econometric" statistically "advanced" methods of modern applied economics.[77]

If those in the professions, in government, and in business and industrial management continued after the war to ignore academics and to assert a belief in the "mythic" superiority of the practical man, economics in the university continued to suffer from an educational heritage that made the union between university and praxis difficult. Professor Anthony Hopwood's comment about the British attitude toward knowledge goes to the root of this postwar educational problem. "The traditional British interest in knowledge," he recalls, "[is that it must be viewed] as a consumption rather than an investment good. So frequently in the UK knowledge tends to be seen as something which generates 'culture,' a particular life style, rather than something which is a resource, a more proactive source of power."[78] This statement describes British academic economics during the postwar period. People who learned economics at Oxbridge were not interested in management careers in British industry. They were destined for nonbusiness or nonindustrial jobs in academia, in government, in parliament, or in the City.

This heritage affected the actual way economics was taught in postwar British universities. The strength of American economics, Professor Sargent has remarked, was its analytical tools which allowed exact

76 C. H. Dodd, "Recruitments to the Administrative Class," *Public Administration* (Spring 1967), quoted in "The Making of Economic Policy," by Roger Opie; in *Crisis in the Civil Service* by Thomas Balogh, Roger Opie, Dudley Seers, and Hugh Thomas (London, 1968), II.

77 Marris, "The Position of Economics," 763.

78 Anthony Hopwood, "Accounting Research & Accounting Practice," paper delivered at the New Challenges for Management Research Conference, Leuven, Belgium, May 23–25, 1984, 6.

definitions and theory to be compared directly with the facts. There was "a lack of distinction between theoretical and applied sciences in the United States" for the one went with the other.[79] These traits resulted from intense specialization which in turn arose from strong graduate programs. The highly professional graduate work of the best American universities produced the new paradigm in the economic policy sciences. At Oxford it was impossible (and still is) to read economics, it being considered only as part of a triple undergraduate major, Politics, Philosophy, and Economics. Although Cambridge in the 1930s, Sir Alex Cairncross noted, was "the leading center of economic study in the world,"[80] his comment really only applied to theory. "Keynes himself," David Winch remembers, "was unsympathetic towards ... [the] mathematical and statistical exercise" involved in econometric policy studies.[81] Although Cambridge economists excelled in the "empyrean realm of pure logic," very little was done there to "narrow the gulf between [it] and the nitty gritty of the real world."[82] At the beginning of the 1930s no economist on the Cambridge staff had a higher degree. The first Ph.D. was awarded there in 1933.[83] After the Second World War Cambridge needed to build up a specialized graduate study program in economics. It did so but later than other universities. Without proper specialist education neither Cambridge nor any other British university could pioneer the development of econometric tools.

Weak British graduate education resulted, too, from the organization of English undergraduate education. Embodied particularly in the Oxbridge college tutorial system, it was the glory of British universities and the basis of that much beloved prewar emphasis on the "gentleman ideal." It was not, however, suitable for teaching specialized economics. "In Oxford and Cambridge," Professor Sargent remarked in 1964,

an insuperable barrier is placed in the way of specialization by the college system, a survival which is about as well adapted to the efficient teaching of undergraduates as the self-sufficient medieval manor to the production of goods

79 Sargent, "Are American Economists Better?," 2.
80 "Academics and Policy Makers," in *Changing Perceptions of Economic Policy*, ed. Francis Cairncross (London, 1981), 7.
81 *Economics and Policy*, 309.
82 Cairncross, "Academics and Policy Makers," 12.
83 Ibid.

and services. The idea that one man should be responsible for almost the total range of instruction of his pupils seems ludicrous to many Americans.[84]

By isolating their students and their tutors in colleges, British universities denied them the specialized instruction taught by acknowledged experts in specific fields of economics, which is the hallmark of American undergraduate and graduate education. The tutorial system did produce brilliant generalists; Professor Sargent thought them (the Oxford P.P.E. students) more advanced than first-year graduates of M.I.T. or Stanford. (On the other hand, the students who took P.P.E. were probably of a much higher calibre at entry than the Stanford or M.I.T. student. Hence the achievement might reflect more quality of entrant than education.) But he also thought that the M.I.T. and Stanford graduate "would finish the course [in economics] better equipped professionally than anyone had the opportunity to become in Oxford."[85] English undergraduate education, therefore, did not, like American, complement specialized graduate studies, the lower leading progressively to the higher. Graduate studies were not related to undergraduate.

As a result the English universities did not fashion the tools that enabled economics to become a macroeconomic policy science. Even though Englishmen had made impressive contributions in the past to mathematical statistics, they made few major contributions to econometrics after the war. R. J. Ball wrote in 1963, "Paradoxically Keynes, whose conceptual apparatus gave such a stimulus to econometric research. . . , himself set the tone towards a continuance of the traditions of armchair economics that had preceded him. . . . The history of quantitative economics in the United Kingdom over the last twenty-five years, particularly in the narrow field of statistical model-building, contains relatively few outstanding features."[86] What advances were made, moreover, often came from Americans like Lawrence Klein who, fleeing McCarthyism to Oxford in the mid-1950s, developed the first econometric models of the British economy (after having developed an American one at the University of Michigan.)[87] Klein, a Nebraskan, studied with Samuelson at Harvard, who himself had been influenced by the great champion of mathematical economics, Joseph

84 "Are American Economists Better?," 5.
85 Ibid.
86 R. J. Ball, "The Cambridge Model of Economic Growth," *Economica* 30:118 (May 1963): 180–90, 180.
87 Sass, *The Pragmatic Imagination.*

Schumpeter. English economists might have been tempted to downplay econometrics, compared to theory, as a lesser accomplishment. But this was the old economics, since Americans, "regarded it as essential to have a grasp of theory and of techniques for testing it, and that not simply for ornament but for use." Only with the American formula could the new paradigm in economic science develop.[88]

But the English university economists were not just behind in macroeconomic techniques. For much too long after the war British professors ignored game theory, linear programming, decision theory, the study of financial flows, indeed the whole bag of analytical tools American economists were borrowing from operations research. Some interest in the firm had been shown at Oxford. An Oxford Economists Research Group started in the late 1930s (although abandoning the task during the war) to question businessmen and manufacturers about how they fixed prices and how interest rates influenced decisions to add plant or equipment.[89] This empirical work produced serious criticism of the marginal theory of the firm (e.g., manufacturers in fact engaged in full cost, not marginal cost, pricing; manufacturers did not seek to maximize profits). The leading figure in the postwar Oxford group (until he was forced to move to Lancaster), P. W. S. Andrews even founded a journal, *The Journal of Industrial Economics,* to support empirical economics. More empirical work also occurred in the London School of Economics and Political Science where the graduate section on commercial education, established in 1932, prospered after the war. It had for its mission, in part, to find and perfect the methods of economic analysis that were susceptible of being used "on practical business problems and to let theoretical analysis guide and at the same time be guided by practical studies."[90]

But the Oxford group, the L.S.E. group, and the armchair economists at Cambridge neglected the analytical instruments with which theory informed practice. Andrews's journal, for instance, ignored linear programming and game theory throughout the 1950s; another economics journal published at the London School of Economics, *Economica* did the same. It printed one article in 1951 on linear programming; the next one, which was written by people at Iowa State University, did not appear until 1963. *The Economic Journal,* prestigious

88 Sargent, "Are American Economists Better?," 5.
89 See initial papers published in the *Oxford Economic Papers.*
90 Locke, *The End of the Practical Man,* 138–39.

organ of the Oxbridge economists, also overlooked these analytical techniques. Occasionally book reviews deplored the ignorance of British economists. Mr. Hain at Churchill College, Cambridge, when reviewing D. Gale's *The Theory of Linear Economic Models* complained, "It is time that users of old tools got themselves the new set and that we stopped equipping students with stone axes."[91] It was actually past time, considering that the American economists had been assimilating these techniques for fifteen years. Not until December 1960 did Professor Hicks publish a little study on "Linear Theory," in *The Economic Journal*. To do it he went to America to find the economists who could explain linear programming to him.[92] That trip alone demonstrated the extent to which preeminence in economic study had shifted across the Atlantic.

The point, then, is that the English educational traditions determined the development of the new policy sciences as much as did the intellectual capacities of students and professors. Professor Hicks did not need to visit America to learn about linear programming. Operational research groups in Great Britain used linear programming regularly. He just did not have sufficient communication with them. But how could he have, even if he had wanted, which he probably did not, considering that O.R. was not being taught in the universities.

It is also understandable that economists did not learn from the engineers since their science was considered intellectually inferior in Oxbridge. And yet the economists needed the engineers and applied scientists. "There is the fact," R. G. Allen observed in 1955, "perhaps reluctantly accepted by many economists – that progress in designing and regulating economic models depends more on heavy computation and the full use of computing devices, than on any attempt to get general solutions. Until the engineer's experience is appreciated and assimilated, there is little hope that the economist can develop macrodynamic models to the point where there is a chance for practical applications."[93] English economists, products of public and grammar school educations that had nothing to do with British industry, isolated from industry in universities, could not acquire these skills as

91 F. H. Hain, review, *The Economic Journal* 71 (1961): 175–76.
92 J. R. Hicks, "Linear Theory," *The Economic Journal* 70:280 (Dec. 1960): 671–709. He wrote H. W. Kuhn of Princeton, Kenneth Arrow, and George Dantzig. Hicks's own education in mathematics had ended in 1923.
93 R. G. Allen, "The Engineer's Approach to Economic Models," *Economica*, NS, 22:86, (1955): 158–68, 168.

quickly as the Americans who, while in business school and engineering school, customarily worked with industry. While Professor Samuelson and his colleagues attended O.R. meetings in America and Europe, while they wrote books (in the mid-1950s) which incorporated linear programming techniques and the new mathematics into neoclassical economic theory, in Britain the academic communication networks made similar initiatives difficult if not impossible. Professor Hicks, apparently, had to visit fellow economists in America to find out about linear programming because British economists did not talk to the few mathematicians, scientists, and engineers who knew the subject in Britain.

R. J. Ball drew the consequences which such an approach to economics has had for the firm. He wrote in 1967 that "[e]conomists were concerned more with what deductions could be drawn from the supposed behaviour of firms for the theory of markets and subsequently for general economic welfare than with solving the actual problems management encountered in the firm."[94] The result:

In the absence of empirical inquiry geared to sound analytical theory economics has developed into a non-quantitative subject. . . . This means that the application of economic principles has to be seen against (a) information systems that exist in firms including the role of the accountant and accounting data, and the staff economists and statisticians, (b) the organisational framework in which decisions are made and the pressures that operate to modify decisions taken within that framework. If the economist knows nothing of this and cannot relate this to his own teaching which is thus put into perspective the danger arises that all that results is a compartmentalised body of knowledge, which the student is unable to relate to the world as he finds it as a manager.[95]

French economists were also ill prepared to adopt the new paradigm after the war. The dual system of higher education, which separated the *grandes écoles* from the university sector, prevented the professors of economics in the law faculties and their students from participating fully in the exciting work of the *ingénieurs-économistes*. This left the university economists struggling to cope with the new ideas on their own. Pareto noted, "When the existence of certain problems is ignored, evidently one does not perceive the need to resolve them."[96]

94 "Economics in the Business Schools," in K. J. W. Alexander, A. G. Kemp, and T. M. Rybczynski, *The Economist in Business* (Oxford, 1967), 184–85.
95 Ibid.
96 Quoted in G. H. Bousquet, "Gaëtan Pirou et l'école de Lausanne," *Revue d'économie politique* 57 (1947): 689–701, 691; my translation.

French university economists had chosen in the past to ignore marginal utility and general equilibrium theory in order to concentrate on the social institutional framework of economic activity. Professor G. H. Bousquet reflected on the consequences of the decision in 1957. "I did all my studies at the Paris law faculty and at the School of Political Science ('Science Po') without anybody ever citing the name Walras to me."[97] If it is remembered that most of the people in the nontechnical *grands corps* (*Conseil d'état, Cour des Comptes,* etc.) were educated at the "Science Po," this signified that the nontechnical *hauts fonctionnaires* who ran France before the war, even if they had studied economics, had learned precious little about marginal utility or general equilibrium theory. In terms of knowledge, therefore, the contrast between French and British prewar economists could not have been more complete. When after the war the French began to wake up from their Rip van Winkle economic sleep, they discovered that it was very hard to change.

Economics students always had literary *baccalauréats* (people with mathematics and science *baccalauréats* went to the *grandes écoles* of engineering). No attempt was made, moreover, to repair this secondary school deficiency while studying at university. Imagine the cri de coeur emitted when the professors faced the technical discussions of the new paradigm. Professor Guitton observed with dismay in 1950 when he tried to review T. C. Koopmans's *Statistical Inference in Dynamic Economic Models:*

[This] exposition is inaccessible to the noninitiate in mathematical language. I know subscribers of the journal *Econométrica* who are completely discouraged, despite persevering in an effort to comprehend. One has to be an accomplished mathematician to follow these developments. But life is short. To learn advanced mathematics is a Herculean task. The way to econometrics is thus definitively closed to us.[98]

Without an adequate knowledge of mathematics it was difficult, if not impossible, to assimilate new ideas in economics. Charles Rist la-

97 Ibid.
98 Henri Guitton, review of *Statistical Influence in Dynamic Economic Models,* ed. T. C. Koopmans, in *Revue d'économie politique* 58 (1948): 706–07; my translation. The journal's editors observed when they published G. Tintner's article "Les Programmes linéaires stochastiques," 66 (1956): 208–15, that "the nonmathematicians would have trouble understanding the article. [One] needed to know matrix algebra and probability theory" (my translation). Thus the journal had a problem: publish articles that were scientifically obsolete but which the readers could understand, or publish highly mathematicized modern studies that its readership could not understand.

mented in 1955 that an ignorance of mathematics had prevented him from understanding Léon Walras. René Courtin, in an article written in 1956, observed:

Apparently, economic thought in the university suffers from a malaise: It only became conscious of the "Keynesian revolution" in 1945, that is with an eight-year delay, when [elsewhere] disciples and adversaries of the "master" had already been at work. And the enthusiasm for innovation was only a flash in the pan [*feu de paille*]. Soon the French had to recognize that their techniques were insufficient and the controversy petered out. [Moreover], throughout the world . . . our contemporaries turned, rightly or wrongly, toward economet-rics as the science of tomorrow. But, this way was also closed to most profes-sors of the law faculties who lacked mathematics.[99]

This defect apparently even stopped people from translating books into French. Samuelson's *Principles of Economics,* which appeared in 1945, was not published in French for twenty years. Its reviewer, S. Wickham, explained the delay in terms of translation difficulties. "To translate, it is necessary that the translation not be a 'treason'; it needs a competent mind, schooled both by mathematics and economics, which is difficult, if exacting, work."[100] Indeed, the application of modern mathematics to economic problems – games theory, linear programming, input–output analysis – was clearly beyond postwar French university econo-mists. There were mathematicians in France, of course, but, as André Marchal commented in an article about Swedish economists, "we de-plore . . . the gulf which too often separates [French but not Swedish] economists without sufficient mathematics from those mathematicians without any veritable knowledge of economics."[101]

Yet mathematics was not the only problem. Professor Gaëtan Pirou claimed before the war that classical and neoclassical economics were too abstract, too logical, not in touch with the reality of human exis-tence. There was no such thing as the "economic man." P. L. Reynard in an article (1945) announced that economics needed modern psychology not econometrics. This was indeed the position that the critics of the new paradigm took when doubts arose about the efficacy of model

99 "De l'Ambiguité des critères de distinction à la prétendue opposition de la micro et de la macro-économie," *Revue d'économie politique* 66 (1956): 19–63, 22; my translation.
100 "Fonction et avenir de l'économiste d'entreprise," *Revue d'économie politique* 75 (1965): 258–69, 268; my translation.
101 "La Pensée économique suédoise contemporaine," *Revue d'économie politique* 57 (1947): 65–111, 108; my translation.

building; they questioned modern economics' social-psychological assumptions about profit maximization and rational economic behavior. But the professors in the French law faculties were no more capable of developing a sophisticated social-psychological-organizational critique of mathematical economics than they were of employing mathematical economics. They were not trained in sociology, psychology, or organization theory. The law faculties offered no courses in these subjects. Indeed the faculties of letters in French universities did not officially give courses in the human sciences (sociology, ethnology, demography, cultural geography) until 1948. Nor did the law students learn industrial, commercial, or banking techniques. They and their students were technically unable to do financial or market analysis.[102]

What then did students of political economy study? They studied the history of law, civil and criminal law, legal procedures, and international law. Students could not acquire a degree (*licence*) in political economy after the war. Until the late 1950s all *licences* awarded in the law faculties were officially law degrees (*licence en droit*) with special mention in one of three subjects: political economy, public law, or private law. Such designations were justifiable because the first two years of the three-year course for the *licence en droit* were a *tronc commun,* the same for all students in the law faculty. Only in the third year did the students in political economy take courses that differed from those in civil or private law options. As for doctoral programs, they did not allow the candidates to specialize sufficiently either. In order to do a doctorate in political economy students also had to prepare a diploma of advanced studies (D.E.S.) in either history, public law, or private law. There was not much time, then, for economics. Since the candidates for the *agrégation* were recruited exclusively from law doctorates, and an *agrégation* was necessary to obtain a professor's chair in a law faculty, modern economic analysis faced hard sledding.

Thus, the immediate postwar history of French higher education reveals that the heritage had a negative effect on the development of the new paradigm in economics. There had, of course, been exceptions to the trend. Albert Aupetit, a disciple of Léon Walras, taught economics at "Science Po" during the interwar years. The people who worked in the Institute for Statistics in the University of Paris were doing very

102 See *Revue d'économie politique.*

valuable work. Many of them were *ingénieurs-économistes* but many were also university-educated professors. Attempts were made after the war, moreover, to enlighten law faculty professors about modern economics. The *Revue d'économie politique,* the spokesman for the university economists, put Professor Maurice Allais on its editorial board. And when he won a medal from the American Management Science Association for his work in marginal pricing, the award was proudly reported to the review's subscribers.[103]

Still, the university faculties were as poorly equipped in the France of 1960 to teach business as the British faculties. Moreover, the problem could be traced to secondary school education. Whereas all German secondary school leavers (in 1960) were examined in mathematics, the students entering French law faculties continued to be literary *baccalauréats.* Any desire to inform students (much less professors who had come up through the same system) about the new quantitative techniques could not be realized quickly. Indeed, S. Wickham could state as late as 1965 that "economic calculations . . . frequently required a very elaborate technical knowledge that currently is found only in the *ingénieurs-économistes* from the *grandes écoles.*"[104]

Business and commercial education

Finally, a few words can be said about the failure in the postwar period of heritages in business and commercial education to facilitate the establishment of a new paradigm in management studies. The traditions in question were British (the commerce degree in provincial universities) and French (the *grandes écoles* of commerce). The British, impressed by the management of the war and convinced in some circles that this managerial expertise could be transferred to peacetime industry, set about establishing management education after the war. The most significant new institution was the Henley Staff College, which was established in 1945; but other colleges of management education were also

---

103 Allais worked hard to make mathematics, not law, the center of economic studies in the university. See his "Pour la création des facultés de sciences économiques et sociales," *Revue d'économie politique* 63 (1953): 212–20. But the *Polytechnicien* econometrician François Divisia disagreed. He supported law studies on the grounds that abstract calculation was not enough. Economic activities take place in socio-legal settings. See his "Contre une coupure entre études économiques et études juridiques," ibid., 204–11.

104 "Fonction et avenir," 267.

founded. The British Institute of Management (B.I.M.), whose creation in 1947 was itself an expression of an enhanced British professional managerial consciousness, also got involved by sponsoring a new diploma in management studies (D.M.S.). But these initiatives in management education were, from the perspective of the management studies paradigm, praxis not science intended. Henley was not an academic institution. Neither what it taught nor the way it taught had much to do with the application of science to management. On the contrary, it presumed that experience alone was the best teacher; its pedagogic methods, which consisted of having experienced managers learn from each other in groups (syndicates), smacked more of the old paradigm than the new. The Diploma in Management Studies, moreover, suffered from the prejudices engendered by the traditional schism between English science and practice. The D.M.S. was earned in a short course, taught in a nonacademic institution (college of further education) by nonscientifically trained teachers to nonacademically qualified and oriented students (the D.M.S. students usually were not qualified for university study). Besides, in a highly class-conscious society where higher education was a "consumption" not an "investment" good, the D.M.S. bore the stigma of a working-class diploma. Management high flyers, therefore, shunned it and the B.I.M., wishing to avoid the stigma it carried, withdrew its sponsorship.

French achievements in commercial higher education overshadowed the British. The *grandes écoles* of commerce, particularly those in Paris (H.E.C, E.S.S.E.C., E.S.C.P.), had connections in banking and commerce. Their students, if not equal to those in the *grandes écoles* of engineering, were every bit as accomplished as those admitted to the universities. But two characteristics prevented them from playing any role in the implementation of the new paradigm in French higher education after 1945. First, they were teaching, not research, institutions. Their professors were still *vacataires* (part-time); research was alien to them. Second, their students were primarily literary *baccalauréats*; they did not know mathematics. Hence even the most prestigious of the *grandes écoles* of commerce could neither develop science-based management research methods nor teach techniques developed elsewhere to their students. Educational reform occurred but not until the late 1950s. At H.E.C. the graduates, consequently, did not have a real education in marketing, management *contrôle,* and the social and psychological problems of the firm before the 1960s. Until then the graduates of the *grandes écoles* of commerce, including those who were instrumental in introducing new managerial techniques into French firms after the war, owed much more to the Americans than to any scientific instruction acquired in school.[105]

In each country, the ability of reformers to establish a new paradigm in management studies differed considerably according to the degree of resistance inherited educational institutions presented. Generally it can be said that people in nontechnical forms of education (business economics, commercial studies, economics) had a more difficult time, because of methodological hurdles, than engineers and natural scientists adjusting to the new paradigm. The high level of mathematics, which was indispensable for the conduct of serious work, was not part of the intellectual baggage required in nontechnical, nonscientific education. This was true, if less so, of German business economists, too, who had trouble with advanced mathematics. With greater technical competence, therefore, engineers and natural scientists could lead in establishing a paradigm based on the application of science to management, providing, of course, that they perceived the need for such an application.

Because of the positions they held in the technical *grands corps* and in industrial administration, because of their scientific education, and because of their connections with the *grandes écoles* of engineering after graduation, the French *ingénieurs-économistes* led the way. The British engineers, mathematicians, and natural scientists who had the technical capacity to apply science and mathematics to management did not have the necessary contacts with institutions of higher education in Great Britain to spawn an educational-management complex. Nor did they have the influence in the state administration, which was still dominated by nonscientifically educated generalists, that Jacques Massé and his group had in France. The German engineers, mathematicians, and natural scientists also lacked the state managerial responsibilities (commensurate with the French) which could spark interest in scientific management. Because they had the technical skills and the educational connections, however, the Germans absorbed the new paradigm relatively quickly once it had spread from military and nationalized industrial activity to private business and industry.

Engineers, mathematicians, and natural scientists did not pay much

---

105 Meuleau, "Les HEC," 22.

attention to the behavioral sciences in any of these countries, but neither, during the postwar era, with rare exceptions, did the business
economists, the economists, or the business studies people. By 1960,
therefore, the extent to which the new paradigm in management studies
had penetrated European higher education varied considerably. Everywhere, however, even the most hidebound conservative educational
establishments could no longer ignore the scientific siren. The computer
made mathematized model building de rigueur, and the transitional
period which, in retrospect, the postwar era clearly constituted, gave
way in the 1960s to the new era of management education. After 1960,
the engineers, applied mathematicians, and natural scientists continued
to develop the management-science educational programs, within their
educational bailiwicks, that they had pioneered.[106] Yet the really significant management educational changes occurred in the nontechnical
business and economic science where people set about gaining technical
competence in order to shift to the new paradigm. This effort brought in
every country business educational reform.

106 See Professor Claude Riveline for information about the management course at the
Ecole Nationale Supérieure des Mines de Paris. Several brochures are available on
the programs. René Alquier, "L'Enseignement de la gestion dans les écoles
d'ingénieurs," *Hommes et commerce,* 19:113 (May–June 1970): 50–62.

5. Why not business schools?

Among the nontechnical and nonscientific forms of American education covered in this book two stand out: economics and business studies. Each has very different origins; economics developed as an academic department in American universities, and business studies as a separate faculty or school that was much closer to business praxis. Before the Second World War the American university economists, like the English, looked down their collective noses at business schools. The difference between Britain and America, however, is that business schools grew vigorously in America, despite the economists' disdain, while in England they did not. After the Second World War, the separation between the academic (read "intellectually challenging") American university departments of economics and the practical (read "nonintellectually stimulating, vocational") American business schools narrowed. Intellectual stimulation in the business schools came through the introduction into their curricula of the new paradigm in management studies. The change for economics came through an increased practicality (Keynes, input–output analysis, and econometrics transformed economics from a theoretical into a policy science). Economists and business studies people, then, collected methods from the same formal science toolshed. But the economists tended to ignore management problems, except, of course, at macroeconomic levels. The growth of the new paradigm in management studies has, therefore, been almost synonymous with the extraordinary growth in size and influence after the Second World War of the American business school.

Many prestigious American business schools (like Harvard and Wharton) not only started before the Second World War, they predate the First. Hence they were well-established educational institutions before the new paradigm in business studies arrived on campus. These older schools did not, moreover, pioneer its adoption. This was true especially of Harvard, by far the most prestigious and influential, particularly abroad, of American business schools. Taking its cue from the law school, the Harvard Graduate School of Business Administration adopted a case method of instruction. Students read and discussed résumés of hundreds of actual or theoretical business cases designed to give them a taste for real business problems from which they (since experience, plus common sense and intelligence, is the best teacher) learned. There is, however, nothing about the case study method which entails in itself the application of science to business problems. Indeed, scientific method cannot be taught particularly well through cases, nor are they very useful in research. Harvard, despite its importance, did not initiate the new paradigm in management studies; it has, in this regard, allegedly been a laggard.[1] The same accusation could be directed at other older business schools but to do so serves no purpose; institutions that predated the new paradigm, those without the faculty and students necessary to it, would inevitably be behind.

Not surprisingly, therefore, schools or departments of industrial administration, often in engineering institutions, innovated. The work of the O.R. teams at the Case Institute of Technology and at M.I.T., which has been mentioned, is a good example. Another is the Graduate School of Industrial Administration established at the Carnegie Institute of Technology in 1949. The G.S.I.A. "which had an impact out of all proportion to its seniority," promoted the new paradigm in business schools. It required at entry a minimum mathematical prerequisite of calculus and it employed "the analytic, normative, mathematical, and scientific mode of instruction."[2] Since schools of industrial administration had traditionally been preoccupied with production problems, scientific techniques (e.g., linear programming) were applied there to the work of engineers. But the researchers, realizing that marketing, finance, and organization theory could employ the same methods, expanded far beyond the customary confines of industrial administration. The new name given at M.I.T. to the Sloan School of Industrial Administration (it became the Sloan School of Business Administration) indicates broadening interest; but schools did not have

1 The school was attacked by the president of Harvard for this failure. See the business school's defense in The Associates of Harvard Business School, *The Success of a Strategy: An Assessment of Harvard University Graduate School of Business Administration by the Board of Directors* (Boston, 1979).
2 John E. Jeuck, "Business Education: Some Popular Models," *The Library Quarterly* 43:4 (Oct. 1973): 281–92, 287.

to change their names to expand their horizons. Herbert Simon's work in organizational theory at the Carnegie G.S.I.A. is sufficient testimony to this fact. If technical schools led, by the mid-1950s a strenuous effort was underway in business schools, led "most notably perhaps" by a Ford Foundation team, to get rid of the "unimaginative, nontheoretical faculties teaching from descriptive practice-oriented texts to classes of second-rate vocationally-minded students."[3] Consequently, the new paradigm developed rapidly in the American business school. Mathematics requirements were raised. New scientifically qualified staff were brought in – exemplified by the move of Russell Ackoff's O.R. team from the Case Institute of Technology to the Wharton School of Finance.

Because the application of science to management affected the behavioral sciences in business schools almost as much as the traditional management sciences (finance, marketing, etc.), there was a greater emphasis on research and publication. American scientific literature, concentrated increasingly in specialist journals, mushroomed. Scientists used the new analytical tools, while maintaining close contact with management practice, in project work, surveys, and other forms of consultancy. This scientizing did not occur quite the same everywhere. Business schools in institutes of technology had the most heavily ladened mathematical systems of analysis. The Harvard Graduate School of Business Administration, at the opposite extreme, although it assimilated such analytical tools as game theory and linear programming, retained almost exclusively a case method of instruction. At the University of Chicago, the business school emphasized neoclassical economics. Whatever the emphasis or the degree of assimilation of science, the trend after the mid-1950s was unmistakably toward the introduction of the new paradigm into business schools.[4]

At the same time business schools underwent institutional transformation. The United States Office of Education reported that bachelor's degrees in business increased from 3.2 percent of all undergraduates in 1919–20 to 10 percent in 1939–40. In 1949–50, business baccalaureates numbered 72,187, almost 17 percent of all baccalaureate degrees, and in 1968–69, 93,356, 13 percent of all baccalaureate degrees conferred.[5] If the popularity of undergraduate business studies

3 Ibid., 284.
4 Ibid.
5 Ibid.

grew after the war, even more impressive has been the growth in graduate business studies. Harvard began as a graduate school (they were exceptional before the war); so did Carnegie in 1949. Some undergraduate institutions (e.g., U.C.L.A.) transformed themselves into graduate schools. Others, while retaining undergraduate degrees, added graduate studies to their programs. Enrollments reflected this postwar emphasis on graduate education. For the ten-year period 1953–54 to 1963–64, the number of master's degrees awarded doubled; from 1964–65 to 1968–69, they tripled (6,375 to 19,335), while bachelor's degrees in business during the same five-year period just doubled (from 56,088 to 93,561). And the popularity of the M.B.A. throughout the 1970s and 1980s has continued to produce a steady and expanding stream of degree holders (over 100,000 M.B.A.s a year). Obviously an upgraded curriculum in business studies did not dampen undergraduate demand. But the real institutional innovation was in graduate education.

Prewar business education in the United States was almost exclusively preexperience undergraduate education. It was predicated on the assumption that the business knowledge acquired in school would serve the recipient throughout his career. The postwar reformers, operating on the principle that "the rate of change in the internal and external environment of business has increased greatly over the last generation and will accelerate in the years to come," perceived a different educational need.[6] Graduate work, therefore, sought to serve this new conception of management education, for it permitted people schooled in life experiences on the job to benefit from academic instruction at a more mature age than ever before. The best graduate schools of business in America still admit students directly from undergraduate studies, but they prefer to bring students who have worked into M.B.A. programs. To the M.B.A. long-term, postexperience graduate education, moreover, was added enhanced involvement in short-term junior and senior business executive instruction. The idea that the manager required a continual upgrading in his managerial skills and that the business schools, with their postexperience executive programs, could play a prominent if not central role in this education, gained apace.

But the American business school contributed a more significant

6 Ibid., 285.

idea to management education than scientific management studies and postexperience education: It propagated, if it did not invent, the idea of management itself. Businessmen and industrialists have always engaged in managerial problem solving; the American business school promoted the professionalization of the managerial function per se. It became an art and a science combined, to be taught and learned through such courses as business policy and decision theory and applied, whatever the particular context (e.g., marketing, banking, manufacturing), by properly qualified practitioners, i.e., by those who had acquired degrees in business administration. Whereas prewar business studies consisted of a number of subjects intended to help managers carry out their tasks, after the war the business schools made the manager's task itself the object of study. The business schools pretended, therefore, like law and medical schools, to prepare people for a profession.

The American business school aroused some interest in Europe before the Second World War. During the 1920s an effort to construct a business barometer at the Harvard Graduate School of Business Administration, which would forecast the business cycle, drew lots of attention; then interest collapsed after the great crash (1929), which the Harvard group had not foreseen.[7] More pedagogically significant, the Harvard case method drew French attention. When the Centre de Préparation aux Affaires (C.P.A.) was set up by the Paris Chambre de Commerce in 1931, it was as a postexperience management education center.[8] Shortly after the Second World War, European productivity teams, seeking explanations for American managerial superiority, visited business schools during American fact-finding tours.[9] Thereafter, European interest in business schools grew steadily, especially when the Americans set about installing in them the new paradigm in management studies. Such educational dynamism convinced Europeans that they had to follow suit or fall hopelessly behind in managerial

7 Locke, *The End of the Practical Man*, 228.
8 Actually, Pierre Jolly introduced the case method into France in 1923. Harvard cases were used; but a French *Central* for the preparation of cases did not appear until 1971. See *Bibliographie de cas: gestion et entreprises* (Paris, 1983), published by the Paris Chamber of Commerce and Industry.
9 *La Comptabilité, mesure et facteur de productivité. Rapport de la mission française des experts comptables aux Etats-Unis* (Paris, 1952); *Productivity Report, Management Accounting*, report of a specialist team which visited the United States in 1950 (Leicester, 1950). Published with many other studies of the Anglo-American Council of Productivity.

know-how. Consequently, the 1960s and 1970s brought rapid and profound changes to European educational systems. But reform, despite ardent desires on the part of many to emulate the American business school, did not in any country mirror the American experience. Why?

The German case

Of all the educational heritages, only the German, with a business economics devoted to the study of the firm, rivaled the American. Nonetheless, German B.W.L. was quite different in 1960 from American business studies. That difference can be most summarily described with the familiar word *Wissenschaft*. Professor Albach, who was a student in America briefly in the 1950s, remarked that at the time 95 percent of American education in the business school consisted of cases without theory, in German B.W.L. of theory without cases.[10] Schmalenbach, stuck in the halfway house to the new paradigm, had insisted that B.W.L. was a *Kunstlehre*, a skill exercised to solve business problems. But the institutionalization of learning that *Wissenschaft* occasioned, with long years of study and research, had discouraged German professors from establishing contacts with people in praxis. The penchant toward academic isolation had been reinforced by Gutenberg's postwar influence in the evolution of B.W.L. Seeking to usher in the new paradigm, he realized that people studying business economics had to improve their scientific education greatly; they had to learn economics and higher mathematics – become fluent in research methodology. Although he insisted on the need for practical experience, too, the effect of the Gutenberg revolution on German business economics was to direct people more toward science than praxis.

This effect, moreover, was matched by a standoffish attitude in praxis toward the university professors' involvement in postexperience management education. In the early 1950s German businessmen crossed the Atlantic to undergo postexperience management training in American business schools. Dr. Ludwig Vaubel's book *Unternehmer gehen zur Schule* (*Entrepreneurs Go to School*), which described his experiences in a senior executive course at Harvard, helped

10 Interview, July 13, 1982, Bonn. The viewpoints expressed in this chapter depend on personal interviews and surveys conducted in Europe. See the Bibliography.

introduce the German business community to American management education. But, when in the winter of 1952–53 various business and industrial leaders set about organizing a German "*Unternehmer-Akademie*" there were two educational models before them. One was the Henley Management College in England, which had no contact with academia. The other was the American where business schools had, as people like Vaubel knew, gotten deeply involved in postexperience education. Dr. Vaubel acknowledged that "the first postexperience management training courses had taken place, relying on the teaching faculties of business schools like Harvard."[11] He and his colleagues found the American example to be quite attractive. But they feared that a different academic tradition, centered on science, had saddled Germany with inexperienced, *praxisfremd* (praxis alienated) professors. The pragmatically minded German businessmen and industrialists, therefore, ignored university business economics when setting up postexperience management educational programs.

Thus in 1955 when the first Baden-Baden Managers Conference (*Unternehmer-Gespräch*) gathered, groups of senior managers met, as at Henley, for relatively unstructured discussions among themselves about management. When the Deutsche Vereinigung zur Förderung der Weiterbildung von Führungskräften (Wuppertaler-Kreis) was organized in 1955, seven organizations (R.K.W., R.E.F.A., V.D.I., etc.) joined the association, none of which had academic credentials.[12] They were sponsored by business, industrial, trade, or professional groups, associations interested in technical and administrative efficiency. The *Wissenschaft* tradition had kept the German professors of business economics and the men in praxis apart.

Within academia, as the American business school model entered into the consciousness of professors during the 1950s, emulation began to take place. Armed with the new mathematics, students, a perusal of German periodical literature after 1960 attests, embraced mathematical model building.[13] The behavioral sciences also penetrated German business economics faculties. Advocates of behavioral science had to overcome Gutenberg's influence; but in the late 1960s

11 *Führungskräfte für die Zukunft der Unternehmen*, 10.
12 The Association for the Promotion of Postexperience Management Education, The Wuppertal Circle. This is an organization of organizations. See the various brochures the association issues, e.g., *25 Jahre Wuppertaler-Kreis* (Wuppertal, 1980).
13 *Zeitschrift für Betriebswirtschaft* and the *Zeitschrift für betriebswirtschaftliche Forschung*, especially after 1965, are full of these studies.

and especially the 1970s, the introduction of new professorships – in organizational theory, in personnel – fostered the introduction of behavioral science approaches to business problems.[14] In terms of numbers, the traditional fields (accounting, banking, insurance, etc.) were still more strongly represented in university faculties, but by the mid-1970s great efforts had been made to incorporate behavioral science into German B.W.L. Behavioral sciences, moreover, also effected changes in teaching techniques: The case method and small group project work during the 1960s supplemented traditional lectures and seminars. There is no need to belabor the achievement; any German college catalogue confirms it quite clearly. Professor Albach, in fact, had made the previously quoted remark about the inverse relationship between experience (cases) and theory in Germany and America not to disparage Germans (or Americans) but to show how much things had changed. After noting the situation in the 1950s, he observed that by 1982 (when he was talking) the case method of instruction was about as prevalent in German B.W.L. as in the American business schools.

In the late 1960s, moreover, efforts were made to establish closer contacts betweeen professors and people in praxis. Industrialists took the initiative. A self-appointed group contacted (1966) the minister of education in North Rhine Westphalia asking him to support "post-experience management education carried out as a cooperative venture with the universities."[15] The initiative produced in 1968 the *Universitätsseminar der Wirtschaft* (University Seminar on the Economy – U.S.W.) The U.S.W. brought (and brings, because it is thriving today) professors of business economics and managers together in postexperience management seminars where active managers are exposed to the ideas of academics and academics to the hardheaded realism ex-

14 Eduard Gaugler, "Gegenstandsbereich und Erkenntnisstand des Personal-Management," *BFuP* 34 (July 1982): 285–92; Eduard Gaugler and Bernhard Ling, "Die Betriebswirtschaftslehre an den wissenschaftlichen Hochschulen in der Bundesrepublik Deutschland, in Osterreich und in der deutschsprachigen Schweiz," *Die Betriebswirtschaft* 37:4 (1977): 559–74; Karl-Friedrich Ackermann, "Hauptströmungen und gegenwärtiger Entwicklungsstand der Personalwirtschaftslehre an den Hochschulen in der Bundesrepublik Deutschland," in *Das Personalwesen in Europa, Standard und Entwicklung des Personalwesens in den einzelnen europäischen Ländern,* ed. Fritz Bisani and Hans Friedrichs (Essen, 1977).
15 Hans-Joachim Arndt, Siegfried Fassbender, and Hans Hellwig, *Weiterbildung wirtschaftlicher Führungskräfte an der Universität* (Düsseldorf, 1968), vi; my translation. The group was composed of Dr. Horn (of Felen-Guillaume), Dr. Jacobi (of Baeyer), Herr Schmidt (of Ford), Dr. Sonne (of Kloechner-Humboldt-Deutz), and Dr. Vaubel (of Glansdorf and the Wuppertaler-Kreis).

pressed by those in praxis. Dr. Vaubel reflected recently about the reforms:

In 1952 I wrote: "The conditions in the Harvard Business School are particularly favorable because an excellent teaching staff has assembled a rich case material over decades that is at the disposal of the business school. . . . But this can succeed only if the material serves practical business needs, . . . a task which the *Hochschule* tradition in Germany, as elsewhere in Europe, does not fulfill." [He is quoting his 1952 report *Unternehmer gehen zur Schule*.]

This has changed in the meantime. Almost all faculties of German universities try to complete their classical teaching in microeconomics through special programmes with lectures of outstanding practitioners. Some (Münster, Augsburg) are organizing, in addition, special courses for the development of young managers. . . . For the foundation of the *"Universitätsseminar der Wirtschaft"* a new generation of academic teachers in *"Betriebswirtschaft"* has become available, men who also know about the efforts – results and sometimes unavoidable weaknesses – of American Business Schools are prepared to try something similar here. In the beginning we financed two of them, Prof. Albach, Bonn, and Prof. Busse von Colbe, Bochum, to make extended studies on the spot over there before offering a final concept suited for our situation here. It needed years, and disappointments could not be excluded before a workable concept could be found. But we think that the U.S.W. now is to the German business world an institution able to combine the results of the permanent scientific work done at various German universities with the needs of the industrial world (banking, insurance, trade included).[16]

Still German business economics faculties did not transform themselves into American business schools, for German professors, if they accepted a need to work with industry, never forgot the call of *Wissenschaft*. A conflict persists, therefore, between the aims of *Hochschule* and those of praxis. The exchange of views that took place in 1965 between a German businessman, Hans Dichgans, and a group of twenty prominent professors of business economics illustrates how German academia resisted practice-related, less theoretical forms of business education. Dichgans had complained in public that German business economics was not willing to be judged on how well it accommodated business. "Everything must the more so serve an abstract idea of higher science. Our young professors have less and less contact with praxis."[17] He recommended that more professors work for extended periods in business and industry and that their students prepare for

16 Letter to Sir Arthur Knight, Dec. 15, 1986.
17 "Betriebswirtschaftslehre, Theorie und Praxis im Streitgespräch," *Der Volkswirt – Wirtschafts- und Finanz- Zeitung* 19 (July 9, 1965): 1426–28, 1427; my translation.

business rather than academic careers. Students "should learn enough in a three-year course to qualify for a beginning position in the economy, from which they could then improve their knowledge through post-experience education."[18] The reforms he suggested would have seemed quite acceptable and desirable to people in American business schools.

The professors were not insensitive to the call for more contacts between business and industry, but they could not imagine accomplishing it in the manner Dichgans outlined. To the suggestion that professors acquire practical experience, Professor Wolfgang Kilger, of Saarbrücken University, replied that for both academics and practicing managers the crucial years in a career occurred between ages thirty and forty. Since it took a student four years to become a *Diplom-Kaufmann*, two to complete a doctorate, and three to write a *Habilitationsschrift*, it was not possible for the prospective professor to complete his education before age thirty.[19] As a young professor he then had to devote effort to academic science to advance his discipline (and his career) – so there was not much time to work in business. To Dichgans's suggestion that the *Habilitationsschrift* be eliminated as a requirement for professorship, in order to attract more men from business into academia (which is what the engineers do), they also objected. One professor observed that a man who had worked for years as an accountant was ill-suited to teach academic accounting. Another pointed out that "business does not understand reality, which is getting more complicated every day."[20] It stands to reason, therefore, another professor intoned, that *Praktiker* needed the professors and their science because of its abstractions, or, as still another professor explained, precisely because most scientists are interested in generalities, not, like the *Praktiker*, in particulars.[21]

The men at Dichgans's conference also questioned his request that the undergraduate course be shortened from four to three years so that students could begin work earlier. "How would people in business," one professor queried, "be able to understand science later if they were not taught its theoretical principles during their studies?"[22] Once again

18 Ibid.
19 Ibid.
20 Ibid.
21 Ibid.
22 Ibid.

Dichgans's insistence on practical knowledge at the undergraduate level ran up against the *Wissenschaft* tradition. To be certified as a *Diplom-Kaufmann* the student had to pass a comprehensive examination laid out by professors after the first two years of study. This examination tested students' grasp of basic issues in economics, business economics, law, and statistics. After two more years students were again tested on subjects in economics and business economics as well as on their knowledge of a chosen specialty. To have accepted Dichgans's proposal would have meant abandoning this scientific training. This the professors were not willing to do.

In short, as the confrontation between Dichgans and the professors reveals, the academics would not compromise the canons of *Wissenschaft* even when they might be at odds with the needs of praxis. This critique applied to teaching method and degree study periods.

Professors often object to the use of case method in instruction. They rightly observe that it is not suited to scientific instruction, especially when a body of thought has to be learned. Lectures are better. The case method, moreover, does not fit German professorial temperament. "To be an effective learning instrument," an American advocate of the method maintains, "the case must be skillfully used by a well-trained teacher. His role is to lead a discussion so that student ideas, experiences, and viewpoints are interchanged and become part of the learning process. The teacher listens; students talk. The teacher questions, but does not give 'the answer' because there is usually no one answer."[23] German professors are not, however, comfortable with this Socratic method. Paragons of knowledge, they do not let students decide. When they use the case method, therefore, they often misuse it. Professor Ackermann notes, for example, that in his lectures he cites cases in order to illustrate theoretical points, that is, instead of using them as a medium for the student's self-realization, he uses them to impart his knowledge.[24] Because the German professor dominates the student in this master-disciple relationship, he has difficulty adapting to the peer relationship that the case method (and project work typical in praxis) requires.

The canons of scholarship, moreover, have shaped the nature of academic research. When a scholar approaches a problem, he does so in terms of a discipline. He not only looks at the problem, something

23 Associates of Harvard Business School, *The Success of a Strategy*, 27.
24 In a conversation with the author.

people in praxis desire, but he considers it in terms of scholarship, that is, how scholars have handled the problems in the past. This requires thorough discussion of the scientific literature, a treatment of the problem from a methodological and theoretical point of view. Germans who have worked in American business schools note the difference in research procedure in the two countries. Professor Hermann Simon observes, for example, how German doctoral dissertations devote much more space than American to theoretical discussions and much less to empirical investigation.[25] The contrast is startling. A Dr. Struven, of the Boston Consulting Group (B.C.G.) (Munich office), attended a course on business policy at the Technical University in Berlin (where he received his degree as a *Wirtschafts-Ingenieur*) and another at the Stanford Business School (which is known in America for its theoretical approach). He calculated that one-fifth of the Stanford course was devoted to discussion of method and its theoretical justification and four-fifths to application in praxis. In Berlin the ratio was the reverse.[26] Simon reports that he was obliged, in his thesis, to discuss literature and theory extensively, much more so than would have been necessary in America, where research on his subject (marketing) consists of field work and where American dissertations reflect this orientation.[27] Simon, incidentally, worked for a professor (Albach) with good relations in praxis (he appreciates a practical application of science); nonetheless, the traditional German academic mode of research prevailed.

Perhaps stress on theory and neglect of field work are inevitable; one hears frequent complaints from German professors about the noncooperation, the secrecy even, of German firms. American business and industry by contrast have always been open, willing, that is, to let the professors use their facilities for research purposes. But Germans claim just as often that this estrangement occurs because the professor is content to lock himself up in an ivory tower and do *Wissenschaft*. The result is bad theory as well as bad praxis because a theory that is not grounded in praxis goes astray. Testimony to the success of the *Universitätsseminar der Wirtschaft* notwithstanding, there is much talk still about German professors being estranged from praxis. Dr. Struven observes that his firm works frequently with American business school professors, seldom if ever with German professors of busi-

25 Hermann Simon, Bielefeld University, personal interview, Bonn, June 14, 1984.
26 Boston Consulting Group, Munich, Feb. 10, 1983, personal interview.
27 Simon interview.

Table 5.1. *Students in first-degree programs in West Germany*

	1960-61	1964-65	1970-71	1974-75	1980-81
Law	16,841	19,909	34,442	45,689	69,778
VWL	6,873	11,521	10,620	11,502	13,978
BWL	11,324	16,340	19,294	27,806	44,808
VWL & BWL	527	2,130	3,139	20,810	33,585

	Doctorate				
	1960	1965	1970	1975	1980
Law	648	594	721	518	457
Economic Sciences	38	?	545	463	592
VWL	30	121	174	127	135
BWL	98	189	188	179	158
BWL & VWL	110	?	?	140	196

Source: *Statistische Jahrbücher* (Wiesbaden), 1960–1980.

ness economics, because of the latter's lack of experience.[28] Dr. Karl-Hermann Baumann, a manager in Siemens, notes that his firm never calls in German professors of business economics, again because they are too inexperienced. Yet Siemens, he goes on to say, uses American professors, especially when innovations in strategic planning are being discussed.[29] Professor Specht, a business economist by training but one who teaches at an engineering school (Darmstadt Technische Hochschule), states that he has close contacts with people in practice.[30] His affirmation, however, does not gainsay the point, for business economists in engineering schools enjoy good relations with people in praxis only because they profit from the generally excellent relations that business and industry have with engineering schools. Specht believes that people in praxis do not, when there is a problem, turn to business economists in universities.

The business economists' resistance to American-style business education even after 1960 can also be discerned from the structural evolution of graduate and postexperience education in Germany. The statistics in Table 5.1 tell the story. These classifications show that German education, despite some experiments at Augsburg and elsewhere,

28 Personal interview.
29 Dr. Karl-Hermann Baumann, Munich, Mar. 17, 1984, personal interview.
30 Personal interview, Vienna meeting of German Association of Professors of Business Economics, May 25, 1983.

Figure 5.1. <u>Comparative business education in West Germany and the United States</u>

Source: Interview with Professor Reber in Vienna (May 25, 1983).

never adopted the most important innovation of postwar American business schools, the M.B.A. As explained in a student guide to management education, "those Germans who want to acquire a 'Masters of Business Administration' (M.B.A.) must go to the United States, to England, to France, or to Switzerland."[31] There are two hundred business schools in the United States that offer a two-year M.B.A. program and over sixty thousand graduates each year, but in the Federal Republic of Germany there is none.[32] To earn a first degree takes time, so much time that Professor Gerhard Reber believes the first degree in the German Federal Republic, Austria, or Switzerland is equivalent to an American M.B.A. (see Figure 5.1).

In terms of years spent in school, indeed, with regard to the difficulties of studies, Reber's view seems plausible. The Germans actually study longer for the first degree than Americans do for an M.B.A. But there are fundamental differences between the two courses of study. First, the American B.A. is a genuine first degree, the M.B.A. a graduate one. People with quite diverse B.A.s and B.S.s embark on M.B.A. programs. No such recruitment diversity is possible in Germany – the move from the *Grundstudium* to the *Hauptstudium* (advanced studies) in B.W.L. is a first degree study process: The completion of the *Grundstudium* is not, therefore, equivalent to a bachelor's degree in America. Secondly, and more importantly, the break between the B.A. and the M.B.A. can entail prolonged work experience. The German

31 Joerg E. Staufenbiel, *Berufsplanung für den Management Nachwuchs: Trainee-Programme und Stellenangebote von über 100 Unternehmen für Wirtschaftsakademiker,* 5th ed. (Cologne, 1981), 88; my translation. See also Hans D. Werner's article, "Die verschenkte Chance," *Die Zeit* (Mar. 3, 1980), in which he describes the lack of M.B.A.s in Germany.

32 Staufenbiel, *Berufsplanung für den Management Nachwuchs.*

Diplom-Kaufmann course permits no such break; it is preexperience – the more so since (with the exception of Nuremberg) the requirement that the students have a *Praktikum* has been dropped. Third, the M.B.A. is generalist and the German B.W.L. specialist management education.

German doctoral education also differs from American. In America doctorates are usually obtained by people who want to have academic careers; people with praxis in mind take a bachelor's degree and/or an M.B.A. In West Germany, Staufenbiel writes, 8 to 9 percent of the *Diplom-Kaufleute* got doctorates between 1966 and 1975 [13 to 14 percent of first degree holders in economics (V.W.L.) also got doctorates].[33] A large number, considering the time and expense involved, it can be explained, Staufenbiel states, by the fact that "of top managers in big firms who have first degrees in economics or business economics about two-thirds have doctorates. The doctorate is today a great aid to [managerial] advancement."[34] Since the German doctorate is a specialist research degree, German managers, in contradistinction to Americans with their generalist M.B.A. degrees, have quite different business educations. It is the *Wissenschaft* ideal for the former, the provision of general management know-how for the latter.

Because of *Wissenschaft* German business economists still refrain from becoming fully engaged in postexperience education. Siegfried Fassbender, who worked for decades as business agent of the Wuppertaler-Kreis and who actively supported efforts to bring German faculties of business economics into postexperience education, avers that the effort failed.[35] Among the four reasons he cites for the failure are that (1) professors and (2) businessmen were not sufficiently interested in establishing links with each other.[36] Consequently, academic business economics is still not engaged institutionally in postexperience business education – notwithstanding even U.S.W., the im-

33 Ibid.
34 Ibid., 80. The American Ph.D. makes greater academic demands (in good universities) on its candidates than the German doctorate. Whereas the German prepares a thesis, the American has to complete a rigorous comprehensive examination before doing an equally demanding research dissertation.
35 Interview, Cologne, Aug. 13, 1982.
36 The other two reasons arise from the immediate situation in which the reform movement took place: (1) students, because of leftist leanings, were particularly hostile in the late 1960s to universities establishing linkages with capitalistic industry, and (2) university administrators, with all the student unrest, were not interested in provoking by such a reform any more trouble than necessary.

pressive recent success in academic-praxis, postexperience cooperative education. Fassbender observed, "The *Universitätsseminar der
Wirtschaft* is really a professor's *Seminar der Wirtschaft,* for the
universities are not formally involved as are the Harvard, the London, and the Manchester business schools in postexperience education.[37] Fassbender's successor at the Wuppertaler-Kreis, Dr. Wippermann, and members of his staff do not work with, or show much
enthusiasm for working with, faculties of business economics on
postexperience management education.[38] To them the academic viewpoint is too theoretical and the professors, with obvious exceptions,
too divorced from praxis. *Wissenschaft* resists praxis, Professor Ackermann of Stuttgart University attests. He works regularly with business and industry in the Stuttgart area but he does so uniquely as a
scientist, i.e., if a suggested project has no scientific merit, he refuses
to do it, even if its accomplishment would help the firm solve a
problem.[39]

The pull of *Wissenschaft* remains, then, a powerful force in German
education. German professors who are especially under American influence, those in marketing, for instance, who are highly conscious of
the need for extensive field research, complain particularly about the
German professors' failure to work closely, even when developing
research projects, with business and industry.[40] Often, attempts to
defend the professors condemn them. Professor Hans-Jürgen Drumm
in Regensburg observes, for instance, that people in praxis, in contrast
to academics, are interested in the present not the future. His claim, in
short, is that *Wissenschaft* is important to people in praxis even if they
do not appreciate it, an attitude not calculated to rally many from
praxis to the professors' banner.[41]

Since the *Wissenschaft* idea exists within the greater educated German community, it sets the tone beyond the confines of the university's
business faculties for undergraduate and graduate work. The reforms
that created the *Fachhochschulen* show this quite clearly. Traditionally the technical and commercial schools (the *Handelsschulen* and
Ingenieurschulen) out of which the *Fachhochschulen* were fashioned

37 Interview, Cologne, Aug. 13, 1982.
38 Interview, Cologne, July 18, 1984.
39 Personal interview.
40 E.g., Dr. Gerd Wagner of Bochum University, Dr. Sönke Albers and Professor Klaus
   Brockhoff of Kiel University, and Professor Hermann Simon of Bielefeld University.
41 Personal interview, Regensburg, May 28, 1982.

in the early 1970s had escaped the *Wissenschaft* tradition. They were subuniversity institutions that taught practical skills in commerce and engineering. Although it was customary for these schools to recruit faculty from the ranks of the *Diplom-Ingenieure* and the *Diplom-Kaufleute*, i.e., from university-trained people, all faculty had to have at least five years' experience in business and industry. Moreover, students were required to have completed an apprenticeship (*Lehre*) in engineering or commerce. Graduates from these schools were very popular in industry and commerce because of their great practical skill. But *Wissenschaft* existed in them in the form of the university graduates on their faculties. Their *Wissenschaft* training evoked emulative strivings among faculty to raise the schools to the status of *Hochschulen*. Ambition bore fruit when Sozialdemokratishe Partei Deutschland (S.P.D.) governments turned the higher technical and commercial schools into technical and commercial colleges (*Fachhochschulen*). The "promotion to *Hochschule* and therewith incorporation into the university system," was possible only because people in these lower schools, recognizing the validity of *Wissenschaft,* wished to adopt the "research outlook."[42] Their attitude illustrates how the university-inspired *Wissenschaft* tradition acted like a magnet, drawing lower echelon schools almost inexorably into the research science orbit, much to the disgust of many businessmen and industrialists who have seen the practically useful graduates of these schools subjected to much more theoretical research and nonpractical education in the now transformed *Fachhochschulen*. The requirements that the professors have five years' work experience and that the students do an apprenticeship were dropped as the *Fachhochschulen* moved closer to the universities in their entrance and curricula requirements. As Norbert Kluge, Ayla Neusel, and Ulrich Teichler judged:

[This] promotion to a *Hochschule* . . . very quickly produced an identity crisis: On the one hand, the old specific value of the commercial secondary school as a training center for craftsmen was lost; on the other, the adoption of a research outlook has been only conditionally possible, for it has harmed the schools' traditional relationship with praxis. After a decade the *Fachhochschule* dilemma about which identity to choose has not been resolved.[43]

42 Norbert Kluge, Ayla Neusel, and Ulrich Teichler, *Beispiele praxisorientierten Studiums* (Bonn, 1981), 8; my translation.
43 Ibid., 11. In Baden Württemberg this elevation of *Fachhochschulen* has led to the creation of *Wirtschafts-Akademien* which try to give the practical training which the *Fachhochschulen* seem to have lost.

German B.W.L. today, therefore, differs from American management studies because it is primarily undergraduate preexperience and specialist research graduate education. Postexperience education is not, as in America, the province of academic institutions.

Great Britain

Since British universities had almost ignored management education, in one sense it was easier for them to copy American management education: they did not have, as did the Germans, a tradition in business education that could resist change. Many influential British businessmen, moreover, had attended Harvard Business School senior executive courses where they learned about American business education. In 1963 a group of industrialists, during a series of luncheon meetings with M.P.s at the House of Commons, created the Foundation for Management Education (F.M.E.) which collected funds for the promotion of management teaching in universities. Shortly after this group sparked public debate, a second one, which met at the Savoy Hotel, also launched a campaign for management education but outside the traditional universities: They wanted an independent Harvardlike business school located in London.[44] In the meantime, the National Economic Development Council (N.E.D.C.), which had been created in 1961 to foment discussions among people in government, industry, and trade unions about economic planning, reported in April 1963 that there was a "need for at least one very high-level new school or institute, somewhat on the lines of the Harvard Busineess School, or the School of Industrial Management at the Massachusetts Institute of Technology." Lord Franks was commissioned by the F.M.E., the Savoy group, the British Institute of Management, the Federation of British Industries, and N.E.D.C. to formulate a concrete set of proposals. Franks's job was simplified by the recommendations of the Robbins Committee whose report on the reform of British higher education, published a month before (1963), recommended that "two major post-graduate schools . . . be built up in addition to other developments already probable in universities and other institutions."[45] The relative stagnation in business edu-

44 Interview with Sir Douglas Hague, Athenaeum, London, Dec. 7, 1982.
45 Whitley, Thomas, and Marceau, *Masters of Business?*, 45. Also "British Business Schools," report by the Rt. Hon. Lord Franks, the British Institute of Management, 1963.

cation of the 1950s was succeeded everywhere by an almost universal clamor for fundamental reform which would make it an important aspect of higher education.

The two elite schools which resulted from the reforms, one in London and the other in Manchester, were inspired, and their educational structure deeply influenced, by American business schools' examples. "London," Richard Whitley, Alan Thomas, and Jane Marceau observe,

was particularly keen to acknowledge its debt to the United States. The full title of the School, for example, the London Graduate School of Business Studies, was a borrowing from Harvard practice, and its literature spoke of "Programmes" (Senior Executive Programme, London Executive Programme, Master's Programme, etc.), an "Alumni Association," and "electives." Manchester stuck to the more parsimonious "Manchester Business School," and was more inclined to talk of "courses," a "Manchester Business School Association," and "course options." Even so, in 1968 it drew particular attention to the number of staff who were training in the major American schools, such opportunities being particularly welcome "in view of the fully established and highly advanced state of graduate business education in the United States today."[46]

These British schools borrowed much more extensively, then, from the Americans after 1960 than did the Germans. London and Manchester adopted the two-year Masters programs; certain functional courses were taught (accounting, finance, law, economics, quantitative methods, psychology, organizational theory) in order to familiarize everyone in the program with business functions and managerial disciplines, but the courses also dealt with "decision making, resource allocation and policy making," that is with management per se.[47]

The graduate schools at London and Manchester were the first (1965) university-affiliated business schools in Britain. They were followed in the late 1960s and early 1970s by others which promoted management education, sometimes at the undergraduate (e.g., Bath), as well as graduate and postexperience levels of education. Even the older nonacademic management colleges underwent academic transformation. Henley Management College affiliated with Brunel University and added a Ph.D. program to its studies. By 1980, the Business Graduates' Association, itself a self-conscious product of educational reform, recognized fourteen business schools in Great Britain.[48] All

46 Page 50.
47 Ibid.; also, London Business School, *Two Decades of Excellence, 1965–1985*, Annual Report 1984/5.
48 *The Business Graduate.*

had followed London and Manchester along the road to academic achievement. Ph.D. programs were offered, but the interest had not focused primarily on *Wissenschaft*. Rather there was great concern for the education of professional managers. As Professor Newbigging remarked, "Important cultural overlays strongly influenced by the Americans . . . promoted management as a profession – a kind of separate elite – whose status and expertise is based upon a putative body of knowledge called 'management' with which the word science is frequently linked."[49] The Masters and executive programs in the British businesss schools and the business graduate association illustrate the reformers' desire to promote an American-style management profession and the education suited to its advancement.

Thus British higher education was not only reformed during the early 1960s with the establishment of university institutes of technology and the founding of new universities, but, within this reform movement specifically, business education held a premier place. Nonetheless, reforms begun with such high hopes have disappointed. They have failed for some because they have not really created an American business education; for others, and this is more important, they, because the traditional forms of British education have proven intractable, frustrated the intent of educational reform. This happened because of the way three groups – businessmen and industrialists, the general public, and the university community – reacted to business education.

At no time did the move to develop an American-style business school go unchallenged in British business and industrial management. Lord Franks's report recommending the establishment of two business schools noted how wary industry was of academic involvement in management education. The report recommended an M.B.A. of one-year duration, a recommendation which was rejected by the academics in the business schools in favor of an American-style two-year program. The extra year appeared to be a waste of time to businessmen.[50] The reluctance to accept a university-based business school was also reflected in the failure of businessmen and industrialists to respond to a call for funds. A second committee, under Lord Normanbrook, in

---

49 Eric Newbigging, "Management Development: Panacea, Placebo or Punk," inaugural lecture given by Eric Newbigging, Head of Management Studies in the Polytechnic of Central London (Feb. 1982). Typewritten.
50 Alan B. Thomas, "Management and Education," 91.

order to finance the new business schools, recommended in May 1964 a pound-for-pound funding shared between government and industry. Although £5 million was collected from industry within six months, £2 million above the target, most of it came from a few firms. "Only 47 companies," Alan B. Thomas observed "donated £25,000 or more to the 1964 appeal; and of these only 41 were among the largest 100 firms of the day, which suggests that most large firms did not support Franks's proposals, or at least did not back them with substantial donations."[51]

Subsequent to creation, business and industry continued to react to the business schools with suspicion, if not outright hostility. While trying to establish themselves they were constantly criticized. Not four years after their foundation a management education advisory panel, sponsored by the British Institute of Management and the Confederation of British Industry, expressed concern "at the growing unease and doubts in industry about some developments in the rapid expansion of undergraduate and postgraduate courses in business studies."[52] Business and industry did not send their employees to the schools or hire their graduates. Thomas reports that of the three hundred organizations that gave money to the schools in their first ten years only forty-six sent people on Masters' courses and they were sent on one-year not two-year courses (not to London and Manchester).[53] Of them only ten firms sent more than two (Shell sent the most, sixteen). Organizations that had given money to establish the business schools only sponsored ninety students.[54] Of the big contributors (sixty-three firms gave £25,000 or more) just twenty actually sent people on M.B.A. courses. And the numbers sent declined over the decade. Records at the Manchester Business School indicate, furthermore, more public than private organizational support for postexperience courses. Forty-two percent of its students came from nationalized industries and only fourteen from the financial sector. And the public sector's proportion increased over the years. Thomas comments that "recent analysis of 158 press advertisements for managerial posts, . . . over the period 1962 to 1977, showed that fewer than half asked for any formal qualifications at all. A similar analysis covering the period March 1965 to March 1976 did not dis-

51 Ibid.
52 Ibid.
53 Ibid.
54 Ibid.

cover a single request for an academic management qualification."[55] Large firms did hire masters from British business schools, but about 40 percent of them went into British-located American firms.[56] Such support explains the poor growth rates of British masters programs (with only eight hundred M.B.A.s a year), especially when compared to those of American business schools.

British management people attribute this great numerical discrepancy to different systems of management education. Professor Tom Lupton claims, for instance, that the British do not, in contrast to the Americans, believe that management can be taught to the inexperienced.[57] Whereas a person in America normally moves directly from undergraduate education to an M.B.A. program, in Britain he or she does not. The British masters programs are small, according to this logic, because people, after completing undergraduate degrees, work. Inasmuch as management education is effectively postexperience education in Britain, the numbers enrolled in M.B.A. courses will automatically be much smaller than in America. The view that management education is profitable (or even possible) only when combined with actual business experience shifts business school education away from M.B.A. programs to joint firm-school developed activities. Patterns of attendance at the London Business School show that the company course, designed and taught for the specific management needs inside the company, has shown spectacular growth in recent years (see Table 5.2). At the London Business School student weeks in the postexperience executive programs amounted to almost half the student weeks devoted to masters' programs. Company courses tailored for and taught inside the companies by the business school are shown in the item, Company Courses C.M.D. It shows that the London Business School not only teaches the longer and shorter executive courses, which are attended on an individual basis, but that it serves the management training needs of the specific firms. No university-affiliated German institution has such relations with business and industry.

Programs from the beginning at the Manchester Business School courted similar contacts with business and industry. One, for execu-

55 Ibid., 97.
56 Ibid.
57 Lupton's ideas are expressed in a number of manuscripts available through Manchester Business School. See, e.g., "Management Development in Western Europe" (March 1982); "Business Schools in the '80s and Beyond" (1980); and "The Functions and Organisation of University Business Schools" (1982).

Table 5.2. *Attendance at London Business School*

	Longer Executive (10 Weeks)	Short Courses (4-6 Weeks)	Company Courses LBS CMD (1 Week)		LBS Executive Total	Post-Graduate Masters	Grand Total
1972-73	1966	325	–	–	2291	5610	7891
1973-74	1862	735	–	–	2597	5580	8177
1974-75	1812	727	75	166	2780	5250	8030
1975-76	1948	522	90	358	2918	6090	9008
1976-77	2028	490	191	548	3257	6750	10007
1977-78	2340	556	288	617	3801	6390	10191
1978-79	2346	646	332	568	3892	6540	10432
1979-80	2192	642	224	786	3844	6900	10744
1980-81	2128	539	320	750	3737	7080	10817
1981-82	1940	490	350	650	3430	7140	10570
1982-83	1959	555	334	754	3602	7550	11152
1983-84	2133	651	345	846	3975	8960	12935
1984-85	2368	771	251	1098	4448	10620	15109
1985-86	2300	803	–	1086	4189	10740	14929

Source: Report of London Business School, 1987 (unpublished), Annex 5, Table 3.

tives, had long and short postexperience courses and joint development activities which tailored management education to the specified needs of individual firms. The M.B.A. program also worked closely with praxis. Two-thirds of the M.B.A. students at Manchester (1983) were postexperience (one-third entered directly from undergraduate studies).[58] Most Manchester M.B.A. students, moreover, work in business during the break betweeen the first and second year "and are expected to use this inter-term experience as a basis for a 10,000 word dissertation," required of all Manchester M.B.A. degree-holders. Project work is emphasized the second year; groups of students work on open-ended problems which operating companies sometimes provide (projects have included topics in operations management, industrial relations, entrepreneurship, and international business).[59] Students in German business faculties often work on projects in close cooperation with industry, too, but the Germans are either Ph.D. candidates, working on individual dissertations, or they are preexperience first degree students who lack the maturity and the experience of the Manchester M.B.A.

   Philip Nind, recently retired head of the Foundation for Management Education, stresses the peculiarity of British management education:

When FME was formed twenty years ago as Britain was entering a new era of management education, it was natural that we should lean heavily upon the

58 Interview, Tom Lupton, Feb. 24, 1983.
59 Whitley, Thomas, and Marceau, *Masters of Business?*, 51.

advice and assistance of the Americans – and we are immensely grateful for the help. . . . By the end of the 1960s it was clear that our cultural environment, our education system and our social attitudes were so distinctive on this side . . . that our academic institutions would have to shift their emphasis to suit a different form of relationship with their clients. This is in fact what happened. Without in any way reducing the value and importance of the Master's degree and advanced management-type programmes held within the walls of the schools themselves, it is perhaps the work embraced by the phrase "joint development activities", "action learning," "action research" which is having the most influential impact upon the acceptance by companies and their boards of the importance of each learning process as an essential aid, even pre-requisite to better management. And now we are entering a decade in which the activities of teaching, research and consultancy on the part of management school graduates will become more integrated and interdependent, merging into what Professor Tom Lupton has called "clinical experience."[60]

"In a business school," Lupton notes, "the disciplines are only relevant for their contributions to the solution of problems in the world of organization and management."[61] Relevance is not indirect, in the sense that German professors might conceive of a practical spin-off from *Wissenschaft*, but a direct application to actual problems. That is what Lupton means by business education being a "clinical experience." The analogy is with medicine, where the learning and teaching (and the healing) go on in the hospital or, in the case of business, in the firm. The joint development activity, which is akin to Rig Revans's technique of "action learning," brings active managers together with business school faculty to work on a company problem.[62] Here the German claim that *Wissenschaft*, if it might be helpful to praxis, is its own *raison d'être*, is denied, for academia has no other purpose in Lupton's view than to serve praxis. Nind's claim, then, is that British management exhibits, more than American, this sort of intense cooperation between academia and praxis. They work together on actual problems.

Philip Nind is right about the nature of British management education. He is also right when he attributes the British emphasis on joint development activities, action learning, and action research to "our

60 Philip Nind, "The Challenge of the Eighties," *The Business Graduate,* special issue (1981): 34–35.
61 Social Science Research Council (S.S.R.C.), *Report on Research and Doctoral Training,* 1978.
62 For a description, see R. W. Revans, "The Nature of Action Learning," *OMEGA* 9:1 (1981): 9–24.

cultural environment, our education system and our social attitudes."[63] But in this instance he is making a virtue out of necessity, for
the peculiarities of British management education reflect the deep-
seated distrust of academia that bewitches British managers. Because
of this distrust, the M.B.A., who is hired regularly in America, is
rejected in Great Britain. British business schools have turned to joint
development schemes, whatever their intrinsic educational merits, for
a very practical reason: to keep their doors open.

A need to accommodate has not been forced on schools uniquely by
business and industry. The greater educational establishment, too, is
suspicious of the business school. The business schools have really
never been fully incorporated into the university. Their professors do
not have proper scientific qualifications, many not possessing Ph.D.s.
Their publications are skimpy (in both bulk and content). Often, for
certain fields like accounting, professors have the professional qualification (which satisfies the demands of powerful professional associations, e.g., Chartered Accountants) rather than the Ph.D. (which satisfies those of science). It is poignant to observe how business school
professors downplay their academic interests and qualifications when
approaching praxis.[64] What a contrast to German professors of business economics who insist that their discipline, as *Wissenschaft,* has
much to offer business and industry! What a contrast with the best
American business schools, with their Nobel Prize winners and respectability within the academic community! Even the financial position of
business studies within the university makes them academically un-
sure. Business schools, at least many of them, including the most prestigious (London, Manchester, Cranfield, etc.) are not, although technically classified as such, normal university institutions. Much funding
must, unlike in other university departments, be earned from outside
sources, from services rendered to, and paid for by, government and
business organizations. The British business school, therefore, is not so
institutionally insulated, like the German, from the outside world. The
financial independence which permits the German professors to develop disciplines according to the dictates of *Wissenschaft* does not

63 He is probably wrong, at least partially, when he discusses American education.
   Although Americans move, without experience, from undergraduate to M.B.A. programs, this is not true in elite schools which insist on work experience. The work
   experience had by the American M.B.A. students in elite schools does not suffer by
   comparison.
64 Brochures about programs stress the years of practical experience the staff has had.

exist for the British business school, and there is a dark suspicion that this is true because the rest of the British university's scientific community does not think business studies are respectable *Wissenschaft*. A kind of hucksterism results in British business schools, born of the necessity to earn money from a business clientele that has no use for academics and never did.

It must not be thought, however, that the business schools are just the poor victims of a conservative educational establishment. The situation is much more complicated, and in order to see just how complicated, the development of the binary educational policy in British higher education must be considered. When the universities expanded rapidly in the early 1960s, people did not talk about a binary system of higher education that would permit nonuniversity institutions of higher education to issue degrees. The growing university sector alone sufficed. In the mid-1960s, however, a C.N.A.A., Council for National Academic Achievement, was created. The C.N.A.A. is not an educational institution; it is a supervisory body that awards degrees to people who study in programs at certain institutions, institutions that are not, like universities, empowered to grant degrees. Obviously, in order for its degrees to attain a university equivalency, the C.N.A.A. needed to find appropriate nonuniversity institutions to carry on the instruction. Hence with the C.N.A.A. came the polytechnics, that is, institutions, financed by local authorities, created either outright or by the upgrading of subuniversity schools (technical colleges, commercial colleges, normal schools, and colleges of continuing education) that had existed for decades. The polytechnics, then, became the institutions in which people who got C.N.A.A. degrees received their education. They, with the universities, constituted this binary system of higher education.

Until recently, when the C.N.A.A. authorized M.B.A. programs in selected schools, polytechnics had neglected graduate management education.[65] In them, therefore, management education has been undertaken primarily at the first-degree level. Since first degrees in management studies can now also be obtained at British universities, a full array of management degrees (from first degrees, to masters, and Ph.D.s) is offered there (see Table 5.3). British university education does not resemble American, not, at least, in its recent evolution.

65 Dr. Anthony Saw, C.N.A.A., London, Dec. 10, 1983, personal interview.

Table 5.3. *First degrees in Great Britain*

	1976	1977	1978	1979	1980	1981	1982
Polytechnics							
Management Studies	895	968	1,149	1,417	1,616	1,684	1,850
Economics	413	330	423	498	578	521	533
Accountancy (after 1981 + banking & finance)	100	166	249	366	210	526	541
Universities							
Business & Management	700	785	788	905	1,024	1,209	1,271
Economics	1,791	1,855	2,151	2,174	2,174	2,272	2,425
Accountancy	299	498	747	784	866	837	949
Totals							
Management Studies	1,595	1,753	1,937	2,322	2,640	2,893	3,121
Economics	2,204	2,185	2,574	2,672	2,752	2,793	2,958
Accountancy	399	664	996	1,150	1,076	1,363	1,490

Source: C.N.A.A., "Directions of First Degree and Diploma of Higher Education Courses, 1976–82"; U.C.C.A., *Annual Reports*, 1–22, 1963–84, published with annual, *Statistical Supplement.*

Table 5.4. *Degrees awarded in British universities*

	1975	1976	1977	1978	1979	1980
Business Management Studies	856	817	939	1,051	1,102	1,102
Economics	602	678	758	702	690	633
Accountancy	45	62	52	58	73	77

Note: These statistics combine all graduate degrees. Therefore masters and Ph.D.s are included. Since most of the degrees are masters (M.B.A.s or equivalent masters under business management studies), very few could be Ph.D.s. Hence, in numbers, doctorates are few in comparison to those awarded in Germany and in the United States.
Source: University Central Council on Admissions, *Statistical Supplements,* 1975–80.

Management education started in graduate schools, primarily in the M.B.A. program (see Table 5.4); then it moved in the late 1970s to undergraduate levels. The quite different American tradition began with undergraduate education, which was the mainstay of business schools before the war and, if less important than graduate, also grew rapidly immediately after.

Why create a binary system of higher education when the universities were expanding so rapidly? The answer was, and is, to provide a different sort of higher education. The polytechnics stress practicality. The C.N.A.A. business studies degrees are earned in sandwich

Table 5.5. *Numbers of reported arts and sciences publications (1970–1979)*

Institution	Arts	Sciences	Institution	Arts	Sciences
Universities			Polytechnics		
Bangor	2,161	2,575	Hatfield	209	650
Bath	1,638	2,584	Huddersfield	1,188	589
Belfast	2,445	6,105	Kingston	707	920
Durham	2,720	2,785	Central London	488	664
Kent	1,950	1,590	Oxford	803	672
Leicester	3,077	4,577	Paisley	213	686
Salford	834	4,668	Plymouth	407	1,090
Stirling	1,632	1,455	Sunderland	492	948
Warwick	2,457	2,461	Wales	364	751
York	2,919	1,956	Wolverhampton	406	274
Total	21,833	30,756		5,277	7,244
Percentage	41.5	58.5		42.2	57.8

Source: W. O. George and B. C. Thomas, "When the Lines Become Blurred," *Times Higher Educational Supplement,* no. 593 (March 16, 1984), 13.

courses, that is, with periods of on-the-job training alternating with periods of classroom instruction. Sandwich courses at the undergraduate level are seldom encountered in universities. Pedagogical arguments can be made in favor of sandwich schemes, and they will be considered in the next chapter. At this juncture what matters is how binary education reflects British educational cultural heritages. The attitude of people in praxis should be apparent by now. Polytechnics are popular with them because of their practical orientation. Since university-educated businessmen would not want their children educated in polytechnics, the old class view seems inescapable: The polytechnics are vocational and hence for the laboring classes; the children of top managers are destined for the university elite. What about the educational establishment? A study of comparable institutions in the university and the polytechnic sectors shows that research (measured in terms of publications) is much stronger among university academics (see Table 5.5). Since research depends on funding, these studies do not tell whether the funding agencies are prejudiced against polytechnic professors, as opposed to university, and hence discriminate when awarding grants. If that were the case, then fewer publications might reveal less about research talents than institutional snobbism.[66] That the polytechnics are looked upon as inferior

66 Who sits on the agencies that grant the research money? One Economic and Social Research Council (E.S.R.C.) committee, on which the author sat, did not have a single person from a polytechnic on it, and this committee was involved in drafting guidelines for research that led to numerous grants.

certainly is the case. Witness the controversy in the *Times Higher Educational Supplement* over the failure of the universities to adopt the sandwich teaching method, leaving it to the polytechnics.[67] Assumptions are made that the sandwich method is suited more to vocational than scientific instruction, i.e., to the polytechnics rather than the universities. Witness, too, the fact that polytechnics take students that universities reject (A-level grades of polytechnic entrants are two points lower than those of university entrants). The binary policy, if not itself a reflection of the prejudices of universities against low-status technical and commercial education, perpetuates that prejudice through the different status accorded polytechnics and universities.

The social prejudices voiced within the academic community, on both sides of the binary line, are also directed at business schools; for, if they are attacked by university people in the older, established disciplines, they are also attacked by professors in the polytechnics. Professor Newbigging, of the Central London Polytechnic, evaluating Britain's elite business schools, observed that

[T]he so-called classical or liberal education, [with its] call for the education of generalists, and the Anglo-Saxon model of "profession" have all promoted a middle class professional ethic which continues to maintain a dubious distinction from a world of work. The development of UK management education has reinforced the idea of the manager as a separate profession. Strengthened by the growth of management science it has encouraged the pursuit of personal status within organisations rather than a concern with the excellence of the product.[68]

Newbigging, then, echoes the criticism raised against the traditional professions in Britain, that they express the gentleman's disdain for industry and trade. The accusation seems incongruous in a business school context since the schools propose to improve management. But the critics say, and there is much merit in their argument, that the business schools, especially London, recruit people working in production, engineering, and manufacturing functions, retrain them for finance, banking, and consultancy or, if for industry, not for the technical functions they did before attending business school. This educational process shifts managerial talent away from the economic sector that needs it so desperately. The argument is interesting as much for its

67 Fall 1983.
68 "Management Development," 11.

very existence as its intrinsic merits. The attack on the business schools manifests the perennial clash between low-status, low-class, technical manufacturing and upper-class, commercial-financial, professional, gentry-aristocratic Britain. Expressed originally in the advocacy of a technical education for the lower classes and a useless classical education for the elite, during the educational expansion period after 1960 it continues in the binary system of management education. Newbigging's annoyance with the business schools' attempt to create a managerial profession need not be a class reaction. In America criticism of business schools and their alumni carries no such connotation. But when the idea of a professional manager moves across the Atlantic it absorbs class distinctions. Commenting on the German failure to develop either a professional corps or the concept of manager, Newbigging remarks:

The Germans distinguish *Führung* (entrepreneurial management) from *Leitung* (line management) and have established identities such as *Techniker* (engineer/technologist). These differences stem from the culture and the development of managers in Germany – which is specifically vocational. The special British emphasis upon some generalized activity called management has been at the expense of those who carry out more specific activities particularly those concerned with manufacturing.[69]

He and others in polytechnics resent the business schools for the same reason they resent the public schools: They express themselves, with their professional strivings, in class terms.

The resentments are not imaginary. Recently at lunch a business school professor seemed startled by the question: "What contribution does this school make toward improving British productivity?" He acted as if the question had never crossed his mind. What had occurred to him and to others at the school, since it is very much a part of its public relations propaganda, is how attendance there enhances the student's subsequent career. Abundant data are given out about that to prospective students. It is, in short, entirely possible for an elite to improve its status within a community at the expense of the community. And the suspicion among some that this has happened with business schools is very strong.

That suspicion colors relationships, moreover, among business schools as well as between business schools and polytechnics. Man-

69 Ibid., 10.

chester and London suffer from status conflicts that go beyond normal school rivalry. Manchester recruits more students (15 percent to London's 0 percent) from the working classes. London's graduates get better jobs at higher pay. London's graduates, however, suffer themselves vis à vis Harvard's and those of other major American business schools (and some continental European, e.g., I.N.S.E.A.D.). The personnel recruitment policies, for instance, at the Boston Consulting Group, London office, reflect this status consciousness. The company is looking for "high flyers," very bright men and women who can talk to top people in top firms about major business problems (i.e., strategy).[70] The firm recruits from the best American business schools and from Oxbridge. Thus London and other British business schools especially are overlooked, for, if graduates from Oxford and Cambridge might attend a short postexperience course in a business school, it is their undergraduate education that constitutes the decisive employment factor. Since Oxford and Cambridge espouse traditional forms of education (i.e., engineering is downgraded and no business schools have been founded there), to prefer their graduates to those of the business schools and management faculties of other universities is to prefer students in the classics, modern history, economics, and natural science, i.e., to frustrate the educational reforms embodied in the business schools and perpetuate not only the traditional elites but the traditional forms of education.

Talk among businessmen about the relative effectiveness of experience versus formal management education also seems a less objective evaluation of skills than a defense of vested social interests which business schools threaten. A. Robertson observed in 1970 that

British business regards general management posts as *rewards* for performance in other things. What the young business school alumnus is asking for, then, is looked upon as a status post, and to insist on it will not only put up the backs of senior management and of peers in the company, but may act in the long run as a deterrent to firms sending young men and women on long courses that may engender such awkward ambitions. Resistance to extending formal education for management will harden if the redundant army of middle managers and its core of top managers is thought to be endangered by every wave of intake from the schools.[71]

70 Interview with Mauricio Gonzales Sfeir, B.C.G., London, Apr. 13, 1984.
71 A. Robertson, "Business Schools: Is the Backlash Justified?" *Management Decisions* 4:3 (Autumn 1970): 14; cited in Thomas, "Management and Education," 101.

This is a serious accusation, for it means that the senior managers are not promoting into middle management on merit perceived during years of experience but on old school ties. That is what promotion criteria like innate qualities (leadership, courage, decisiveness, judgment) as opposed to business knowledge acquired in the schools can mean. The former express class as much as individual qualities. Business schools, by making business learnable, open management ranks to individuals of merit, the wrong sort of people. So a double snobbery is at play. Educated in public schools, the traditional elite, in order to maintain its position, discriminates against the business school graduate; the business school graduate resents this discrimination but, fleeing the low-status manufacturing employments, discriminates himself against the low-status polytechnic's graduate.

The antimanagement education prejudices encountered in praxis and in academia permeate broad elements of British society. They show up especially in secondary education. Table 5.6 compares the top twenty subjects selected over a fifteen-year period by entering university students in Great Britain and West Germany. Among the subjects many are common to both lists. Law, medicine, mathematics, the physical sciences, the national language, and the engineering sciences count among the top twenty in each country throughout the period examined. But the differences are most significant. First, the humanities (history, classics) hold a more prominent place in British studies than in German. Only foreign languages, which have roots in the humanities, are strongly represented in Germany. But modern foreign languages (English and French) are also considered to be practical subjects. Historically their adoption in the curricula meant that the old humanistic view of education was giving way to the needs of a commercial and industrial society. A second difference is the German emphasis on education. This stress includes teacher training for vocational schools. Third, although economics ranks among the top twenty subjects studied in both countries, the position of business studies on the lists is different. Business economics (B.W.L.) is very high on the German lists; business studies does not appear on the British list until 1980, and then it appears in seventeenth place when it ranked second in Germany. This comparison confirms the low status of undergraduate business education in Britain. It demonstrates how certain features of British education persistently shape university education, i.e., the humanistic-science emphasis and the

Table 5.6. *Top subjects studied in Britain and West Germany (number of students)*

Britain		West Germany		Britain		West Germany	
1966 (56,222 total)		1967 (57,898 total)		1971 (64,985 total)		1970 (66,108 total)	
1. Chemistry	3,308	1. Law	6,271	1. Mathematics	3,800	1. Educ.	14,451
2. Mathematics	3,292	2. Medicine	4,462	2. Medicine	3,289	2. Mathematics	4,984
3. Medicine	2,655	3. German	3,318	3. Law	2,745	3. Law	4,286
4. Elec. Eng.	2,443	4. Mathematics	2,823	4. English	2,618	4. German	3,122
5. English	2,329	5. Life Sciences	2,808	5. Chemistry	2,526	5. Bus. Econ.	2,681
6. Physics	2,315	6. Bus. Econ.	2,762	6. Physics	2,377	6. English	2,520
7. Law	2,102	7. English	2,595	7. Elec. Eng.	2,377	7. Second. Educ.	2,478
8. Sociology	2,097	8. Chemistry	2,352	8. Civ. Eng.	2,152	8. Chemistry	2,289
9. Mech. Eng.	2,027	9. Pri. Educ.	2,330	9. History	2,086	9. Medicine	2,241
10. Civ. Eng.	1,920	10. Physical Sc.	2,056	10. Geography	1,765	10. Mech. Eng.	2,137
11. History	1,895	11. Economics	2,024	11. Mech. Eng.	1,765	11. Physical Sc.	2,016
12. Geography	1,604	12. Elec. Eng.	1,750	12. Econ.	1,724	12. Elec. Eng.	1,723
13. Econ.	1,566	13. Psychology	1,737	13. Sociology	1,313	13. Life Sc.	1,662
14. French	1,028	14. Sec. Educ.	1,585	14. French	1,183	14. Civ. Eng.	1,379
15. Chem. Eng.	869	15. Mech. Eng.	1,568	15. Biology	1,024	15. Econ.	1,239
16. Biology	836	16. Pharmacy	1,342	16. Dentistry	933	16. Voc. Educ.	1,116
17. Dentistry	796	17. French	1,268	17. Psychology	833	17. Psychology	1,076
18. Zoology	723	18. Sociology	1,114	18. Biochem.	858	18. Gen. Pedagogy	999
19. Psychology	691	19. Dentistry	1,098	19. Pharmacy	748	19. Econ. Sc.	935
20. Classics	680	20. Vet. Med.	901	20. Business	744	20. Sociology	911
1976 (77,830 total)		1976 (85,337 total)		1980 (81,013 total)		1980 (116,349 total)	
1. Mathematics	3,809	1. Elec. Eng.	10,639	1. Medicine	3,997	1. Law	11,350
2. Medicine	3,742	2. Mech. Eng.	9,552	2. Law	3,566	2. Bus. Econ.	8,619
3. Law	3,389	3. Law	8,856	3. Elec. Eng.	3,257	3. Adm. Scs.	8,469
4. English	3,031	4. Econ. Scs.	7,022	4. Mathematics	3,066	4. Econ. Scs.	8,268
5. Elec. Eng..	2,848	5. Sociology	5,834	5. English	3,030	5. Elec. Eng.	8,251
6. History	2,626	6. Bus. Econ.	5,652	6. Physics	2,853	6. Mech. Eng.	8,078
7. Chemistry	2,545	7. Medicine	5,094	7. Chemistry	2,693	7. German	7,971
8. Civ. Eng.	2,451	8. Civ. Eng.	5,043	8. History	2,554	8. Medicine	6,871
9. Mech. Eng.	2,222	9. Architecture	4,160	9. Mech. Eng.	2,191	9. Architecture	5,708
10. Physics	2,218	10. Chemistry	3,583	10. Geography	2,095	10. Biology	5,150
11. Economics	2,073	11. Mathematics	3,380	11. Computers	2,085	11. Chemistry	4,841
12. Geography	2,073	12. Pedagogy	2,962	12. Economics	1,983	12. Mathematics	4,805
13. Biology	1,781	13. Physics	2,931	13. Biology	1,920	13. Civ. Eng.	4,600
14. Sociology	1,391	14. Economics	2,651	14. Civ. Eng.	1,885	14. Pedagogy	4,406
15. Business	1,330	15. Communicat.	1,836	15. Psychology	1,396	15. English	4,388
16. Psychology	1,255	16. Psychology	1,721	16. Sociology	1,332	16. Physics	3,514
17. Biochemistry	1,184	17. Biology	1,598	17. Business	1,262	17. Sociology	3,157
18. French	1,175	18. Sociology	1,418	18. French	1,143	18. Psychology	2,571
19. Dentistry	946	(Last two missing)		19. Biochemistry	1,084	19. History	2,438
20. Chem. Eng.	914			20. Chem. Eng.	978	20. Sports	2,894

Source: Compiled from The University Central Council on Admissions, *Statistical Supplements,* "Examination Qualifications and Subjects of Acceptances,"1966–81, and from the *Statistische Jahrbücher* (Wiesbaden), 1966–80.

weakness of economic purposeful education despite a period of significant reform (post-1960).

Other studies confirm these conclusions. A survey of British graduates' career choices at the beginning of the reform period (the class of 1960) shows 50 percent of those with first class honors degrees and one-third of those with upper seconds wished to ignore employment in business and industry by staying within the university community. "There was no question," the investigators observed, "that in terms of

Table 5.7. *British university admissions*

Subject	Proportion of Students with Good A levels admitted
Top three (of 13 subjects)	
Medicine	45
Classics	38
Mathematics	36
Bottom three (of 13 subjects)	
Civil Engineering	12
Mechanical Engineering	11
Business Management	5

Source: Hermann Bayer and Peter Lawrence, "Engineering Education and the Status of Industry," *European Journal of Engineering Education* 2 (1977): 223-27, 224.

preferences the professions and perhaps most seriously of all, management, appealed particularly to the academically less qualified man. . . . Key posts in the industrial sectors are for one reason or another distinctly unattractive to those who have shown themselves most able to absorb intellectual heritage."[72] Hermann Bayer and Peter Lawrence, using statistics published by the Universities Central Council on Admissions, found similar preferences for a later period. They observed that top British sixth form A-level students opted for the humanities or pure sciences. Table 5.7 shows, for example, the proportion of students admitted to British universities with good A levels, by field study, in 1974.

A comparison of the British and the German experience with the Japanese is also instructive. Professor Michio Morishima remarks that

the first clause of the Imperial University Edict of 1886 . . . states [that] the Imperial University shall have as its purpose instruction in the arts and sciences such as accords with the cardinal principles of the state and research into their deepest mysteries. Japanese higher education did not exist for the sake of the individual; the individual was educated for the state in accordance with the needs of the state.[73]

Since the Japanese state engaged in a relentless quest to overcome, indeed to end, the technological-industrial supremacy of the West, the Japanese system of higher education, from its reform in the nineteenth

72 R. K. Kelsall, Ann Pool, and Annette Kuhn, *Graduates: The Sociology of an Elite* (London, 1972), 85.
73 *The Production of Technologists and Robotization in Japan* (London, n.d.), 2. Suntory Toyota, International Centre for Economics and Related Disciplines, London School of Economics and Political Science.

Table 5.8. *Students obtaining degrees in Britain and Japan (1982)*

	Japan		Britain		3* Together
Science	Graduate School	2,821	Higher Degree	5,520	10,322
	National University	6,024	First Degree	20,839	38,969
	Private University	7,773	Higher Natl. Diploma	2,209	4,130
Engineering	Graduate School	7,489	Higher Degree	3,855	7,209
	National University	21,936	First Degree	15,350	28,704
	Private University	41,696	Higher Natl. Diploma	15,471	28,931

*Column 3 adjusts the Japanese figures to population. In 1980 "the economically active population working in Japan's industrial sector . . . was around 1.87 times the figure for the U.K. in the same year." The figures in column 3 are obtained by multiplying British numbers by 1.87. The result is the number of Japanese needed to have equivalency with Britain when population differences are considered. (The statistics for Junior Colleges and Technological Colleges [Japan] and for the Ordinary National Diploma, which are on original chart, have been omitted because they are not considered to be representative of higher education.)
Source: Japanese figures calculated from Statistics Bureau, Prime Minister's Office, Japan Statistical Yearbook, 1983. British figures in Department of Education and Science and Others, *Education Statistics for the United Kingdom,* 1984. From Michio Morishima, *The Production of Technologists and Robotization in Japan* (London, n.d.), 15.

century to the present, acted accordingly. Professor Morishima's chart (see Table 5.8) indicates how this policy has affected the patterns of study in Japanese universities. Obviously these statistics mirror traditional British respect for pure, as opposed to applied, sciences and engineering. Inasmuch as they include C.N.A.A. degrees as well as university degrees and since most of the engineering degrees are probably C.N.A.A. degrees, they surely hide the extent to which British universities avoid engineering. The statistics also record the results of the Japanese state's systematic encouragement of technologies instead of *Wissenschaft*. Although Japanese numerical superiority in such degrees cannot in itself explain the country's ability to sustain rapid high-tech growth (just as important, Professor Morishima observes, is very efficient management of available manpower), the numbers do affirm a much greater emphasis in Japan on practical purposive education.[74]

In this respect the German system of higher education resembles the Japanese more than the British. Professor Morishima, using foreign membership in the American Academy of Arts and Sciences as a yardstick for measuring a country's prowess in basic research, constructed a chart (see Table 5.9) that suggests a similarity. Morishima's point is that Japan's emphasis on technologists instead of scientists has led to

74 Morishima, *The Production of Technologists*, 15–16. He says that in fact Japan has a great shortage of technicians for its needs and only through their expert utilization has management been able to prevent the shortage from having harmful results.

Table 5.9. *The American Academy of Arts and Sciences' international distribution of foreign honorary members (1985)*

	Mathematical & Physical Sciences	Biological Sciences	Social Arts & Soc. Sc.	Humanities	Total
UK	39	50	39	54	182
France	18	10	14	17	59
Soviet Union	21	5	2	4	32
W. Germany	7	10	4	10	31
Japan	7	8	4	3	22
Italy	3	3	1	9	16
Others	41	44	41	31	157

Source: Michio Morishima, *The Production of Technologists and Robotization in Japan* (London, n.d.), p. 28.

Table 5.10. *Balance of payments – money earned from patents acquired abroad*

	With USA	With Others	Total
England	-61	+38	-23
France	-48	+14	-34
West Germany	-55	+14	-41
Japan	-80	-30	-110
USA	--	--	+298

Source: "Importer de la matière grise," *Hommes et techniques* 25: 292 (Feb. 1969): 117.

the country's "poverty in basic knowledge."[75] Whether the West Germans' contribution to basic knowledge is also minimal is perhaps debatable. But the once-dominant position German universities held in scientific discovery has certainly been eroded since the war. If Morishima's comparison is correct, the small number of Germans in the American Academy of Arts and Sciences could be attributed to the German emphasis on occupational purposive study rather than value-free research. Could it have had a similar effect on Germany's capacity to produce basic knowledge? *Hommes et techniques* (see Table 5.10) in 1969 registered the "balance of payments" for money earned on patents in foreign countries (balance of payments with the United States.) West Germany is tops among European countries for borrowers of ideas, although the Japanese are the great borrowers.[76]

Morishima's conclusion that Japanese "industry has ended up by putting learning in a totally dependent position," might seem surprising, considering the nature of Japanese postexperience education.[77]

75 Ibid.
76 "Importer de la matière grise," 25:292 [Feb. 1969]: 117.
77 Ibid., 30.

Like the Germans, but more so, Japanese industry either trains its own people or sends them to nonuniversity training centers. Japanese universities would seem to be independent of business and industry. British industry, by contrast, is more closely integrated with universities and polytechnics than Japanese or German when it comes to project work and postexperience education. But the Japanese and, if to a lesser degree, the German systems of education channel university students, in number and quality, into more economically useful studies than does the English. All the talk about the estrangement in Germany between praxis and *Wissenschaft* and about British practicality (sandwich courses, joint development activity) is deceiving.

Why not business schools in Britain? The answer is that there are business schools which are the creation of the serious reforms in British education which came after 1960. But the answer is also that they are very different from American, different in their structure, with more emphasis on graduate postexperience education, and in their clientele. Structure and clientele are in fact interrelated, and that interrelationship has been affected by the ability of advocates of pre-reform educational traditions to circumvent reform. The B.C.G. episode illustrates how it works. Although the elite business schools have been in existence for almost twenty years, a major business consultancy firm chooses to ignore the premier British business schools for the elite educated in the traditional way. The choice probably makes sense as far as B.C.G.'s clientele is concerned. A B.C.G. consultant would be dealing with top management, with a social type (e.g., public school, Oxbridge, of those who conform to their modes of behavior), whose favor they would have to curry to succeed. To gain their confidence, to appear intelligent and capable, the consultant has to be like them. A person from the wrong school, with the wrong accent, has an uphill struggle, not because he is incapable or unintelligent but because perceptions of ability and intelligence are socially shaped.

The survival of the traditional modes of education, indeed their capacity to flourish side by side with the reform system, is a peculiarity of the British system. It has a lot to do with the absence of a bureaucratic state tradition.[78] The government has never tried to dictate curricula content to the schools. Consequently, conservative educators could resist the new. It makes the polytechnic not only a place where one can get a

---

78 Archer, *Social Origins of Educational Systems.*

university degree (first or graduate through the C.N.A.A.) but a place where the ordinary national certificate (O.N.C.), the higher national certificate (H.N.C.), the diploma in management studies (D.M.S.), and other subuniversity diplomas can be earned.[79] Because these subsystems are not just a different but an inferior kind of education, one the upper classes have shunned because of its vulgar connotations, to perpetuate it in the polytechnic is to perpetuate the stigma of social inferiority in this institution. Students are not stupid and they will avoid the place if possible. For the bright ones it is possible. Hence they opt to go to the universities.

As for the universities, they do not want to be tarred with the brush of inferiority either. That, traditionally, had been the fate of the redbricks, the civic universities that did so much, compared to Oxbridge, to further engineering education in England. But they did comparatively less well in business education, especially at the undergraduate level. The past tense must be used, of course, for in recent years undergraduate enrollment in business studies has grown impressively in British universities. If the trend continues the business studies first degree might, as a percentage of university graduates, rival the German. And this change would undoubtedly have an impact on graduate studies in British business schools. But it has not happened yet. Oxford and Cambridge in particular, with their powerful networks, hold out against business studies just as they did against commerce degrees between the wars. With Oxbridge, unless it loses its influence, the business studies major will always look and perhaps remain second-rate.[80]

The pre-reform university's capacity to survive, moreover, is deeply rooted in the education order. The roots extend into the secondary school system. That secondary system survived the Second World War in the tripartite scheme recognized by the Education Act of 1944: grammar schools for the university-bound, classically educated scholars; technical schools for those going into industry; and secondary modern for most of the British population – for those whose education was neither vocational nor scholarly, i.e., inferior in every respect. The Labour Party succeeded in abolishing the tripartite system and

79 All nondegrees of vocational repute.
80 Witness the writing done by management professors in a section of the *Times Higher Educational Supplement* 13:4 (1984): i–vii on "Management Education." In terms of analytical and literary skills the writing, compared to that of other academics in the issue, is quite mediocre.

replacing it with modern comprehensive schools. This brought the dismantlement of a system of state-supported elite schools. The result has, however, been the opposite of that intended. If the destruction of the grammar schools ended elite state education, elitism has continued unabated in the form of fee-paying independent public schools. The independent public schools had always been there, of course, educating the privileged few. They found themselves strengthened by the egalitarian reform, for the good grammar schools have chosen to renounce state funding in order to remain elitist, but now financially independent public schools, rather than convert themselves into state-financed comprehensives. And the great British middle-class public has responded by sending their children to them. The result is the resurgence of public schools in Britain.[81]

From an engineering and business perspective, the independent schools do not necessarily continue to provide people with antiquated educations. Anthony Sampson writes:

The ignorance is less marked than it was. Over the last twenty years headmasters, with some prodding from industry, have encouraged boys towards science and engineering, and many more public school boys now take engineering degrees. Some headmasters looked forward to an ultimate breakdown of the barriers between the arts and sciences. The headmaster of Eton in 1961, Robert Birley, told me: "Our ambition is to have the head of Harwell Research Station, an Old Etonian who learnt Greek at Eton and read the lesson at Harwell Parish Church." But the gulf between arts graduates and scientists remains as wide as ever, and the strands of politics and science remain very separate, even under a scientist prime minister. "Scientists are still narrowly educated," said John Rae. "There's really a three-way split between scientists, technicians and the arts."[82]

It is indeed the survival of this three-way split that the secondary schools, despite the abolition of the tripartite system and the adoption of comprehensives, protect. The key to survival is the A-level examination which every sixth form (16 to 18 years) has to take to enter a university. The English sixth form is unique because of the degree of specialization it permits or rather requires, since its education is shaped by university-set A-level examination requirements. "Students," A. G. Howson observes,

81 Anthony Sampson, *The Changing Anatomy of Britain* (New York, 1984); see chap. 7 "Schools: The Private Resurgence" for a good discussion.
82 *The Times,* Sept. 30, 1975, quoted in Sampson, *The Changing Anatomy of Britain,* 127.

need only study three main subjects (in addition to physical and religious education and the odd hour or two devoted to "culture"). These could be "Pure Mathematics," "Applied Mathematics," and "Physics" – scarcely a balanced education. On the other hand they might be English, French, and German. Thus many very bright and mathematically able children study no more mathematics after the age of 16.[83]

The specialization necessitates that only the best-prepared students, an elite, do A levels in mathematics, for the examination is rigorous. And it also means that the attempted democratization of the school system (the comprehensives) had to fail because of the failure simultaneously to democratize A levels. No parent in his right mind would send his children through comprehensive schools when the chances to pass the A levels would be improved by attending an independent public school.

The narrow degree of specialization, moreover, contributes to the survival of the two cultures in English academia because it permits the sciences and humanities – it almost forces them in fact – to ignore each other. More significantly, the specialization separates the arts and sciences from the technologies. The new paradigm in business studies requires minimal skills in mathematics (statistics, probability theory, matrix algebra) that sixth-form students who avoided mathematics do not have. If they wish to study business in university they have to acquire numerate skills, a daunting prospect. Sixth-form students who prepare mathematics at A level could certainly do the mathematics needed in business studies and engineering. But they are few in number. Moreover, because of specialization, the good A-level mathematics students intend to do mathematics or physical science in the university. If business studies at university required A-level mathematics for entry, they would not attract mathematicians and they would eliminate arts majors. A-level specialization, therefore, channels the best mathematicians away from business and engineering.

The French post-1960 reform experience

The American business school offered comprehensive education: undergraduate degrees, taught masters, research doctorates, and postexperience education. This education forms a self-contained whole because it is self-perpetuating: The professors who educate the students

83 A. G. Howson, "Changes in Mathematics Education," 192.

are themselves trained in the system which they help develop. Of all the educational traditions studied here, the German is closest to the American in this respect. Although it stays out of postexperience education, it is self-contained; it generates researchers and teachers. The British system, which had to be created almost from scratch after 1960, lacks the research tradition. Indeed, it suffers from a schizophrenia, for to it the idea that business studies is a *Wissenschaft* is an alien concept. The French reforms in business studies suffered from different prejudices. Since French *grandes écoles* of commerce had existed for decades and since graduates from these schools had found top positions in management, French business employed many management school graduates. The French problem was not one of establishing relationships between educational establishment and praxis but of introducing the new management science paradigm into business educational establishments.[84]

The difficulty arises from the inherited educational effects within their dual system of higher education. The university system is self-contained, that is, it provides for the education of the professors who develop the disciplines (the researchers and teachers) that are imparted to the students. Had the universities been involved in management education, they could have quickly learned about the new paradigm from the Americans, assimilated it, developed it through research, and trained the requisite teachers to pass it on to the students. But the universities did not teach business economics or management. They did not even, as stressed in the last chapter, teach modern economics after the war. That went on in the *grandes écoles* of engineering. The *grandes écoles* of commerce, the French equivalent of business schools, did teach business, but because they were not research institutions they did not possess properly qualified researchers or teachers, or have the capacity, institutionally, to generate them. During the post-1960s reforms, institutional habits seriously hindered the development of the new management paradigm in both educational sectors.

The 1950s had not left universities unreformed. But reforms in the faculties of law, with one exception (the creation of the I.A.E., *Instituts d'administration des entreprises*), sought to modernize economics.[85] By 1963, with the establishment of a new faculty of economic

---

84 Meuleau, "Les HEC."
85 First came general reforms. Wickham noted the need to change the education of law students: "Rather than a highly diversified *culture générale* and good humor and

sciences, the old guard finally lost. A particularly important point, moreover, had been conceded even before the Second World War, with the creation of an *agrégation* in economics. The *agrégation* is a degree essential to the existence of a university discipline, for it is the qualification Frenchmen must have to be professors. Before 1935 there was no *agrégation* in economics, hence professors who taught economics usually had an *agrégation* in law, a very unsatisfactory situation for the self-conscious, ambitious, young discipline. As a result of these reforms by the beginning of the 1960s there were separate faculties for economic studies that offered the full gamut of degrees in economics from the *licence* through the *diplôme d'études supérieures,* third cycle doctorates, state doctorates, and *agrégation.*

Obviously Frenchmen, impressed with American management education, had come to appreciate neoclassical economics as an intellectual tool, useful for understanding business problems. But economics is not management; the management enthusiasts wanted their own discipline. A second fight, therefore, had to take place within economics before management-study programs developed. The reformers got what they wanted after considerable delay. The first step had come when Gaston Berger started the I.A.E. in the faculties of law. But who taught in the I.A.E.? Since there was no *agrégation* in the field yet, it could not be people who had studied management in French universities. Moreover, the doctoral problem was not solved. If instructors had doctorates, if they were French, they were in economics not in management.

The other sector, the *grandes écoles* of commerce, beginning in the late 1950s, entered a period of reform. Quantitatively the reform did

sociability" (the goals of traditional education), education had to obtain "not just applied economics but pure mathematics, moral philosophy – a demanding critical sense, even though it might be detrimental to civilized living" (Wickham, "Fonction et avenir," 268). In 1955 the curriculum for the law degree (*license*) was lengthened from three to four years, ex cathedra teaching in large lecture halls was partially replaced by seminars (Paris law faculty had to hire forty new *chargés de cours* [instructors] to handle these seminars). In 1959 mathematics was made obligatory for economics majors (in 1966 similar courses were introduced for majors in humanities). These courses covered mathematics, statistics, and computer programming (*informatique*), "not in order to train mathematicians ... but to enable the future professional economist to be able to cooperate with mathematicians who work in the same organization with him" (72). Since most economic students in law faculties had literary *baccalauréats* and, like their professors, "not only insignificant knowledge about but a distaste for everything scientific" (72), (*Revue de l'enseignement supérieur,* "Roles des Maths"), these reforms helped get rid of the "easy going manner" for which the faculty was known and were important for inculcating "the demanding critical mind" in students and faculty the reformers desired.

Table 5.11. *Enrollment in* grandes écoles *of commerce*

	1974	1975	1976	1977	1978	1979	1980	1981	1982
ESCAE (19 schools)	1,021*	1,518	1,306	1,238	1,559	1,467	1,355	1,324	1,363
HEC	274	267	265	261	265	261	279	303	297
Others, i.e., ESSEC, ESCP		611	870	880	1,378				
Total	1,957*	2,296	2,441	2,379	3,202	3,084	2,914	2,996	3,113

*Statistics missing for two schools.
Source: Ministère de l'Education Nationale, Service des Etudes Informatiques et Statistiques, *Statistiques des Elèves des Etablissements de Haut Enseignement Commercial*, various years.

not match German or American expansionism. The *grandes écoles* of commerce remained, quite proudly, elitist and selective (see Table 5.11). Nonetheless, reforms were significant. At the leading school, H.E.C. (*Ecole des hautes études commerciales*), a 1957 reform altered the entrance examination (the *concours*) and the composition of the faculty. H.E.C. had always pegged its *concours* on French secondary education, that is, on an education that had nothing whatsoever to do with the education the student received at H.E.C. Other than the dead languages, all the important subjects covered on the *baccalauréat* figured in the *concours* (French composition, modern languages, mathematics, physics, chemistry, history, and geography). The new *concours* treated the same subject areas but not the same material and not in the same way, or for the same purpose. Marc Meuleau notes: "Memorization was abandoned. French composition, limited before to the national literature, was replaced by several tests in science and human sciences, e.g., psychology, sociology, and philosophy. Economic history and geography replaced old-fashioned descriptive geography and political history."[86] Candidates were no longer examined on an acquired body of knowledge. In order to determine how well they could reflect upon and examine the implications of a topic, the *concours* now focused more on the education that existed in the H.E.C. than on what was taught in secondary school.

The second great reform created a permanent teaching faculty. Be-

86 Meuleau, "Les HEC," 48. Also see René Puiraveaux and Jean-Pierre Bertiet, "Dialogue sur l'école HEC," *Hommes et commerce*, nos. 101–103 (March–July 1968): 165–86, where, through a dialogue between two former students, one prereform and one postreform, the old H.E.C. is compared with the new.

Table 5.12. *Faculty at H.E.C.*

	1886	1895	1905	1911	1923	1936	1947	1954	1963	1972	1980
Number of Professors	30	40	44	58	63	55	93	113	179	88	101
Number of Examinateurs	7	19	29	33	40	39	60	58	--	--	--
Vacataires	--*	--	--	--	--	--	--	--	169	220	250

*Until 1963 everybody was a *vacataire*. After 1963, therefore, the permanent faculty is the professors.
Source: Marc Meuleau, *Histoire d'une grande école, H.E.C. 1881–1981* (Paris: Bordas-Dunod, 1981), 83.

fore 1963 part-time lecturers (the *vacataires*) did all the teaching at H.E.C. After, a gulf opened up between a new permanent staff and part-timers. By 1968 permanent professors taught 88 hours of courses a year to the part-timers' 47; in 1980 the respective hours were 118 to 40.[87] The appearance of a permanent corps of professors enabled H.E.C. for the first time (and other business schools in France, which also began to employ permanent professors) to develop a discipline, for the permanent professors were not, like *vacataires,* teaching non-management disciplines to a business school audience, but developing business studies itself as a discipline. To do that the permanent staff had to teach, to research, and to publish. Table 5.12 shows the evolution of the professorial corps at H.E.C.

In addition, curriculum and teaching methods changed. The undergraduate curriculum dropped the commercial and science courses that had been its mainstay. The first year was now devoted to general studies and to an introduction to management, the second to more advanced management studies and an analysis of the nature of the firm, the third to a special management project that was often done with a firm. Nineteen sixty-eight brought computer programming (by 1980 thirty terminals were available to students). Teaching methods were also reformed. "In fact," Meuleau remarked,

the reform of 1957 amounted to the adoption of American management education. . . . The school took up most of the methods it had discovered in the 1950s and the inauguration of its new installations at Jouy-en-Josas (1963) was done in the presence of the American ambassador. The organization of studies at Columbia University in 1956 – 40% lectures, 20% case studies,

87 Meuleau, "Les HEC," 82.

20% discussions after lectures, 20% seminars where students make reports that are criticized by their classmates – could be found at the school c. 1965–67. It also agreed to accept engineers seeking management education, a common practice in the United States.[88]

The other *grandes écoles* of commerce, particularly the most prestigious rivals of H.E.C. – Ecole Supérieure des Sciences Economiques et Commerciales (E.S.S.E.C.) and Ecole Supérieure de Commerce de Paris (E.S.C.P.) – introduced similar reforms *à l'américaine*. The lesser schools adapted more slowly but they could not escape the fallout from the American-induced management education explosion of the late 1960s. With the immense popularity of Jean-Jacques Schreiber's book *The American Challenge,* an aroused French public opinion made the American business school the model for business education. Great changes had occurred, too, in the new university faculties set up after the student unrest in 1968. Students were now permitted to take undergraduate degrees in applied economics, in managerial economics, in the administration of financial and banking institutions, in financial accounting and financial management, and in the management of public health and social organizations – nothing short of a major revolution in preexperience business education had happened in both sectors of education during these years (late 1960s and early 1970s).[89]

The major obstacle to reform, even in preexperience education, was an absence of qualified teachers. This obstacle neither sector could quickly overcome. Hence the creation of the F.N.E.G.E., the Fondation Nationale pour l'Enseignement de la Gestion. According to the law of "orientation," December 3, 1966, half of F.N.E.G.E.'s board would be bureaucrats (designated by government bodies [foreign affairs, finance and economics, vocational education]) and half drawn from professional groups (from a national committee of French businessmen [Conseil National du Patronat Français]). Unlike English and German organizations (the Foundation for Management Education,

---

88 Ibid., 91.
89 For the range of new studies permitted in university faculties of economics, see Ministère de l'éducation nationale, statistiques des enseignements, tableaux et information. No. 18/1982. No. 6.3. Les examens et les diplômes dans les universités. The reorganization after 1968 led to the formation of the U.E.R. in French universities. The Unité d'Enseignement et de Recherche replaced the old university faculties. The former were smaller and considered to be more logical educationally than the latter, for they were divided into fields of specialization.

Table 5.13. *French academic management education abroad*

	1969	1970	1971	1972
Source of Income				
Public (State)	FF3,950,000	1,000,000	2,100,000	5,950,000
Private	320,000	2,100,000	2,100,000	2,700,000
Complémentaire et/ ou affectés		2,300,000	3,300,000	2,600,000
Total	4,270,000	5,400,000	7,500,000	11,250,000
Annual Expenses in %				
Programs for foreign education	44	68	63	51
Programs for education in France and in Europe	3	6	14	19
Programs for conferences and study groups	20		3.5	6
Programs for pedagogical and methodological research		3	3.5	5

Source: F.N.E.G.E., "Rapport d'activité exercise 1972," *Enseignement et gestion*, no. 5 (1972).

Wuppertaler-Kreis), F.N.E.G.E. was government supported. It was hoped that through this organizational structure, the government, educational institutions, businessmen, and industrialists would get behind management education.

Since French higher education in 1969 could not train professors and since American business schools could, F.N.E.G.E. decided to send prospective French professors of management to America. From 1969 to 1973, in fact, the organization centered its efforts on *formation de formateurs* (educating the educators) in America. The statistics in Table 5.13 show the extent of the effort. Although French students could and did study on individual scholarships awarded by F.N.E.G.E., the foundation worked out special programs with business schools at Northwestern, the University of Texas (Austin), and Sherbrooke (Canada). Usually the students spent some time on study programs and meetings before leaving France (*programmes d'études, d'échanges, et de rencontres* [study programs, exchanges, and meetings]). Then about 30 percent of them entered three-year doctoral programs while the others took either one-year individual courses or a one-year course tailored by the host school especially for the French. In the years 1969–72, 210 people underwent such education.[90] It was, with the program of the Collège Interuniversitaire d'Etudes Doctorales dans les Sciences du Management (C.I.M.) in Belgium, the most direct appeal to American business school expertise in Europe.[91] It led, consequently, to the importation into France of American teaching and research methods. French management literature, if not actually American (in English or translated), leans heavily, when written by these returning students, on American works.

Recourse to America was an expediency. In order to be self-sufficient French higher education had to educate its own management professors. F.N.E.G.E. began to shift its resources away from the foreign management-education programs in 1973; in fact, the shift can already be discerned in 1972 when 19 percent of the foundation's expenditures went into a program for education of management professors in France and in Europe. This meant that the French sought to provide their own management instructors. In the universities there was an inevitable period of transition required for management science to insinuate itself into every level of the educational process.[92] Since the first two years of university work, for the D.E.U.G. (*Diplôme d'études universitaires générales*), was rather general, the D.E.U.G. could be pursued only in the broad category of economic science. The same was true of the *licence*. The ability to distinguish between a

90 The results of the program are clearly discernible in the *Annuaire des Enseignements de Gestion* (most recent edition published in 1984), where the educational backgrounds of French management professors are often given (although, not consistently, thereby precluding using the book as a source for a statistical analysis).

91 C.I.M. is the Belgian program. Organized by Fondation-Industrie-Université, it sponsored doctoral candidates between 1970 and 1980, who studied in the United States. Over half of them became professors of management in Belgium.

92 Here is the normal progression of French university studies in the 1960s. First the *baccalauréat*, which ends secondary studies and is the formal qualification for university entry. Next, in the university, two years of general study leading to the D.E.U.G., i.e., university general studies diploma (*Diplôme d'études universitaires générales*). Then follows a year's study for the *licence*. After that, another year and the student gets the maîtrise (masters). This masters is attained, therefore, after four years, i.e., four years after receiving the *baccalauréat*. It is at this point that graduate school, in the American sense, begins. This is the so-called third level of education. The first degree at this level is called D.E.S. (*diplôme d'études supérieures*), or was called that in the 1960s until it was divided into two degrees: D.E.S.S. (*diplôme d'études supérieures spéciales*) and D.E.A. (*diplôme d'études approfondies*). The division was introduced to allow greater range of choice. After receiving a D.E.S., D.E.S.S., or D.E.A. the student worked on the third cycle doctorate. That took two years after the one year spent on the D.E.S., D.E.S.S., or D.E.A. Then came the state doctorate (*doctorat d'état*). It could take decades, as could the *agrégation* which was required for the professorship.

Table 5.14. *Economic and management studies*

	1972	1973	1976	1977	1979	1981
DEUG or DEEG	5,300	4,775	4,706	4,468	4,781	5,020
LICENCE	4,730	3,786	3,965	3,557	3,586	3,670
MAITRISE IN MANAGEMENT			698	672	776	841
DES	1,196	971	700	142		
DESS				858	2,050	2,440
DEA				1,198	1,111	1,257
DOCTORATE (3RD CYCLE)	88	151	237	304	377	577
STATE DOC	115	158	145	127 Econ.	53	89
				25 Manage.	4	19
CAAE	886	1,602	1,583	1,586	1,104	

Source: Ministère de l'Education Nationale, Statistiques des enseignements, *Tableaux et Informations, Les Examens et Les Diplômes dans les universités,* for years given.

degree in economics and in management began, therefore, with the *maîtrise,* that is, in American parlance, the four-year degree. Until 1972 the official statistics did not distinguish between the *maîtrise* in management (*gestion*) and the *maîtrise* in economics. Still university students with a *maîtrise* had been permitted, once they had obtained the diploma of advanced studies (D.E.S.) or an equivalent first degree, to take a third cycle doctorate in management as early as 1963 (that year the I.A.E. at Grenoble awarded its first third cycle management doctorate). In 1972 there were twenty-eight students in that program. Paris IX started its doctorates when the school was founded in 1968; the I.A.E. at Aix-Marseille began with third cycle doctorates in 1970.[93] People were getting third cycle doctorates in management (*gestion*) before it was possible to acquire the *maîtrise* in management.

Since the Paris IX third cycle doctorate program was by far the largest and since most other programs began in the late 1960s, these doctorates did not really become significant in the French university until the 1970s. The *doctorat d'état* in management was not adopted until 1974 (except for Paris IX where it had existed since 1968). These doctorates appear in official statistics as a separate category only in

93 Paris IX at Porte Dauphine is the most important *unité d'enseignement et de recherche* for economic sciences in France. It not only has more students in economics and, especially, in management than any other French U.E.R., but it once had more privileges. In effect, Paris IX has the right to award third cycle management doctorates, but, since other universities have this right too, it was Paris IX's initial monopoly of state doctorates (*doctorat d'état*) upon which its position as a management research center was built. The monopoly was ended in 1974 when other U.E.R. were permitted to grant state doctorates in management.

Table 5.15. *Paris IX (Dauphine)*

	1972	1973	1976	1977	1979	1981
Maîtrise (Management)	426	366	392	355	427	403
Doctorate (3rd Cycle)	31	38	58	56	59	97
Doctorate (State)	3	6	11	7 Econ. 6 Manage.	0 0	8 8

Source: Ministère de l'Education Nationale, Statistiques des enseignements, *Tableaux et Informations, Les Examens et les Diplômes dans les universités,* for years given.

1977. The first *agrégation* in management was also conferred that year. The evolution of these degrees can be seen in Table 5.14. The figures do not distinguish between economics and management below the *maîtrise*. Those for the D.E.S. do not make this distinction either. The distinction between *doctorats d'état* in management and in economics appears in 1977, with economics options dominating. Statistics for third cycle doctorates also do not separate management from economics. The Certificat d'Aptitude d'Administration des Entreprises (C.A.A.E.), which had been obtained in the I.A.E.s since 1955, are postexperience M.B.A.-type degrees. The dominant role that Paris IX plays in doctoral education can be seen in Table 5.15. There were twelve successful candidates for the *agrégation* in management in 1977, fifteen in 1979, twenty-two in 1981, and twenty in 1984.

Thus the universities did not complete their reforms of graduate management education until quite recently. Still it is now possible for people to undergo all their graduate education in the university. What significance did this have for the *grandes écoles* of commerce? When the universities developed graduate management degrees and management became a science, the second sector, the traditional elitist sector of French higher education, felt threatened. There was the danger that they would be turned into inferior undergraduate teaching institutions vis à vis superior university graduate business faculties, that the *grandes écoles* of commerce would be incorporated, as second-level schools, into the university's primary, secondary, and tertiary organization of higher education.

But the *grandes écoles* declined to become a *stage* in a university-dominated higher education. They insisted that their education was not a step in, but a culmination of, preexperience management education. And they refused to be left out of two new but significant instructional areas: postexperience, short-term executive and long-term graduate research education. At Jouy-en-Josas, where H.E.C. had moved in 1963, a postexperience school (la Formation Continue) for managers was created in 1967. At Cergy-Pontoise, E.S.S.E.C. founded a similar institute in 1968. Research, which had always been done by universities, was handled in different ways. In 1969, the Paris Chamber of Commerce created I.S.A., the Institut Supérieur des Affaires, a "center for intensive education in management," for all people whatever their origin or age. In effect I.S.A. was not meant to be just a graduate school for H.E.C. but a place that "brought people of vision from very diverse backgrounds with very different advanced degrees and qualifications" together (engineers, people with graduate degrees from the universities, people with experience in managerial functions). In this sense it was clearly the *grandes écoles'* answer to the university's I.A.E. (Instituts d'administration des entreprises). In fact, in 1975, to train their own professors of management, a doctoral program was created. In order to coordinate H.E.C., postexperience education, and I.S.A., the Chamber of Commerce created, in 1970, a Centre d'Enseignement Supérieur des Affaires (C.E.S.A.) to provide the necessary administrative structure for this polynuclear complex of institutions.[94] E.S.S.E.C. started its own research center at Cergy-Pontoise, complete with a program for the *doctorat d'état* in management. Because only a university could actually grant such a degree, the E.S.S.E.C. doctorate was developed in liaison with the university of Aix-Marseille III. Other programs were adopted along the same lines throughout France.[95]

Therefore, the development of French management education after 1960 clearly ended that neat division of educational labors which had traditionally separated the *grandes écoles* from the university. In a sense both sectors became rivals. Because of the prestige of the *grandes écoles* that rivalry was most uneven at the preexperience, first-degree level. There the *grandes écoles* reigned supreme and the poor university undergraduates struggled for recognition. Such publications as *Le Monde d'Education,* which rank schools, indicate that the university sector still has a long way to go, for the most prestigious management institutions on their lists are the *grandes écoles.*[96]

94 Meuleau, "Les HEC," 63–64.
95 Yvette Ménissez, *L'Enseignement de la gestion en France* (Paris, 1970), 145.
96 "Palmares des universités '85," *Le Monde de l'Education* 118 (June–Aug. 1985):

But the management education story at the postexperience executive and, especially, the research-degree level is somewhat different. The steady growth of the C.A.A.E. degrees earned in the I.A.E. indicates how successful the postexperience masters-level programs have become in the university-affiliated institutions. These programs readily appeal to graduates of the *grandes écoles*. The same is true of the university doctoral programs. Of the 450 third cycle doctoral students enrolled at Paris IX in 1972, for instance, 25 percent had the *licence* in economics, 25 percent the *maîtrise* in management, and 10 percent the *maîtrise* in science – all university degrees – but 30 percent had degrees from *grandes écoles* of commerce or engineering (10 percent were classified as "other").[97] No doubt these statistics spurred the *grandes écoles* to develop their own doctoral programs in the mid-1970s. But E.S.S.E.C., it must be remembered, did so in conjunction with the University Aix-Marseille III.

Graduates from the *grandes écoles* also participated in the educational venture F.N.E.G.E. organized in American business schools, and their graduates readily sought, in order to become professors, the university *agrégation* in management. The preliminary qualifications for the *agrégation* stipulate, in fact, that the candidate can have a third cycle doctorate, or a degree from a science faculty (physics, e.g.), or a first degree from a *grande école* of engineering or commerce. Or, of course, the candidate could have a Ph.D. from a foreign university, meaning, mostly, an American graduate degree.

Both sectors have been very greatly influenced at the graduate level by the Americans. C.E.S.A. started sponsoring postgraduate education for H.E.C. students in American business schools in 1965. Graduates from the *grandes écoles* and the universities participated in the business education program F.N.E.G.E. organized in American business schools after 1969. But this heavy American influence can

---

85. The magazine ranks schools (1) in terms of the quality of their management education, and (2) as vehicles into higher management. In terms of quality of education, the top ten schools in descending order (i.e., H.E.C. was ranked first) were: H.E.C., E.S.S.E.C., E.S.C. Paris, E.S.C. Lyon, I.N.S.E.A.D., Paris IX, Harvard, E.S.C. Reims, E.S.C. Toulouse, and Clermont-Ferrand. As vehicles into higher management, the top ten were: H.E.C.-I.S.A., E.S.S.E.C., E.S.C. Paris, E.S.C. Lyon, I.N.S.E.A.D., Paris IX, Polytechnique (engineering), E.S.C. Reims, E.S.C. Clermont-Ferrand, and E.S.C. Montpellier.

97 Birgitta Wadell, "Doctoral Programs in Management: An Overview of Eight Programs in Belgium, France, Great Britain, and Sweden, 1971–1972," report 721–3. E.I.A.S.M., Brussels, Nov. 1972.

be illustrated most graphically perhaps, because of its importance to the creation of the professoriat in university and *grande école,* by the *agrégés.* Out of the twelve successful candidates in the 1977 competition, six had studied extensively in American business schools. Five out of the next group of fifteen successful *agrégés* (1978) were also American trained (Texas, Northwestern, Harvard, California, M.I.T., and Columbia).[98] As another example, of ten deans (all Frenchmen) who have run the I.A.E. at Aix-Marseille, all but one have had American degrees (Harvard, Chicago, Texas, Northwestern, M.I.T.). There is a working informal association between Aix-Marseille and the business schools at Texas and Northwestern just as there is between E.S.S.E.C. and Northwestern. And if the Ph.D. program arrangement between E.S.S.E.C. and Aix-Marseille is remembered, the connection between the Americans and these two French schools is all the closer. This Americanization of the French business school faculty has led, according to Professor Saias, himself a U.C.L.A. graduate, to the accusation that I.A.E. equals C.I.A.[99]

Thus the French developed a business education after 1960 that, like the education in Britain, clearly followed American lines. But it also continued, like the British, to reflect the native educational traditions. This was true first of all because it took place within the framework of the two French education sectors, the university and the *grandes écoles.* Their presence is significant primarily because it assured weakness in research, for the universities did not have the relationships with praxis and the *grandes écoles* the experience in research necessary to develop and sustain good research habits in management. Despite the support of F.N.E.G.E., French scientific periodicals in management are sparse. Indeed, the scientific community does not pay much attention to the idea of research in management. The chief funding agency for scientific research in France, the Centre National de la Recherche Scientifique (C.N.R.S.), does not recognize management as a field of research (management is included among the economic sciences and must in consequence compete for the limited research funds available with the much more respected tradition in economics). The whole research ethos has had difficulty taking root in French management

98 Interview with Maurice Saias, I.A.E., Paris, Aug. 1984.
99 Ibid.

higher education.[100] In this respect the French are probably no worse than the British. Management researchers in both countries still look to American business schools for the great names in management science and to American publications for the best work.

100 *La Recherche française en gestion: Bilan et propositions,* numéro spécial (1983), Enseignement et Gestion, F.N.E.G.E., colloque de Nancy, Dec. 1, 1982.

6. Knowledge and achievement

So far we have been concerned with society's impact on the evolution of business studies. The time has come to look at how business studies in their various manifestations relate to managerial performance and to draw some conclusions about how well educational arrangements work. How one judges educational efficacy depends on the yardsticks applied. In the final chapters two will be considered: (1) how well higher education provides and transmits knowledge that is managerially useful (this chapter), and (2) how well it motivates people to perform tasks whose accomplishments are desired by managers (the next). Knowledge and motivation are, thus, considered to be the wellspring of performance. Before dealing with these topics, however, something needs to be said about prior efforts to match education and performance. Here a subject raised briefly in the second chapter, the ahistorical nature of statistical analysis, calls for comment. Since it constitutes the principal shortcomings of previous efforts to correlate education with performance, it serves as an introduction to our own.

The British educational system has been severely chastised for its insufficiencies. Yet there are comparative studies that do not reach this conclusion. Table 6.1, which is taken from Albu's "British Attitudes to Engineering Education," illustrates what is meant. These statistics are interesting because they show that far more engineers with university degrees and far fewer with nonuniversity diplomas, that is, inferior qualifications, graduated in Great Britain than in West Germany. If this is true, then, what about the connection between education and performance? Either the British should have done better economically than the Germans (which nobody suggests), or no correlation exists between performance and the quality of engineering education. But are the numbers accurate? In the British statistics Council for National Academic Achievement (C.N.A.A.) first degrees, acquired primarily in the polytechnics, are listed under university; in the German statistics

Table 6.1. *Number of engineers qualifying annually*

	University or Equivalent	Non-university
USA (1976)	37,970	25,089
France (1975)	11,105	12,778
West Germany (1976)	3,960	11,830
Great Britain (1976)	11,025	6,594
Japan (1973)	62,025	8,235

Source: Austen Albu, "British Attitudes to Engineering Education," in *Technical Innovation and British Economic Performance*, ed. Keith Pavitt (London, 1980), 67–87, 80.

for nonuniversity graduates, those from the *Fachhochschulen* are not. Is it proper to classify C.N.A.A. polytechnic degrees in a different category than those from *Fachhochschulen?* The answer is no. Students in both establishments study four years for their degrees. The course in the *Fachhochschulen* involves more practical work than in the German technical universities but the same is true in the polytechnics. They, not the university, have the sandwich courses. What about the entry requirements? They are somewhat lower for the *Fachhochschulen* than for the German technical *Hochschulen* (institutes), but so are they in Britain; people who enter polytechnics have lower A-level scores than those who go to universities. Consider, too, those classified under nonuniversity qualified in Great Britain. They are holders of higher national certificates or higher national diplomas. To equate the graduates of *Fachhochschulen* with H.N.C. or H.N.D. holders is wrong, if for no other reason than that most (4,791 out of 6,594) H.N.D. candidates were part-time students and all *Fachhochschulen* students were full-time. And if the 11,830 nonuniversity qualified from the German *Fachhochschulen* are moved to the category "university or equivalent," the West Germans have many more university-qualified engineers than the British.

From a purely legal standpoint Albu's classification makes sense. In Britain the C.N.A.A. is the recognized legal equivalent of a university degree; in Germany the *graduierter Ingenieur* diploma (from the *Ingenieurschulen*) was not. Had, however, Albu's survey been done two years later, after the *Ingenieurschulen* had been upgraded to *Fachhochschulen*, the legal situation would have changed. This time lapse did not have any great de facto short-term signficance since the new *Fachhochschulen* were about the same educationally as the old *Ingenieurschulen*. Only a shift in legal status has taken place. By this

Table 6.2. *Percentage of chief executives with university or equivalent education*

	France	Great Britain	West Germany
Engineering or science	59	42.7	54.3
Business or economics	34	46.7	29.8
Law or social science	6.9	10.7	17.1

Source: David Hall, H.-Cl de Bettignies, and G. Amado-Fischgrund, "The European Business Elite," *European Business* (Oct. 1969): 45–55, 45.

sort of ahistorical analysis statistical categorizers go awry, with potentially very misleading results for the historically unwary.

The same ahistorical categorization appears in comparative studies about the educational backgrounds of European managers. Thus, David Hall, H.-Cl. de Bettignies, and G. Amado-Fischgrund's study presents the qualifications of European chief executives about 1970 (see Table 6.2). From these statistics it would appear that, although degree holders are much fewer in Britain, the degrees they received scarcely differed from those awarded in France and Germany. But the categories hide the significant differences. A 1978 British Institute of Management (B.I.M.) survey shows that 38 percent of its respondents had degrees in engineering and 19 percent in science/mathematics.[1] Considering that almost no French and less than 5 percent of German managers had science/mathematics degrees, the British science/mathematics qualification is much more prevalent. The statistics seemingly support the contention made by Peter Lawrence, Derek Channon, Michael Fores, and others that there is a confusion in Britain among those who think engineering is just applied science. It is but it is also much more. Therefore, the higher use of scientists in engineering jobs is a misuse of educational resources; they would be better off trained as engineers. Because of engineering's low status in the educational pecking order, however, it does not get the best students.[2] This book has argued that engineering and science have different historical roots and constitute

1 The educational profile of *Survey of British Managers* (B.I.M., 1978); questionnaires sent out to 10,000 of B.I.M.'s own members, nationwide. The response rate was 45% (4,000), all ranks from company chairman to junior managers. The following qualifications were claimed by the respondents: two or more "O" levels or the equivalent, 58% of the sample; two or more "A" levels or equivalent, 45%; ordinary national certificate or ordinary national diploma, 21%; higher national certificate or higher national diploma, 27%; first degree, 28%; diploma in management studies, 36%; other postgraduate diplomas, 9%; and higher degrees (M.A., M.Sc., Ph.D.), 8%.
2 Lawrence, *Managers and Management in West Germany*, 97.

very different forms of education, especially when viewed from the perspective of industrial management. Science majors are so poorly prepared to carry through industrial innovation, as opposed to scientific creation, that Derek Channon blames Britain's poor technological performance on the presence of many scientists in British management ranks:

Britain was heavily committed to basic research on aerospace. . . . The poor success rate on the conversion of discoveries to innovations was attributed to deficiencies in the supply of engineers as distinct from basic scientists. One reason for Britain's comparative failure has been attributed to a national shortage of suitable engineers capable of developing the ideas generated by primary research. This shortage of qualified engineers inevitably led to the substitution of pure scientists less well-equipped to exploit discoveries.[3]

The French and German statistics, on the other hand, show that this misuse (assuming of course that the guess is true) does not take place in either country. Remember, too, the sort of educational system extant in Japan. Engineers are not replaced by scientists there, although the reverse (engineers replace scientists in scientific research) could be the case.[4] In any event, lumping English, French, and British managers into an "engineering or science" group is meaningless.

Statistics on "business or economics" in the Hall, de Bettignies, and Amado-Fischgrund survey are equally misleading. The 1978 B.I.M. survey shows that only 6 percent of the managers surveyed had first degrees in business/management, compared to 15 percent in economics. If these percentages held true for the Hall, de Bettignies, and Amado-Fischgrund survey, it would mean that only a small number of the 46.7 percent of British executives had first degrees in business; a far greater number had them in economics and in the accounting equivalency. The German figure in the "business or economics" category refers primarily to first-degree holders in business economics. One did not really study business, in the British sense or rather the American; there was no equivalency accounting qualification. A large number of Germans, however, would have degrees in economics. On the other hand, almost all the people of the 34 percent classified under

---

3 *Strategy and Structure of British Enterprise*, 29. He is quoting R. E. Caves, and Associates, *Britain's Economic Prospects*, 248–84, about the failure of R and D resulting from the substitution of scientists for engineers. The missing engineers would be those with top scientific training and capability, but those who were nonetheless engineers.
4 Morishima, *The Production of Technologists*.

"business or economics" for France would have first degrees in business and not economics. They would mostly be graduates of the *grandes écoles* of commerce.

Finally, difficulties also arise with the "law or social sciences" category. In Germany, which has by far the greatest percentage of degree holders in the Hall, de Bettignies, and Amado-Fischgrund chart, "or social science" could be dropped. Law is and has always been a popular form of education for business and industrial managers; lawyers, accordingly, predominate in the group. The same is true in France, although the group is very small. French university-trained lawyers do not rival the engineers and business studies degree holders. The number of law graduates among the 10.7 percent of British managers classified under "law or social science" could not be very great. In the 1978 B.I.M. survey there were, among first-degree holders, as many with degrees in social services (4 percent) as in law (4 percent) and twice as many (8 percent) in the arts, a degree scarcely encountered in German and French managerial ranks.

Another classification that misleads finds its way into almost every comparative study when the British are involved (it is present in both the Albu and the Hall, de Bettignies, and Amado-Fischgrund surveys): the term *equivalent* as in "university education or its equivalent" is used. What is this equivalent? It is not, as in France, another school, as a *grande école* that is equivalent to a university faculty. It is, in fact, no school at all, in an academic sense, but a qualification granted by a professional body, in the case of technical managers from an engineering society (mechanical engineers, electrical engineers, etc.) and in the case of nonengineers usually from an accountancy group. It is accounting that is of interest, for engineers have held university degrees for some time now. Hall, de Bettignies, and Amado-Fischgrund pointed out that "20% of the British executives" were chartered accountants "who are not university graduates." That is a large number. British chartered accountants usually attend public schools before being articled to a firm. Since these are secondary schools the young articled clerk might even have taken A levels. But that 20 percent did not attend the university, or, at least, did not graduate if they attended. Then why classify their education as university-equivalent? There seems to be no real justification in an academic sense. Rather, the justification appears to be social. Since it is unthinkable that these public school boys be grouped with nonuniversity people (putting them in the same category as the rough-hewn workers who climbed up from the shop floor), they are, despite the fact that they may not have entered a university door, given a university-equivalent education. It is another example of treating education as a consumption rather than an investment good.

And, as a final example, classification difficulties also materialize, when international secondary-school comparisons are made. Thus the German *Abitur* and the English A levels are listed as comparable diplomas. But the point made about English secondary-school education, as against German and French, is that it is very specialized; students can in Britain concentrate either on science-mathematics or on arts-humanities at A levels. The German *Abitur* and the French *baccalauréat* are much more balanced between science and the humanities. To say that German and French managers had *Abiturs* and *baccalauréats* signifies that they had a good education in science, mathematics, and the humanities. A levels mean nothing of the sort in Britain.

Matching educational backgrounds with managers creates problems for comparative analysis because, although admitting the possibility that education might affect managerial behavior, it does not in itself explain how the specific education of the designated category fulfills the needs of the manager. The questions (1) what do people need to know in order to do their jobs and (2) how can what they need to know best be developed and taught are left unexplored. This chapter confronts these questions in terms of the knowledge component of management and it does so from the historians' perspective, a perspective that permits different answers for different countries to the two questions just posed.

To succeed a modern business community and a modern business firm within that community have to mold a lot of disparate functions into a self-supporting whole. That, at least, is what the American firms and then the Japanese taught the managerial world. Success in industry, in particular, requires a close coordination of sales, design, production, and financial planning, and it requires governmental encouragement if not guidance. People able to maximize the effectiveness of this coordination have to be knowledgeable and capable. And there are two types of knowledge and capability that management communities need to command. One is functional (knowledge of accounting, marketing, etc.) and the other is general (ability to decide, to lead, to work with and within groups, to assimilate new ideas, etc.). How can schools best teach, and how have schools in these countries best taught, both types of skills and knowledge to people at different stages in their student and working careers?

There is, besides, more to educating people than just preparing them for a specific functional job or occupation. There are, in fact, good reasons to believe that the ability of a society to cope with economic and technical change has more to do with general literacy and numeracy than with training. Studies done by the European Parliament show

that the time it takes for the content of education to become outmoded and the speed with which it takes place can be positively correlated with its concreteness [closeness to praxis] and negatively correlated with its level of abstraction. It follows, therefore, that during periods of sudden social change the basic education needed to prepare us for life is worse the more it is related to concrete practical needs.[5]

This conclusion is very interesting because it means that one should not just attempt to teach what goes on in praxis. It is better, when organizing secondary and higher education, to teach what Peter Mertens has called "key qualifications" (*Schlüsselqualifikationen*).[6] Among these key qualifications are, according to him, basic and lateral ones. Basic qualifications are those necessary to learn. Lateral qualifications are those that permit the individual, who is properly equipped with basic qualifications, to tap the information that is available in society. Table 6.3, which is much abridged from the original, indicates the nature of the two kinds of qualification. Key qualifications are not really qualifications in the sense that they qualify a person for a particular job or occupation (accounting, electrical engineering, etc.) in a specific technology. During periods of change such qualifications rapidly become outmoded. Indeed, the Institute for Job Market and Occupational Research (Das Institut für Arbeitsmarkt- und Berufsforschung) in West Germany has concluded that "it is illusory to believe that quick changes can be made in the training structure, the educational curricula, or in continuing education in order to keep them synchronized with the sudden and constantly changing work world."[7] There is no way, especially

5 Hartmut Wächter, *Praxisbezug des wirtschaftswissenschaftlichen Studiums*, Expertise für die Studienreformkommission: Wirtschaftswissenschaften (Sept. 1980), 34; my translation.
6 Ibid.
7 Ibid., 35.

Table 6.3. *Key qualifications*

BASIC QUALIFICATIONS		
As Education Goals	Expressed Concretely	Acquired Educationally By
logical thinking	logical conclusions	formal logic, algebra
analytical procedures	technical analytical processes	linguistics, analytical geometry
critical thinking	capacity to discuss and dispute	dialectics
structural thinking	classification skill	priority ordering of phenomena
management thinking (*dispositives Denken*)		organizational theory, principles of economics
conceptual thinking		planning techniques

LATERAL QUALIFICATIONS		
As Education Goals	Expressed Concretely	Acquired Educationally By
information acquisition capacity	nature of information	semantics, information science
	information acquisition	library science, statistics, media science
	understanding information	foreign languages, language structures, speech, knowledge of symbols, graphics, mathematical symbols
	assimilation of information	speed reading, acquisition of specialized vocabularies, elimination of redundancies and repetitions

Source: Adapted from a table in Hartmut Wächter, *Praxisbezug des wirtschaftswissenschaftlichen Studiums*, Expertise für die Studienreformkommission: Wirtschaftswissenschaften (Sept. 1980).

during periods of great ferment, to make educational institutions serve directly the specific professional and occupational needs of the economy. "Mertens believes," Professor Wächter reports,

that such a response is not really necessary: For most jobs the bosses in a business or firm find that they want people with entirely different qualifications than those imagined when the original position was advertised. Also positions offered can be filled by people of quite diverse training. Mertens concludes that in numerous cases a complete elimination of bottlenecks and surpluses on the labor market occurs, even if calculations about future educational and occupational structures are wrong. The imminent elasticity of the system is important.[8]

8 Ibid.

Since the system seems to be self-regulating and (in West Germany at least) no real bottlenecks appear, we have to ask ourselves why the labor market is capable of adjusting. What in the education makes this flexibility possible? The answer is the acquisition of key qualifications. The implication also is that we should not try to educate people for specific tasks because we cannot succeed and it is not even necessary. Professor Igor Ansoff's comment about business schools always being twenty years behind praxis is, therefore, less a call for reform than a statement of fact.[9] Since the gap is inevitable and unbridgeable, the importance of a key-qualification educational policy is enhanced.

Thus judgments about the relative effectiveness of higher education depend, as far as the knowledge and skill components are concerned, on

1. how well the systems deal with functional education;
2. how well they encourage generalist skills; and
3. how well they cultivate key qualifications in the population.

Two other criteria, besides, have to be weighed. One is the extent to which the right knowledge and skills are imparted to groups outside the firm whose jobs are important to the success of business and industrial enterprise (people in government, banks, and in certain professions). The other is the problem of knowledge creation. Functional knowledge, generalist skills, and key qualifications can be taught. But if business studies are like those in the natural sciences there is a creative (research) as well as a distributive (teaching) dimension to education. The research point will be considered first.

Research

Two things said about research in this book seem contradictory. One (in the second chapter) is that business economics is no science; research does not produce a body of scientific knowledge which can, as in engineering, be applied in praxis. For the British and the French this realization has not posed much of a problem, for they have no academic, management-research tradition. For the Germans it has. The fact that social science is attacked and that German professors of business economics are self-conscious members of a scientific community has cre-

9 H. Igor Ansoff, "The Changing Manager," in *Management Education in the '80s* (La Hulpe, n.d.), 29–38. International Seminar.

ated a particularly painful situation for them. Raised on the ethos of nineteenth-century positivism, anxious to justify the inclusion of business studies among the sciences, they have spent much time debating epistemological questions.[10] Ironically, debates about method and purpose eat into research time.[11]

The second point is that the Germans have been, as a result of *Wissenschaft,* cut off from German praxis. How much they have been cut off is an open question. Professor Albach denies this estrangement; others stress it. A questionnaire circulated to the members of the German Association of Academic Business Economists (Verband der Hochschullehrer für Betriebswirtschaft) in 1983 provides some statistical basis for judgment; it revealed that 46.5 percent of the respondents (185 professors out of c. 400 queried) had engaged, since they had become professors, in research projects in cooperation with a firm.[12] The head of a Frauenhofer Institute, one of the research institutes that works closely with industry, reported in 1983 that *Wirtschafts-Ingenieure* were on his permanent research staff. Although this staff has no pure business economists (*Diplom-Kaufleute*), professors of business economics are frequently called in to work with the researchers on particular problems.[13] Although these figures show that the picture is by no means as somber as some would have us think, academic aloofness is still a constant theme in the literature.

Academic researchers need to have close contact with praxis. Profes-

---

10 The Germans insisted on the usefulness of their science. Erich Kosiol observes that the *Denkschulung,* which is the chief aim (*Kernziel*) of scientific education in B.W.L., "enables one to apply the theoretical knowledge that conforms to the thought system [*Denksystem*] to concrete events in the real world and in given cases to apply it to purposeful economic activities" ("Das Bildungsziel der Betriebswirtschaftslehre an wissenschaftlichen Hochschulen," *ZfbF* 12 (1960): 445–57, 453); my translation. But the reverse is also true, i.e., one studies reality to develop the science which has existence in its own right quite apart from the demands of praxis. This is what separates Kosiol from Lupton.

11 Articles appear regularly in the journals and in collections of edited papers, e.g., Raffée and Abel, *Wissenschaftstheoretische Grundfragen der Wirtshaftswissenschaften; Paradigmawechsel in der Betriebswirtschaftslehre?,* ed. Fischer-Winkelmann; Gerd Walger, *Das Ziel betriebswirtschaftlicher Theorie* (Spardorf, 1982).

12 Only people who attended the annual meeting of the association in Vienna, in 1983, were interviewed. Those agreeing to this interview were Professors Biermann, Meyer zu Selhausen, Wolfgang Weber, Gaugler, Ackermann, Reber, Albers, and Specht.

13 There are twenty-five Frauenhofer Institutes in the German Federal Republic. The one at Stuttgart is magnificently laid out. About 10% of the permanent staff were *Wirtschafts-Ingenieure*. Professor Warnecke, the director, a professor of engineering, observed that the hiring at Stuttgart of *Wirtschafts-Ingenieure* was not exceptional. (Interview, Oct. 13, 1983.)

sor Meyer zu Selhausen of the Hochschule der Bundeswehr (Munich), who has strongly criticized German business economists for praxis-alienated research, explains why.[14] The problems these professors handle, he observed, do not resemble those with which managers actually grapple. Problems in praxis are simpler intellectually; they are less general and operate at a lower level of abstraction than problems professors concoct. On the other hand, they are more complex than those of professors because the professors, in order to engage in mathematical modeling, define away 95 percent of the conditions that affect problems in the business world. Moreover, professors, unrealistic in their problem selection, do not have to suffer the consequences of mistakes. In the real world if propositions are false, they must have definite consequences. For the doctor the patient dies; for the engineer the bridge collapses; for industrialists the company goes broke. For the professors nothing happens; they keep their jobs and continue to solve problems whose solutions, if attempted in practice, would not work. Meyer zu Selhausen's viewpoint echoes those of Professor Lupton and Professor Schmalenbach. They are saying that research should be judged in practical terms pure and simple, not in terms of scientific achievement. In the German case, to the extent that it curtails contacts with praxis, preoccupation with science is bad.

But does this mean if contact with praxis helps academia that research in academia is necessary to performance in praxis? If Professor Ansoff is right about academia being twenty years behind, obviously innovation comes from business. Ansoff, moreover, was, when he made the remark, thinking about American management academics not German. He was saying, then, that even in America academia profits more than business from mutual research contacts because the former learn from the latter. A further conclusion is also implied. Business could make the same progress without much academic research. Professor Katsuyuki Nagaoka points out that

large [Japanese] firms with a lifetime employment and a seniority system . . . made it a rule to employ fresh graduates from college according to their overall abilities rather than their special competence and to assign them various jobs. They trained and educated them on these jobs and/or in their own training centers. They did not employ students from graduate courses except those in

14 In an interview at the Vienna meeting in 1983.

the natural sciences and technology. This employment practice prevented higher business education in graduate courses from developing.[15]

The absence of graduate research programs thus discouraged business school academics from doing research in cooperation with management. Yet Japanese firms have managed to develop excellent management practices.

Research may be of value but it does not have to take place in academic institutions. It is possible, epecially in countries where firms do not spend money or time on management questions, for business schools to do research that helps people in praxis. In Britain, the failure of firms to promote management studies themselves suggests that they can profit from joint efforts with academia. But, inasmuch as the development in praxis of management science does not depend exclusively on the work done in academic research institutions, business does not need academic research. The reverse is true; academia needs business cooperation in order to discover what goes on managerially in the firm, for academic research is not about the creation of knowledge that is of value to practitioners as much as about the dissemination of knowledge of the firm to academicians. From the academics' perspective this activity smacks more of the teaching than the research function.

The teaching function

The potential usefulness of modern business studies, then, comes from efforts to teach a body of knowledge and skills that assist managerial work. To evaluate teaching effectiveness two subjects must be discussed: (1) what people need to know in order to do their jobs, and (2) how what they need to know can best be taught to them. Which system of business studies that grew up in the postwar world has succeeded best teaching people what they need to know: the West German, the French, or the British? Which best contributed to the incorporation of management knowledge and skills into praxis?

Teaching the key qualifications to managers and other responsible

15 "Business Management Study in Japan: Its Development under the Influence of Germany and the USA," paper given at Symposium on Academic Business Education and Industrial Performance in Europe, America, and Japan, EIASM, Brussels, May 21–22, 1987, 9.

people in society is one important educational goal. A look at Table
6.3 shows that these qualifications result primarily from a good, general mathematic-scientific and literary education. The capabilities of
the West German and French educational systems differ very little in
this respect. The French managers, whose educational backgrounds
are described in the surveys, probably enjoyed a slight advantage over
the German because their secondary schools and postsecondary preparatory classes for the *grandes écoles* emphasize mathematics. But the
German secondary schools offered a balanced education which was
only a cut below the best French schools in quantification and probably a cut above in foreign languages. The British system neglected
mathematics. Consequently, in terms of the quality of general education and the numbers involved, the British manager had less command
of the key qualifications than the French or the German.[16]

But what about business studies per se? The response depends on
which group of managers is being talked about, in which country and
at what time. Not only do different managerial positions require different educations, but the needs in the same functions vary between
countries. Moreover, occupational categories are no different than
educational. If to say that a person was educated as an engineer in
England does not mean the same thing as stating that he was educated
as an engineer in West Germany, it also does not mean the same thing
to say that he worked as an engineer or a manager in one country as it
does in the other. It is just as misleading to compare occupation categories as categories as it is educational categories; they have to be discussed in terms of their very different manifestations in each culture
and the correlation between both educational and occupational categories does too. This will be demonstrated by considering the educational requirements of five managerial groups: bureaucrats and bankers (who work primarily outside the firm but who can have influence

16 The 1977 B.I.M. survey reports less than half (45%) of its members (who responded)
   with A levels. Up to 90% of German top managers (depending on the survey) and
   even more of the French had an *Abitur* or a *baccalauréat*. Lethbridge and Miles
   observed of British managers that mathematical training is confined to the arithmetic, geometry, and algebra that they took in school. Very rarely do they have a
   knowledge of statistical techniques such as probability and sampling which are vital
   to sound management practice. Peter Wilby observed in 1986, "the average Japanese
   child is above the O level standard achieved at 16 by only ¼ of British children."
   David G. Lethbridge and Roger Miles, "Pathways to Management Numeracy,"
   OMEGA 4:4 (1976): 397–405, 397; and Peter Wilby, "Schools Fail in Test of
   Skills," *The Sunday Times* (Feb. 23, 1986).

upon it) and general, marketing, and production managers (who manage firms from within).

Bureaucrats

Bureaucratic intervention in business and industry is problematic. William Kingston observed:

[T]here can never be a meeting of minds between a bureaucrat and an innovator. However polite the surface exchanges, at heart the true innovator despises the bureaucrat. The "unknowns" to which a bureaucrat's imagination is directed, are not those of business or technology, but of the problems of following a career path within his organization. His underlying interest dictates this, and it also controls the food his imagination receives from his subconscious mind. That imagination consequently cannot be available to be sparked into vision by the innovator's project. Moreover, because bureaucrats are able to contribute so poorly to decisions requiring imagination, they inevitably tend to limit the activity of their bureau to decisions that do *not* require it, i.e., to decisions concerned with anything other than innovation.[17]

Such views are part of the folklore of liberal capitalism, deeply embedded, since Adam Smith, in the Anglo-American psyche. They tend to become a priori contentions that produce equally a priori conclusions: Nothing good can come from bureaucrats qua bureaucrats; the less government the better; our inability to innovate results from the growth of bureaucracy. Although the argument should not be lightly dismissed, evidence exists to the contrary. France has a good, and Japan an enviable, postwar economic record; both have active bureaucracies. No doubt, especially for the Japanese, bureaucracy assisted the rapid modernization of these countries. For some at least, the Japanese Ministry of International Trade (M.I.T.I) and the French Planning Commissariat (to cite two obvious examples) are quite innovative forces in each country's economy.

The opposite argument is not necessarily being sustained, i.e., that bureaucrats are (or potentially are) entrepreneurial. On the contrary, the argument is that the characteristics of bureaucrats are historically, as much as generically, determined. The Japanese bureaucracy, finding itself in an economically backward country in the midnineteenth century, got involved successfully in its modernization; the French did the

---

17 William Kingston, *Innovation: The Creative Impulse in Human Progress* (London, 1977), 141.

same after the Second World War. Success often required renovation of the bureaucracies themselves. That was done and as a result the particular manifestation of bureaucracies in each country today is one of innovative capability. In Great Britain the bureaucracy was not involved in economic modernization, the nation having industrialized itself primarily privately. The attitude of British businessmen, academics, economists, industrialists, and bureaucrats has been determined by this experience, so well expressed in the Kingston quotation. In Germany the bureaucracy was more involved in the modernization process during the nineteenth century than it was in Britain. But, since the Second World War especially, there has never been the interpenetration between the high civil service and management in banking, business, and industry that has taken place in France. The prevailing attitude among West German businessmen and industrialists, moreover, about bureaucracy is similar to that expressed by Kingston: Bureaucrats are temperamentally unfit to manage business and industry.

In short, the specific national historical experience with bureaucracy might be a more significant factor than the occupational category per se when determining the role that bureaucrats play and could play in future business and industrial management. After noting that higher civil servants rarely entered private firms in the past, Anthony Sampson described a "spectacular migration" of higher civil servants into private industry:

In the early sixties there was only a trickle, when Sir Leslie Rowan left the Treasury to take over Vickers; Sir Edward Playfair left Defence for International Computers; Sir Richard Powell left Trade for Albright and Wilson. But the trickle soon turned into a stream and after the head of the civil service himself, Sir William Armstrong, became Chairman of the Midland Bank, the floodgates were opened.[18]

The British experience might seem to parallel the French, where top positions in business and in banking are frequently taken by top civil servants, or that of the Japanese, who move from the higher echelons of the bureaucracy into private industry. But to whose benefit? If the bureaucrats are, through their recruitment and training, a creative force, then this bureaucracy–business interpenetration can produce the beneficial results that many believe have occurred in France and Japan. But if the civil servants are as William Kingston describes them,

18 Sampson, *The Changing Anatomy of Britain*, 181.

if they are careerists without innovating instincts, whose move to industry constituted the last act of old men to achieve financial security in retirement, then the results can be industrially disastrous.

How does the historically specific experience of bureaucracies relate to the education of bureaucrats in business studies? The senior French civil servants are graduates from the *grandes écoles* of engineering, especially but not necessarily, if in technical services, or of the prestige school of administration, E.N.A., if not. Although the engineers are very well equipped to handle the new management techniques, the nonengineers have also acquired a fluency in these matters because of a good grounding in mathematics. The work of the *ingénieur-économiste* after the war sparked a good system of management education for bureaucrats who have close relations with banking and industry. German senior bureaucrats have studied law. Those who have also worked in the Hochschule für Verwaltungs-Wissenschaften (the College of Administrative Sciences at Speyer) have been introduced to management concepts. Young civil service aspirants, moreover, are required to take a course in business economics in the university. Nonetheless, legal education in the Federal Republic is generally more bureaucratic than managerial. Compared to the French civil servants, the *Beamte* are poorly schooled in management studies. But that does not matter so much because they do not move into business and industry.

Table 6.4, from Anthony Sampson's *The Changing Anatomy of Britain*, provides educational information about the top bureaucrats (permanent secretaries) that run the biggest government departments at Whitehall. He notes that men from the top public schools no longer dominate these positons, for, if in 1950 the nine "Clarendon Schools . . . provided a third of the permanent secretaries, in 1981 [they] provided only one in eight."[19] Still, former grammar school pupils are heavily represented. Oxbridge graduates, moreover, clearly predominate and the more prestigious the department, the more Oxbridge "which in 1977 provided 86 percent of the senior officials (deputy secretary and above) in the Foreign Office, 77 percent of the Treasury, 62 percent in the Department of Employment, and 60 percent in Energy."[20] Civil servant entry requirements established in the nineteenth century account for Oxbridge's hegemony. Hence this Oxbridge-oriented, nontechnical, noncommercial, nonmathematical

19 Ibid., 176.
20 Ibid.

Table 6.4. *Education – permanent secretaries*

Name	Department	School	University
Sir Robert Armstrong	Cabinet Office	Eton	Christ Church, Oxford
Sir Ian Bancroft	Civil Service Dept.	Coatham, Redcar	Balliol, Oxford
Sir Douglas Wass	Treasury	Nottingham High	St. John's, Cambridge
Sir Anthony Rawlinson	Treasury	Eton	Christ Church, Oxford
Sir Kenneth Couzens	Treasury	Portsmouth GS	Gonville, Gaius, Cambridge
W. S. Ryrie	Treasury	Mount Hermon, Darjeeling Heriots	Edinburgh
Sir Frank Cooper	Defense	Manchester GS	Pembroke, Oxford
Sir Kenneth Stowe	Health & Social Security	Dagenham GS	Exeter, Oxford
Sir Lawrence Airey	Inland Revenue	RGS Newcastle	Peterhouse, Cambridge
Sir James Hamilton	Education & Science	Penicuik	Edinburgh
Sir Kenneth Barnes	Employment	Accrington GS	Balliol, Oxford
Sir Donald Maitland	Energy	George Watson's College	Edinburgh
Sir Kenneth Clucas	Trade	Kingswood	Emmanuel, Cambridge
Sir Peter Carey	Industry	Portsmouth GS	Oriel, Oxford
Sir Brian Cubbon	Home Office	Bury GS	Trinity, Cambridge
Sir Douglas Lovelock	Customs & Excise	The Bec	--
Sir Brian Hayes	Agri. & Fisheries	Norwich	Corpus Christi, Cambridge
Sir Peter Baldwin	Transport	City of London	Corpus Christi, Cambridge

Source: Anthony Sampson, *The Changing Anatomy of Britain* (New York, 1984), 178–79.

emphasis in the civil service entry examination has, despite attempts to reform the system in the 1960s, persisted until today.

The question is, has the educational background of top British civil servants affected their performance? Has it mattered that people so educated have been parachuted into important jobs in British management; has it mattered that they run a government that increasingly requires expert managerial skills with a high technical knowledge content? Evidently people have felt it did. The civil service came under sharp attack during the 1960s for its lack of expertise. One result has been a recruitment of economists into Whitehall beginning in 1963. The Oxbridge generalists might still hold down top jobs but they have been joined by the economists. These changes, therefore, seem to reflect events elsewhere, i.e., the employment of statisticians and economists in America, France, and in the Netherlands.

But is this employment necessary? Ryutaro Komiya and Kozo Yamamoto wrote in an article about the Japanese bureaucracy that "one cannot discuss the role of economists in government, since there is not one professional economist employed by the government of Japan. . . . [L]arge organizations in Japan, whether government ministries, banks, or corporations, are run by generalists, administrators, or managers who work in most cases in one organization for their entire careers and reach the top positions after occupying many different posts in the organization."[21] The generalists are recruited primarily, if not exclusively, from the University of Tokyo School of Law, whose students in turn are drawn from those who study Japanese classics and history. From the educational perspective, therefore, the Japanese generalist career civil servant resembles the British. But it is important to stress that it is preexperience education that is at issue. In effect, the Japanese government subjects its generalists to a highly competitive examination at entry and to extensive training on the job thereafter. Those wishing to become career officers in the Japanese civil service must take an examination (in one of twenty-eight fields, i.e., law, economics, civil engineering, etc.) and one in forty pass. After entry the best (five out of twenty-six in the Ministry of Finance, e.g.) are sent abroad (to the United States and Europe) to study economics and business administration; the remainder are withdrawn from administrative assignments and sent through a year's schooling in a subject. The education is set at graduate level; the teachers are frequently university professors. Those studying the course in economics take, for example: microeconomics (25 sessions; sessions are three hours each); macroeconomics (20 sessions); mathematics for economists (35 sessions); statistics (20 sessions) econometrics (20 sessions); input–output analysis (20 sessions); public economics (15 sessions); monetary theory (15 sessions); public finance (13 sessions); international economics (15 sessions); international finance (10 sessions), plus 60 sessions of seminar work and 32 composed of lectures on special topics. It is obviously an intense training, one that, since 1961 when the examination system was adopted, has given the Japanese career officer a good technical qualification. Still, if many are capable of doing specialist work in economic forecasting, etc., the career officers are never considered to be specialists. Indeed, they avoid being so tagged for it is considered to be undesirable to specialize in any single field or to judge a matter from any special viewpoint.

It is not, therefore, as the Japanese achievement shows, detrimental in itself to British civil service to recruit career officers from Oxbridge, from people who have studied the classics or history. It is, however,

21 "Japan: The Officer in Charge of Economic Affairs," *Economists in Government,* ed. Coats, 262.

bad for their generalist education not to have had more mathematics, which was the case in Oxford. The main problem seems, however, to be what happens after the generalists are brought into the service. The cult of amateurism which prevailed in Whitehall certainly was not good. The importation of specialists might have improved technical skills but as long as British academic training in economics was theoretical and generalist and business schools had not come into their own, the advancement of economic forecasting and statistics within the British civil service could not have proceeded apace. In the 1970s economics in British universities became more specialized, as it was in American universities. Belatedly, then, levels of technical skills grew with the recruitment of the economists into Whitehall. But this threatened to set generalists and specialists at each others' throats. The founding of civil service management schools has led to improvement in managerial knowledge among the generalists. Nonetheless, from a knowledge point of view, the British civil servant has not benefited from as good a preentry or postentry education as the French or the Japanese. Despite recent reforms it is questionable whether the general level of expertise in the British civil service will soon rival that of the French or Japanese. The British bureaucratic and educational traditions are against it. To the extent, therefore, that the management-knowledge quotient in the civil service affects British business and industry, they suffer comparatively.

Bankers

A second function, which usually is located outside the firm but is essential to its welfare, is finance-banking. The subject is the dysfunctioning of British banking during industrialization and how it might relate to educational attainment. German education and banking serve as a contrast. Richard Whitley's investigation (1974) of the educational backgrounds of British bankers and insurance executives produced Table 6.5. The pattern is familiar: public schools and Oxbridge. It is a pattern, moreover, which reflects one Sampson found (see Table 6.6) when he charted the educations of chairmen in top banks, i.e. those which have branches all over Britain. Both tables manifest that this is one part of the anatomy of Britain that has not changed.

Heinrich Evers, by contrast, provides the information in Table 6.7 on board (*Vorstand*) memberships in the German service industry.

Table 6.5. *Education – directors*

School	Bank of England	Clearing Banks	Merchant Banks & Discount Houses	Insurance Companies	Industrial Firms
Eton	1	31	37	46	34
Harrow	0	3	7	9	5
Winchester	2	11	5	6	7
Rugby	3	5	6	4	6
Charterhouse	1	2	1	2	1
Marlborough	0	2	1	0	7
Other Public	3	25	25	31	110
Private	0	0	2	1	3
Total fee-paying	10	79	84	99	173
Grammar	5	18	16	17	71
No Secondary	1	0	1	0	0
Overseas	2	2	5	2	8
County Secondary	0	0	0	0	9
Total	18	99	106	118	261
No Data	0	16	50	48	269
Universities					
Oxford:					
Trinity	0	8	2	7	7
New	1	7	5	9	8
Magdalen	1	5	7	4	3
Other	2	11	20	11	35
Cambridge:					
Trinity	2	12	14	14	18
Magdalen	1	4	4	6	0
Other	4	13	13	13	34
Other UK	1	10	5	7	34
Military	0	2	0	3	2
Foreign	0	0	4	1	11
None	6	29	33	43	109
TOTAL	18	101	107	118	261

Source: Richard Whitley, "The City and Industry: The Directors of Large Companies, Their Characteristics and Connections," in *Elites and Power in British Society*, ed. Philip Stanworth and Anthony Giddens (Cambridge, 1974), 65–80, 70.

Table 6.6. *Education – British bank chairmen*

Bank	Gross Deposits in £ millions	Chairman	Education
1. Barclays	42,834	Timothy Bevan	Eton; Guards
2. National Westminister	39,709	Robin Leigh-Pemberton	Eton; Oxford; Guards
3. Midland	38,000	Sir David Barran	Winchester; Cambridge
4. Lloyds	25,309	Sir Jeremy Morse	Winchester; Oxford
5. Royal Bank of Scotland	6,698	Sir Michael Herries	Eton; Cambridge
6. Bank of Scotland	2,524	T. N. Risk	Kevinside; Glasgow

Source: Anthony Sampson, *The Changing Anatomy of Britain* (New York, 1984), 274.

There are two things to be said about his data. First, by *old* the author means the board members who have just retired, and by *new* those currently sitting. The trend by 1974 was clearly in favor of people educated in the economic sciences. Since the survey does not distinguish, there is no way to know if students majored in economics or business economics. But the commonality of the studies in German

Table 6.7. *Education – German bank directors*

Educational Study Area	Old Members (% of)	New Members (% of)	Rate of Change
Engineering	--	--	--
Economic Sciences	11	24	+13
Law	34	40	+6
Natural Science	5	1	-4
Other	13	9	-4
Degree Holders all fields	64	74	+10
Non-University Members	36	26	-10

Source: Heinrich Evers, *Kriterien zur Auslese von Top-Managern in Grossunternehmen. Eine empirische Untersuchung* (Frankfort on the Main, 1974), 103.

universities robs this oversight of great significance. Secondly, since the information pertains to the service sector, it encompasses much more than finance and banking. Evers, however, does state that 88 percent of bank board members had degrees (of them, 64 percent in law and 32 percent in the economic sciences). The banks, therefore, were promoting business economists to top positions as fast as other firms in the service sector.

These British and German surveys evince different patterns of development in finance and banking. Already in the nineteenth century a closeness between big banks and big business was a hallmark of German economic development: Germans financed industrialization on borrowed money. And the banks that lent the money placed representatives on the boards of the companies in which they placed their funds. The practice, as Table 6.8 manifests, began quite early. A recent study (1978), which reported that 14.9 percent of supervisory board members of the top one hundred German companies were from the banks, shows that the practice has continued to today.[22] German bankers and industrialists have traditionally worked together.

Such active financial engagement in business, commerce, and industry requires great expertise. The extent to which the banks foster it can be discerned in Germany. Before German banks could invest in industry, they needed reliable information about financial status and business performance (both actual and potential). To carry out investigatory services, banks organized the first *Treuhand* societies (trustees, executors, but really consultancies in this regard), beginning in the

22 Monopolkommission, Hauptgutachten III, *Fortschreitende Konzentration bei Grossunternehmen* (Baden-Baden, 1978).

Table 6.8. *Industrial corporations on whose boards bank representatives sat*

Name of Bank of Corporations	Total Number Corporations	Total German
Deutsche Bank	221	208
Diskontogesellschaft	92	81
Darmstädter Bank	101	85
Dresdner Bank	133	119
Schaffhausenscher Bankverein	130	116
Berliner Handelsgesellschaft	74	60

Source: Otto Jeidels, *Das Verhältnis der deutschen Grossbanken zur Industrie,* 2d ed. (Leipzig, 1913), 169.

1880s, as adjuncts of their financial operations.[23] The bank-owned *Treuhand* societies recruited auditors who, because they were interested in the industrial as well as the financial strength of their clients, had to learn industrial and financial accounting.

The industrial audit appeared before the First World War. By 1930, Professor Alfred Isaac of the Nuremberg business faculty claimed that "today's auditor is not just an auditor. He needs to examine whether business transactions which the accounts record are open to criticism, for it is necessary to go into organizational questions, to handle questions of costs and pricing, and many others besides."[24] The *Treuhänder* became what Isaac in his brochure about them called an "economic counselor" (*Berater der Wirtschaft*).

Obviously *Treuhänder* needed to know business economics. Considering the demand, the supply of trained personnel was small. Professor Schmalenbach of Cologne's business faculty observed, in 1920, on the eve of great expansion of *Treuhand* companies: "[A]mong *Treuhand* companies there are questionable and even notoriously unsuitable firms; among individual auditors there is, sometimes, shocking incompetence." Paul Gerstner, one of the leading practitioners and an authority on trusteeship, pointed out that "the greatest treasury of experience cannot make up for the lack of theoretical knowledge."[25] Schaer, Schmalenbach, Schmidt, and many other professors of business economics set out to provide it. In 1906 Schmalenbach started courses in *Treuhandwesen* in Cologne. In 1907 Penndorf was named head of a

23 Locke, *The End of the Practical Man,* 260–67.
24 *Die Aufgabe des Treuhänders und die Treuhänderausbildung an der Hochschule für Wirtschafts- und Sozialwissenschaften (Handelshochschule) Nürnberg* (Nuremberg, 1930), 2–3; my translation.
25 Quoted in Locke, *The End of the Practical Man,* 264–65.

newly established training program in Leipzig that led to diplomas in auditing. Professor Rieger, after the First World War, established a *Treuhand* institute in Nuremberg. By 1929 "most schools where business economics was taught [had] set up special exercises and lecturing" in auditing.[26] The bank's habit of recruiting people from business faculties was of long standing.

The City, on the other hand, grew into a world financial center without directly participating in British industralization. The divorce between the two processes is reflected in the bankers' education. Those who study at public schools and Oxbridge pay scant attention to business studies and law. The accountants among them are not well qualified on industrial subjects; they only learned, until quite recently, financial accounting in an accountant's office, as articled clerks. The stigma of industry and commerce is well known. "The people in the City," Sampson observes, "see across the whole globe, but they see it only through money. . . . They are constantly dealing with bits of British industry, restructuring companies, joining their boards, merging them or rationalising them. But they still remain aloof from the real industrial problems; and their business is making money, not things."[27] William Kingston observes that

Japan's Zaibatsu and bank-centered groups are giant holding companies which operate world-wide and include banks, insurance and shipping firms, and trading companies, in addition to manufacturers. Some of the best-known Japanese names abroad, such as Mitsui and Mitsubishi, are Zaibatsu. Keiretsu stands [in Japanese] for the way in which these giant enterprises organize subcontracting upstream for their own operation, from huge numbers of small firms. This Keiretsu relationship is far closer and more complex than anything known in the West, and provides the small firms with orders, management consultancy and finance, without destroying their autonomy.[28]

It would be excessive to blame Britain's industrial decline uniquely on education. But it is fair to say that the separation of higher education from industry, and its association with the City, reinforce each other. If Japanese integration is the future, it behooves people in finance to learn about industry. That is what German banks have done, if on a more modest scale than the Japanese, and what they continue to do.

26 W. Bork and A. E. Weber, 'Treuhand-Auslese,' *ZfhF* 23 (March 1928): 180–86, 180.
27 *The Changing Anatomy of Britain*, 264.
28 Kingston, *Innovation*, 136.

Generalists

Traditionally, the two functions just discussed stood outside the firm. Opinion differs about education for functions that have always been exercised within the firm. One such function, whose development has epitomized modern management and its education, is that of the generalist. During the heyday of the American business schools in the 1960s, educational reformers believed that British corporate directors were inadequately educated. The attack was directed at the Oxbridge arts and science degree, but it was especially pronounced against engineers. The reformers believed, as Nuala Swords-Isherwood observed, "that scientific or technical training is in some way narrow and does not fit a person to take general and far sighted decisions. It is less difficult (in their eyes) for the nontechnically educated person to take sensible decisions in a technically sophisticated industry without technical knowledge."[29] German managers, as a Booz, Allen, and Hamilton survey testifies, were also criticized for the inadequacies of their education. "The German economy has had," an article in *Die Zeit* observed in 1980, "an increasing need for internationally educated managers. Specialists we have aplenty but specialists with broad vision . . . capable of dealing with international tasks . . . , we have few. German firms have had to turn to English, Dutch, and Luxembourgers educated in European business schools."[30] Much the same thing was said in France, but since France identified so closely with the American business school movement and, in any event, had a strong tradition in encyclopedic learning, the Germans were considered to be educationally bad and obstinate in their refusal to adapt education to generalists' needs.

Since the 1960s, views have altered. In 1980 two Harvard Business School professors, Robert H. Hayes and William J. Abernathy, questioned the skills of American corporate businessmen. "Since the mid 1950s," they observed,

there has been a rather substantial increase in the percentage of new company presidents whose primary interests and expertise lie in financial and legal areas and not in production. . . . High level American executives come and go. . . .

29 Nuala Swords-Isherwood, "British Management Compared," in *Technical Innovation and British Economic Performance,* ed. Keith Pavitt (London, 1980), 88–99, 89.
30 Werner, "Die verschenkte Chance," *Die Zeit,* Mar. 3, 1980; my translation.

Top management posts are filled from the outside. . . . The business community . . . has developed a preoccupation with a false and shallow concept of the professional manager, a "pseudo-professional" really, an individual having no special expertise.[31]

This is an interesting indictment of American top corporate management. It is echoed in recurrent attacks on faddish, cookbook-recipe management policies – return on investment, market share, portfolio diversification – which at one time or another were used, almost exclusively, as yardsticks, particularly by consultancy firms, with which to measure performance. The current emphasis on product design and production, on engineering, on disinvestment, on in-house recruitment of top men attempts to correct the superficiality of the generalist M.B.A. approach to corporate management that Hayes and Abernathy think got American industry into trouble. Although the new emphasis does not deny the need for top corporate management to be engaged in general policy formulation, strategic planning, etc. – functions essentially different, and requiring different knowledge and skills, from those of operations managers – engineering knowledge has again gained fashion.

With the changed criteria the stock of German managers and, with them, German education, has gone up and the stock of American managers down. German managers, condemned twenty years ago for their technical outlook, find themselves praised for being product-oriented, for their failure to succumb to the generalist approach to management, for their thorough knowledge of functions within the firm (that they had learned during years spent in various departments before being promoted up the hierarchy to command). People recognized that American management methods were different but they no longer assumed that they were better. The German corporate executives think, Peter Lawrence explained, about the functionally specific rather than the managerially general.[32] The Germans do not even think about management at all. One manages something, one does not just manage. The emphasis on functional education in German engineering schools and in departments of business economics supports this view of management. Nobody claimed that firms could ignore managers with generalist skills. They just argued that the generalists

31 Robert H. Hayes and William J. Abernathy, "Managing Your Way to Economic Decline," *Harvard Business Review* 58:4 (July–Aug. 1980): 67–77, 74.
32 *Managers and Management*, 183.

had to be people with functionally specific business and, especially, technical knowledge and skill. Viewed accordingly, German education serves the generalist needs of the firm because it provides the solid education very good generalists require.

If this American climb down has helped to restore the reputation of the German general manager and German managerial education, the same has not happened in Britain. Because the British emulated American business education in the 1960s, the dross of the now tarnished American reputation rubbed off on them. Whether this attack on the Americans is justified, indeed whether the critique of American M.B.A.s is justified, remains unsettled. Debate about what general managers need to be taught depends on the criteria deemed necessary to the job, and since those criteria have changed, so have views about management education.

Marketing and production managers

Opinions about the educational criteria of other managerial specialties seem less subject to change. Marketing and production functions are good examples. In 1981 a book appeared that examined how British, French, and German managers fared in marketing. The study is based on interviews of eight hundred marketing and purchasing agents in five countries. Each interviewee was asked about the nature of his marketing and purchasing experience with people in firms outside his country (i.e., in the other four). British firms were rated by the non-British agents poor in meeting delivery deadlines (which requires close cooperation between production and marketing) and in offering new technology to their customers (which requires close cooperation between research and marketing). The British were, in fact, at or near the bottom and the Germans almost at or near the top (second only to the Swedes) in every category judged. The French were in the middle (the Italians were next to last sometimes, last sometimes – just before or behind the British). The investigators explained:

The marketing staff in German companies have an exceptionally high reputation, not only for their technical competence but also for their commercial ability. In technical matters, the German suppliers are found to be innovative and at the forefront of development. They stress technical excellence and high quality, rather than emphasizing price. . . . They keep buyers informed of developments and follow up on product application in customer firms. Their export experience has given them a very sound knowledge of how foreign firms operate. They are outstanding in speed and punctuality of deliveries.[33]

British marketing fell down particularly on technical competence, on keeping suppliers informed about product development, and on meeting delivery dates. To some extent these results cannot be attributed to the performance of marketing agents; delivery dates require the full cooperation of production units. But there is ample evidence that the marketing people themselves were responsible for their ranking.

This occurred particularly when marketing agents handled technical matters. German firms have always employed engineers as salesmen, especially when the products are very sophisticated.[34] In English firms nontechnically trained people usually handle marketing; indeed, if university graduates are used, they are frequently arts majors.[35] Much of the training received is done in the firm, even in Germany. Certainly the engineers used in marketing learned little about the subject in engineering school, although the *Wirtschafts-Ingenieur* could.[36] But the status of engineering studies in both countries clearly influenced the ability of a firm to employ engineers in a marketing capacity. Not only were engineering graduates fewer in number in British firms, they were also less suited for nontechnical work. To some extent this amounted to a self-fulfilling prophesy: Because technical education

33 Peter Turnbull and Malcolm Cunningham, *International Marketing and Purchasing: A Survey among Marketing and Purchasing Executives in Five European Countries* (London, 1981), 123.
34 Herr Knoben observed in 1976: "The good technical education of salesmen, the efforts to go see the client in order to get acquainted with his problems and to help him overcome them, putting your research facilities at his disposal in order to build durable relations with him, have always been more important than price. The client is regularly informed about new products in his sector by an immense information service." These remarks apply to Bayer. Also, same comment about the "technical-commercial" cooperation producing Siemens's success. Hans-Konrad Knoben, "Les Facteurs du succès des exportations allemandes (Queleques cas majeurs)," a thesis for the third cycle doctorate, University of Paris IX-Dauphine, 1976, 76; my translation. The same thing was being said about German firms in 1905. See an excellent description in Sydney Higgins, *Dyeing in Germany and America, with a Chapter on Colour Production, a Report* (Manchester, 1907), 92–100.
35 *The Action Study of Arts Graduates in Industry* gives "The Functions in Which Arts Graduates Were Used" as follows: administration, 16% of total of arts students surveyed; production, 12%; sales, 33%; finance and accounts, 7%; research, development, and design, 4%; buying and stores, 4%; personnel, 15%; legal, 4%; economics, statistics, 2%; public relations, 2%.
36 It is interesting to observe that German marketing professors complain about how German marketing research, compared to American, has been neglected in universities. This again suggests how unimportant academic research is for praxis.

was judged inferior, it got inferior people, people that could not, like the bright and eager young German *Dipl.-Ing.*, be sent out to deal with top management in customer firms. The result was the generally inferior marketing and procurement in British firms reported in the Turnbull and Cunningham survey.

Peter Lawrence wrote that the Germans and the British have different views of the production function. Germans tend to "treat production as connoting the whole company minus sales and finance."[37] The British think of it in a much narrower sense. They exclude not only research and development and design from production but quality control, engineering, production c ontrol, and maintenance. These disparate concepts reflect different n anagerial career patterns. Of thirty production managers interviewed in Germany, Lawrence found only two who had spent their working lives in production exclusively (in the British sense). All the others worked in every management job: sales, R and D, design, maintenance, and engineering. "If one compares this finding with the figures for a much larger sample in Britain, it would appear that German production managers are more mobile functionally than their British colleagues" who tend to stay in the function as narrowly defined.[38] Lawrence describes the qualifications held by these production people: In production (narrowly defined) and in associated technical jobs, i.e., design, maintenance, engineering, few people in German firms have less than the *Graduierter Ingenieur* diploma, that is, they have studied in what is now called the *Fachhochschule*. Some have university-level engineering degrees (*Dipl.-Ing.*) and a few even have doctorates in engineering. Those who work in R and D are better educated and "there are more graduates and PhDs in engineering and quality control than in production or maintenance." But, generally speaking, the educational level is high enough for people to be able to move from function to function inside and outside production, narrowly defined, and they do. The *Grad.-Ing.* degree is "sufficiently high for no one (who has it) to be seriously disadvantaged educationally when dealing with anybody else."[39]

This educational homogeneity does not exist in the British firm. It is not "unusual for [production] managers to make mildly self-deprecatory remarks about their education, along the lines of 'of

37 Lawrence, *Managers and Management*, 137.
38 Ibid., 141.
39 Ibid., 140.

course, I can't claim any kind of superior education' and 'Afraid I left school at 14 and anything I've learned I've learned here.' "[40] Production leaders tend to be promoted from the shop floor. The maintenance and engineering managers, to say nothing of those in research and development, have at least subuniversity qualifications (H.N.C., H.N.D.) or even degrees in engineering. A failure to achieve great mobility between management functions can result from causes other than education. The French seem, in this respect, to be closer to the British in their production management, despite educational qualifications that are much higher.[41] But apparently the nonformally educated English production leader cannot be moved easily to more knowledge-demanding functions (engineering, maintenance, design, sales). Neither can arts graduates be moved, like German engineers, from sales into production. A poorer coordination of efforts in the English factory and between the factory and the customers must be a result.

Because what civil servants, bankers, general managers, salesmen, and production people need to know, to work inside and/or outside the firm, varies in time according to institutional circumstances, so do estimates of the education that best suits people for tasks. Yet one thing seems sure. Whatever the need, English education, because of a crippling heritage, has most trouble meeting it. With increased undergraduate business education and management education for engineers, the educational levels of British managers are clearly improving. There was evidence of this already when B.I.M. surveyed its members in 1977. Forty-four percent had studied business management (in the university but mostly at the subuniversity level). The percentages by age group were 25–35 years old (72 percent), 36–45 years old (56 percent), 46–55 (30 percent), 56–65 (31 percent), and over 65 (18 percent). Nonetheless, old habits persist. The best people still avoid

40 Ibid., 140–41.
41 The lack of mobility between functions in France has been attributed to the bureaucratic tradition; see Michael Crozier, *The Bureaucratic Phenomenon* (Chicago, 1964). Still, the Belgian Wallonian experience is so different from the Flemish, despite coexisting in the same state, as to suggest deep cultural causes. In fact, Wallonian bureaucratic behavior resembles French much more than it does that of the Flemish. See the interesting study by Michael Aiken and Samuel B. Bacharach, "Culture and Organizational Structure and Process: A Comparative Study of Local Government Administrative Bureaucracies in the Walloon and Flemish Regions of Belgium," in *Organizations Alike and Unlike*, ed. Cornelis J. Lammers and David J. Hickson (London, 1979), 215–50.

production engineering because it is a despised profession; the elite who go into banking and civil service continue to neglect management education. Even if British undergraduate and graduate studies were as good as French and German (which seems not to be the case), the effect on praxis would not be equal since fewer managers have a business education (only 7 percent of those in the B.I.M. survey had first degrees in management) and the educations the other managers received prepared them poorly for managerial careers.

What distinctions can be made between German and French managers? Because educational fields (business and engineering) and educational levels (a higher percentage of university graduates) are quite similar, it is more difficult to distinguish between the societal effects of French and German business studies. But it is not impossible. Two evaluations, done by managers reflecting after several years on the job about their own preexperience education, evidence how well each system taught what managers need to know.

The first is Andreas Kallmann's questionnaire sent out to thirteen hundred firms which employed people who had been out of school for about five years. The degrees the recipients held were all in the economic sciences (57 percent *Diplom-Kaufleute*, 11 percent *Diplom-Ökonome*, 10 percent *Diplom-Volkswirte*, 22 percent *Wirtschafts-Ingenieure* or *Diplom-Betriebswirte*). Kallmann set out to measure two things. First, he wanted active managers to evaluate how well school had prepared them for specialties. The study areas asked about were accounting; finance; sales, marketing, commerce; personnel; production economics; taxation; auditing; industrial administration; banking; insurance; operations research; electronic data processing; planning, organization, and management.[42] Second, Kallmann wanted to know about generalist education, i.e., how well their education had prepared them to do the following: (1) to think analytically and synthetically, (2) to structure problems, (3) to solve problems, (4) to work independently and methodically, (5) to think in terms of economic interrelatedness, (6) to be ready to take up tasks, (7) to be creative, (8) to work in teams, (9) to convince and persuade, (10) to lead.[43]

42 Andreas Kallmann, "Beziehung zwischen Wirtschaftswissenschaft und Wirtschafts-praxis – Ergebnisse einer schriftlichen Befragung der Schmalenbach-Gesellschaft-Deutsche Gesellschaft für Betriebswirtschaft," *ZfbF* 9 (1981): 827–43, 833; my translation.
43 Ibid., 837.

The Hay-France Society did a survey about the same time (1979) for F.N.E.G.E.[44] The investigators sent out 11,522 questionnaires to former students of the *grandes écoles* of commerce who had graduated between 1970 and 1974. The response was poor; only 782 usable questionnaires were returned. Nonetheless, the researchers felt the results warranted publication. The difference between the design of the French questionnaire and that of the German is the initial comparative point. Whereas the Kallmann study had two lists of appreciations (specialist education and generalist skills), the French had one. French managers were called upon to measure how well their education dealt with the following: (1) extent and combination of specialization, diversity of courses, (2) acquisition of knowledge, (3) fostering of analytical skills, (4) arousing critical senses, (5) quality of pedagogical methods, (6) fostering of communication skills, (7) development of a sense of organization, (8) teaching how to evaluate knowledge, (9) fostering decision-making ability, (10) fostering savoir faire, (11) teaching sense of the reality of the enterprise.

Obviously the German and French questionnaires had, to a very large extent, different aims and these aims projected the different conceptions of business studies that were themselves products of quite distinct educational traditions. The Germans favored specialized education. Indeed, this emphasis in the Kallmann questionnaires is not exceptional. It is characteristic of German surveys that attempt to relate business education to performance in praxis. Traditional fields of business knowledge (accounting, marketing, organizations, commercial law, taxation, finance) and newer fields (statistics, electronic data processing, operations research) are covered. These educational specialties, moreover, correspond to the fields in which German managers show the most interest in their recruitment of business economists. Professor Drumm's poll of managers, conducted about the same time as Kallmann's survey, ranked the educational backgrounds business and industry most demand by descending preference:[45] (1) accounting (by far), (2) planning, (3) marketing, (4) finance, (5) personnel/organization, (6) taxation, (7) auditing, (8) computer science, (9) operations research. A second group, composed of educational qualifica-

44 The survey is reported in Yvette Ménissez, *L'Enseignement de la gestion et ses publics* (Paris, 1981).
45 Hans-Jürgen Drumm, "Die Nachfrage der Praxis nach wirtschaftswissenschaftlichen Studienfächern," *Zeitschrift für Betriebswirtschaft* 50:9 (Sept. 1980): 997–1015.

tions employers least demanded was, descending in order of demand: (1) statisticians, (2) econometricians, (3) business historians, (4) people in private law, (5) people in public law, (6) sociologists. Low demand for law is surprising, but perhaps it only means that companies preferred to hire lawyers, not legally instructed business economists. Employers preferred specialties that have a hard core of technical knowledge (unlike sociology and business history). Another study, which lists accounting (by far), general business economics (*allgemeine B.W.L.*), marketing, organization, law, and electronic data processing among sixteen fields of knowledge, observed: "The relatively high number of references to accounting underscores the great meaning to employers that this field has. It also means that praxis perceived accounting as the central field in economic science."[46] Such a view of economic science is at variance with the one held at Oxford or Cambridge; it underscores the extent to which praxis appreciates the heavy emphasis on specialist knowledge in German B.W.L.

The Hay-France questionnaire ignored questions that deal with functional education (just one or two references to how well special education was done, but no breakdown by specialties.) Rather, it asked people about leadership and decision making, questions designed not for specialists but for *chefs de file*. That is what the students and their schools thought would be the destiny of graduates from *grandes écoles de commerce*. Such ambition sparked some resentment in praxis. A survey of senior managers (in-depth interviews in 1979) revealed that they were annoyed by the "competition that exists between the education establishments and particularly management schools . . . because it provoked them into making unrealistic statements about the brilliant prospects of their students."[47] Nobody had a mediocre career, nobody was normal. But these pretensions obviously beset experienced middle managers from *grandes écoles* of commerce as well as the preexperience students still in school. Table 6.9, compiled from the survey, lists the areas in which the managers believed they would work in the future. Since 63 percent thought they would be involved more in general management, these middle managers (six to nine years' work experience after graduation) expected to arrive at the top.

Yet the actual answers are more interesting than the design of the

46 Hans Hörschgen, "Wirtschaftswissenschaftler: Wie die Praxis sie sieht," *Der Arbeitgeber* 11:31 (1979): 647–50, 647; my translation.
47 Ménissez, *L'Enseignement de la gestion et ses publics*, 157; my translation.

Table 6.9. *French managers estimate future work orientation (in %)*

	More	Less	As Much as in the Present	No Response
General Management	63	3	20	14
Personnel and Social Relations	45	10	30	15
Finance, Accounting, Management Control Systems	42	11	39	12
International Business	41	8	32	19
Marketing, Commerce, Sales	41	12	33	14
Data Processing & Organization	36	16	33	15
Research & Economic Studies	29	16	37	18
Legal & Fiscal Matters	22	19	42	17
Headquarter's Staff	21	19	38	22
Production Management	16	20	42	22

Source: Yvette Ménissez, *L'Enseignement de la gestion et ses publics* (Paris, 1981), 129.

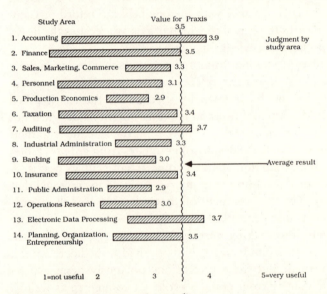

Figure 6.1. Germán managers evaluate studies

Source: Andreas Kallmann, "Beziehung zwischen Wirtschaftswissenschaft und Wirtschaftspraxis," *Zeitschrift für betriebswirtschaftliche Forschung,* 33:9 (1981): 827–43, 831.

questionnaires. Kallmann's survey results (see Figure 6.1) show that the managers believed the business faculties had done the best job teaching them accounting and auditing, the worst, teaching production economics and public administration. Despite variations in estimates, however, on the whole German managers thought their specialist education had prepared them well. Information about how French managers evalu-

Table 6.10. *Educational preparation for* grandes écoles *of commerce*

Students graduating from a *grande école* of Commerce. *Baccalauréat* obtained before entry.

Series of Baccalauréats	Schools	
	ESCAE (in %)	HEC, ESSEC, ESCP (in %)
A	4	5
B	19	5
C	46	75
D	23	5
Equivalent Diploma		1
Not Responding	8	9

Students preparing the competitive entry (*concours*) for the *grandes écoles*.

Series of Baccalauréats	Preparing HEC (in %)	Preparing ESCAE (in %)
A	1	3
B	3	30
C	84	32
D	12	34
G	--	1

Source: Yvette Ménissez, *L'Enseignement de la gestion et ses publics* (Paris, 1981), 13, 42.

ated their education in functional subjects, since it was not collected in detail, is much more sparse. But there are hints at dissatisfaction. Students graduating from the Ecoles supérieures de commerce et d'administration des entreprises (E.S.C.A.E.) named accounting, along with foreign languages and personnel, among the three subjects that "had an insufficient place in the programs."[48]

Information about the managers' secondary school education charts a similar educational pattern. Table 6.10 indicates the more elite the school (H.E.C., E.S.S.E.C., E.S.C.P.), the more students intending to prepare for them had studied mathematics (Baccalauréat C). This emphasis, moreover, is stressed even more for the students in special schools preparing for the *grandes écoles de commerce*. Considering that during these two or three preparatory years after the *baccalauréat*, the surveyed did not learn any business subjects, they arrived in the *grandes écoles* of commerce completely uninstructed in them. The relative neglect of such subjects as finance, accounting, and marketing in the *grandes écoles*, coupled with the complete neglect of practical subjects before the *grandes écoles*, left these Frenchmen, compared to the Germans, badly prepared in functional specialties.

The German managers' appreciation of what they had learned

48 Ibid., 72.

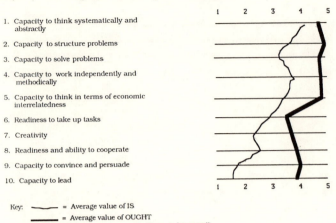

1. Capacity to think systematically and abstractly

2. Capacity to structure problems

3. Capacity to solve problems

4. Capacity to work independently and methodically

5. Capacity to think in terms of economic interrelatedness

6. Readiness to take up tasks

7. Creativity

8. Readiness and ability to cooperate

9. Capacity to convince and persuade

10. Capacity to lead

Key: ——— = Average value of IS
        ▬▬▬ = Average value of OUGHT
        1 = Did not promote ---------- 5 = Promoted very well

Figure 6.2.   An "is-ought" chart

Note: This chart indicates how their studies had promoted general management skills, according to the former students after several years in praxis (IS), and how they would like to see certain skills stressed more in academic studies, because of their importance in praxis (OUGHT).

Source: Andreas Kallmann, "Beziehung zwischen Wirtschaftswissenschaft und Wirtschaftspraxis," *Zeitschrift für betriebswirtschaftliche Forschung,* 33:9 (1981): 827–43, 837.

about general management is much less positive. Kallmann constructed an "is-ought" chart (Figure 6.2) from the managers' responses to his questionnaire. It shows the greatest dissatisfaction with the academic's attempt to teach these skills: ability to solve problems, creativity, team work, capacity to convince and persuade, and, the worst of all, leadership.

It might be tempting to conclude that the poor results are caused by poor German education in general management. The *grandes écoles* pride themselves on their close relationship with people in praxis. Managers from the public and private sector regularly lecture in the schools. Since the French *grandes écoles,* moreover, stressed leadership, it might be thought that teaching this, not specialty education, is what they do best. Table 6.11 indicates how the managers surveyed in the Hay-France report evaluated these aspects of their education at the *grandes écoles* of commerce.

The areas in which the managers thought their education (they had been educated in *grandes écoles* of commerce after management education was clearly "in") had been less than satisfactory or insufficient were (in order of negation) practical experience in the firm (62 percent of the answers), savoir faire (60 percent), decision making (53 per-

Table 6.11. *French managers evaluate education in* grandes écoles *of commerce (in %)*

Aspect	No Reply	Excellent	Satisfactory	Average	Insufficient
Extent and combination of specializations. Diversity of courses	2	25	51	18	4
Acquisition of knowledge	1	14	62	21	2
Fostering of analytical skill	1	28	44	21	6
Arouses critical sense	--	27	36	27	10
Quality of pedagogical methods	1	13	44	34	8
Fostering of communication skills	1	20	34	28	17
Development of a sense of organization	1	13	39	31	16
Teaches how to evaluate knowledge	3	6	45	38	8
Fosters decision-making ability	1	14	32	35	18
Fosters savoir faire	1	7	32	42	18
Teaches sense of reality of enterprise	1	11	26	32	30

Source: Yvette Ménissez, *L'Enseignement de la gestion et ses publics* (Paris, 1981), 114.

cent), how to evaluate knowledge (46 percent), and sense of organization (47 percent). Despite having stressed these management skills in their propaganda and in their education and having voiced a desire to teach people how to manage rather than just do functional jobs, the pedagogical results the graduates later judged among the least helpful were precisely those educational objectives the schools stressed.

Does this mean that the French *grandes écoles* taught these subjects as poorly as the Germans, or does it mean that they cannot really be taught to twenty-year-olds without any practical experience, students, who in France more than in Germany, had never done anything but study intellectual subjects? If the latter is the proper conclusion, then, the pretense of the French *grandes écoles* to teach these subjects is misplaced and so is their relative neglect of specialization. Because, as the evidence suggests, the German system of education does as good a job teaching leadership skills to its students as the French (which is not very good in both cases) and a much better job teaching specialized skills than the French, it seems to be, in terms of teaching knowledge and skills, a more beneficial system.

It is true that we often hear about the superiority of the French student. Vincent Degot, when comparing graduates from the top fifteen *grandes écoles* of engineering with those of the lesser, specialized *grandes écoles,* expressed it this way:

Here again we encounter the difference between the two types of schools: the *grandes écoles* graduates, who have attained a more abstract level of knowledge, are better equipped than the others to face the new developments. Moreover, they are adept at transforming the content of their academic training to suit new disciplines, often to the detriment of the disciplines that were the very *raison d'être* of these schools (e.g., *écoles des mines*).[49]

Degot's claim that the French students in the top *grandes écoles* have a greater sense of leadership than those in the lesser schools and the oft heard claim in France that the same is true of German students (they are less capable) might be true, but it can have nothing to do with the pedagogical prowess of the French *grandes écoles*. Rather, it appears to be a result of a selection process that creates a psychology of self-conscious, self-confident elitism in the very bright students at the *grandes écoles,* one that does not occur at the German universities and *Fachhochschulen* to anywhere near the same extent.

These conclusions probably raise as many questions as they answer. Assuming that the managers queried knew what they were talking about, does their evaluation signify, since German education is at least as good as French, that contact with praxis is not necessary for praxis-effective teaching? This question emerges because of the ivory tower reputation German academics have acquired. It is important, of course, not to exaggerate the state of this isolation in terms of teaching any more than in terms of research.[50] Still, the accusation persists that

49 "Types of French Engineers and the Implementation of Company Policies," *International Studies of Management and Organization* 10:1–2 (1980): 165–84, 176.
50 Results from the 1983 survey, conducted by the author, of German professors of business economics provide some useful data in this analytical context. To the question, are you involved in postexperience education for courses organized inside the firm, 53.5% of the respondents answered yes. To the question, do you engage in consultancy regularly, 60.5% answered yes and 15.2% that they were either partners in or owned their own consultancy firm. To the question, do you leave academia to do work-study in praxis, 11.4% answered yes. To the question, do you invite honorary professors from praxis to give courses to the students, 23.9% answered never, 27.7% sometimes, 58.4% frequently. To the question, do you invite experts from praxis to talk with your students, 6.1% answered never, 49.7% sometimes, 44.1% frequently. To the question, do you get reaction from people in praxis to your work, 6.6% answered never, 58.8% sometimes, 35.6% frequently. Finally, to the statement, "curricula structure and teaching methods are not relevant to business and industrial praxis," 81.0% either disagreed (46.2%) or strongly disagreed (34.8%). Only 2.5% strongly agreed with the statement, i.e., that their teaching was not praxis relevant. The teaching experience is not, apparently, one that just happens in the ivory tower.

the *Wissenshaft* tradition isolates the German professors of business economics from praxis much more than the educational traditions of the *grandes écoles* have kept praxis and teacher apart in France.

Here the key-qualifications argument can be invoked. It is not used to prove that the quality of German education was generally superior to the French. The reverse, as far as secondary education is concerned, is probably true. But the concept of key qualifications is applicable to business studies programs. Professor Karl-Hermann Ackermann remarked that in Germany academics make a distinction between *Berufsfähigkeit* (ability to do a job) and *Berufsfertigkeit* (readiness to do a job) when questions about business education crop up.[51] The first is what schools do, that is, they make people able to do a job by teaching them how to analyze, to plan, and to think. They also teach them how to synthesize special areas of knowledge (finance, law, etc.) in ways that are useful to people in business. Such distinctions are what the German business economists were talking about when discussing *Wissenschaft*. When Erich Schneider and Erich Gutenberg emphasized *Denkschulung*, they never pretended that it would actually train people how to manage. It only helped them to become capable of managing. People in praxis, moreover, make the same distinction as the academics. "It is not readiness to work [*Berufsfertigkeit*] that business and industry expect to find in the graduate," Hans Dichgans said, "but the capacity [*Fähigkeit*] during special training in praxis quickly to make himself occupationally ready [*berufsfertig*]."[52] Ihno Schneevoigt, chief of personnel (I.B.M. Germany) agrees. The young business graduate (*Diplom-Kaufmann*) needs to know, he observes, "how decisions in a firm are made, . . . how the firm operates, . . . how specific planning processes run." But he added that this assignment "cannot be undertaken by the university. It is a time-consuming task, that the firm itself must fulfill."[53] Ackermann's distinction is operative. To concentrate on *Denkschulung* is, even from the viewpoint of praxis, not a bad thing. British management education, especially with its sandwich courses in polytechnics, confounds the two tasks. The French, like the Germans, also wish to make their students *berufsfähig* in preex-

51 Interview.
52 Quoted in Joachim Kienbaum and Peter Paschek, "Das beste Sprungbrett ist ein breites Wissen," *DUZ* (1981): 854–57, 857; my translation.
53 Ihno Schneevoigt, "Die Ausbildung der Wirtschaftler aus der Sicht der IBM Deutschland GmbH," *Bildung und Wettbewerbsfähigkeit*, special issue, *ZfbF* (1981), 96; my translation.

perience education at the *grandes écoles*. But the Germans, because they deal more thoroughly with the specialties (to make people *fähig* not *fertig* in them) than the French, provide a more professionally useful *Denkschulung*.

The benefits of this division of educational labors, moreover, extend to postexperience German education. Because the private sector and the nonacademic teaching bodies it directly supports (e.g., the Wuppertal Circle) take up postexperience education almost exclusively, they assume it at the point where the state system's usefulness ends; for, if the division of labor between the universities (preparing students to be professionally able) and education in praxis (to make them ready) makes sense in functional fields (learning finance, accounting, marketing, etc.), teaching leadership, where praxis is really the best teacher, does not. German academic B.W.L. leaves such teaching to praxis. Inasmuch as the French concentrate on teaching these general managerial qualities at the preexperience level in *grandes écoles,* it would appear that German business education (and Japanese, too, it might be added), through this division of labors, has its priorities right.

7. Motivation and achievement

Napoleon Bonaparte is reputed to have said that, in battle, morale is to physical as three is to one. Armies with the same number of men, the same organizational structure, the same strategy, and the same tactics can be most unequal opponents because their shared values, their spiritual cohesion, their motivational forces differ. Indeed, the type of organizational structure adoptable or the strategy realizable can hinge on levels of motivation. So the question to be answered in this final chapter is quite simple: How have the academic traditions examined in this book influenced motivation and, with it, organizational efficiency in the countries studied – how do they today, and how might they in the future? Something quite different from knowledge is being discussed, indeed something different from a sociology of knowledge. The last chapter considered how educational systems have affected the managers' ability to acquire useful knowledge. Irrational factors were involved because historically shaped educational systems had social-psychological features which proved to be beneficial or detrimental to the teaching of a managerially useful knowledge. The English public school and the Oxbridge educational tradition were the most obvious cases. Socially based educational prejudices, like "engineering is not 'done,' " produced an upper class that lacked requisite knowledge. Now, however, the impact of the same historically created psycho-social educational systems on motivation, rather than knowledge, is at issue. The shift in focus is important, for an educational system could favor knowledge acquisition and be demotivating, that is, it could (but need not) have excellent results in terms of imparting knowledge to managers but have bad effects on morale. In other words, judgments made about the effectiveness of educational systems from a motivational viewpoint can be quite different from those made about it from the knowledge perspective.

In order to evaluate motivation and to relate it to educational cultures, more yardsticks are needed. When considering knowledge, the key qualifications seemed appropriate. Since these are thought categories, however, they do not fit a scheme of evaluations concerned with motivation. But a considerable literature about motivation in business and industrial organizations has emerged. Abraham Maslow posited a needs hierarchy to explain what drives people: self-actualization, esteem or status, affiliation or acceptance, security or safety, psychological needs. Douglas MacGregor developed what he called a Theory X (the average man dislikes work and must be coerced, directed, and controlled) and a Theory Y (individuals like to work if they set their own standards of achievement). There is no need to evaluate this body of theory because it is all quite arbitrary (one scheme often contradicts another) and because, since the validity of a scheme seems to vary from country to country, it is relative. As Geert Hofstede points out: "We found evidence . . . that agreement with MacGregor's Theory X is more frequently found among subordinates in large power distinct countries [where people respect authority] than in others, and that the perceived leadership behavior between 'task' and 'people' orientation (Blake and Mouton) is a function of a country's power distance level (the extent to which people respect authority)."[1] Hofstede maintains that American authors are unaware of this relativity. As scientists they seek to find the hierarchy of needs that motivates man from within the man not the culture. He observes:

The only U.S. history of leadership that allows for a certain amount of cultural relativity, although indirectly, is Fiedler's. . . . Fiedler states that different leaders' personalities are needed for "difficult" and "easy" situations, and a cultural gap between superior and subordinates is one of the factors that makes a situation "difficult." However, his theory does not consider the *kind* of cultural gap.[2]

Perhaps the Americans' failure to appreciate the cultural origins of needs in organizations is itself cultural. People who deal with motivation in America approach it the same way that they do knowledge. The Americans invented general management as a field of knowledge to fit the new man, the manager. The hierarchy of needs (self-actualization, achievement), about which Americans so often speak when treating motivation and leadership, fits well the concept of the manager as a

1 *Culture's Consequences: International Differences in Work-Related Values* (London, 1980), 378.
2 Ibid., 380.

member of a special class, an extracultural super-elite. But it is not a scientifically determined universal set of motivations that is at stake as much as it is an expression of values that are America-specific.

These American ideas about motivation, whether they stress profit maximization, self-actualization, Theory X, or Theory Y, have one thing in common; they are concerned with the individual. There are needs, however, which spring from social values. It is not just a cultural factor that is being discussed, for it is possible to affirm that individuals have different values in different cultures and still be talking about individuals. Geert Hofstede does as much when he reports how Scandinavian social scientists reacted to the American Herzberg's remarks about workers' participation in management: "You [Herzberg] are against participation for the very reasons we are in favor of it – one doesn't know where it will stop. We think that is good."[3] Or, as Hofstede concludes, "If leadership is only a complement to subordinateship, a key to leadership is the type of subordinate expectations we are likely to find in a country."[4] Hofstede is well aware of the variety of culturally based responses that occur when questions like individual versus collective responsibility or authority versus power sharing arise. But he still considers these subjects from the individual's perspective.

Although group values have to be internalized in individuals, social or group motivation differs from individual motivation because it expresses the community's morale. This distinction is frequently accented in studies comparing Japan with the West. Arthur Whitehill and Schin-Ichi Takezawa, in *The Other Worker,* remark:

[O]rganizational goals have been defined in terms of "worker responses sought by management," and would include such universally sought responses as subordination, loyalty, and diligence. Individual needs have been represented by the hierarchy of human needs as developed in the literature of psychology, and include those related to physiology, safety, love, esteem, and self-actualization. Even though both organizational goals and individual needs may be culturally conditioned in the ways they are perceived and satisfied, we would seem warranted in assuming this central dichotomy of organizational versus individual in our cross-cultural analysis of industrial relations.[5]

Because, these authors claim, the individual gains his satisfaction through subordination, loyalty, and diligent work for the organiza-

3 Ibid., 378.
4 Ibid., 379.
5 Page 360.

tion, the organization's goals become more important than the individual's. The study showed that "In the U.S. system of industrial relations, the involvement between an individual and his organizations seems both less intensive and less extensive than in the Japanese system."[6] Dore's comparative study of workers in Hitachi and in English Electric reached the same conclusion, for, by loyalty to a labor market instead of a company (by defining a job as an occupational not a company function) the workers in the English Electric company were motivated by individual needs; the Hitachi worker, by contrast (expressing his need in company terms), as a Hitachi man, automatically places the community's welfare ahead of his or rather, makes it synonymous with his own.

Thus motivation has an individual and a community dimension. The cultural manifestation of individual and community motivation, moreover, must take organizational situations into account; for just as some organizations and some positions in organizations require different kinds of managerial knowledge, so do they require different kinds of motivation. Accordingly, the usefulness of educational systems will vary to the extent to which they foster an individual or a community motivational ethic and, since these ethics relate differently to organizations, to the extent to which the managerial structures need a particular motivational ethic.

Witness Professor Chandler's argument. He stressed the relationship between strategy and structure, that the creation of the M form multiproduct, multifunctional firm required the creation of a headquarters' staff that could deal with strategic planning as opposed to the operational planning and control going on in divisions. This new structure required a new kind of knowledge, that of the headquarters' staff manager, and a new kind of motivation, that of the high flyer. The American business schools satisfied these organizational needs.

6 Ibid. The survey of Japanese and American workers, upon which the study was based, took place at the end of the 1950s. Whitehill and Takezawa repeated their survey twenty years later. The result: "[A] striking difference persists with Japanese workers placing their company in a far more central life-role than U.S. workers. Furthermore, the willingness to at least equate work life with personal life among Japanese workers has tended to strengthen during the interim between surveys. In contrast, U.S. workers, particularly the young, demonstrated an increasingly alienated, separatist view of the work-life sector." *Workways: Japan and America* (Tokyo: The Japan Institute of Labor, 1981), 123. Hence, in terms of organizational as opposed to individual motivation, no convergence in motivation had taken place. The Japanese worker, as he lived longer in an industrial world, did not become more like the American.

But critics of this system complain about the divorce between management and operations. Indeed, the critics believe that knowledge of specific technologies and businesses is considered essential to success. The American tendency to separate management and product knowledge allegedly brought about a decline in American manufacturing capability. If this is true, then the knowledge needed at headquarters changes, and so the motivation for the personally motivated high flyer, the manager moving from company headquarters to company headquarters in his career, gives way to the hardworking, functionally competent, company-oriented team man whose experience in the company is critical to headquarters' management. A three-corner connection, then, is made: (1) historically shaped educational cultures in each country are matched with (2) the kinds of motivation they induced and with (3) organizational needs in motivational terms. This chapter looks at individual motivation and community motivation and then assesses the motivational efficacy of the educational systems.

Individual motivation

That business exists within an educational culture and, from a motivational as well as a knowledge standpoint, responds to that culture has been implicitly if not explicitly discussed throughout this book. There is no need, therefore, to rehash unduly points already made about systems of education. One story, told by John Egan, the current head of Jaguar Cars, illustrates how the public school/Oxbridge experience discouraged entry into industrial careers. He spoke at Oxford University, he relates, about the need for university graduates to take industrial jobs. The talk was well attended by eager and concerned (concerned about Britain's industrial decline) students. When, during the question period, Egan asked how many in his audience planned to work in manufacturing, not one hand went up. Considering that the Oxford undergraduate did not study business management the result might seem desirable. But knowledge implies key qualifications as well as specific professional training. If Oxford students lacked the latter they were well endowed with the former. Inasmuch as intelligence is as significant as education to success and Oxford students are among Britain's intellectual best, to deprive industry of them is, whatever the specific shortcomings of their education, a bad thing. Besides, Oxford students enter the City and civil service; for a sizable number of them not to enter industry means that industry is deprived of contacts with the national elite.

Surveys of students at the London Business School also show that industrial demotivation exists in schools founded to lead Britain's economic renaissance. "Engineers in particular," Nicholas Newman concluded in his work,

tend to use business schools to escape from the notoriously limited furrows into which their qualifications lead them. "Why did I go to business school?" says one Citibank M.B.A.: "To get out of engineering!" . . . The problem is hard to cure: "Production management in the country has traditionally been poor because it is a low status job," says one lecturer, "and that won't change until the management gets better. But then you can't get the good management in because it's low in status." . . . Not that the teaching of production management is bad, the difficulty is rather that, out of London's 77 strong faculty, for example, 33 teach finance-related subjects, while only one a piece teach production and industrial relations.[7]

The business school undoubtedly taught useful management knowledge to its students; but, from the production engineers' perspective, its program was just as demotivational as that at Oxford, indeed more so since it took people who were already there away from production engineering.

The motivational patterns characteristic of those in French higher education also affect career entry. Once the *baccalauréat* is finished a decision has to be made about preparing for a *grande école*. Because of the railway-line nature of French secondary education, choice depends largely on previous success in mathematics.[8] The best students in mathematics enter the best *grandes écoles* of engineering; the good but less-accomplished in mathematics enter the best (Parisian) *grandes écoles* of commerce; and the mediocre students in mathematics enter the university faculties or the less important *grandes écoles* in the provinces. The school selection process itself, then, because of the prestige of the schools involved and the extent to which attendance at them opens career possibilities, motivates individuals.

Study choice and hence career entry can be prompted less by interest and aptitude than by social enticements. It is not easy for the student who is very good in mathematics but has a passionate interest in

7 Nicholas Newman, "The MBA Credibility Gap," *Management Today* (Dec. 1981): 46–49, 110–12, 49.
8 Whitley, Thomas, and Marceau, *Masters of Business?*, 99.

literature or art to resist the siren of the Ecole Polytechnique. But the dysfunctional effects that this educational system has should not be exaggerated. If the very best students are drawn away from business studies, they are not, as in Great Britain, taken into nonutilitarian subjects. The encyclopedic character of the education, moreover, assures reasonably interesting, varied, and respected career prospects.

Inasmuch as schools in Germany do not cream off the elite and send them into bureaucratic or nonbusiness and nonmanufacturing careers, West German education has an even less dysfunctional motivational effect on entry into business and industrial management than the French. The Germans put great stress on educational qualifications, but it matters more what you study in the German Federal Republic than where. Industry in West Germany, moreover, is a high-prestige occupation, much more so than in Great Britain and, perhaps more so than in France where the superstate bureaucrats, the *hauts-fonctionnaires*, dominate the nation's elite. "Salary data," Peter Lawrence observes, "do on the whole suggest that in Germany, an American rather than a British evaluation of the worth of the manager prevails."[9] He also observes that "pay relativities for engineers as between the public and private sectors are reverse in Britain (compared to West Germany); here [in Britain] every type of public sector employment for engineers is on average more highly remunerated than employment in industry."[10] The high prestige of business and industrial management is a recent phenomenon. Although the German middle class channeled its energies into business and industry, traditionally a civil and military-service elite dominated the German state. The old aristocracy, the high-status master of militarism, was not only discredited by two lost wars but, with the disappearance of its landed estates in the East, destroyed as a dominant class. And the *Beamte*, if still respected, scarcely have in the German Federal Republic the prestige of those who ran the great German superstate. The leadership default of the old military-bureaucratic elite and the status enhancement of the business and industrial managers resulted from much greater historical processes than those which pro-

---

9 *Managers and Management*, 164. Lawrence states: "German managers are well paid. [Professors] . . . are about level pegging with a middle manager. . . . The professor is outranked by the personnel chief and by the 55-year-old graduate engineer in industry. A major general . . . is on a similar footing to the head of sales. . . . The *Geschäftsführer* of a small GmbH type of company with 1,000 employees outranks the major general," 172.
10 Ibid., 172.

duced the educational system. But German higher education played its part in the change because it did not make entry or level of entry into business and industry depend on schools attended.

Similar statements can be made about the influence of higher education on individual motivation during careers. Much was said in the last chapter about how education affected a person's ability to rise in the hierarchy. Those from the German university and, if to a lesser extent, from the *Fachhochschulen,* could set their sights at the top because people with both educational backgrounds were sitting there. Lawrence found that among German managers, even at the top, "there is qualification heterogeneity. Members of a Board of Directors (*Vorstand*) are usually graduates and often PhDs. The top management, where companies tend to be smaller, often has a membership where the range of qualification is considerable. . . . One finds similar variation at lower levels in the management hierarchy, even though the average qualification level is high."[11] Lawrence telescoped comments made by German managers on the subject of how to get ahead into the following dialogue:

Does the professor's son have an advantage over the welder's son [Lawrence asked]? The answer is no. . . . Does it help to be a graduate of any particular university (say Heidelberg) one asks hopefully? No, universities as such do not have different prestige levels, only particular faculties or departments. . . . Is it a good idea to start in some prestige function? No, one should do that for which one has the most talent and interest. . . . Is it desirable to get experience in a number of different functions? No, at any rate there is no managerial folk wisdom on this point. Should one alternate between line and staff posts? No, and staff posts do not have much standing anyway. So what do you have to do to get on, one demands in desperation? Just have *Fachkompetenz* (ability in your field), work hard and show *Leistung* (achievement). Yes, they say (repeatedly). *Es geht um persönliche Leistung* (It is a matter of personal achievement.) This view is, in the author's [Lawrence's] experience, expressed consistently by German managers.[12]

Another feature of German management is that qualification differences inspire relatively little envy among German managers. In a survey of German engineers, conducted by Lawrence, the *Graduierte-Ingenieure* (i.e., nongraduates) were asked how they would explain the higher average pay of the graduate engineers. The majority answered in a straight, unhostile way: The *Dipl.-Ing.* underwent longer training,

11 Ibid., 112.
12 Ibid., 110–11.

had a higher level qualification, and so on.[13] Lawrence says there was no conflict in the management because of this diversity. A Ph.D. egghead was not hated by nongraduate engineers. But no, he was in fact picked out for praise by colleagues, not on account of his academic prowess but because "he sets the highest standards, and drives himself the hardest." Such an attitude prevailed because it was also possible for those without the highest qualification to rise to the top. Or, as Lawrence writes, "It is [his experience] to come across quite senior people in Personnel, Administration and Sales who started as commercial apprentices and in some cases have not added any qualification."[14]

In France the beginning employee has quite different prospects. One graduate from a lesser school noted:

I saw in my firm that graduates of ENA and the *Polytechnique* were very well placed and those of [the *Ecole*] *Centrale* also. But those from HEC did much worse, and people like myself did very poorly.... I could see that I needed something extra.... It is important to say that in France people are obsessed by the level of their qualifications . . . and it is quite painful, when it happens that one has failed to get into a so-called *grande école*, so then one finds onself not really inferior but left with the impression that one has not done as well as other people, and is somehow an idiot or stupid. It is certain, nevertheless, that the difficulty of the entrance examination does impose a degree of selection, and I would not pretend that I have the mathematical ability of a *polytechnicien*, but I also believe that what makes the difference afterwards is the different cultural milieu (*formation*) of the schools themselves. There is no doubt that in the French *grandes écoles* students are educated into a way of seeing things which enables them to behave differently in the environment they enter afterwards. From the moment you tell someone he will be a manager (*dirigeant*), that he is destined for responsibility, he behaves completely differently from someone to whom this has not been said, and that, I think, is important. So, very often, someone who graduates from a French *grande école* is quickly associated with positions of power, and is promoted rapidly and develops quickly.... There is, in that, a phenomenon which places everybody else in an inferior position at least to some extent.[15]

When a select group dominates top positions, there is always (even when that selection, as in the case of the *grandes écoles*, is based ostensibly on merit) a controversy about whether they are there because of performance or privilege. Obviously, graduates from the *grandes écoles* believe they deserve the top spots; they have earned

13 Ibid., 112.
14 Ibid., 165.
15 Whitley, Thomas, and Marceau, *Masters of Business?*, 138.

them by gaining access to the best schools in the country. But graduates of the *grandes écoles* run a terrible patronage system. It is alleged that the *anciens élèves* from the very renowned *grandes écoles* protect their own, so much so that they promote the mediocre in order to insure that graduates from their school do not fail. There is no reason to join a debate over the objective skills of the graduates from prestige schools. In any event, it is the others that are of interest. These others are not inferior members of French society. Graduates from the university faculties and from lesser *grandes écoles* of engineering or commerce, they really belong to the French social elite as much as most graduates from German universities and *Fachhochschulen* do to the German. But, unlike the Germans, they are, because of their schools, excluded from the pool of people from which top managers in French business, industry, and bureaucracy are selected. The demotivation, therefore, as the quotation just cited illustrates, that the French system of higher education has on the others throughout their careers, is, compared to the German, severe.

The long-term, postexperience motivational effect of English higher education on individuals differs from both the German and the French. Peter Lawrence, after discussing the heterogeneity of the educational requirements in German management, compared them with those in Great Britain: "Although the proportion of graduates was smaller and the number of PhDs few, the same phenomenon is to be observed: a heterogeneity of qualifications at any particular level."[16] If, then, public school and Oxbridge prejudices divert people from business and industry, prejudices about school origins do not, as in France, harm career possibilities excessively once people start work. Still the similarity with Germany is only partially and, indeed, deceptively true. The British managers without university qualification do resent the egghead university man. They even resent the man with a business education. As a secretary of an engineering company observed: "You've got to put business graduates in senior positions, to satisfy their expectations – and then you run the risk of their lack of experience. They're bloody good on statistics and graphs, but often they can't motivate their team as people with a track record might do."[17] German managers want practical-minded people, too, for they are hardheaded realists who are wary of the theory boys. But, as

16 *Managers and Management*, 112.
17 Newman, "The MBA Credibility Gap," 49.

Lawrence himself writes, "The difference is that those in England who press the claim of experience and practical aptitude are often arguing that these commodities satisfactorily replace further and higher education . . . [and] . . . in West Germany those arguing the case usually have formal qualifications, take this for granted, but plead for the practical as well."[18] British disputes about the value of a practical outlook express, on one side, hostility toward the university man and, on the other, contempt for the practical nonuniversity-educated one. This is not true in Germany.

Actually, the heterogeneity of qualifications current in British management at any level does not signify so much that people put performance and hard work above educational qualifications (which happens in Germany) as that the British are finally catching up with the rest of the world by hiring university graduates. It represents a management undergoing qualification upgrading, one where the old, nonuniversity-trained man resents the college arrival. The heterogeneity of British management educational qualifications is deceiving in another way. They are not broadly based. The point was made in the last chapter when the failure of engineers to enter nontechnical positions was noted. Although engineers with or without degrees can be found in top and middle technical jobs, thus confirming the heterogeneity of qualifications at any level, the nontechnical positions are, especially in large firms, reserved pretty much for public school products. Here class attitudes expressed in educational attainment obviously continue to demotivate people throughout their careers. To escape the low-status jobs for which their engineering degrees destined them, engineers enter the business school.

How community motivation relates to higher education

So much, then, for how the French, West German, and English systems of higher education motivate individuals in their careers both at entry and postexperience levels. But what about community as opposed to individual motivation? If individual motivation is not the same as community motivation, group motivation is not necessarily community motivation. People have written extensively about elite motivations in relationship to systems of education. Pierre Bourdieu and his

18 *Managers and Management*, 116.

associates describe how the French bourgeoisie utilizes the *grandes écoles* in order to maintain a dominance over French business and industry.[19] The managerial revolution brought by the new large-scale corporation (the shift from owner managers to professional managers) posed no threat to the old *patronat,* for the scions of this *patronat,* through qualifications acquired in the *grandes écoles,* became the "new" managerial class. The managerial revolution was not a social revolution. The question is not, however, whether the elites perpetuate their power – a subject which seems to obsess left-wing sociologists – but how well they are able to carry through their managerial functions. It is a different question essentially from the social one because there is no guarantee that any elite, whether they perpetuate their power or comprise a new group, will manage an economy efficiently. Are they, in short, good managers in respect to their knowledge and their ability to inspire community motivation?

For a group to be highly motivated every individual within it has to be ambitious and hardworking. But for community motivation to be high, individual goals have to coincide with community goals. The individual or group cannot think of herself or himself or itself as a victim (feeling separated from and exploited by the group) or as a parasite (using the organized community for personal or group advancement without regard to community goals). It is not necessary that there be job satisfaction for the individual. As Constance A. Nathanson and Marshall H. Becker have noted, "the absence of a consistent relationship between job satisfaction and job performance has been documented."[20] Indeed a ten-country management survey indicates that it was "not U.S. executives [that] suffer from the highest level of stress but rather the Japanese. . . . On a comparative scale the Japanese respondents are more depressed than everybody except the Brazilian and Nigerian participants. They also have the highest percentage of respondents who are

19 "Reproduction culturelle et reproduction sociale," *Social Science Information* 10:2 (Apr. 1971): 45–79; "L'Ecole conservatrice, les inégalités devant la culture," *Revue française de sociologie* 7 (1966): 325–47; Pierre Bourdieu and Jean-Claude Passeron, *La Reproduction, éléments pour une théorie du système d'enseignement* (Paris, 1970); and Pierre Bourdieu, Luc Boltanski, and Monique de Saint-Martin, "Les Stratégies de reconversion: Les classes sociales et le système d'enseignement," *Social Science Information* 12:5 (Oct. 1973): 61–113.
20 "Job Satisfaction and Job Performance: An Empirical Test of Some Theoretical Propositions," *Organizational Behavior and Human Performance* 9 (1973): 267–79, 267.

potentially unstable."[21] Productivity, profits, and technological leadership, not happiness, are goals of business and industrial firms. As long as the employees bend their wills to these ends, whether they are happy or not does not seem, from a performance angle, to matter.[22] Stress, therefore, and the unhappiness that results are not, apparently, since actual performance in terms of keeping up with technology does not correlate with stress, of much significance. More important than individual happiness to the highly motivated community is an appropriate ideology – common beliefs about collective goals – and an organizational structure and style that convince people that the ideology is true. Educational systems influence both.

Community motivation, as just defined, conflicts with the Anglo-Saxon ideology of individualism. There are, however, nonliberal traditions which have to be considered. Here the corporate conceptions that reached their culmination under fascism are not at issue. They were swept away by the Second World War. It is a question rather of long-standing, extraliberal, antiindividualistic ideologies that still strongly determine organizational cultures. One of these traditions is French; it is the product of the Napoleonic state. This heritage, embodied in the elite group of state servants, has been treated in a variety of contexts. It is, however, important to look at it specifically as it affects community motivation. Neither the training of this elite in the *grandes écoles* (primarily in the Ecole Polytechnique and in the Ecole Nationale d'Administration) nor their careers in the grand corps "predispose them to the business world." Even after they enter business or industry, moreover, there persists "a certain mental structure which summarily condemns, on the basis of a certain ethic, all that involves economic gain, everything that has to do with profit."[23] By their esprit de corps, by their sense of state service, the French corporate executives drawn from these *grandes écoles* constitute a very different kind of leadership group than the liberal, capitalistic, individualistic American or British M.B.A.s.

A second extraliberal attitude can be found in West Germany. Peter Lawrence notes that when the German manager is asked about the purpose of his enterprise, he never says that it is to make money. He is

21 Cary L. Cooper, interview, UMIST, Feb. 1983.
22 Hence, both the British and the Japanese manager are most stressed about keeping up with new technology, the German and Swedes the least under stress.
23 Ezra Suleiman, *Elites in French Society* (Princeton, N.J., 1978), 241.

like the Japanese who, if pushed on the subject, will simply say that profit making is incidental to the greater purpose of the firm, which is to provide a service to its customers, to benefit mankind. Americans are usually skeptical about such pronouncements; they think the Americans are more honest when they admit their pecuniary desires. In other words the Americans have trouble understanding the Japanese because they do not share their values. The same is true of the Germans. Whereas, as Lawrence observes, Americans believe "if you can pay you're equal," Germans think "if you are *leistungsfähig* (capable of achievement) you're equal."[24] In both countries a man's value is not determined by his origins, but the basis of judgments about individual worth differs. In Germany it is performance not money that matters. This belief, moreover, produces corollaries. One is the conviction in German firms that the product is the thing and superior performance means superior products. The second is the idea (discussed in the third chapter) of *Technik*. *Technik* is the combination of knowledge and know-how necessary to make a product. Lawrence asserts that this idea permeates German industry, that it accounts "for the uncomplicated view taken by top managers of company goals and the means to achieve them."[25] German managers do not need to discuss company strategy. The goal is clear, to produce the best possible product. Nor do they need to have a special group of managers to plan, control, and make decisions, for "*Technik* is in the foreground and managerial techniques and corporate strategy take second place."[26] People must work hard and efficiently to produce the product and it sells itself. Pierre-Alain Schieb observes that the Germans believe "that the market is elastic in terms of products, the crisis comes only when the consumer abandons the product."[27] This outlook explains the German emphasis on specialist education. Not only do they specialize in education, they also remain throughout their careers in a single business organization.[28] This respect for experts explains Peter Lawrence's comment about why various product managers are represented on the boards of directors of German firms. Not only is the production engineer there but so is an engineer from Design; often, in fact, more

24 *Managers and Management,* 106.
25 Ibid., 98.
26 Ibid.
27 Pierre-Alain Schieb, "Dessin industriel: une comparaison France-Allemagne," *Revue française de gestion* 32 (Sept. – Oct. 1981): 80–86, 86; my translation.
28 See Evers, *Kriterien zur Auslese,* 128.

than one is on a board if the firm has more than one product line. With the German firm "*Technik* is," Lawrence states, "a force for integration. The German company is *Technik* in organizational form. The skilled worker, the foreman, the superintendent, the technical director are all participants in *Technik*. Of course there are many things which they do not have in common, but *Technik* is something which transcends hierarchy."[29]

Thus the technocratic view of the French statist elite and the German idea of *Technik* make German and French managers more group oriented than the liberally educated American and British individualists. Does this mean that group motivation is higher among the French and the Germans? Undoubtedly it is high among the French elite who look upon themselves as the brightest and the best. All graduates of *grandes écoles* believe this and the grander the *école* the higher the group's opinion of itself. This is particularly true of the members of the *grands corps* (mines, bridges and roads, inspectors of finance, etc.) who move so freely into top jobs in industry and banking.

Still, since the *grandes écoles* and the *grands corps* exist outside the business and industrial firms, they are not synonymous with them. In other words, the elite really do not belong to the firms in which they work. Their educational qualification (their *grandes écoles*) rather than their performance on the job affects their placement and advancement in the firm. They do not, in fact, as do the Germans, begin at the bottom of the managerial hierarchy in specialist functions and steadily work their way to the top. They do not even necessarily know much about the firm where they work. As a member of the Corps of Bridges and Roads noted in 1967:

I have the opportunity of changing posts every three or four years. Let's say that I am offered a post at the Caisse des Depôts – and this post would only be offered to a member of the grands corps (I don't have to explain why – friendship, corporatism, the telephone, etc.) – I come to it, as to other posts, with the great merit of ignorance. This is what allows for a new view of things. The general and relative incompetence of members of the grands corps is a great advantage: it allows them to take a fresh view, which the others cannot.[30]

This might, from an intellectual viewpoint, give the Frenchman a freshness of approach to his task, but it makes him an outsider. The elite are

29 *Managers and Management*, 98.
30 J. Mantes, "Reflexion sur l'orientation du corps des ponts et chaussées," *Bulletin du PCM* 64 (Mar. 1967), cited in *Elites in French Society*, by Suleiman, 169.

not members of the organizational community in which they work, neither in the sense of having grown to maturity within it or in the sense of identifying their destiny with it.

As a method of decision making, moreover, French elitism contrasts sharply with the famous Japanese Ringi. Rin (a proposition made by a subaltern) Gi (which brings about a formal group discussion of all people involved by the proposition) is a formalized bottom up system of consultation that permits, with a hierarchy based on seniority, younger people in the Japanese firm to express their ideas. It is, moreover, perfectly compatible with, indeed it is part of, the collective decision-making that is typical of Japanese firms. The French generalist approach, therefore, is a top down method of decision making in which the claims of the brilliant *chef de file* are vaunted against those of the regular organization's members whose opinions are disregarded. Whereas the Ringi system cements community sentiment and therewith the idea of community motivation, the French system has just the opposite effect.

Indeed, it seems to reinforce the French penchant for bureaucratic formalism in organizational culture. Michael Crozier ascribes four major components to French bureaucracies:

First the bureaucracies are characterized by an extensive development of impersonal rules which are generated by strata who are not directly involved in the day-to-day operation of the plant. Second, the occupational groups have clear boundaries, high cohesion and there is no movement between them. The groups and their members are, therefore, isolated from each other. Third, authority to decide exceptional cases and to change the rules of the game is centralized and local plant managers have little autonomy. Fourth, around these areas in which it is not possible to specify all activities through rules, there are sources of uncertainty which are matched by these various groups organizing themselves in "parallel power relations."[31]

Not having risen from the shop floor, the *grandes écoles*-educated elite have no real knowledge of the day-to-day operation of the plant. Being an exclusive group, they are isolated from the other non-*grandes écoles*-qualified members of the hierarchy with whom they have little interchange. And, as the centralized super-elite in a top down hierarchy, they set the rules of the game. As outsiders, then, this French elite

31 Quoted in Peter Clark, "Cultural Contexts as a Determinant of Organizational Rationality: A Comparison of the Tobacco Industries in Britain and France," in *Organizations Alike and Unlike*, ed. Lammers and Hickson, 272–82, 274.

reinforces the penchant of impersonal bureaucratization in French organizational life and, with it, contributes to the destruction of a sense of community.

The German concept of *Technik,* by contrast, since it is a yardstick with which every echelon within the hierarchy can identify and against which each can be measured, reinforces the sense of community. The sentiment, moreover, buttresses certain community traits that Germans, like Japanese, share in their organizations, for instance, an inclination to avoid uncertainty by engaging in collective decision making.[32] It also intensifies the German idea of worker participation in management, for it provides the performance standards which the workers, like the managers, must meet when faced with decision making. The Japanese have been praised for their consultative forms of decision making; if it takes longer, it is more effective because everybody works harder to implement what is a commonly derived policy. A study of workers' participation in ten West German companies reached the same conclusions: higher workers' participation in policy formulation does not mean that management control lessened. Effective management control actually increased because participation by the workers in management brought the duty and responsibility with it to submit to control.[33] Schieb's comparative study of innovation in the French and German electric appliance industries reveals that product innovation in German firms is done by groups:

The [group] participants' place in the hierarchy differs. Decisions are made and have to be made by group consensus. Every member of the group has to shed the particular interest of the service department he comes from. . . . Decisions are made unanimously and are written up formally. . . . Vertical integration of the hierarchy allows people to explain and communicate the decision more easily – and to integrate the youngest managers into the pro-

32 Hofstede, *Culture's Consequences.*
33 Klaus Barthhölke, Walter Eschweiler, Dieter Flechsenberger, and Arnold S. Tannenbaum, "Workers' Participation and the Distribution of Control as Perceived by Members of Ten German Companies," *Administrative Science Quarterly* 27:3 (Sept. 1982): 380–97, 384. P. W. Turnbull and T. Yamada note that "team approaches" also characterize West German and Swedish companies' international marketing. They observe that firms in these countries are, therefore, unlike British companies where "individual approaches" to international marketing prevail but like Japanese where "[i]nteractive marketing strategies based on the 'team approaches' or collective 'organisation approaches' of Japanese companies have greatly contributed to the success of Japan in world markets." ("The Japanese Approach to International Marketing," University of Manchester Institute of Science and Technology, *Occasional Papers,* no. 8407, Dept. of Management Sciences [July 1984], 21).

cess. The integration of the functional hierarchy and horizontal integration avoids isolating the various services from each other and permits collaborators to have a global view of the enterprise: its goals, its problems, its norms. . . . The engineers assimilate the concepts, the techniques, the appreciations (*valeurs*) of the commercial people and vice versa. . . . The "benjamins" are often charged with drafting committee reports and above all with visiting each participant [on the product innovation team] to get his signature on the definitive document.[34]

No elaborate consultative process takes place in this industry, Schieb reports, in French factories – factories, he also reports, that are far behind those in Germany in product development. There the sense of *Technik* presides over the community of workers. It provides the ideology of community motivation, the common purpose.

Thus *Technik* constitutes the ideology necessary to the development of community motivation that the French ideology of elite service and the Anglo-American of liberal individualism do not. The material conditions of work, moreover, make the German ideology believable. In the French case, an elitist rationale permits French underlings to accept the idea of a supermanagerial class that serves the public. The graduates of the *grandes écoles* and the members of the *grands corps* are generally admired for their brilliance and their capacity, so much so that even the socialist left makes no plans to abolish the *grandes écoles*.[35] Unlike the Germans, the French more readily accept the *chef de file* who, without the participation of the lower elements, makes the decisions. (Geert Hofstede in *Culture's Consequences* calls this a Power-Distance Index, according to which there is a greater distance between the governed and the governor in the French than in the German firm.)

Systems of material reward within the firm undermine the concept of service. Because of the philosophy of individualism, Americans accept great income differentials between a corporation's board members, who might make hundreds of thousands of dollars, and its lowest paid employees, who might make the minimum wage. Japanese are prone to accept an elite which, like the French, are recruited from a few prestige schools, an elite which preach an ideology of community motivation, because the salary differentials in the firms are not very great and promotion is decided by seniority. But this material sanction

34 "Dessin industriel," 84.
35 Suleiman, *Elites in French Society*, 107.

is missing in France where the distance between the income of the elite and the underlings is one of the greatest in Europe. J. J. Sylvestre's study of wage differentials in France and West Germany demonstrates that

salary differences, not just absolute but in terms of internal relativities, exist between the French and German companies. The most general way to express that difference is to say that the salary hierarchy – the gap between the highest paid person and the lowest paid person – was shorter in the German companies. And several more detailed propositions consistent with this general fact of a narrower overall salary rank in the German companies, are also valid. The gaps between the skilled average wage and the unskilled average, between the manual average wage and the non-manual average, and between the managerial average and other white collar average, were all smaller in the German companies.[36]

It is hard to support an ideology of community solidarity – especially if a class-conflict, anticommunity alternative like Marxism is at hand – when some people are gaining disproportionate material rewards from the firm. That is the case to a much greater degree in France than in West Germany.

Factory organization, moreover, makes the community ideology more acceptable in West Germany than in France or in Great Britain. Studies done by Marc Maurice, J. J. Sylvestre, Arndt Sorge, and Malcolm Warner which compare British, French, and German firms show the motivational effects of organizational difference at factory levels.[37] The researchers compared firms, paired and matched for similarity according to size, production type, and kinds of operational problems. They drew up the ideal scheme of the operational managerial hierar-

---

36 "Industrial Wage Differentials: A Two-Way Comparison," *International Labour Review* 110:6 (Dec. 1974), quoted in Lawrence, *Managers and Management,* 51–52. Salary differences are manifested, moreover, according to educational background. The journal *l'Expansion* for June 1974, e.g., gave salary figures for the *cadres debutants* showing graduates of the Ecole Polytechnique at the top, followed by those of the Ecole Centrale (Paris), the Ecole Nationale Supérieure d'Electricité, the Ecole Nationale Supérieure d'Aéronautique, and the schools of Télécommunications and Mines (Paris, Nancy, and St. Etienne), and the three major Parisian commercial schools (H.E.C., E.S.S.E.C., E.S.C.P.). These were followed by holders of doctorates in economics at the university, graduates of the smaller engineering schools, commercial schools and "Sciences Po," and holders of first degrees (maîtrises) from the business faculties at the university, Paris IX (Dauphine) in Paris, and then by holders of first degrees in other university business faculties (Whitley, Thomas, and Marceau, *Masters of Business?,* 136.)
37 "Societal Differences in Organizing Manufacturing Units: A Comparison of France, West Germany, and Great Britain," *Organization Studies* 1:4 (1980): 59–88.

Figure 7.1. <u>Factory personnel structure</u>

Source: Marc Maurice, Arndt Sorge, and Malcolm Warner, "Societal Differences in Organizing and Manufacturing Units: A Comparison of France, West Germany, and Great Britain," *Organization Studies* 1:4 (1980): 59–88, 69.

chy that appears in Figure 7.1. And they evaluated the firm's management hierarchy in terms of three blocks of variables:

1. *The configuration of the organization;* breakdown of the labor force into categories as shown in the hierarchy in Figure 7.1 and numerical ratios between the sizes of components, as well as sizes relative to the total work force.
2. The joining of individual tasks to work positions, and the coordination of work activities; this could be called *work structuring and coordination.*
3. The acquisition of qualifications and competence and the progression of individuals within typical careers; these constitute the *qualification and career systems.*

Comparisons under the first category show that, although in every branch of technology (unit production, large batch/mass production, continuous process production) the German work units were substantially larger than the British or the French (and hence should be more bureaucratic), staff size was larger in the British and the French than in the German units (see Table 7.1). Although these statistics reveal a smaller German staff than British and French in relationship to the line, this was not always the case. German managerial and supervisory staff was larger than British, but British technical staff was larger than German. The difference indicates that German managerial hierarchies in the firm were not as tall as British (or French) and German managers' spans of control were much greater. If the technical staff is thought of as being engaged in advisory functions, moreover, the line dominated the staff in German factories even more.

Work structuring and coordination, the second variable, also differed. The flexibility and cooperation between different production jobs were greater in Germany than in Britain or France; the differentiation between the functions of production and maintenance was sharp-

Table 7.1. *Work–function relations in German, French, and British factories*

		Germany	Britain	France
Percentage of foremen in works	Unit production	4.0	5.7	9.6
	Large batch/mass production	3.5	3.8	9.5
	Continuous process production	15.8	16.5	22.2
Percentage of managerial & supervisory staff in works	Unit production	28.8	21.6	46.6
	Large batch/mass production		(no data available)	
	Continuous process production	37.4	25.5	55.0
Percentage of technical staff employees/works	Unit production	25.0	39.9	46.2
	Large batch/mass	2.3	6.5	7.2
	Continuous process production	11.3	16.7	39.8

Source: Marc Maurice, Arndt Sorge, and Malcolm Warner, "Societal Differences in Organizing Manufacturing Units: A Comparison of France, West Germany, and Great Britain," *Organization Studies* I:4 (1980): 59-88, 66-70.

est in France and Britain. Both sets of activities were clearly separated in the two countries and workers rarely crossed over from one area into another. On the British and French shop floors, supervisory activities were dominated by the technical services. German foremen, on the other hand, were freer to detail workers to other jobs during a shift. German production workers often did easy repair and maintenance jobs themselves (thereby eliminating the necessity to call in technical services). In other words, the style of work and management differs in German factories from that in British and French factories.

With the third variable, the qualification and career system, the flatter an organizational structure, the greater the spans of control, and the more, as Professor John Child notes, "the competence of manager and subordinates needs to rise."[38] Hence not only were the style of work and the nature of individual tasks different in the British, French, and German factories but the skills were, too, the German manager's being much broader in scope and of a higher technical quality than the British and perhaps the French. Higher skills permitted production workers in German factories to cross over to maintenance and production managers to become part of technical staff at some point in their careers, and vice versa. Style and skill, therefore,

38 *Organization: A Guide to Problems and Practice* (London, 1977), 148.

had considerable influence on the structure of these firms. German firms were not as tall as British and French and were less formal. The border between line and technical expert in Germany tended to disappear; in Britain and in France it was quite pronounced.

Other studies substantiated the view about French, West German, and British organizational cultures presented in these microcomparisons. Michael Crozier's description of the French bureaucracy confirms the sharp isolation between staff and line in France at the factory level. The paucity of verbal as opposed to written communication in French organizations illustrates rule-laden bureaucratic relationships in French firms. Comments about the poor correlation between research and production in British and the good relations in German factories evoke the predominance of the line over the staff in Germany and the separation of the staff (in R and D) from the line in the British example. The broader spans of control found in the German factories explain the greater status that German foremen, compared to English or French, have in their firms. "If one spends time in German manufacturing companies," Peter Lawrence observed, "it becomes clear that the foremen are doing quite a lot for their superiors. They are able to do it in terms of skill and knowledge, they are allowed to do so and they expect to do so. German foremen often attend meetings alongside managers of higher rank . . . they discuss investment plans and machinery purchases."[39] Lawrence observes that the broader spans of control, the line's dominance of the staff, or rather the fuzziness of the interface between the two, also seem to clarify why German views about

who should do what and how is remarkably free from stereotyping. The sort of antitheses which are often felt to exist between theory and practice, thought and action, specialist knowledge and generalist judgments, commercial and technical aptitude, even line and staff, do not seem to bother the Germans. They do not show much zeal for putting people in boxes. One is less likely to hear remarks like "He has a good honours degree in engineering – put him in Research and Development" or "What we really want our Sales people to have is personality." The Germans do not seem to see any incompatibility between intellectual ability and educational attainment on the one hand and working in industry on the other, in line positions or even in "sharp end" functions like Maintenance and Production. They do not seem to fear that clever people will be bad at "action." If one looks at advertisements for executive posts in German newspa-

39 *Managers and Management*, 159.

pers it is again quite clear that there is no perceived incompatibility between technical knowledge and commercial attitude.[40]

The factory organizational culture, in short, reinforces or indeed reflects the community motivation, for it brings the group together. Perhaps this greater reciprocity explains the better work satisfaction. Jean-Claude Pelissolo and Robert de Metz report, for example, from a 1978 survey, that among those who prefer being at work to being away from it, 30 percent in Japan prefer work, 28 percent in West Germany, and 14 percent in France.[41]

Even the so-called shortcomings of top corporate German management can be explained by a community motivation based on the idea of *Technik*. Heinz Thanheiser concluded after studying fifteen West German firms (with at least DM70 billion turnover) that "the great majority have no system for strategic planning" and the three firms that did were, compared to Americans, not doing it very well. "The success of the German enterprises that we studied cannot be explained by advanced planning techniques."[42] The Germans were not uninformed about these techniques; they just did not have any faith in them or in the management philosophies the techniques projected. Thanheiser observed:

The managers at the highest level, even on the board, were extremely skeptical about the idea of professionalism in management. They did not, then, share the confidence that their American colleagues had in the transfer of "management know-how," confidence which gave them the courage to create the "conglomerates." The German leaders [*dirigeants*] view diversification from a different angle: "we have seriously studied the potential of Sector X (close to us from a technological standpoint) into which we could have easily entered. But nobody on the Board of Directors knows the market, the competitors, the clients. . . . Consequently we don't touch it." Such a view differs greatly from the viewpoint on diversification and decentralization advanced in Anglo-Saxon writings.[43]

At issue are not just the different conceptions that the Germans have vis à vis the Americans or the British or the French but the different

40 Ibid., 111–12.
41 "L'Industrie au futur," rapport de mission au Ministère d'Etat, Ministère du Plan et de l'Aménagement du territoire, Jan. 1983 (Paris, 1983), 106.
42 "Stratégie et planification allemandes," *Revue française de gestion* 21 (May–June 1979): 6–13, 8; my translation.
43 Ibid., 8.

organizational cultures out of which the ideas originate. Because, Heinrich Evers concluded from his study, "one half [the top managers] work exclusively in one firm before joining the board [and] only one in eight changed firms more than twice in their careers," they had long-term associations with their firms.[44] Seventy-seven percent of the board members, moreover, worked in a functional capacity (*Sacharbeit*) for years at the beginning of their careers. They were not only experts in something, therefore, but they were experts on that something in the firms where they had moved to the board. Board members were promoted from operational specialist jobs; their usefulness to the board, as the above quotation suggests (nobody knows the market, the competition, the clients) stemmed from operational experience. Since German boards were recruited from the highly motivated operational community, all this American talk about headquarters' management differing from divisional/operational did not make much sense to them. Confident that a good product sold itself, convinced that attention to *Technik* assured a quality product, they saw all managers' tasks as essentially the same. Only a staff which had not come from or had cut itself off from the operational community could deal in strategic concepts that would put a petroleum company into the motion picture business or take a famous steel company out of steel.

Two points need to be stressed. First, the German system of higher education supports the community motivation that is embodied in the organizational culture just described. The combination of *Wissenschaft* with practical purposiveness in German engineering education obviously fostered the disappearance, at the operational level, of the contradiction between thought and action, and the ability of German engineering managers to move back and forth between technical staff services and production blurred the distinction between staff and line and nourished the task-oriented atmosphere which is another strength of German operational management.

Academic business economics contributed to shared community values. Eugen Schmalenbach had affirmed from the beginning that the science of business economics should abet the productivity of the national economy as well as that of the firm. Efficiency (*Wirtschaftlichkeit*) within the firm was not defined in German business econom-

---

44 *Kriterien zur Auslese*, 129.

ics solely in money-making terms.[45] Community (*Gemeinschaft*) ends also had to be served or rather were involved in the very concept of efficiency. The disdain that profit-minded American M.B.A.s have for the engineer's pride in product is quite alien to German business economics. *Technik* could become one of its shared values. That acceptance is expressed most directly in the *Wirtschafts-Ingenieur* educational programs at technical universities but it is also expressed in programs like that of the business faculty at Stuttgart University where all business economics majors, regardless of study emphasis (marketing, personnel, accounting) have to take a quarter of their courses in engineering-technical subjects. In praxis the business economists' accommodation of *Technik* is expressed in the person of the *Wirtschafts-Ingenieur,* who is frequently employed in controller functions; in the close cooperation between commercial and technical staff in product-development and marketing functions; in the high technical knowledge at every management echelon and the excellent specialist knowledge in nontechnical, managerial positions, which corresponds to equally advanced educational preparations and which contributes to the ability of German managers to exercise larger spans of control and, hence, to the balance in favor of more line than staff managers.

An examination of the same categories of British and French educational-management relationships produces inverse results. The taller management structures, the shorter spans of management control, the higher proportion of staff to line employees, the dominance of the line by the technical services – all these attributes of the British and/ or the French operational units, ascertained in comparative factory studies, reflect the contempt of the scientist for the technologist, the generalist for the specialist, the man of knowledge for the man of action,

45 Professor Katsuyuki Nagaoka points out that German business economists distinguish between *Betrieb* (firm), a public or private independent productive unit whose "aim is not necessarily profit but economic efficiency," and *Unternehmung* (enterprise), a form of ownership, public or private, "that has no goal." The distinction is made by Marx when discussing the transformation of capital from its money form to its thing form and vice versa, that is, between labor process that goes on in the firm (*Betrieb*) and value formation that occurs in the enterprise (*Unternehmung*). "It is," Nagaoka writes, "not too much to say that what is characteristic of German business economics right up through the system of Erich Gutenberg and has made it different from the American management theories and the English and American economic theories of the firm, is the use of the concept of transformation of capital and the distinction of *Betrieb* and *Unternehmung*." These conceptions have permitted the German business economists to think more than in profit terms when dealing with their subject. See Nagaoka, "Business Management Study in Japan," 9.

which is engrained in the English and/or the French system of higher education.[46] The fact that the *grandes écoles* trained men for the board-rooms of corporate France – a self-conscious elite – encouraged them to perceive their interests and managerial functions – as strategic generalists – separately from those of the managers at lower levels of the hierarchy.[47] And the fact that English top management is composed of accountants and arts graduates rather than engineers, and that it puts profit ahead of inventiveness, must certainly result, at least in part, from an educational system that looks on technologists as narrow-minded specialists incapable of appreciating the overall view. And the fact that British production engineers are not as well educated as German must have something to do with their relative incapacity to unify thought and action, intellectual ability and practical-prowess on the job. All these particular educational features combine in Britain with the generally lower educational level of managers to create the less homogeneous, less flexible, less united British operational organization.

The second point has to do with the economic effectiveness of the educationally related organizational cultures. That a high percentage of German managers, especially at upper levels, possess postgraduate re-search doctorates helps explain why German management sees no con-tradiction between inventiveness and profit and why German firms have succeeded particularly well in high-technology manufacturing. Active German managers willingly participate in the work of the techni-cal and scientific community. Peter Lawrence says that, among German

46 In addition to the Maurice et al. study already cited, see Pierre Dubois, "Manning Levels and Wage Hierarchies: The Case of French and English Maintenance Workers in Serial (Batch) Industries," *British Journal of Industrial Relations* 20:2 (Mar. 1982): 76–82; Pierre Dubois, "Niveaux de main-d'oeuvre et organisation du travail ouvrier. Etude des cas français et anglais," *Sociologie du travail* 16:4 (1974): 257–74; Pierre Dubois, "Workers' Control over the Organization of Work: French and English Maintenance Workers in Mass Production Industry," *Organisation Studies* 1:4 (1981): 347–60; Donald Gerwin and Jean-Claude Tarondeau, "Ateliers flexi-bles: une analyse internationale," *Revue française de gestion* 31 (May–Aug. 1981): 80–93; Gert Hartmann, Ian Nicholas, Arndt Sorge, and Malcolm Warner, "Com-puterised Machine Tools, Manpower Consequences and Skill Utilisation: A Study of British and West German Manufacturing Firms," *British Journal of Industrial Rela-tions* 21:2 (July 1983): 221–31.
47 That wider spans of control correspond to greater capacities arising from better training throughout the factory hierarchy seems true. Pelissolo and Metz give the following qualification comparisons for the French and West German labor force: higher education degree, 3.5% Fr., 4.5% W. Ger.; professional but nonuniversity qualification, 27% Fr., 60% W. Ger.; no professional qualification, 69.5% Fr., 27% W. Ger. The gap between the top and bottom is smaller educationally as well as monetarily in West Germany.

Table 7.2. *Education and achievement – highest salaried German engineers*

	Entire Sample	Highest Paid	Engineers with good university final exams
-Percentage with technical publications (books and articles)	30	44	55
-Percentage who give technical talks or lectures 'outside' their firm	36	53	54
-Percentage with patented 'discoveries'	24	37	31

Source: Peter A. Lawrence, *Technische Intelligenz und Soziale Theorie* (Munich, 1981), 83.

engineers, those with the highest salaries (those higher in the employment hierarchy and hence those most probably higher in management) are engaged in "technical-scholarly activities." The data he recorded on the German engineers queried in a survey appears in Table 7.2. The study confirms the research orientation of engineers in German management. Lawrence has concluded that "technical-scholarly activities are very much more common among German engineers than among their British colleagues."[48] No doubt the relative degree of exposure to scientific culture in educational systems has prompted different patterns of behavior in the managers' active professional careers.

Professor Christer Karlsson has also noticed a relationship between education and the ability of an organization to increase its volume of production: unit costs for production decrease by accumulated production volume.[49] In order to accumulate volume, an organization has to learn to do so; to do that promptly the organization has to learn quickly. If a firm, therefore, can increase accumulated production in a shorter time than its competitor, its organization is smarter. The rate of increase in accumulated volume is charted on an experience curve. Karlsson observes that Japanese experience curves (the rate at which an organization learns to accumulate production volume) are steeper than American. Karlsson's description of how Japanese work the assembly line at Honda suggests why. Teams, not individuals, are assigned tasks; every person on the team can perform every task necessary to the accomplishment of the team task, so that each team member can work where the work needs to be done. This work method requires a labor force with high work skills and knowledge, i.e., better education. It also requires a

48 Lawrence, *Technische Intelligenz und soziale Theorie* (Munich, 1981), 83; my translation.
49 In conversation.

management that acts as a consultant for the workers (to help them overcome problems) not as an instrument of command. The logic of Karlsson's explanation transfers particularly well to German factory organizations, with their broader spans of control, shorter management hierarchies, higher qualifications, and the community motivation which this educational-organizational culture and the ideology of *Technik-Wirtschaftlichkeit* provide.

These examples illustrate how educational systems reinforce organizational and motivational as much as knowledge patterns. If drawn from manufacturing firms, they could just as easily have come from other organizations. Ryutaro Koyiya and Kozo Yamamoto, speaking of the civil servants in the Japanese Ministry of Finance (M.O.F.), the Ministry of International Trade and Industry (M.I.T.I.) and the Bank of Japan (B.O.J.), observed:

Most of the occupants of these posts are highly intelligent and capable men. . . . In practice they often play the role of an economist. [But, a]ll are basically generalist administrators, diplomats, or central bank officers; none is a professional economist. They are influential in the economic policy making process not because they apply advanced knowledge of economics or economic theory to the issues under consideration but because they have wide experience as generalist administrators and can react promptly to new problems and changing circumstances, mobilize the information, knowledge, and capabilities available among their subordinate staff, and build up a consensus among those concerned through deliberate persuasion and skillful negotiations.[50]

The quotation's principal point is motivational not informational, for the intelligence and knowledge of the manager are useless unless they are implemented by an ability to motivate the organization. The Japanese organizations, who know what they want, promote the desired results (knowledge plus motivation) in employees by taking over employee education themselves. And this makes sense, for they could not leave the motivational aspect of education to the academic community and expect much. The distinction made when discussing knowledge and achievement between *berufsfähig* and *berufsfertig* applies very much to the subject of this chapter, too. By taking on postexperience education the Japanese and the German firms improve the motivational climate of their organizations. The British and the French firms, leaving education to the academic community, weaken motivation

50 "Japan: The Officer in Charge of Economic Affairs," 267.

within their organizations, for outside academic institutions are ill-equipped to carry out organizational-specific motivational tasks.

The present is future

This book began by presenting the new paradigm in management studies and then citing reasons for questioning its validity, not to imply that the application of science to management was valueless, but to show that the new paradigm could not explain management reality. The point is important because those who embraced the new paradigm had high hopes that it could. These hopes were so pronounced, in fact, that the advocates of the new paradigm tended to change science into ideology. This has occurred especially in economic science. Japanese success has shown that the growth of the modern economy cannot be explained by the ethos of the economic man. Consequently, if Western man behaves like economic man, he does so for cultural reasons: The economic man is the phenomenon of a specific culture, not a universal norm.[51] The contention supported here, therefore, has been that managerial behavior in every society, including the West, is culturally distinct.

These considerations directly affect another point that was made in the introductory chapter, that comments would be made about future as well as past and present relationships between higher education and economic performance. Nancy McNulty observed in 1980:

The Japanese showed great astuteness in refusing to adopt all the management practices recommended by the United States. Generally speaking, they took what could be easily transferred – production management techniques, financial management, some aspects of marketing – and put them to good use. In areas subject to cultural factors, especially those of organization and personnel management, they stuck firmly to their traditional practices and values with great benefit.[52]

McNulty's comment is an interesting example of historical relativity, for such a statement would not have been made twenty years before. Then the American cultural values, embodied in business organization and personnel were considered to be just as responsible for the superi-

---

51 David Bergmanini notes in a democracy "the Anglo-American type of government was too individualistic to be compatible with Japanese society." *Japan's Imperial Conspiracy* (London, 1971), 135.
52 Nancy G. McNulty, *Management Development Programs, The World's Best* (Amsterdam, 1980), 17.

ority of American business and industry as the technical instruments employed – production management techniques, financial management, some aspects of marketing. But there is another sense in which the quotation is misleading: It gives too much credit to the Japanese. The Japanese should not be praised for retaining cultural traits. If they had had a choice they might have abandoned them for the American after the war, but, as the quote itself indicates, they had no choice; for cultural factors are most difficult to change. The Japanese merit, then, resided in their ability to bend their cultural habits, which at one time were blamed for their backwardness, sufficiently to be able to borrow those management practices from the West needed to promote a modern economy.

Comments about the future relationship between higher education and economic performance depend on what one thinks that relationship will be. Historians doubt people's ability to predict accurately in this respect, and the comments demonstrate why. In the 1960s everyone predicted that the American manager was the model for the future; few made the same predictions twenty years later. Japanese management methods – which are in some respects very different from the American – had caught people's eye. Will these management methods be admired in twenty years? Who knows? It depends on how well the Japanese and others manage their affairs.

Yet the real problem is not the predictability of the future as much as it is the ability to deal with it, however unexpected, when it comes. From an educational viewpoint, this ability varies according to whether a technical or a cultural management factor is at stake. Obviously, inasmuch as advanced management techniques (financial analysis, modeling, etc.) are intellectually demanding, they cannot easily be learned in backward countries. The techniques of management are, however, not much of a problem for people living in advanced industrial-educational states. Even if German managers are poorer than American in long-range planning because German universities do not teach it well, even if it can be learned more easily in British, French, or American business schools, the obstacles German firms face are hardly insurmountable. German firms can send their people abroad to get proper education or recruit people from abroad who have been properly educated. Since the numbers involved in strategic planning are relatively few, getting the properly schooled people is relatively easy. A reliance on foreigners would not pose problems because the expertise required – strategic planning, portfolio analysis, etc. – is of a cognitive order, easy to learn by people of diverse cultural backgrounds, and, because of its relatively culture-free character, taught much the same way whether in Singapore, London, or Munich. Consequently, discrepancies in the teaching of management techniques that have existed between advanced countries in the past are quickly disappearing. The English, with the rapid accumulation of undergraduates reading business subjects, will close the gap with the Germans and the French soon. It is difficult, therefore, to believe that any advanced country will suffer comparative educational disadvantage in the future in terms of knowledge about management techniques, for, if they do not develop the techniques themselves, they can, as the Japanese and Europeans did after the Second World War, borrow them from abroad (America).

The problems arise with the culturally dependent forms of management education. This is true because the difficult-to-transfer, culturally based educational factor becomes more important as countries achieve educational parity in the more easily transferable and assimilative education in management techniques. Whatever comparative advantages the Americans had in this respect have been lost; whatever comparative advantages the Japanese have gained, which have grown as a result of the attainment of parity in techniques, are easier to retain.

Education is not just a part of the solution to the management problem but a part of the problem itself. This book has stressed how inherited culture-specific educational systems have affected the acquisition of managerially useful knowledge and how they have influenced community motivation. In Great Britain there persists, as a result of the educational system, a great prejudice against education throughout every level of society. This means, at the mass level, that people who must work do not value education per se: Education is good for them only when they see how it directly affects their ability to do their specific job. It means, at the upper levels of society, that employers, like the workers, do not think education is useful unless it can be shown to be directly responsible for improving profits and that people who do not have to do useful things cling to the gentleman's ideal of education. Assuming that the general level of numeracy and literacy within society has the least apparent immediate impact but the most real, long-term economic usefulness, the British educational system is indeed part of the problem.

The same is true, of course, of the other educational systems treated in this study. That the French do not have a problem promoting utilitarianism can be attributed to an educational heritage which produced, through the *grandes écoles,* an action-oriented civil servant and technocratic elite. That France, on the other hand, has a problem with community motivation can also be attributed to this system because it demotivates Frenchmen who, not having passed through the *grandes écoles,* find themselves hindered in their careers. The German success in community motivation and in knowledge qualifications, moreover, can also be attributed to this educational heritage, not because it causes everything to turn out as it does but because it is part of a system that permits these results to occur.

One management educational task is apparent. Western European institutions of higher education are knowledge oriented and the chief problem is motivation, not knowledge. How exactly business and engineering schools or departments can cultivate community motivation is not known. The educators, as it now stands, have no ideology with which to inspire community motivational goals, nor do they seem to be possessed with a sense of urgency about acquiring them and the pedagogical techniques necessary to their teaching.

The real problem is not that people's cultural values are difficult to change but that there is no agreement about what should be done. Despite the American and now Japanese example, it is hard to find interchangeable variables in cultural situations, for what might work in one cultural context might not work in another. The German refusal to adopt the M.B.A., the French to emulate the American graduate business school, and the English to get rid of public schools are not prompted by blind prejudices alone. The Japanese firm's heavy financial commitment to thoroughly educating its employees, which echoes German experience, and seems, by blending motivation with knowledge, to provide optimum managerial education, might not be possible in English firms. There are concerns about the transferability of these educational examples, concerns that are well grounded because of the uniqueness of cultural experience.

What the future requires is therefore not some super educational-reform program in Europe patterned on American or Japanese education. It requires honesty. Europe is threatened now in a way that it has not been for half a millennium; its economic survival is at stake. In the past fifty years it has lost its technological leadership first to America and then to Asia and there is a danger of this becoming an irreversible decline. The economic threat menaces the ability of Europeans to maintain their prosperity and their civilization. This technological crisis is the latest in a series of disasters. Three generations ago, largely through their own doing, the peoples of Europe destroyed their world political hegemony. The generation of 1914, which lived in a world dominated by Europe, one in which the end of European hegemony was almost unthinkable, could at least claim that it was ignorant about the consequences of its actions. But this excuse is no longer possible. Europeans cannot afford the luxury of ignorance and dishonesty any more.

The dishonesty is expressed particularly by the beneficiaries of higher education, the so-called directing classes. They are a privileged, primarily middle-class group in every country which does not understand, or does not wish to understand, the responsibilities it has towards tax-paying people. One part, if small, of the educated elite indulges in the luxury of Marxism. To sincere, eager generations in the past Marxist ideology seemed a plausible directive to human happiness. But with the evidence plainly before our eyes – the economic failure, moral bankruptcy, and political hypocrisy of Marxist states everywhere – to advocate seriously Marxist solutions to problems is dishonest. It is dishonest because, without any real prospects of providing anything better and with real prospects of furnishing worse, it foments class conflict and noncooperation in societies that need community. The majority, those intellectuals, businessmen, and non-thinking white-collar and blue-collar workers who have embraced the philosophy of the economic man, are perhaps more at fault. In the pursuit of personal profit and class advantage, they too, demotivate their economic communities. It is not a question of intellectual arguments about supply-side economics or similar stuff. It is one of actions that are dishonest, for one cannot expect enthusiasm within a work community when a few people get most of the material rewards. Successful management education in the future requires people who are interested in an educational system that really advances the community's welfare. If reformers follow such an aim with enthusiasm and talent, they might find the specific educational solutions tailored to the requirements of the particular cultures in the particular age. But if cultural heritage does not permit people to be honest about their problems, then they are indeed doomed; for it is not written in the stars that Western Europe or Western Civilization must survive and prosper.

Bibliography

Statistics

France. Ministère de l'Education. Secrétariat d'état aux universités. Statistiques des enseignements. Tableaux et informations. 6.3. *Les Examens et les diplômes dans les universités*. Nos. 1–20, 1962–83.

Ministère de l'Education. Service de l'informatique de gestion et des statistiques. Sous-direction des enquêtes statistiques et des études. *Recueil des codes. Code des titres et des diplômes.*

Ministère de l'Education. Service de l'informatique de gestion et des gestions et des statistiques. Tableaux statistiques. *Statistiques des élèves des établissements de haut enseignement commercial. Diplômes délivrés, 1970–1984.*

German Federal Republic. Statistisches Bundesamt. Wiesbaden. *Bestandene Abschlussprüfungen, 1950–1984.*

Statistisches Bundesamt. Wiesbaden. *Statistische Jahrbücher, 1962–1984.*

Great Britain. Central Services Unit for Careers and Appointments Services. AGCAS Statistics Sub-Committee. *First Destination of University Graduates, 1976–77.* Central Services Unit, Manchester, 1977.

Council for National Academic Awards (C.N.A.A.). *Annual Reports. 1964–1984.*

Council for National Academic Awards (C.N.A.A.). *Directory of First Degree and Diploma of Higher Education Courses.* Published yearly.

Pickman, S. P. *The Output of UK Universities by Institution and Discipline,* Manchester. *Central Services Unit for University and Polytechnic Careers and Appointments Services.* Published yearly.

Polytechnic Careers Advisers. Statistics Working Party. *First Destinations of Polytechnic Students Qualifying in. . . . A Statistical Report on Those Obtaining First Degrees and Higher Diplomas by Full-Time and Sandwich Course Study, 1980–1984.* Before 1980 published as *A Statistical Report on Those Obtaining First Degree and Higher Diplomas by Full-Time and Sandwich Course Study, Polytechnic First Degree and HND Students. Some Details of First Destination and Employment.*

The Universities Central Council on Admissions (U.C.C.A.). *Annual Reports 1–22, 1963–84.* Published with annual *Statistical Supplement.*

University Grants Committee. *Details of First Destinations of University Graduates.* University Statistical Record. Cheltenham.

United States. National Research Council. Office of Scientific and Engineering Personnel. *Summary Report 1981 Doctorate Recipients from United States Universities.* Conducted by the National Research Council for the National Science Foundation, the U.S. Office of Education. Peter D.

Syverson, Operations Manager, Doctorate Records Project. National Academy Press, 1982.

Books, articles, brochures, and personal interviews

To save space, works cited in the footnotes are, on the whole, not repeated in this Bibliography. The Bibliography consists, therefore, of studies not previously cited but which were of use in preparing this book.

Nonauthored secondary works

"Augsburger Modell nach Ablauf der Erprobungszeit als regulärer Studiengang eingerichtet." *Informationen, Bildung, Wissenschaft* (Sept. 1982): 180–81.

Berufsakademie. *Studienführer, Ausbildungsbereich Wirtschaft.* Stuttgart: Berufsakademie, n.d.

"Le Centre Consulaire de Recherche et d'Enseignement de la Gestion des Entreprises de Reims (C.C.R.E.G.E.)." *Enseignement et gestion,* no. 14 (1976): 73–82.

Le Centre de gestion scientifique, Ecole nationale supérieure des mines de Paris. Paris: E.N.S.U.L.P., 1982.

Centre National de la Recherche Scientifique. *La Politique de l'énergie.* Proceedings of the Seminar of Professor Allais, 1959–1960. Paris, 1962.

    La Décision. Paris, 1961.

    Econométrie, fondements et applications de la théorie du risque en économétrie. Paris. 1953.

"Ce que veulent les 'Sup de Co.," Nouvelles de l'enseignement de la gestion, actualités." *Enseignement et gestion,* no. 5 (1972).

"Le C.N.P.F. et la formation au management." *Hommes et commerce,* no. 117 (Jan.–Feb. 1971): 10–23.

"Le Comité d'études sur les formations d'ingénieurs." *Cahiers, C.E.F.I. Technologie et formations des ingénieurs,* no. 1 (Mar. 1982).

"Contrôle de Gestion, L'Enseignment du contrôle de gestion." *Enseignement et gestion,* no. 14 (May 1976).

"Création d'un troisième cycle d'enseignement dans les facultés des sciences." *Revue de l'enseignement supérieur,* no. 1 (Jan.–Mar. 1956): 57–64.

Ecole nationale supérieure des mines de Paris: Cycle de formation des ingénieurs civils. Ecole Nationale Supérieure des Mines de Paris, n.d.

Enquiry into the Flow of Candidates in Science and Technology into Higher Education. Dainton Report. London, 1968.

"L'Enseignement des relations industrielles dans les établissements de gestion." Une étude de "Travail et Société." *Enseignement et gestion,* no. 1 NS (Spring 1977).

"Les Enseignements de gestion scientifique à L'Ecole des Mines, Synthèse des discussions du département des sciences économiques et sociales sur les différents cours de la section gestion scientifique." Working Paper, Direction des Etudes, Ecole National Supérieure des Mines de Paris, June 1980. Mimeographed.

"Les Entreprises jugent l'enseignement commercial français, Nouvelles de l'enseignement de la gestion." *Enseignement et gestion,* no. 5 (1972).

"Etude sur les jeux et simulateurs d'entreprise utilisés dans l'enseignement de la gestion, nouvelles de l'enseignement de la gestion, actualités." *Enseignement et gestion*, no. 5 (1972).

Etude sur les présidents directeurs généraux des 1000 premières sociétés françaises. Paris: Russell Reynolds Associates, n.d.

50 Jahre Wirtschaftsingenieurwesen. VWI-Zeitschrift, Berlin, 1977. A festschrift.

Fondation nationale pour l'enseignement de la gestion des entreprises. *Rapport d'activités, 1982.* Paris: F.N.E.G.E., 1982.

Annuaire des enseignants de gestion, 1984. Paris: Marchand, 1985.

"Formation au Japon." *Enseignement et gestion.* Special issue of the series "Cahiers de la fondation nationale pour la gestion des entreprises" (Winter 1981–82).

"La Formation des ingénieurs en question?" Quelques propositions inspirées par les méthodes nord-américaines de formation d'ingénieurs, observées au cours d'un voyage aux Etats-Unis et au Canada (Nov. 19–Dec. 2, 1973). *Enseignement et gestion*, no. 9 (Oct. 1974).

Führungskräfte für die Zukunft der Unternehmen. Zehn Jahre Baden-Badener Unternehmergespräche. Fünf Vorträge. Essen: Verlag W. Girardet, 1966.

"The Great Debate: A Post-Robbins Mould?" *THES*, no. 593 (Mar. 16, 1984): 32.

"Le Groupe, E.S.S.E.C." *Enseignement et gestion*, no. 13 (Jan. 1976): 33–67.

Hommes et commerce, 17th year, no. 104 (Sept.–Oct. 1968). Issue devoted to L'Homme et l'informatique.

Hommes et commerce, 18th year, no. 109. Issue devoted to La Formation continue.

I.D.E., "Participation: Formal Rules, Influence, and Involvement." *Industrial Relations: A Journal of Economy and Society* 18:3 (Fall 1979): 273–94.

"Importer de la matière grise." *Hommes et techniques*, 25th year, no. 292 (Feb. 1969): 117.

"Improper profits." *The Economist* (Nov. 5–11, 1983): 19–20.

Information, Consultancy, Training. RKW, Rationalisierung – RKW-Annual Review '78. Eschborn: RKW, 1978.

Information, Consulting, Further Training. RKW, Rationalisierung – RKW-Annual Review '80. Eschborn: RKW, 1980.

"Japanische Literatur über Plankostenrechnung." *ZfbF* 17 (1965): 636–37.

"Le Lancement des programmes doctoraux." *Enseignement et question*, no. 10 (Jan. 1975): 17–40.

Liaison Office of the grandes écoles and technische Hochschulen. "The Education of Professional Engineers in West Germany and France and the Equivalence of Studies." Translated by Anthony Beaty. *European Journal of Engineering Education* 2 (1977): 167–83.

"Management Education." *THES* (Apr. 13, 1984), a special section, i–viii.

Management Education in the 80s. Brussels: A.I.E.S.E.C. (L'Association Internationale des Etudiants en Sciences Economiques et Commerciales), 1979.

"Der Mensch im Betrieb." Report on the workshop of the Seminar on Economic Sciences of the Darmstadt TH and Chamber of Commerce, June 19 and 20, 1950. *ZfbF* (1950): 355–58.

"Mitteilungen – Betriebswirtschaftslehre und Business Economics." *ZfbF*, NF 1 (1949): 356.

"Mitteilungen – Festschrift für Eugen Schmalenbach in Japan." *ZfbF* 6 (1954): 548.

"Mitteilungen." *ZfbF* 16 (Sept. 1, 1922): 84.

"The New Curriculum in the French Facultés de Droit." *The Economic Journal* 67 (Mar. 1957): 145–48.

"Obituary – Eric Charles Williams, 15 May 1915–8 January 1980." *Journal of the Operational Research Society* 31 (1980): 559–61.

"Obituary – Professor W. Ross Ashby – Pioneer of Cybernetics." *Operational Research Quarterly* 24:1 (Mar. 1973): 1–2.

"Obituary – Sir Charles Frederick Goodeve, OBE, FRS." *Journal of the Operational Research Society* 31 (1980): 961–64.

Postgraduate Courses in Business Studies, Management, and Related Subjects, CUMS at Universities and Business Schools in the United Kingdom. London: The Conference of University Management Schools, 1975.

"Problems and Prospects of Management. Education and Research in Germany. Developments in Organizational Theory and Organizational Practice." Summary Report of the 12th annual I.U.C. Conference held in Nuremberg, June 17–21, 1965. I.U.C. Secretariat, 1965. Typescript.

"Proceedings of the Seminar on Management Decision Making," Oslo, June 3–4, 1982. Institute Report no. 82–5. E.I.A.S.M., Sept. 1982.

"Quelques exemples de centres de perfectionnement." *Enseignement et gestion*, NS, no. 24 (Winter 1982–83): 27.

Reichskuratorium für Wirtschaftlichkeit. *Jahresbericht, 1932/33.* RKW-Veröffentlichungen, no. 95, 14.

Sekretariat der Ständigen Konferenz der Kultusminister der Länder in der Bundesrepublik Deutschland – Geschäftsstelle für die Studienreformkommissionen. *Entwurf, Empfehlungen der Studienreformkommission Wirtschaftswissenschaften und Stellungnahme der Ständigen Kommission für die Studienreform.* Bonn: Sekretariat der Kultusministerkonferenz – Geschäftsstelle für die Studienreformkommissionen, 1982.

Studies on the Need of Management Education in the European Community. Brussels: European Foundation for Management Development, 1974.

"Technikfeindlichkeit können wir uns nicht leisten." *Deutsche-Universitäts-Zeitung* (1981): 452–55.

"25 Jahre Wuppertaler Kreis." Wuppertal, 1980. Brochure.

"Von Amerika lernen?" *Der Volkswirt*, no. 38 (1952): 5.

"Was sich in den Wirtschaftswissenschaften ändern sollte." *Hochschulpolitische Informationen – HPI*, no. 10 (May 22, 1981): 11–14.

"Zahl und Alter der betriebswirtschaftlichen Hochschullehrer in der Bundesrepublik Deutschland einschliesslich West-Berlins und in Österreich." *ZfbF* 17 (1965): 37–49.

ZfbF, Heft 1 (Jan. 1982). Issue devoted to the German, Japanese, and American comparisons.

"Zu wenig qualifizierte Marktforscher?" *Der Volkswirt* 13:18 (May 2, 1959).

Authored works

Abdalla, Ikhlas H. "Impact of Influence and Skill on Managerial Performance." *OMEGA* 11:3 (1983), 263–72.

Abrams, Mark. Review of *Principles of Market Research,* by A. H. R. Delens. *The Economic Journal* 61 (1951) 405–49.

Ackermann, Karl-Friedrich. "Eine interdisziplinäre Projekstudie für Betriebswirte und Ingenieure an der Universität Stuttgart." In *Betriebswirtschaftliche Hochschulausbildung – Neue Formen – Experimente – Praxisbezug,* by Horst Albach, Eduard Gaugler, and Peter Mertens. *ZfB Ergänzungsheft* (Jan. 1982): 79–90.

"Tutorenkurse für Betriebswirte im Mannheimer Modell." In *Betriebswirtschaftliche Hochschuldidaktik – Materialien und Untersuchungsergebnisse,* 2d ed., edited by Peter Mertens, 65–68. Wiesbaden: Betriebswirtschaftlicher Verlag Dr. Th. Gabler, 1971.

Ackoff, Russell L. "A Comparison of Operational Research in the U.S.A. and in Great Britain." *Operational Research Quarterly* 8:1 (Mar. 1957): 88–100.

"Does Quality of Life Have to Be Quantified?" *Operational Research Quarterly* 27:2 (1976): 289–303.

Adler, John, and Cherrington, Paul. "Management Education in West Germany." An occasional paper. The Administrative Staff College Henley-on-Thames, 1966.

Aftalion, Florin; Evrard, Yves; and Trahand, Jacques. "La Recherche dans les établissements français d'enseignement de la gestion." *Enseignement et gestion,* F.N.E.G.E., no. 14 (May 1976): 57–69.

Albach, Horst. "Entwicklung und Aufgaben der Unternehmensforschung." *Die Wirtschaftsprüfung* 18:5 (1965): 113–20.

"Lineare Planungsrechnung." *ZfbF* 11 (1959): 482–86.

Uberwindung des Gegensatzes zwischen Volks-und Betriebswirtschaftslehre." *FAZ* (Dec. 13, 1977).

"Zur Theorie der Unternehmensorganisation." *ZfbF* 11 (1959): 238–59.

Albach, Horst; Gaugler, Eduard; and Mertens, Peter. *Betriebswirtschaftliche Hochschulausbildung – Neue Formen – Experimente – Praxisbezug. ZfB Ergänzungsheft* (Jan. 1982).

Alchian, Armen A. "The Basis of Some Recent Advances in the Theory of Management of the Firm." *The Journal of Industrial Economics* 14:1 (Nov. 1965): 30–41.

Allais, Maurice. "Croissance et dangers de l'utilisation de l'outil mathématique en économique." *Nouvelle Revue de l'économie contemporaine* (Jan. 1955).

"L'Emploi des mathématiques en économique." *Metroéconomica* (Oct. 1949).

"Le Problème de la coordination des transports et la théorie économique." *Bulletin des Ponts et Chaussées et des Mines* (Oct. 1947). Reprinted in *Revue d'économie politique,* no. 2 (1948): 212–71.

Allen, David. "Report of the S.S.R.C. Management and Industrial Relations Committee Seminars on Research and Doctoral Training." Institute Report no. 80–1, E.I.A.S.M., Mar. 1980.

Allen, G. C. Review of *Investment in Innovation,* by C. F. Carter and B. R. Williams. *The Economic Journal* 69 (1959): 558–60.

Allen, J. M. "A Survey into the R & D Evaluation and Control Procedures Currently Used in Industry." *Journal of Industrial Economics* 18:2 (Apr. 1970): 161–81.

Allusson, R. "Les Centres universitaires d'administration des entreprises." *Hommes et techniques* 203 (Oct. 1961): 1153–57.

Alquier, René. "L'Enseignement de la gestion dans les écoles d'ingénieurs." *Hommes et commerce,* 19th year, no. 113 (May–June 1970): 50–62.

Amako, Tetsuo. "Quand les entreprises japonaises intègrent la gestion américaine." *Revue française de gestion* 32 (Mar.–Apr. 1982): 59–63.

Anderson, Brian. C.N.N.A. London (Dec. 9, 1983). Personal interview.

Andrews, P. W. S. "Industrial Economics as Specialist Subject." *Journal of Industrial Economics* 1 (1952–53): 72–79.

———. "Strategic Dimensions of Internationalization." Working Paper no. 82–37, E.I.A.S.M., 1982.

Ansoff, H. Igor. "The Next Twenty Years in Management Education." Paper presented at the University of Chicago, Graduate Library School, 36th Annual Conference, April 9–10, 1973.

Anweiler, Oskar, and Hearnden, Arthur G. *From Secondary to Higher Education.* Beiheft 1, *Bildung und Erziehung.* Cologne: Boehlau Verlag, 1983.

Bacon, Robert, and Eltis, Walter. *Britain's Economic Problem: Too Few Producers.* 2d ed. London: The Macmillan Press, 1978.

Baker, Charles. "A Retreat from Franks." *The Business Graduate,* special issue (1979 – 1980): 14–16.

Ball, R. J. "The London Business School." *The Business Graduate,* special issue (1979–1980): 3–6.

Bardey, Emil. "Wo stehen die deutschen Volkswirte?" *Der Volkswirt,* no. 39 (1950): 13–15.

Barou, Yves. "Spécificité et exemplarité de la crise économique du Royaume Uni. Un essai d'interprétation des principaux enchaînements depuis 1945. Productivité, rentabilité, compétitivité." A thesis for the degree of *doctorat d'état* in applied economics, University of Paris-Dauphine, U.E.R. Sciences des Organisations.

Bass, Bernard, and Franke, Richard H. "Societal Influences on Student Perceptions of How to Succeed in Organizations: A Cross-National Analysis." *Journal of Applied Psychology* 56:4 (1972): 312–18.

Bassière, F. Review of *Jeux de stratègie: théorie et application,* by M. Dresher. Translation from American, in *Revue d'économie politique,* 76th year (1966): 529.

Baumann, Dr. Karl-Hermann. Siemens. Munich (Mar. 17, 1984). Personal interview.

Baumgarten, H., and Feilhauer, H. *Berufsbild des Wirtschaftsingenieurs.* Berlin: Verband Deutscher Wirtschaftsingenieure e. V., 1981.

Bayer, Hermann, and Lawrence, Peter. "Engineering Education and the Status of Industry." *European Journal of Engineering Education* 2 (1977): 223–27.

Becker, Curt; Baudisch, Roman; Birck, Heinrich; Braun, Hedwig; Krelle, Wilhelm; Rühle von Lilienstern, Hans; von Medem, Eberhard; Schnutenhaus, Otto R.; and Stöhr, Rudolf W. *Führungskrafte für die Wirtschaft, Praktiken und Methoden der Aus- und Weiterbildung in den USA und ihre Nutzanwendung in der Bundesrepublik.* Düsseldorf: Econ-Verlag, 1962.

Behrens, K. Chr. "Methoden der Marktforschung und ihre Bedeutung für Absatzplanung und Marktbeeinflussung." *ZfbF* 10 (1958): 485–99.

Beinke, Lothar. "Integrierter Studiengang Sozial- und Wirtschaftswissenschaften an der Gesamthochschule Kassel." *Wirtschaft und Erziehung,*
no. 4 (1981): 117–19.

Beinke, Lothar, and Stuber, Fritz. *Fachhochschule und Weiterstudium. Eine
empirische Untersuchung der Fachhochschulstudenten.* Bad Honnef:
Boch-Herchen Verlag, 1979.

Bellah, Robert N. *Tokugawa Religion: The Values of Pre-Industrial Japan.*
Glencoe, Ill.: The Free Press, 1957.

Bernard, Michel. F.N.E.G.E. Paris (Sept. 30, 1983). Personal interview.

Bernard, Michel, and Citeau, Jean-Pierre. "L'Option: gestion du personnel
dans les instituts universitaires de technologie." *Enseignement et gestion,*
NS, no. 1 (Spring 1977).

Bernhard, Ludwig. "Die Stellung der Ingenieure in der heutigen Staatswirtschaft." *Schmollers Jahrbuch für Gesetzgebung, Verwaltung und
Volkswirtschaft* 28:1 (1904): 127.

Bertonèche, Marc, and Teulié, Jacques. "Que devons-nous enseigner en finance?" *Enseignement et gestion,* no. 14 (May 1976), a small article in
brochure, 9–15.

Best, Michael, and Humphries, Jan. "The City and the Decline of British
Industry: Liquidity without Commitment." A paper presented at the
Anglo-American Conference on the Decline of the British Economy, Bos-
ton University, 1983.

Beuret, Geoff, and Webb, Anne. "Goals of Engineering Education: Final Report." A D.E.S./CNAA sponsored project conducted by Leicester Polytechnic School of Electronic and Electrical Engineering, October 1983.

Bhagat, Rabi S., and McQuaid, Sara. "Role of Subjective Culture in Organizations: A Review and Directions for Future Research." *Journal of Applied
Psychology Monograph* 67:5 (Oct. 1982), 653–85.

Bienaymé, Alain. "Le Centre universitaire Dauphine." *Hommes et commerce*
(Nov.–Dec. 1969): 23–37.

Binsted, Don. "The Training of Teachers of Management Subjects." *Journal
of the Operational Research Society* 31 (1980): 29–41.

Bisani, Fritz, and Friedrichs, Hans. *Das Personalwesen in Europa. Part I:
Ergebnisse des internationalen wissenschaftlichen Kolloquiums am 13/14
Oktober in Essen.* Essen: Hanstein, 1977.

Bishop, B. C. "A Contribution to a Discussion on the Methodology of Operational Research." *Operational Research Quarterly* 23:3 (1972): 251–60.

Bize, Pierre. "Les I.U.T. de gestion: Une Nouvelle Contribution à la formation
au management." *Hommes et commerce* (Nov.–Dec. 1969): 39–45.

Blaug, M. "Approaches to Educational Planning." *The Economic Journal* 77
(1967): 262–87.

Bleicher, Knut. "Sind die Amerikaner wirklich schlechter?" *FAZ* (Mar. 3,
1981).

Blondeau, André "Options nouvelles en matière d'enseignement des affaires."
Hommes et commerce, 19th year, no. 114 (Sept. 1970): 13–18.

Böcker, Franz. "Perspektiven der Internationalisierung der deutschen Marketingwissenschaft." *Zeitschrift für Betriebswirtschaft,* Supplement 1/81 –
Internationale Betriebswirtschaftslehre, 91–97.

"Zur internationalen Positionierung der deutschen Marketingwissenschaft –
Auf dem Weg zu einer Repositionierung." *ZfB,* heft 4 (Dec. 1979): 283–
86.

Boddewyn, J. J., ed. *European Industrial Managers, West and East.* White Plains, N.Y.: International Arts and Sciences Press, 1976.

Böhringer, Rudolf. "Das britische System: Der Finniston-Report und die Folgen." *DUZ* 1 (1981): 14–15.

Boiteux, Marcel. Le Choix des équipements de production d'énergie électrique." *Revue française de recherche opérationelle* 1:1 (4th quarter 1956): 45–60.

"L'Énergie électrique: données, problèmes et perspectives." *Annales des mines* (Oct. 1960): 35–51.

"Le Tarif vert d'Electricité de France." *Revue française de l'énergie* (Jan. 1957).

"La Tarification des demandes en pointe." *Revue générale de l'électricité* 58 (1949), 321–40. (Translated as "Peak-load Pricing," *The Journal of Business* 33:2 [1960]: 157–79.)

"La Vente au coût marginal." *Revue française de l'énergie* (Dec. 1956).

Boiteux, Marcel, and Bessière, F. "Sur l'emploi des méthodes globales et marginales dans le choix des investissements." *Revue française de recherche opérationnelle* 20 (1961): 259–69.

Boiteux, Marcel, and Stasi, Paul. "Sur la détermination des prix de revient de développement dans un système interconnecté de production-distribution." Union Internationale des Producteurs et Distributeurs d'Energie Electrique (U.N.I.P.E.D.E.), Rome Meetings, vol. 10, 1952.

Böning, Eberhard. "Hochschulpolitik, der 80er Jahre." Report no. 21. Wuppertaler Kreis, 1982.

"Die veränderte Rolle des Hochschulasolventen." *DUZ/HD* 17/18 (1976): 466–71.

Bonzon, Pierre. "L'Opinion des employeurs." *Hommes et commerce* 16:101–03 (1968): 187–92.

Booz, Allen, and Hamilton, "German Management." *International Studies of Management and Organization.* Report. Arts and Science Press, Inc. (Spring/Summer 1973).

"German Management: Challenges and Responses – A Pragmatic Evaluation." In *European Industrial Managers,* edited by J. J. Boddewyn, 251–338. White Plains, N.Y.: International Arts and Sciences Press, 1976.

Boulanger, J. J. "Chances d'une économique appliquée – le problème des interdépendances." *Revue d'économie politique* 63 (1953): 185–200.

Boulding, K. E., and Spivey, W. A. *Linear Programming and the Theory of the Firm.* New York: The Macmillan Co., 1951.

Bowen, K. C. "Formalization of the O. R. Process: An Extended Review." *Operational Research Quarterly* 28:2:2 (1977): 369–76.

"Purposeful Systems and Operational Research." *Operational Research Quarterly* 26:1:2 (1975): 125–31.

Bradley, K., and Hill, S. "After Japan: The Quality Circle Transplant and Productive Efficiency." *British Journal of Industrial Relations* 21:3 (Nov. 1982): 291–311.

Brauchitsch, Eberhard V. "Bildung und Beschäftigung im Wandel." *Bildung und Wettbewerbsfähigkeit,* by Klaus von Wysocki, 29–39. Wiesbaden: Gabler, 1981.

Brauer, Dr. K. M. "Grundstudium der BWL an der TU Berlin." In *Betriebswirtschaftliche Hochschuldidaktik,* 2d ed., edited by Peter Mertens, 70–73. Wiesbaden: Betriebswirtschaftlicher Verlag Dr. Th. Gabler, 1971.

Braunstein, Daniel N. "Oh, Harvard (Business Review)." *Interfaces* 4:2 (1974): 39–51.

Bredt, Otto. "Programmierung der Unternehmung." *Die Wirtschaftsprüfung* 12:4 (1959): 85–88.

Bridenne, Alain. "La Révolution silencieuse des Business Schools." *Enseignement et gestion*, no. 5 (1972).

Brinkmann, Gerhard. *Berufsanforderungen und Berufsausbildung: Zur Bestimmung des Bedarfs an hochqualifizierten Arbeitskräften.* Tübingen: J. C. B. Mohr, 1970.

Brittan, Samuel. "How British Is the British Sickness?" *The Journal of Law and Economics* 21:2 (Oct. 1978): 245–68.

Brooke, Michael Z., and Remmers, H. Lee, eds. *The Multinational Company in Europe: Some Key Problems.* London: Longman, 1972.

Brossard, Michel, and Maurice, Marc. "Existe-t-il un modèle universel des structures d'organisation?" *Sociologie du travail*, 16th year, 4/74 (Oct.–Dec.), 402–26.

Brown, E. H. Phelps. "The Brookings Study of the Poor Performance of the British Economy." *Economica*, NS 36:143 (Aug. 1969): 235–52.

Brown, Margaret. King's College. London (Aug. 13, 1986). Personal interview.

Buchanan, Sherry. "Japanese Most Stressed, Swedes Calmest, Says Study." *Herald Tribune, International, Business/Finance* (May 2, 1984): 11, 13.

Buhler, Nicolas, and Trahand, Jacques. "Systèmes de contrôle de gestion et caractéristiques organisationnelles." *Enseignement et gestion*, no. 14 (May 1976): 33–39.

Buquet, Leon. "L'Evolution des facultés de droit, rapport statistique." *Revue de l'enseignement supérieur*, no. 1 (1963): 32–36.

Cardebas, Colette. "Quelques réflexions sur la pensée économique contemporaine." *Revue d'économie contemporaine* 73 (1963): 259–77.

Carroll, Daniel T. "A Disappointing Search for Excellence." *Harvard Business Review* (Nov.–Dec. 1983): 78–88.

Carr-Saunders, A. "The Place of Economics and Allied Subjects in the Curriculum, Presidential Address." *The Economic Journal* 68 (1958): 433–48.

Carter, C. F., and Williams, B. R. "Industry and Technical Progress." *The Economic Journal* 68 (1958): 366–68.

Chadwick, Owen. "Looking beyond Two Cultures." *THES* (Apr. 20, 1984): 13.

Champvillard, Pierre-Denis. "Les Problèmes de management des chemins de fer britanniques (1960–1970)." A thesis for the degree of Doctor of Economic Sciences, University of Paris IX (Dauphine), 1971.

Chandler, Alfred D., Jr., and Redlich, Fritz. "Recent Developments in American Business Administration and Their Conceptualization." *Business History Review* 35:1 (1961): 1–27.

Chandrasekar, Krishanamurti. "U.S. and French Productivity in 19 Manufacturing Industries." *The Journal of Industrial Economics* 21 (1972–73): 110–15.

Charlot, Alain. *Les Universités et le marché du travail: Enquête sur les étudiants à la sortie des universités et sur leurs débouches professionnels.* Paris: La Documentation française, 1977.

Charney, Craig. "Inequality Combats Inequality." *THES* (May 18, 1984): 12.

Chenery, H. B. "Engineering Production Functions." *Quarterly Journal of Economics* (1949).

Child, John. *British Management Thought: A Critical Analysis.* London: Allen and Unwin Ltd., 1969.

"The 'Non-productive' component within the Productive Sector: A Problem of Management Control." *Manufacturing and Management,* by Michael Fores and Ian Glover, 51–68. London: HMSO, 1978.

Child, John; Fores, Michael; Glover, Ian; and Lawrence, Peter. "A Price to Pay? Professionalism and Work Organization in Britain and West Germany." *Sociology* 17:1 (Feb. 1983): 65–78.

Child, John, and Kieser, Alfred. "Organizational and Managerial Roles in British and West German Companies: An examination of the Culture-Free Thesis." In *Organizations Alike and Unlike,* edited by Cornelis J. Lammers and David J. Hickson, 251–71. London: Routledge & Kegan Paul, 1979.

Child, John; Pearce, Sandra; and King, Lisa. "Class Perceptions and Social Identification of Industrial Supervisors." *Sociology* 14:3 (Aug. 1980): 363–99.

Chmielewicz, Prof. Dr. Klaus. Bonn (June 14, 1984). Personal interview.

Cibert, André. Dauphine. Paris (June 28, 1984). Personal interview.

Clementson, A. T., and Clewett, A. J. "Management, Operational Research and the Micro: A Critical Review of What Is Available." *Journal of the Operational Research Society* 32 (1981): 255–68.

Colliard, Claude-Albert. "Présent et avenir des facultés de droit et des sciences économiques." *Revue de l'enseignement supérieur,* no. 1 (1963): 8–19.

Collignon, Etienne. "Compétivité et industries traditionelles." *Revue française de gestion,* no. 41 (June–July–Aug. 1983): 31–36.

Collin, Audrey; Rees, Anthony M.; and Utting, John. *The Arts Graduate in Industry.* London: Action Society Trust, 1962.

Collins, Glenn Michael. *A Statistical Analysis of Applications and Admissions to United Kingdom Universities through the U.C.C.A. Scheme.* Final Year Project, Management Sciences IV, Loughborough University, 1982, under supervision of Peter Lawrence.

Colson, C. *Cours d'économie politique.* Vol. 6, *Les travaux publics et les transports.* Paris, 1910.

Courtin, René. "De l'ambiguité des critères de distinction à la prétendue opposition de la micro et de la macro-économie." *Revue d'écomonie politique* (1956): 19–63.

Crew, Bob. "MBA Business Trip." *Graduate Post,* no. 4 (Aug. 27, 1982): 6–7.

Cruson, Claude. "L'Utilisation de la sociologie par les services publics et par les services privés." *Revue de l'enseignement supérieur,* no. 1 (1965): 99–106.

Daems, Herman. "The Rise of the Modern Industrial Enterprise." In *Managerial Hierarchies: Comparative Perspectives on the Rise of the Modern Industrial Enterprise,* by Alfred D. Chandler, Jr., and Herman Daems, 203–23. Cambridge, Mass.: Harvard University Press, 1980.

Daham, ESCP, Personal interview, June 26, 1984.

Danert, Dr. Gunter. "Zur Vorbereitung von unternehmerischen Entscheidungen." *ZfbF* 10 (1958): 311–23.

Darmois, Georges. "La Statistique." *Revue de l'enseignement supérieur,* no. 1 (1960): 31–42.

de Bettignies, H. C. "Japanese Organizational Behavior: A Psychocultural Approach." In *Management Research,* edited by Desmond Graves, 75–93. Amsterdam: Elsevier, 1973.

Delarue, Julien. "Pour une critique des modèles de prévision économique." Extract from *Critique de l'économie politique* (Apr.–June 1980), published in the series "Problèmes économiques, sélection de textes français et étrangers," *La Documentation française,* no. 1.690 (Sept. 24, 1980), 11–19.

Delay-Termoz, Roger. "La Simulation de gestion – Support de l'enseignement universitaire de l'administration des entreprises?" *Revue d'économie politique* 73 (1963): 289–304.

Desmarez, Pierre. "La Sociologie industrielle fille de la thermodynamique d'équilibre?" *Sociologie du travail,* no. 3 (1983), 261–74.

Desreumaux, Alain. "Histoire et structures des entreprises." *Revue française de gestion,* no. 32 (Sept.–Oct. 1981): 87–97.

Devaux, Louis. "Essai sur le rôle de l'économiste d'entreprise." A General Essay, typewritten. Association française des économistes d'entreprises, Dec. 1, 1980.

Dichgans, Hans. "Zur praktischen Ausbildung der Betriebswirte." *ZfbF* 11 (1959): 199–204.

Dichtl, Erwin. "Die Berufschancen des wissenschaftlichen Nachwuchses in der Betriebswirtschaftslehre." *DUZ/HD* 7 (1977), 206.

Didszun, Klaus-Dietrich. *Zum Problem der Integration der Höheren Wirtschaftsfachschulen in den Hochschulbereich.* Bad Honnef: Verlag Karl Heinrich Bock, 1973.

Ditlmann, Klaus. "Höhere Wirtschaftsfachschule, Aus der Praxis für die Praxis." *Der Volkswirt* 17:37 (Sept. 13, 1963): 2120–22.

Dribbusch, Friedrich. "Personalführung in multinationalen Unternehmen." *ZfbF,* Sonderheft (Apr. 1975).

Drumm, Hans-Jürgen, and Scholtz, Christian. "OR/MS Methods in Manpower Planning. The Theorem of Acceptance." No. 145 in the [Regensburger Diskussionsbeiträge zur Wirtschaftswissenschaft,] Universität Regensburg, Wirtschaftswissenschaftliche Fakultät.

Duerr, Michael G. *Are Today's Schools Preparing Tomorrow's Business Leaders? A Worldwide Survey of Chief Executives.* A Report from the Conference Board, Inc., 845 Third Avenue, New York, N. Y. 10022, n.d.

Dumon, Jacques. "Le Poids des qualités humaines." *Enseignement et gestion,* no. 5 (1972).

Dupriez, Leon H. "Rapport général au congrès des économistes de langue française, Mai 1966." *Revue d'économie politique,* 76th year (1966): 409–32.

Dworkin, James B.; Feuille, Peter; and Wolters, Roger. "Ph.D. Education and Research in IR, 1949–1976." *Industrial Relations* 19 (Winter 1980): 74–80.

Earley, James S. "Business Budgeting and the Theory of the Firm." *Journal of Industrial Economics* 9:1 (Nov. 1960): 23–42.

Earley, James S., and Carleton, Willard T. "Budgeting and the Theory of the

Firm: New Findings." *Journal of Industrial Economics* 10:3 (July 1962): 165–73.

Eden, Colin, and Sims, David. "On the Nature of Problems in Consulting Practice." *The International Journal of Management Science* 7:2 (1979): 119–27.

Edey, H. C. Review of *Accounting for Economists,* by R. Mathews. *The Economic Journal* 76 (1966): 627–28.

Edwardes, Michael. "British Industry and Industry in Britain." In *Manufacturing and Management,* by Michael Fores and Ian Glover, 9–23. London: HMSO, 1978.

Eilon, Samuel. "Ackoff's Fables." *OMEGA* 7:2 (1979): 89–99.

"Editorial – Who Says Production Control Is Dead?" *OMEGA* 5:2 (1977): 107–12.

"In-Company Training." *OMEGA* 4:2 (1976): 119–23.

"The Role of Management Science." *Journal of the Operational Research Society* 31:1 (1980): 17–28.

Eilon, Samuel, and Jenkins, John. "On Education in Management." *The Business Graduate,* special issue (1979–1980): 16–18.

Ellinghaus, W. "Berufsausbildung und Berufsaussichten der Wirtschaftswissenschaftler." *Schriften des Vereins für Sozialpolitik,* NF (1949): 86 ff.

Emshoff, James R. "Behavioural Theory for OR Applications." *Operational Research Quarterly* 26:4 (1965): 675–92.

Endres, Walter. "Die Allgemeine Betriebswirtschaftslehre in Forschung und Lehre." *ZfbF* 33:5 (1981): 416–18.

Engelhardt, Werner, and Hammann, Peter. "Die Verwertbarkeit der Marketingausbildung an deutschen Hochschulen in der Praxis – Eine empirische Untersuchung." Working paper no. 8, Ruhr-Universität, Bochum.

Engholm, Björn; Giescke, Ludwig; Schindler, Götz; Frank, Martin A.; Löhn, Johann; Dalheimer, Rolf. "F-H Spezial." *DUZ* 17 (1980): 519–34.

England, George W., and Lee, Raymond. "The Relationship between Managerial Values and Managerial Success in the United States, Japan, India, and Australia." *Journal of Applied Psychology* 59:4 (1974): 411–19.

Engwall, Lars, and Johanson, Jan. "Business Administration: Then – Now – Later." Manuscript. Department of Business Administration, Uppsala University, Sweden, 1982.

Erdmann, Ernst-Gerhard. "The Impact of Participation on Management in Germany." *OMEGA* 2:3 (1974): 389–93.

Escoube, Pierre. *Les grands de l'état.* Paris: PUF, 1971.

Fallows, James. "America's Changing Economic Landscape." *The Atlantic Monthly* (Mar. 1985): 47–68.

Farrell, Michael. "Philip Andrews and Manufacturing Business." *Journal of Industrial Economics* 20:1 (Nov. 1971): 10–13.

Farrell, M. J. Reviews of *Econometric Methods,* by J. Johnston; *Méthode statistique de l'économétrie,* by E. Malinvaud; *Econometrics,* by S. Valavanis. *The Economic Journal* 75 (1965): 416–18.

Review of *Linear Programming and the Theory of the Firm,* by K. E. Boulding, W. A. Spivey, et al. *The Economic Journal* 73 (1963): 499–500.

Fassbender, Siegfried. *Die Beurteilung von Weiterbildungskursen durch die Teilnehmer.* Bonn: Hanstein, 1974.

Wie lehrt und lernt man Management? Ziele und Methoden der Weiter-bildung von Führungskräften. Frankfurt am Main: Fritz Knapp Verlag, 1973.

Wuppertal Kreis. Cologne (Aug. 13, 1982). Personal interview.

Fassbender, Siegfried, and Bierfelder, Wilhelm. *Erziehung zum unterneh-merischen Handeln: Studienberichte über Weiterbildungsmassnahmen in Frankreich und Grossbritannien* (EPA Projekt 422). Essen: Verlag W. Girardet.

Fassbender, Siegfried, and Groenewald, Horst. *Zweitausend Führungskräfte über ihre Weiterbildung.* Cologne: Peter Hanstein Verlag, 1977.

Fassin, Yves. "Ce que nous pouvons apprendre des Japonais." *Annales de sciences économiques appliquées* 38:1 (1982): 108–31.

Fidler, John. *The British Business Elite: Its Attitudes to Class, Status and Power.* London: Routledge & Kegan Paul, 1981.

Fiedler, F. E. *A Theory of Leadership Effectiveness.* New York: McGraw-Hill, 1967.

Fiedler-Winter, Rosemarie. *Die Management-Schulen.* Düsseldorf: Econ Verlag, 1973.

Fisher, Malcolm R. Review of *Introduction to Operations Research,* by C. W. Churchman, R. L. Ackoff, and E. L. Arnoff. *The Economic Journal* 69 (1959): 558–59.

Flather, Paul. "Calls for Four-Year Degrees." *THES* (Apr. 20, 1984): 4.

"Deans Challenge Science Shift." *THES* (Apr. 20, 1984): 4.

Fliegel, Frederick; Sofranko, Andrew J.; Williams, James D.; and Sharma, Navin C. "Technology and Cultural Convergence." *Journal of Cross-Cultural Psychology* 10:1 (Mar. 1979): 3–22.

Florence, Philip Sargent. "Philip Andrews and the Empirical Approach." *Journal of Industrial Economics* 20:1 (Nov. 1971): 3–13.

Foldes, Lucien. "Uncertainty, Probability and Potential Surprise." *Economica* 25:99 (Aug. 1958): 246–55.

Fores, Michael. "A Proper Use of Science." In *Manufacturing and Management,* by Michael Fores and Ian Glover, 141–55. London: HMSO, 1978.

Fores, Michael, and Glover, Ian. *Manufacturing and Management.* London: HMSO, 1978.

Fores, Michael; Lawrence, Peter; and Sorge, Arndt. "Fertigung ist ein schmutziges Geschäft." *Management* (Apr. 1979): 96–99.

"Germany's Front-Line Force." *Management Today* 13 (Mar. 1978): 87–89.

Forrester, Peter. "Cranfield Prepares for the Future." *The Business Graduate,* Special edition (1979–1980): 10–12.

Fortelle, Gerard de la. La Tour Fiat, la Défense. Paris (June 26, 1984). Personal interview.

Fossati, Eraldo. "Considérations sur des tendences actuelles de la science économique." *Revue d'économie politique,* 68th year (1958): 1007–25.

Foy, Nancy. "The Missing Links: British Management Education in the Eighties." A brochure from the Oxford Centre for Management Studies, 1978.

"Priority for the Eighties: Better Linkage." *The Business Graduate,* Special edition (1979–1980): 32–34.

Frank, Franz-Wilhelm. "Die Ausbildung der Wirtschaftler aus der Sicht der Daimler-Benz AG." In *Bildung und Wettbewerbsfähigkeit,* edited by

Klaus von Wysocki, 89–91. Sonderheft of *ZfbF*. Wiesbaden: Gabler, 1981.

Franko, Lawrence G. "The Move toward a Multidivisional Structure in European Organizations." *Administrative Science Quarterly* 19:4 (Dec. 1974): 493–506.

Frechet, Maurice. "Le Rôle d'Emile Borel dans la théorie des jeux." *Revue d'économie politique*, 69th year (1959): 139–67.

Frederichs, W., and Kübler, K. "Die Leistungsfähigkeit ökonometrischer Prognose-Systeme." *Operations Research Verfahren* 26 (1977): 814–26. Symposium on Operations Research, University of Heidelberg, Sept. 1–3, 1976.

Freemank, C. Review of *Management of Scientific Talent*, by J. W. Blood. *The Economic Journal* 74 (1964): 649–50.

Frenckner, T. Paulsson. "Bestimmung des Produktionsprogramms als Anwendungsbeispiel der Linearplanung." *ZfbF* 10:2 (1958): 565–94.

Unternehmungsumwelt, Unternehmungsplanung und Controlling. Entwicklung in den letzten 50 Jahren." In *Unternehmensplanung*, edited by K. Brockhoff and W. Krelle. Berlin: Springer Verlag, 1981.

Friday, Frank A. "The Problem of Business Forecasting." *Journal of Industrial Economics* 1 (1952–1953): 55–71.

Friend, John. Tavistock Institute. London (July 24, 1986). Personal interview.

Fritsche, Klaus. "Erfahrungen mit der Eingliederung von Hochschulabsolventen der Wirtschaftswissenschaften in die Praxis." *ZfbF*, Sonderheft (Dec. 1981): 55–62.

Galliano, Alain. "Les PME françaises sur le marché américain." *Revue française de gestion*, no. 6 (Sept.–Oct. 1976): 99–107.

Gasser, Chr. "Der Mensch im modernen Industriebetrieb." *ZfbF* 2 (1950): 359–86.

Gasser, Chr.; Gsell, E.; Lisowsky, A; and Moetteli, H. "Deutschlandreise der St. Gallener Betriebswirte." *ZfbF* 2 (1950): 358.

Gaugler, Eduard. "Betriebswirtschaft-Gedanken zum Studium und Beruf." *DUZ/HD* (Mar. 1976): 71–75.

Gaugler, Eduard; Hirsch-Weber, Wolfgang; Kobler, Michael; and Schlenke, Manfred, eds. *Die Universität Mannheim in Vergangenheit und Gegenwart*. Mannheim: Mannheimer Morgen Grossdruckerei und Verlag, 1976.

Gaugler, Eduard, and Ling, Bernhard. "Die Betriebswirtschaftslehre an den wissenschaftlichen Hochschulen in der Bundesrepublik Deutschland, in Österreich und in der deutschsprachigen Schweiz." *Die Betriebswirtschaft* 37:4 (1977): 559–74.

Gaussen, Frédéric. "Les Universités allemandes saisies par la réforme." *Le Monde* (Mar. 5, 1975): 17; (Mar. 6, 1975): 15.

George, W. O., and Thomas, B. C. "When the Lines Become Blurred." *THES*, no. 593 (Mar. 16, 1984): 13.

Giglioni, G. B., and Bedeian, A. G. "A Conspectus of Management Control Theory: 1900–1972." *Academy of Management Journal* 17 (1974): 292–305.

Gilbert, Xavier. "Le Contrôle de gestion dans la formation à la gestion, problèmes pédagogiques." *L'Enseignement du contrôle* (May 14, 1976).

Giraud, Charles. "La Formation des professeurs de gestion." *Hommes et commerce* (Nov.–Dec. 1969): 99–102.

Glover, Ian. "Executive Career Patterns: Britain, France, Germany, Sweden." In *Manufacturing and Management,* by Michael Fores and Ian Glover, 157–80. London: HMSO, 1978.

Goetz-Girey, Robert. "Une Création récente: le certificat d'aptitude à l'administration des enterprises." *Revue de l'enseignement supérieur,* no. 4 (1956): 81–84.

"Une Expérience de deux années: les centres et instituts universitaires d'administration des entreprises." *Revue de l'enseignement supérieur,* no. 1 (1958), 89–93.

"Promotion sociale et administration des entreprises." *Revue de l'enseignement supérieur,* no. 4 (1961): 27–31.

Gold, Bela. "New Perspectives on Cost Theory and Empirical Findings." *Journal of Industrial Economics* 14:2 (Apr. 1966): 164–89.

Goodman, L. Landon. "The Status of Engineers and Their Contribution to Society." Typescript of the British Association Annual Meeting, University of Lancaster, Sept. 1–8, 1976.

Gordon, Paul J. "The Unfinished Business of Business Education: A Commentary on U. S. and European Trends in Response to 'European Management Education Comes of Age.'" *The Conference Board Record* (Jan. 1976).

Graefe zu Baringdorf, B., and Hergel, K. "Education for Management at Institutes of Technology in Germany." Survey, the International University Contact for Management Education, Rotterdam, the Netherlands, June 1965. Typewritten manuscript.

Graham, Robert R. "Is Management Science Arcane?" *Interfaces* 7:2 (Feb. 1977): 63–67.

Graves, Desmond, ed. *Management Research: A Cross-Cultural Perspective.* Amsterdam: Elsevier, 1973.

"The Impact of Culture upon Managerial Attitudes, Beliefs and Behavior in England and France." *Management Research,* edited by Desmond Graves, 283–304. Amsterdam: Elsevier, 1973.

Grayson, C. Jackson, Jr. "Management Science and Business Practice: Management Science Has Now Become Arcane, or Nearly So; a Bridge Must Be Built between It and the Real World of the Executive." *Harvard Business Review* (July–Aug. 1973): 41–48.

Green, V. "Systems Engineering as a Possible Undergraduate Option." *European Journal of Engineering Education* 7 (1982): 147–58.

Grochla, Erwin. "Die Träger der Betriebsplanung." *ZfbF* 10 (1958): 511–24.

Grosset, Serge. *Management: European and American Styles.* Belmont, Calif.: Wadsworth, 1970.

Grossfield, K., and Heath, J. B. "The Benefit and Cost of Government Support for Research and Development: A Case Study." *The Economic Journal* 76 (1966): 537–49.

Gruber, William H., and Niles, John S. "Problems in the Utilization of Management Science/Operations Research: A State of the Art Survey." *Interfaces* 2:1 (1971): 12–19.

Gueudet, Dominique. "La Technologie française face au défi japonais." *Revue française de gestion,* no. 9 (Nov.–Dec. 1984): 72–77.

Guitton, Henri. Review of *Applications et prolongement de la programmation linéaire,* by G. B. Dantzig. *Revue d'économie politique,* 76th year (1966): 1257.

Review of *Les fondements de l'analyse économique*, by Paul Samuelson. *Revue d'économie politique*, 76th year (1965): 1118.

Review of *Statistical Influence in Dynamic Economic Models*, by T. C. Koopmans. *Revue d'économie politique*, 58th year (1948): 706–07.

Günther, Max. "Internationale Wettbewerbsfähigkeit der Unternehmen in Japan, den USA und der Bundesrepublik Deutschland." *ZfbF* 34:1 (1982): 1–7.

Gunz, Hugh. "Generalists, Specialists, and the Reproduction of Managerial Structures." *International Studies of Management and Organization* 10:1–2 (Spring–Summer 1980): 137–64.

Gutenberg, Erich. "Der Stand der wissenschaftlichen Forschung auf dem Gebiet der betrieblichen Investitionsplanung." *ZfbF* 6 (1954): 50.

Haehling v. Lanzenauer, Chr. *Operations Research und betriebliche Entscheidungsprobleme*. Frankfurt am Main: Fritz Knapp Verlag, 1972.

Hague, Sir Douglas. Athenaeum Club. London (Dec. 7, 1982). Personal interview.

Haley, K. B. "O.R. as Apocrypha," *Journal of the Operational Research Society* 33 (1982): 207–10.

Hall, David J. Boston Consulting Group. London (Apr. 13, 1984). Personal interview.

Hall, David J., and Amado-Fischgrund, G. "Chief Executives in Britain." *European Business* (Jan. 20, 1969).

Hall, David J., and de Bettignies, H.-Cl. "L'Elite française des dirigeants d'entreprise." *Hommes et techniques*, 25th year, 291 (1969): 19–27.

"The French Business Elite." *European Business* 19 (Oct. 1968): 230–36.

Hall, Peter. "Control Type and the Market for Corporate Control in Large U. S. Corporations." *Journal of Industrial Economics* 25:4 (June 1977): 259–73.

"Effect and Control Type in the Performance of the Firm in the U. K." *Journal of Industrial Economics* 23:4 (June 1975): 257–71.

Harris, D. J. "Corporate Planning and Operational Research." *Journal of the Operational Research Society* 29:1 (1978): 9–17.

Hartmann, Heinz. "Appraisal of the Report 'German Management: Challenges and Responses.' " In *European Industrial Managers, West and East*, edited by J. J. Boddewyn, 237–50. White Plains, N.Y.: International Arts and Sciences Press, 1976.

Hasenack, Wilhelm. "Zum Problem des betriebswirtschaftlichen Hochschullehrer-Nachwuchses." *ZfbF* 7 (1955): 464–91.

Haug, Dieter. "Die Ausbildung der Wirtschaftler aus der Sicht der Robert Bosch, GmbH." In *Bildung und Wettbewerbsfähigkeit*, edited by Klaus von Wysocki, 91. Wiesbaden: Gabler, 1981.

Hax, Karl. "Die Ausbildung und Weiterbildung des Unternehmernachwuchses: Neue Methoden in den USA und Grossbritannien." *ZfbF* 5 (1953): 235–49.

"Betriebswirtschaftslehre, Betriebswissenschaft und Rationalisierung." *ZfbF* 2 (1950): 184–87.

"50 Jahre Zeitschrift für handelswissenschaftliche Forschung." *ZfbF* 8 (1956): 1–6.

"Gründung einer Industrial Administration Research Group an der Universität Osaka." *ZfbF* 8 (1956): 342.

"Die menschlichen Beziehungen im Betrieb als Gegenstand wissenschaftlicher Forschung." *ZfbF*, NF, 2 (1950): 390–99.

"Rationalisierung der Warenverteilung." *ZfbF*, NF, 4 (1952): 379–86.

"Stand und Aufgaben der Betriebswirtschaftslehre in der Gegenwart." *ZfbF* 8 (1956): 133–49.

Hayes, Robert H. "Why Japanese Factories Work." *Harvard Business Review* (July–Aug. 1981): 57–66.

Heinen, Edmund. "Der entscheidungsorientierte Ansatz der Betriebswirtschaftslehre." Report of the Annual Meeting of Verband der HSL für BWL, St.-Gallen, 1971, pp. 21–37. Berlin: 1971.

"Fortschritte der betriebswirtschaftlichen Lehre und Forschung in Frankreich." *ZfbF* 8 (1956): 126–28.

Heinhold, M.; Nitsche, C.; and Papandopolos, G. "Empirische Untersuchung von Schwerpunkten der OR Praxis in 525 Industriebetrieben der BRD." *ZfOR* 22 (1978): B185–B218.

Heller, Robert. "The State of British Boardrooms." *Management Today* (May 1973): 81–88.

Hempel, Sandra. "Market Attitudes." *THES* (Apr. 13, 1984): 12.

Henderson, P. D. "The Use of Economists in British Administration." *Oxford Economic Papers* 13:1 (Feb. 1961): 5–26.

Hetlebower, Richard B. "Observations on Decentralization in Large Enterprises." *Journal of Industrial Economics* 9:1 (Nov. 1960): 7–22.

Hicks, D. "Education for Operational Research." *OMEGA* 1:1 (1973): 107–16.

Hicks, Donald. "The Origins of Operational Research in the Coal Industry: A Tribute to Sir Charles Drummond Ellis, F. R. S., 1895–1980." *Journal of the Operational Research Society* 34:9 (1983): 845–52.

Hicks, J. R. "Linear Theory." *The Economic Journal* 70:280 (Dec. 1960): 671–709.

Hicks-Beach, Michael. Management Consultants Association. London (Dec. 9, 1983). Personal interview.

Hiscock, M. J. U.C.C.A. Cheltenham, Gloucestershire (Dec. 6, 1983). Personal interview.

Hitpass, Josef; Ohlsson, Rita; and Thomas, Elizabeth. *Studien- und Berufserfolg von Hochschulabsolventen mit unterschiedlichen Studieneingangsvoraussetzungen.* Forschungsberichte des Landes Nordrhein-Westfalen, no. 3183, Institut für Erziehungswissenschaft der Universität Bonn. Opladen: Westdeutscher Verlag, 1984.

Schulreform, Schülerauslese und Hochschulzulassung. Zur Gewissenerforschung der deutschen Bildungspolitik. Stuttgart: Verlag Bonn Aktuell, 1977.

Hitpass, Josef; Mock, Albert; Kammerer, E.; Ohlsson, R.; Thomas, E. *Studenteneskalation. Expansion der Studentenzahlen bis zum Jahr 2000. Studienwünsche der Gymnasiasten und ihre Motive.* Bielefeld: Bertelsmann Universitätsverlag, 1970.

Hjelholt, Gunnar. "Europe Is Different." In *European Contributions to Organization Theory*, edited by Geert Hofstede and M. Sami Kassem, 232–43. Amsterdam: Van Gorcum, 1976.

Höfer, Raimund, and Rober, Manfred. "Einige Bemerkungen zur Entwicklung der Organisationsforschung." *ZfbF* 27 (1975): 171.

Hoflack, Jean, and Dubois, Pierre-Louis. "Les Métamorphoses du marketing." *Revue française de gestion*, no. 39 (Jan.–Feb. 1983): 4–10.

Hofstede, Geert. "Businessmen and Business School Faculty: A Comparison of Value Systems." *Journal of Management Studies* 15:1 (Feb. 1978): 78–87.

Dordrecht (Oct. 25, 1982). Personal interview.

"Nationality and Espoused Values of Managers." *Journal of Applied Psychology* 61:2 (1976): 148–55.

"The Poverty of Management Control Philosophy." *Academy of Management Review* 3 (1978): 450–61.

Hofstede, Geert, and Kassen, M. Sami, eds. *European Contributions to Organization Theory*. Amsterdam: Van Gorcum, 1976.

Hohmeyer, Wolfgang. "Betriebswirtschaftslehre – Wohin? Praktiker Kontra Professoren – Kölner Streitgespräche." *Die Welt* (July 3, 1965).

Holger, Hillmer; Peters, Rolf Wolfgang; and Polke, Martin, eds. *Der Ingenieur in Beruf und Gesellschaft; Studium, Beruf und Qualifikation der Ingenieure*. Düsseldorf: Verlag VDI, 1979.

Holtermann, Sally E. "Market Structure and Economic Performance in U. K. Manufacturing Industry." *Journal of Industrial Economics* 22:2 (Dec. 1973): 119–39.

Horovitz, Jacques. "Allemagne, Grande-Bretagne, France: trois styles de management." *Revue française de gestion*, no. 17 (Sept.–Oct. 1978): 8–17.

Hosmalin, Guy. "Les Travaux pratiques d'économie politique dans le nouveau regime de la licence." *Revue d'économie politique* (1956): 433–44.

Houssiaux, Jacques. "Renouveau de l'expérimentation en sciences économiques: la simulation par les jeux d'entreprises." *Revue d'économie politique* 70th year (1960): 273–300.

Houssiaux, Jacques. Review of *L'Economie au service de l'entreprise*, by R. Henon. *Revue d'économie politique* (1965): 150–51.

Hron, Aemilian; Kompe, Hartmut; Otto, Klaus-P.; and Wächter, Hartmut. *Organisation des Praxisbezugs im wirtschaftswissenschaftlichen Studium: Abschlussbericht eines hochschuldidaktischen Modellversuchs am FBIV der Universität Trier*. Hamburg: Arbeitsgemeinschaft für Hochschuldidaktik e.V., 1980.

Hughes, Thomas Parke. "ENIAC: Invention of a Computer." *Technikgeschichte*, bd 42, no. 2 (1975): 148–50.

Hull, Frank, and Hage, Jerald. "Organizing for Innovation: Beyond Burns and Stalker's Organic Type." *Sociology* 16:14 (Nov. 1982): 564–77.

Hundhausen, Carl. "Amerikanische Literatur zur Wirtschaftswerbung [advertising]." *ZfbF* 17 (1965): 148–52.

Hutton, S. P., and Lawrence, P. A. "The Engineer at School: A Report Based on a Study Made on a Group of over 600 West German School Children." *Energy World* (Feb. 1977): 6–7.

"Production Managers in Britain and Germany." Interim Report of University of Southampton Department of Mechanical Engineering to Department of Industry, Sept. 1978.

"The Work of Production Managers: Case Studies at Manufacturing Companies in West Germany." Interim Report of University of Southampton Department of Mechanical Engineering, Oct. 1979.

Ichihara, Kiichi. "Zwei verdiente Vertreter der japanischen Betriebswirtschaftslehre." *ZfbF* 14 (1962): 518–19.

Iribarne, Philippe d'. "La Gestion à la française." *Revue française de gestion,* no. 1 (Jan.–Feb. 1985): 5–13.

Jackson, Adrienne. L.B.S. London (June 29, 1983). Personal interview.

Jamieson, Ian. "Some Observations on Socio-Cultural Explanations of Economic Behaviour." *The Sociological Review,* NS, 26:4 (Nov. 1978): 777–806.

Jeans, Dr. A. F., and Hurley, Dr. J. "Value of Research." *THES* (May 11, 1984): 2.

Jenkins, B. T. "The Nature of Management Work: The Technical Function." In *Manufacturing and Management,* by Michael Fores and Ian Glover, 25–40. London: HMSO, 1978.

Jenkins, Richard. "Critical Note: Pierre Bourdieu and the Reproduction of Determinism." *Sociology* 16:2 (May 1982): 270–80.

Jonas, H. "A Critique of Cybernetics." *Social Research* 20 (1953): 172–92.

Jones, H. G. "Investment and the Swedish Economy." *OMEGA* 5:5 (1977): 583–92.

Jordan, A. G., and Richardson, J. J. "Policy-Making and Engineering Change: From the Finniston Report to the Engineering Council: An Interim Report." Report No. 7, Politics Department, Strathclyde Papers on Government and Politics, 1983.

Kagono, Tadao, et al. "Mechanistic vs. Organic Management Systems: A Comparative Study of Adaptive Patterns of U.S. and Japanese Firms." Reprinted from *The Annals of the School of Business Administration,* no. 25, Kobe University, 1981.

Kahlert, Helmut. "Forschung an Fachhochschulen?" *DUZ/HD* (1977): 795–97.

Kahn, R. F. "Oxford Studies in the Price Mechanism." *The Economic Journal* (Mar. 1952): 119–30.

Kapferer, Dr. C. "Volkscharakter und Verkaufspolitik in den Vereinigten Staaten." *ZfbF* 1 (1949): 177–83.

Kappler, Ekkehard, ed. *Rekonstruktion der Betriebswirtschaftslehre als ökonomische Theorie.* Spardorf: Wilfer, 1983.

Kasai, Y., and Takada, K. "Die Betriebswirtschaftslehre in Japan nach dem Kriege." *ZfbF* 3 (1951): 518–22.

Kassem, M. Sami. "Introduction: European versus American Organization Theories." In *European Contributions to Organization Theory,* edited by Geert Hofstede and M. Sami Kassem, 1–17. Amsterdam: Van Gorcum, 1976.

Keachie, E. C. "Der Stand der ökonomisch-technischen Betriebsführung (Industrial Engineering) in Deutschland." *ZfbF* 10 (1958): 672–78.

Kelley, J. "Changing Views of Management Efficiency," *Journal of Industrial Economics* 12:2 (Mar. 1964): 108–14.

Kennerley, Prof. Strathclyde Business School. Strathclyde (Feb. 28, 1983). Personal interview.

Kern, Werner. "Studienreform als eine Aufgabe spezifischer Produktgestaltung." *ZfbF* 32:2 (1980): 136–48.

"Unternehmungspolitik als angewandte Betriebswirtschaftslehre." *ZfbF,* 18 NF (1966): 491–97.

Kienast, Philippe. "Le Comportement financier comparé des entreprises allemandes et françaises." A Thesis for the degree of Doctor of Finance, Doctorat 3è Cycle, University of Paris IX-Dauphine, 1980.

King, Edmund J., ed. *Reorganizing Education: Management and Participation for Change.* London and Beverly Hills: Sage Publications, 1977.

Kingston, William. *The Political Economy of Innovation.* The Hague: Martinus Nijhoff, 1984.

Kleine, Meinolf. *Das betriebswirtschaftliche Hochschulstudium: Didaktisch-methodische Analyse und curriculare Elemente.* Stuttgart: Paul Haupt, 1981.

Koch, E. "Mathematik – pro und kontra." *Der Volkswirt* 14:24 (1960): 1176–78.

Koch, Helmut. "Über einige Grundfragen der Betriebswirtschaftslehre." *ZfbF* 9 (1957): 569–97.

Koch, Waldemar. *Aus den Lebenserinnerungen eines Wirtschaftsingenieurs.* Cologne: Westdeutscher Verlag, 1962.

Der Beruf des Wirtschaftsprüfers. Berlin: Funcker & Humblot, 1957.

"Probleme der Hochschulpädagogik." *ZfbF* 11 (1950): 183–84.

Koot, Ronald S., and Walker, David S. "Short-Run Cost Functions of a Multi-Product Firm." *Journal of Industrial Economics* 18:2 (Apr. 1970): 118–28.

Korndörfer, Wolfgang. "Die Fachhochschule für Wirtschaft – eine echte Alternative?" *DUZ* 21 (1973): 895–97.

Kosiol, Erich; Szyperski, Norbert; and Chmielewicz, Klaus. "Zum Standort der Systemforschung im Rahmen der Wissenschaften: einschliesslich ihrer Beziehungen zur Organisations-, Automations- u. Unternehmensforschung." *ZfbF* 17 (1965): 337–41.

Krähe, Dr. Walter. "Die Ausbildung der Diplom-Kaufleute in Hochschule und Wirtschaftspraxis." *ZfbF*, NF 4 (1952): 433–47.

Lammers, Cornelis J., and Hickson, David J., eds. *Organizations Alike and Unlike: International and Inter-Institutional Studies in the Sociology of Organizations.* London: Routledge & Kegan Paul, 1979.

Lanthier, Pierre. "Les Dirigeants des grandes entreprises électriques en France, 1893–1973." Typescript, Business History Unit, London School of Economics, n.d.

Larçon, Jean-Paul. H.E.C. Jouy-en-Josas (July 2, 1984). Personal interview.

Lassibille, Gérard; Lévy-Garbona, Louis; Novarro-Gomez, Lucia; and Orivel, François. *De l'Inéfficacité du système français d'enseignement supérieur.* Paris: CNRS, CREDOC, IREDU, 1980.

Lassman, Gert. "Das gelenkte Pflichtpraktikum an der Ruhr-Universität Bochum." *Betriebswirtschaftliche Hochschulausbildung,* by Horst Albach, Eduard Gaugler, and Peter Mertens, 107–20. *ZfB Ergänzungsheft* (Jan. 1982).

Laudit, Michel. "Les mathématiques et l'ordinateur." *Revue de l'enseignement supérieur,* nos. 46–47 (1969): 91–95.

Lawrence, Peter. "Executive Head-Hunting." *New Society* (May 25, 1978): 416–17.

"A National Culture and Business Policy." *Journal of General Management* 8:3 (Spring 1983): 80–85.

Loughborough University. Loughborough (Dec. 7, 1983). Personal interview.

"Personnel Management in West Germany: Portrait of a Function." Unpublished paper, July 1982.

Leblanc, Bruno. E.A.P. Paris (June 26, 1984). Personal interview.

Leclercq, Jean-Michel. *Le Japon et son système éducatif.* Paris: La Documentation française, 1983.

Lederer, Klaus G. "Die Ausbildung der Wirtschaftler aus der Sicht der Bayerischen Motorenwerke AG." *Bildung und Wettbewerbsfähigkeit,* edited by Klaus von Wysocki, 92–94.

Lefour, Alain. "La Maturité émotive clé de la réussite." *Enseignement et gestion,* no. 5 (1972).

Leggatt, Timothy. "The Status Ranking of Industries." *Journal of Management Studies* 17:1 (Feb. 1980): 56–67.

Legge, Karen. Imperial College. London (Dec. 16, 1983). Personal interview.

Legras, Jean. "Institut universitaire de calcul automatique de Nancy." *Revue de l'enseignement supérieur,* no. 2 (1959): 154–57.

Leigh-Pemberton, Robin. "The Blackett Memorial Lecture 1978 – O. R. and the Changing Banking Scene." *Journal of the Operational Research Society* 30:1 (1979): 1–9.

Leitherer, Eugen. "Mitteilung, Erich Schäfers Beitrag zur Absatzlehre – eine Würdigung zum 75. Geburtstag." *ZfbF,* Heft 1, 28 (Jan. 1, 1976): 53–54.

Lenz, Friedrich. "Die Erforschung der öffentlichen Meinung – Aufgaben und Methoden." *ZfbF,* NF 1 (1949), 511–23.

Lescar, Léon. "Formation et perfectionnement des cadres commerciaux." *Hommes et commerce,* 15th year, no. 97 (June–July 1967): 63–81.

"La Révolution de l'éducation permanente." *Hommes et commerce,* no. 122 (Sept. 1971): 16–26.

Lesourne, Jacques. "Le Comportement des entreprises et certains aspects de l'imprévisibilité." *Revue d'économie politique* 64 (1954): 20–51.

"The Place of Operational Research in the Development of Modern Society." *Operational Research Quarterly* 11:4 (Dec. 1960): 185–96.

"A la recherche d'un critère de rentabilité pour les grands investissements." *Cahiers du séminaire d'économétrie* (1957).

Levinson, H. "Management by Whose Objectives?" *Harvard Business Review* 48:4 (1970): 125–34.

Leyland, Norman H. Review of *Business Economics,* by J. Bates and J. R. Parkinson. *The Economic Journal* 74 (1964): 1010.

Lherault, Guy. "L'Institut supérieur des affaires." *Hommes et commerce,* 18th year, no. 110 (Nov.–Dec. 1969): 11–22.

Lichnérowicz, André. "Les Mathématiques et leurs enseignements." *Revue de l'enseignement supérieur,* nos. 46–47 (1969): 6–14.

Limprecht, Joseph A., and Hayes, Robert H. "Germany's World-Class Manufacturers." *Harvard Business Review* (Nov.–Dec. 1982): 137–45.

Linhardt, H. "Die Stellung der Betriebswirtschaftslehre an den deutschen Hochschulen." *Die Wirtschaftsprüfung* 3:8 (Aug. 1950): 337–39.

Liouville, Jacques. "Un Exemple de recherche décentralisée: la RFA." *Revue française de gestion,* no. 35 (Mar.–Apr.–May 1982): 45–54.

Lisowsky, Arthur. "Käuferschichtung als absatzwirtschaftliches Problem." *ZfbF,* NF, 2 (1950): 527–41.

Liston, David. "Management Education: Are Our Priorities Right?" *The Business Graduate,* special issue (1981): 35–37.

Little, I. M. D. Review of *A la Recherche d'une discipline économique,* by M. Allais. *The Economic Journal* 60 (1950): 559.

Livesey, F. Review of *A Behavioral Theory of the Firm: Attempts to Develop a Theory of the Firm Which Is Based on Empirical Studies of Decision-making within the Firm,* by R. M. Cyert and J. G. March. *The Economic Journal* 74 (1964): 200–02.

Lloyd, I. S. "Operational Research – A New Tool for Management." *Journal of Industrial Economics* 1:3 (1953): 175–86.

Loasby, Brian J. "Management Economics and the Theory of the Firm." *The Journal of Industrial Economics* 15:3 (July 1967): 165–76.

Lowe, E. A., and Shaw, R. W. "The Accuracy of Short-Term Business Forecasting: An Analysis of a Firm's Sales Budgeting" *Journal of Industrial Economics* 18:3 (July 1970): 275–89.

Lowe, E. A., and Tinker, A. M. "New Directions for Management Accounting." *OMEGA* 5:2 (1977): 173–83.

Luthringshausen, Gudrun. *Auswirkungen des Studiums auf Berufs- und Weiterstudienmöglichkeiten von Fachhochschulabsolventen in Hessen – beispielhaft untersucht am Absolventenjahrgang Sommer 1976.* Wiesbaden: Kooperationssystem Studienberatung, 1977.

McClelland, W. G. "Mathematics in Management – How It Looks to the Manager." *OMEGA* 3:2 (1975): 147–55.

McDonald, J. J. "Undergraduate Education for Operational Research." *Organizational Research Quarterly* 28:3 (1977): 615–27.

McDougall, R. H. "Review of Management Education in the United Kingdom." A Report prepared for the EFMD, under commission from the EEC, Mar. 1976.

McNulty, Nancy G. "European Management Education Comes of Age." *The Conference Board Record* (Dec. 1975): 38–43.

Mag, Wolfgang. "Hemmnisse und Fortschritte bei der Entwicklung der Personalplanung in der Bundesrepublik Deutschland." *ZfbF* 37 (Jan. 1985): 3–25.

Maillet, Pierre. "Une Etude d'économie synthétique: Le 'modèle' de Léontief." *Revue d'économie politique* 60 (1950): 669–93.

"Une nouvelle technique économique: les programmes linéaires." *Revue d'économie politique* 63 (Jan.–Feb. 1953): 114–23.

Malin, Howard. "Of Kings and Men, Especially O. R. Men: A Methodological Tale." *Journal of the Operational Research Society* 32 (1981): 953–64.

Malinvaud, Edmond. *Méthodes statistiques de l'économétrie.* Paris: Dunod, 1964.

Mallory, Geoffrey; Butler, Richard J; Gray, David; Hickson, David J.; and Wilson, David C. "Implanted Decision-Making: American Owned Firms in Britain." *Journal of Management Studies* 20:2 (Apr. 1983): 191–212.

Malm, F. T. "Britain's Training Act: A Manpower Revolution." *Industrial Relations: A Journal of Economy and Society* 11:2 (May 1972): 245–59.

Mant, Alistair. "An Open-Systems Model of Business School Activity." Final report submitted to the Social Science Research Council, Oct. 1975.

The Rise and Fall of the British Manager. London: Macmillan Press, 1977.

Marchal, Jean. "Les Travaux pratiques des sciences économiques." *Revue de l'enseignement supérieur,* no. 3 (1958): 73–76.

Marois, Bernard, and Mille, Christian. *L'Organisation de planification financière internationale; L'Exemple de grandes entreprises françaises.* Jouy-en-Josas: CESA. Les Cahiers de Recherche, CDR 231/1983.

Marris, Robin L. "The Higher Education Crisis: A Sermon for Conservatives and Socialists." Published by the Suntory Toyota International Centre for Economics and Related Disciplines, LSE, n.d..

Marschak, Thomas. "Capital Budgeting and Pricing in the French Nationalized Industries." *Journal of Business* 33:2 (1960): 133–56.

Marty, Gabriel. "Le Cours magistral." *Revue de l'enseignement supérieur,* no. 3 (1958): 63–66.

Marx, Fritz Mortstein. "Staborganisation im Grossbetrieb: Amerikanische Ausgangspunkte." *ZfbF* 17 (1965): 529–41.

Massé, Pierre. Suggestions préliminaires pour un essai de programmation mathématique. Commissariat générale du plan. 1960, 1–17. Mimeographed.

"Les Choix économiques dans un monde aléatoire et la notion d'espérance marginale." *Econométrica* 17, Supplément (1949).

Massé, Pierre, and Gibrat, R. "Application of Linear Programming to Investments in the Electric Power Industry." *Management Science* 3:2 (1957): 149–66.

Matsuo, K. "Entwicklungstendenzen des Japanischen Rechnungswesens." *ZfbF* 13 (1961): 172–75.

Mattessich, Richard. "Philosophie der Unternehmungsforschung." *ZfbF* 14 (1962): 249–55.

"Unternehmungsforschung." *ZfbF* 13 (1961): 411–23.

Matthews, William E., and Vasireddi, Prasad, eds. *Directory of Researchers in Marketing in Western European Countries.* Berlin: International Institute of Management; Preprint Series of IIM, July 1973.

Maurice, Marc. "For a Study of 'The Societal Effect': Universality and Specificity in Organization Research." In *Organizations Alike and Unlike,* edited by Cornelis J. Lammers and David J. Hickson, 42–60. London: Routledge & Kegan Paul, 1979.

Meffert, Herbert. "Experimente zur Marktforschungsausbildung an der Universität Münster." In *Betriebswirtschaftliche Hochschulausbildung,* by Horst Albach, Eduard Gaugler, and Peter Mertens, 121–35. *ZfB Ergänzungsheft* (Jan. 1982).

"Gedanken zur Arbeitsgemeinschaft Marketing zwischen Studenten und Praktikern." In *Betriebswirtschaftliche Hochschuldidaktik,* 2d ed., edited by Peter Mertens, 84–90. Wiesbaden: Betriebswirtschaftlicher Verlag Dr. Th. Gabler, 1971.

Meissner, Hans Günther. "Sicherung der internationalen Wettbewerbsfähigkeit als Managementfunktion." *ZfbF* 1 (Jan. 1982): 25–33.

Melese, M., and Barache, M. "La Recherche opérationnelle dans la détermination des stocks et des réapprovisonnements de magasin." *Hommes et techniques,* no. 197 (Apr. 1961): 455–58.

Melrose-Woodman, J. "Profile of the British Manager." Management Survey Report No. 38, V.I.M., 1978.

Mertens, Peter. "Absolventenkritik als Hilfe zur Verbesserung der betriebswirtschaftlichen Hochschulausbildung." In *Betriebswirtschaftliche Hoch-*

schulausbildung, by Horst Albach, Eduard Gaugler, and Peter Mertens, 214–18. *ZfB Ergänzungsheft* (Jan. 1982).

"Acht Jahre computerunterstütztes Entscheidungstraining an der Universität Erlangen-Nürnberg." In *Betriebswirtschaftliche Hochschulausbildung*, by Horst Albach, Eduard Gaugler, and Peter Mertens, 52–63. *ZfB Ergänzungsheft* (Jan. 1982).

"Brauchen wir eine EDV-orientierte Betriebswirtschaftslehre? Anmerkungen zu einem Buch von August-Wilhelm Scheer." *ZfbF* 36 (Dec. 1984): 1050–52.

"Der gegenwärtige Stand von Forschung und Lehre in der Betriebswirtschaft." *Bildung und Wettbewerbsfähigkeit*, edited by Klaus von Wysocki, 40–54. Wiesbaden: Gabler, 1981.

Mertens, Peter, ed. *Betriebswirtschaftliche Hochschuldidaktik – Materialien und Untersuchungsergebnisse*. 2d ed. Wiesbaden: Betriebswirtschaftlicher Verlag Dr. Th. Gabler, 1971.

Meuleau, Marc. Banques des Pays-Bas. Paris (Oct. 7, 1986). Personal interview.

Mey, J. L. "Einige Bemerkungen zum Studium der Betriebswirtschaftslehre." *ZfbF* 12 (1960): 458–63.

Miller, Douglas. "Trade Union Workplace Representations in the Federal Republic of Germany: An Analysis of the Postwar Vertrauensleute Policy of the German Metalworkers Union (1952–1977)." *British Journal of Industrial Relations* 16:3 (Nov. 1978): 335–54.

Miller, James. E. F. Hutton and Co. Honolulu, Hawaii (Oct. 12, 1985). Personal interview.

Miret, Pierre. "Plaidoyer pour une formation sociale des cadres." *Revue française de gestion*, no. 6 (Sept.–Oct. 1976): 47–53.

Mitchell, G. H. "Images of Operational Research." *Journal of Operational Research* 31 (1980): 459–66.

Mohr, Otto. "Ziele für die zukünftige Arbeit der Fraunhofer-Gesellschaft." *DUZ* (Sept. 1–2, 1970): 16–18.

Monjaret, Dominique. "Career Patterns of Company Presidents and Control of the Firm in France." In *European Industrial Managers*, edited by J. J. Boddewyn, 101–20. White Plains, N.Y.: International Arts and Sciences Press, 1976.

Moore, Peter G. "British Business School – The Next Decade." *The Business Graduate*, special issue (1979–1980): 29–32.

"Higher Education: The Next Decade." *Journal of Royal Statistical Society*, A (1983), 146, part 3: 213–45.

"Positioning Business Schools in the UK." *Lloyds Bank Review*, no. 100 (Apr. 1986): 36–51.

London Business School. London (June 28, 1983). Personal interview.

Morikawa, Hidemasa. "The Development of Managerial Enterprise in Japan – Prewar and Postwar." Paper presented at the Anglo-Japanese Conference, Business History Unit, London School of Economics, Aug. 20, 1986.

Morlat, Georges. "Sur la consigne d'exploitation optimum des réservoirs saisonniers." *La Houille blanche* (July–Aug. 1951): 497–509.

Morrell, David. "Diversity Par Excellence." *THES*, no. 593 (Mar. 16, 1984): 15.

Morris, John. "Experience or the Newer Management Training Techniques in Britain." Unpublished paper, Manchester Business School, n.d.

Morsel, Henri. "Pour une histoire de la planification française." Paper, Business History Unit, London School of Economics, n.d.

Morton, G. "Notes on Linear Programming." *Economica,* NS, 18:72 (Nov. 1951): 397–411.

Mowery, David C. "Firm Structure, Government Policy, and the Organization of Industrial Research: Great Britain and the United States, 1900–1950." *Business History Review* (Winter 1984): 504–31.

Muth, Dr. Hans. "Produktivere Unternehmerarbeit durch Management Consultants." *Der Volkswirt,* no. 16 (Apr. 19, 1958): 647–59.

Nées, Danielle. "Le Difficile dialogue des chercheurs et des gestionnaires." *Revue française de gestion,* no. 16 (May–June 1978): 13–19.

Neubauer, Georg. "Praxis lernt man in der Praxis." *DUZ* (July 15, 1980): 455–57.

Neumann, Manfred; Böbel, Ingo; and Haid, Alfred. "Profitability, Risk and Market Structure in West German Industries." *Journal of Industrial Economics* 27:3 (Mar. 1979): 227–42.

New, Colin. "Managing Manufacturing Operations.," *Journal of Operational Research* 34:9 (1983): 861–74.

Newbigging, Erick. Central London Polytechnic. London (Dec. 16, 1983). Personal interview.

Nind, Philip. Foundation for Management Education. Management House, London (Dec. 6, 1982). Personal interview.

"British Industry and the Anti-Intellectual Tradition." Speech given to the Royal Society of Arts, Dec. 12, 1984. Typewritten manuscript.

"Management and Learning." Speech presented at the Yorkshire Regional Management Centre, Sheffield, Mar. 29, 1979. Typewritten manuscript.

Nonaka, Ikujiro, and Yonekura, Seiichiro. "Innovation through Group Dynamics—Organizational Learning in JK Activity at Nippon Steel's Kimitasu Works." Discussion Paper no. 124. Institute of Business Research, Hitotsubashi University, Tokyo, Japan, Dec. 1982 (English version, Mar. 1985).

Oehler, Christoph; Birk, Lothar; Blahusch, Friedrich; and Kazemzadeh, Foad. *Organisation und Reform des Studiums – Eine Hochschullehrerbefragung.* Munich: Verlag Dokumentation Saur, KG., 1978.

Olivier, Gilbert. "ESSEC 1970." *Hommes et commerce* (Sept. 1970): 45–47.

Ortsman, Oscar. "Les Nouveaux Critères de gestion des entreprises américaines." *Revue française de gestion,* no. 41 (June–July–Aug. 1983): 6–10.

Ouzilou, William. "Cadres: l'évolution des qualifications professionnelles." *Enseignement et gestion,* NS, no. 24 (Winter 1982–1983): 1–3.

Page, André. "L'I.A.E. de Grenoble." *Hommes et commerce* (Nov.–Dec. 1969): 65–68.

Pascale, Richard Tanner. "Communication and Decision-Making across Cultures: Japanese and American Comparisons." *Administrative Science Quarterly* 23:1 (Mar. 1978): 91–109.

Pascale, Richard Tanner, and Athos, Anthony G. *The Art of Japanese Management.* New York: Warner Books, 1981.

Pavitt, Keith, ed. *Technical Innovation and British Economic Performance.* London: Macmillan Press, 1980.

Peacock, Alan T. "Recent German Contributions to Economics." *Economica* 17:66 (May 1950): 175–87.

Percerou, Roger. "Pour une politique de la formation en gestion." *Enseignement et gestion* (Fall 1982).

"Les I.A.E." *Hommes et commerce* (Nov.–Dec. 1969): 55–59.

Perkin, Harold J. *Les Nouvelles Universités au Royaume-Uni.* Paris: Organization for Economic Cooperation and Development, 1970.

Perridon, Louis. "Kontaktstudium: Das Augsburger Modell." In *Betriebswirtschaftliche Hochschulausbildung*, by Horst Albach, Eduard Gaugler, and Peter Mertens, 146–58. *ZfB Ergänzungsheft* (Jan. 1982).

Perroux, François. "Une Introduction à l'étude de l'économie politique." *Revue d'économie politique* 54 (1940): 216–34.

"Sur la science économique." *Revue de l'enseignement supérieur*, no. 2 (1960): 119–28.

Pfeffer, G.; Kohl, R. H. "Frankreichs Hochschulsystem im Wandel." *DUZ/HD* 8 (1979): 239–41.

Pickering, Prof. U.M.I.S.T. Manchester (Feb. 25, 1983). Personal interview.

Pickman, Stephen. C.N.A.A. Manchester (Feb. 28, 1983). Personal interview.

Piettre, A. "Economie et mathématiques." *Economie et humanisme* 20:131 (1961): 3–16.

Piganiol, Bernard. "Research in U. S. A. Business Schools – An Example for Europe?" Working Paper no. 74–6. E.I.A.S.M., Feb. 1974.

Portwood, Derek, and Fielding, Alan. "Privilege and the Professions." *Sociological Review* 29:4 (1981): 749–71.

Posner, M.V. Reviews of *Economic Planning in France*, by J. Hackett and A. M. Hackett; *Le IVème Plan français*, by F. Perroux; and *La Planification française*, by P. Bauchet. *The Economic Journal* 74 (1964): 429–33.

Prins, D. J.; Wilpert, B.; and Seeringer, W. "Business Education and the EEC, Report on German Fachhochschulen." Berlin: International Institute of Management, Preprint Series, July 1972.

Priouret, M. "La France et le management." *Hommes et commerce* 16 (1968): 101–03.

Puiraveau, René. "La Formation continue à l'école H. E. C.." *Hommes et commerce*, 17th year, no. 105 (1969): 105–11.

Quirici, Daniel. "Le Comportement des firmes françaises implantées aux Etats-Unis." *Revue française de gestion*, no. 5 (May–June–July–Aug. 1976): 92–98.

Ravier, Jean-Pierre. "La grève, maladie britannique: mythe ou réalité?" *Sociologie du travail* 25:1 (1983): 93–107.

Reber, Gerhard. "Entwicklungslinien der Betriebswirtschaftslehre in Nordamerika." *ZfbF* 21 (1969): 689–705.

Rehder, Robert R. "SMR Forum: American Business Education – Is It Too Late to Change?" *Sloan Management Review* (Winter 1982): 63–71.

Reichel, G. "Operations Research im Versicherungswesen." *ZfOR* 25 (1981): B1–B8.

Reuss, Gerhart E., and Riese, Hajo. "Operations Research – Neues Werkzeug der Unternehmensanalyse." *Die Wirtschaftsprüfung* (1960): 556–60.

Ricard, L. "L'Enseignement commercial en France et les écoles supérieures pratiques de commerce et d'industrie." *Mon Bureau* – (Nov. 1910): 273–78.

Richardson, Bradley M., and Ueda, Taizo. *Business and Society in Japan: Fundamentals for Businessmen.* New York: Praeger, 1981.

Rignault, Alain. "Qui sont les consultants?" *Le Management,* no. 11 (Jan. 1971): 92–99.

Rinnooy, Kan; Alexander, H. G.; and Telgen, Jan. "The Complexity of Linear Programming." Working Paper no. 81–6. E.I.A.S.M., Feb. 1981.

Riveline, Claude. "Les activités de réflexion au sein de l'amicale du corps des mines." *Annales des mines* (Jan. 1983): 1–8.

Ecole Supérieure des Mines. Paris (Sept. 28, 1983). Personal interview.

Rojot, Jacques. "L'Enseignement des relations industrielles." *Enseignement et gestion,* NS, no. 24 (Winter 1982–83): 45–49.

Rose, Harold. Review *The Theory of Financial Management,* by E. Solomon. *The Economic Journal* 76 (1966): 380–82.

Rosenhead, Jonathan. "Planning under Uncertainty: 1. The Inflexibility of Methodologies." *Journal of the Operational Research Society* 31 (1980): 209–16.

Roy, René. "Nécrologie, Henry Schultz." *Revue d'économie politique* 54 (1940): 10.

Ruedi, André, and Lawrence, Paul R. "Organizations in Two Cultures." In *Studies in Organizational Design* edited by Jay W. Lorsch and Paul R. Lawrence, 54–83. Homewood, Ill.: Irwin, 1970.

Sadler, Philip. "O. R. and the Transition to a Post-Industrial Society." *Journal of the Operational Research Society* 29:1 (1978): 1–7.

Saias, Maurice. "L'I.A.E. d'Aix-en-Provence." *Hommes et commerce* (Nov.–Dec. 1969): 61–65.

I.A.E. Paris (Aug. 1984). Personal interview.

Saw, Dr. Anthony. C.N.A.A. London (Dec. 10, 1983). Personal Interview.

Schäfer, Erich. "Markt- und Konjunkturerfassung als Funktion der Unternehmung." *ZfbF* 7 (1955): 555–68.

"Von der statischen zur dynamischen Betriebswirtschaftslehre." *ZfbF* 5 (1953): 205–11.

Schaffhausen, J. Becher. "Besprechungsaufsatz. Der Mensch im Betrieb, Zur deutschen Übersetzung der Werke von Gardner-Moore, Whitehead und Roethlisberger." *ZfbF* 10 (1958): 56–58.

Schanz, Günther. "Die Betriebswirtschaftslehre und ihre sozial-wissenschaftlichen Nachbardisziplinen: Das Integrationsproblem." In *Wirtschaftswissenschaftliches Studium,* heft 11 (1978): 526–32, but in *Wissenschaftstheoretische Grundfragen der Wirtschaftswissenschaften,* by Hans Raffée and Bodo Abel, 12–37.

Scherf, Harald. "Erich Schneiders Keynes-Rezeption." In *Erich Schneider, 1900–1970: Gedenkband und Bibliographie,* edited by Gottfried Bombach and Michael Tacke, 59–67. Kiel: Institut für Weltwirtschaft an der Universität, 1980.

Schiefer, Friedrich. "Faktoren der internationalen Wettbewerbsfähigkeit – aufgezeigt am Vergleich USA, Japan, Deutschland." *ZfbF,* heft 1 (Jan. 1982): 34–51.

Schmalenbach-Gesellschaft. "Diskussion – Wirtschaftswissenschaft als Grundlage der Unternehmensführung." *ZfbF* 10 (1959), 145–76.

Schmidt, Fritz, ed. *Die Handelschochschule, Lehrbuch der Wirtschaftwissen-schaften.* Berlin, 1927.

"Die Zukunft der Betriebswirtschaftslehre." In *Zur Entwicklung der Be-triebswirtschaftslehre,* by Robert Stern 147–59. Berlin, 1927.

Schmidt, Reinhard H. "Zur Entwicklung der Finanztheorie." In *Para-digmawechsel in der Betriebswirtschaftslehre?,* edited by Wolf F. Fischer-Winkelmann, 465–500.

Schneider, Erich. *Volkswirtschaft und Betriebswirtschaft.* Tübingen: J. C. B. Mohr, 1964. See especially the following:

"Geldbedarf, Kapitaldeckung und Liquidität in Handels-und Industrie-unternehmung," 360–68. Originally published in *Nationaløkonomisk Tidsskrift* 79 (1941): 183–94.

"Grundlagen der Betriebswirtschaftslehre," 400–14. Originally published in *Weltwirtschaftliches Archiv* 70/1 (1955): 79–93.

"Grundsätzliches zur Planung und Standardkostenrechnung," 311–59. Originally published in *Zeitschrift für handelswissenschaftliche Forsch-ung* 34 (1940): 235–69.

"Die Problematik der Lehre von den festen Kosten," 369–99. Originally published in *Weltwirtschaftliches Archiv* 60 (1944): 300–28.

"Schumpeter – wie ich ihn kannte," 461–67.

"J. A. Schumpeter – der Theoretiker," 468–82.

"Vilfredo Pareto – Der Ökonom im Lichte seiner Briefe an Walras und Pantaleoni," 525–42.

"Der Weg der Betriebswirtschaftslehre in den letzten 25 Jahren," 452–57. Originally published in *Erhvervolkonomisk Tidsskrift* 4 (1961): 229–35.

Schranz, A. "Recent Tendencies in German Business Economics." *The Ac-counting Review* 12 (1937): 278–85.

Schreiber, Hanns E. "Die Ausbildung der Wirtschaftler aus der Sicht der Siemens AG." In *Bildung und Wettbewerbsfähigkeit,* edited by Klaus von Wysocki, 102–04. Wiesbaden: Gabler, 1981.

Schreyögg, Georg. "Contingency and Choice in Organization Theory." *Orga-nization Studies* 1/4 (1980): 305–26.

Schuster, Herr. K.W.U. Erlangen (July 1983). Personal interview.

Sfeir, Mauricio Gonzales. Boston Consulting Group. London (Apr. 13, 1984). Personal interview.

Shinkai, Yoighi. "Business Pricing Policies in Japanese Manufacturing 'Indus-tries.' " *Journal of Industrial Economics* 22:4 (June 1974): 255–64.

Silver, Morris. "Managerial Discretion and Profit Maximizing Behavior: Some Further Comments." *Journal of Industrial Economics* 15:2 (Apr. 1967): 157–62.

Simon, Hermann. "Challenges and New Research Avenues in Marketing." Paper presented at the Annual Meeting of the European Marketing Acad-emy, Amsterdam-Nijenrode, Apr. 26–27, 1984.

"Management Education in Germany." Typewritten manuscript, University of Bielefeld, West Germany, n.d.

"Zum Stand der Marketingwissenschaft in Deutschland: Historische Per-spektiven und methodologische Bewertung." Paper read at Keio Univer-sity, Japan, Nov. 26, 1983.

Personal interview, Bonn (June 14, 1984).

Simon, Jean-Claude. *L'Education et l'informatisation de la société: Les expéri-ences par pays*. Paris: La Documentation française, 1981.

Simpson, M. G. "Those Who Can't?" *Journal of the Operational Research Society* 29:6 (1978): 517B–522B.

Sitruk, Guy. "A Constantly Evolving O. R. Team." *Journal of the Operational Research Society* 34:3 (1983): 183–91.

Smith, Alan. "Diversified Structures and a Structure for Diversity: Some Recent Trends and Developments in Engineering Education Cooperation in the European Community." *European Journal of Engineering Education* 6 (1981): 221–34.

Snaith, John. "Will the Real Management Education Please Stand Up?" Paper read at European Foundation for Management Education, Dublin Meeting, June 6–9, 1982. Typewritten.

Sonnenfeld, Jeffrey A. "Shedding Light on the Hawthorne Studies." *Journal of Occupational Behaviour* 6 (1985): 111–30.

Sorge, Arndt. "The Management Tradition: A Continental View." In *Manu-facturing and Management*, by Michael Fores and Ian Glover, 87–104. London: HMSO, 1978.

Sorge, Arndt, and Warner, Malcolm. "Manpower Training, Manufacturing Organisation and Workplace Relations in Great Britain and West Germany." *British Journal of Industrial Relations* 17:3 (Nov. 1980): 318–33.

Sprague, Linda G., and Sprague, Christopher R. "Management Science?" *Interfaces* 7:1 (Nov. 1976): 57–62.

Stainton, R. S. "Modelling and Reality." *Journal of the Operational Research Society* 30 (1979): 1031–36.

Stansfield, Ronald G. "Harold Larnder: Founder of Operational Research." *Journal of the Operational Research Society* 34 (1983): 1–7.

Stanworth, Philip, and Giddens, Anthony. "An Economic Elite: A Demographic Profile of Company Chairmen." In *Elites and Power*, edited by Philip Stanworth and Anthony Giddens, 81–101. Cambridge University Press, 1974.

"The Modern Corporate Economy: Interlocking Directorships in Britain 1906–1970." *The Sociological Review*, NS, 23:1 (Feb. 1975): 5–28.

Staufenbiel, Joerg E., and Koetz, Axel G. *Die wirtschaftswissenschaftlichen Fakultäten, Studiengänge und Berufsfelder für Wirtschaftswissenschaftler und Wirtschaftsingenieure, in Deutschland, Osterreich, Schweiz*. 2d ed. Cologne: Staufenbiel Verlage, n.d.

"Wie gut sind Deutschlands WiSo-Fakultäten?" *Wirtschaftswoche*, nos. 31–32 (July 1977): 19–20.

Stein, Helmut. "Hochschulreife für Berufstätige." *Der Volkswirt* 13:50 (Dec. 12, 1959), 2637–39.

Steinmann, Horst, and Braun, Wolfram. "Konstruktivismus und die Kritik am Wertfreiheitsprinzip, zum Prinzip der Wertfreiheit in der Betriebswirt-schaftslehre." In *Wissenschaftstheoretische Grundfragen*, edited by Hans Raffée and Bodo Abel, 191–204.

Stoffaës, Christian. "Les Talents industriels des français." *La Documentation française*, nos. 4627–28 (June 30, 1981): 157–74.

Stone, Richard. "Un Siècle d'économétrie." Published in French in "Problèmes Economiques, sélection de textes français et étrangers," *Documentation française*, no. 1.72 (July 15, 1981): 26–32.

Struven, Herr. Boston Consulting Group. Munich (Feb. 10, 1983). Personal interview.

Sturmey, S. G. "The Management of Research and Development." *Journal of Industrial Economics* 14:2 (Apr. 1966): 91–100.

Susman, Gerald I., and Evered, Roger D. "An Assessment of the Scientific Merits of Action Research." *Administrative Science Quarterly* 23:4 (Dec. 1978): 582–603.

Tabatoni, Pierre. "Une Expérience de promotion sociale: le Centre interentreprises de formation." *Revue de l'enseignment supérieur*, no. 4 (1961): 53–60.

"Les Instituts d'administration des entreprises." *Revue de l'enseignement supérieur*, no. 4 (1956): 85–90.

Tarondeau, Jean-Claude. "Où en est l'industrie française de la machine-outil?" *Revue française de gestion*, no. 32 (Sept.–Oct. 1981): 59–90.

"A propos de la crise technologique aux Etats-Unis." *Revue française de gestion*. no. 24 (Jan.–Feb. 1980): 121–27.

"La Question de la gestion technologique dans la crise de la technologie aux Etats-Unis." *Problèmes économiques*, no. 1 (May 14, 1980): 673.

Taylor, H. J. B. *The Administrative Staff Colleges at Home and Overseas.* Henley on Thames: The Administrative Staff College, 1968.

Thépot, Jacques. University of Strasbourg. Paris (Sept. 26, 1983). Personal interview.

Thirlby, G. F. "The Economist's Description of Business Behaviour." *Economica* 19:74 (May 1952): 148–67.

Thomas, R. Bath University. Bath (Feb. 16, 1983). Personal interview.

Thonet, P. J., and Poensgen, O. H. "Managerial Control and Economics of Performance in Western Germany." *Journal of Industrial Economics* 28:1 (Sept. 1979): 23–37.

Throughton, F. "The Teaching concerning Costs of Production in Introductory Economics." *Journal of Industrial Economics* 11 (1962–63): 96–115.

Timmermann, Manfred. "Erich Schneiders Beitrag zur Betriebswirtschaftslehre." In *Erich Schneider, 1900–1970: Gedenkband und Bibliographie,* edited by Gottfried Bombach and Michael Tacke, 63–90. Kiel: Institut für Weltwirtschaft an der Universität, 1980.

Tisdall, Patricia. *Agents of Change: The Development and Practice of Management Consultancy.* London: Heinemann, 1982.

Tobin, N. R.; Rapley, K.; and Teather, W. "The Changing Role of O. R." *Journal of the Operational Research Society* 31:4 (1980): 279–88.

Tocher, K. D. "The Dilemmas of Operational Research." *Operational Research Quarterly* 23:2 (June 1972): 105–15.

Tscheulin, D. "Leader Behavior Measurement in German Industry." *Journal of Applied Psychology* 57:1 (1973): 28–31.

Turner, I. R. "O. R. in the National Coal Board." *Journal of the Operational Research Society* 32 (1981): 747–53.

Vassen, Paul J. "Aus- und Weiterbildung von Führungskräften in Deutschland." Report no. 5, Wuppertaler Kreis, 1976.

Vigier, Jean. "L'Ecole supérieure de commerce de Paris." *Hommes et commerce,* 19th year, no. 114 (Sept. 1970): 33–44.

Vindry d'Hinvery, E. "Le Haut Enseignement commercial: dans l'évolution de l'enseignement supérieur français." In *Le Défi de la Business School,* 123–51. Special issue of *Hommes et Commerce,* Paris, 1968.

Vogt, Winfried. "Erich Schneider und die Wirtschaftstheorie.' In *Erich Schneider, 1900–1970: Gedenkband und Bibliographie,* edited by Gottfried Bombach and Michael Tacke, 13–48. Kiel: Institut für Weltwirtschaft an der Universität, 1980.

Von Ow, Barbara. "Germans Flock to Polys." *THES* (Apr. 6, 1984): 8.

Wächter, Hartmut. University of Trier. Trier (June 14, 1984). Personal interview.

Wagner, Gerd Rainer. *Lieferzeitpolitik.* Wiesbaden: Gabler, 1975.
  Universität Bochum. Bochum (May 25, 1983). Personal interview.

Wakeford, John, and Wakeford, Frances. "Universities and the Study of Elites." In *Elites and Power,* edited by Philip Stanworth and Anthony Giddens, 185–97. Cambridge University Press, 1974.

Walger, Gerd. *Das Ziel betriebswirtschaftlicher Theorie: Eine konkrete Wiederholung der Gutenbergschen Frage nach den prinzipiellen Möglichkeiten einer betriebswirtschaftlichen Theorie.* Spardorf: Verlag René F. Wilfer, 1982.

Walter, Hans. "Elastiche Absatz- und Produktionsplanung." *Der Volkswirt,* no. 38 (Sept. 1959): 2095.

Ward, R. A. "More Implementation through an OR/Behavioural Science Partnership and Management Training." *Operational Research Quarterly* 25:2 (June 1974): 209–18.

Warnecke, H.-J.; Bullinger, H.-J.; and Hichert, R. *Wirtschaftlichkeitsrechnung für Ingenieure.* Munich and Vienna: Carl Hanser Verlag, 1980.
  Fraunhofer Institut. Struttgart (Oct. 13, 1983). Personal interview.

Weir, David T. H. "Making Sure the Marriage Works." *THES* (Apr. 13, 1984): i.
  "Management Training and Education." In *The British Malaise,* edited by Michael Stephens, 89–106. Falmer Press, 1952.
  University of Glasgow Management School. Glasgow (Feb. 28, 1982). Personal interview.

Wheatcroft, Milfred. *The Revolution in British Management.* London: Pittman Publishers, 1970.

White, Phillip D. "Attitudes of U.S. Purchasing Managers toward Industrial Products Manufactured in Selected Western European Nations." *Journal of International Business Studies* (Spring/Summer 1979): 81–90.

Whitley, Richard D. "The Background and Development of a Business Elite." Working Paper, Research Report Series, Manchester Business School, Centre for Business Research, Mar. 1979.
  "Commonalities and Connections among Directors of Large Financial Institutions." *The Sociological Review,* NS, 21:4 (Nov. 1973): 613–32.
  "The Impact of Changing Industrial Structures on Business Elites, Managerial Careers, and the Roles of Business Schools." *International Studies of Management and Organizations* 10:1–2 (Spring/Summer 1980): 110–36.

Whittington, Geoffrey. "The Profitability and Size of United Kingdom Companies, 1960–74." *Journal of Industrial Economics* 28:4 (June 1980): 335–52.

Wickham, S. "Fonction et avenir de l'économiste d'entreprise." In *Revue d'économie politique* (1965), 258–69.

Wiles, P. "Empirical Research and the Marginal Analysis." *The Economic Journal* 60 (1950): 515–30.

Wilkins, Alan L., and Ouchi, William G. "Efficient Cultures: Exploring the Relationship between Culture and Organizational Performance." *Administrative Science Quarterly* 28 (1982): 268–81.

Willaime, Pierre. "Où-est-ce que la Harvard Business School?" In *Le Défi de la Business School,* by 97–119. Special issue of *Hommes et commerce,* Paris, 1968.

Williams, B. R. "Economics in Unwonted Places." *The Economic Journal* 75 (1965): 20–30.

Williamson, Oliver E. "Emergence of the Visible Hand: Implications for Industrial Organization." In *Managerial Hierarchies: Comparative Perspectives on the Rise of the Modern Industrial Enterprise,* by Alfred D. Chandler, Jr., and Herman Daems, 182–202. Cambridge, Mass.: Harvard University Press, 1980.

Wilpert, Bernhard. *Führung in deutschen Unternehmen.* Berlin: Walter de Gruyter, 1977.

Wilson, T. Review of *Prices and Distribution in Selected British Industries,* by L. Rosta. *The Economic Journal* 61 (1951): 377.

Wilson, Tom. "P.W.S. Andrews, an Appreciation." *Journal of Industrial Economics* 20:1 (Nov. 1971): 3–13.

Wippermann, Rolf. Wuppertal Kreis. Cologne (July 18, 1984). Personal interview.

Wirtschaftsvereinigung – Eisen-und Stahlindustrie. *Trainee-Programm.* Düsseldorf, West Germany. Brochure, n.d.

Wirtz, Carl. "Unternehmensführung und Unternehmensberatung." *ZfbF* 13 (1961): 553–62.

Wiseman, Garth. "Which Way B. G. A.?" *The Business Graduate,* special issue (1980): 47–49.

Wittmann, Waldemar. "Betriebswirtschaftslehre und Operations Research." *ZfbF* 10 (1958): 285–96.

Wood, Stephen. "A Reappraisal of the Contingency Approach to Organization." *Journal of Management Studies* (Oct. 1979): 334–54.

Wood, Stephen, and Kelly, John. "Towards a Critical Management Science." *Journal of Management Studies* 15:1 (Feb. 1978): 1–24.

Woolsey, Gene. "Reflections on the Past of Scientific Management and the Future of Management Science." *Interfaces* 6:3 (May 1976): 1–4.

Wysocki, Klaus von, ed. *Bildung und Wettbewerbsfähigkeit.* Sonderheft of *ZfbF.* Wiesbaden: Gabler, 1981.

Xardel, Dominique. E.S.S.E.C. Cergy Pontoise (June 25, 1984). Personal interview.

Yamashita, Katsuswi. "Die betriebswirtschaftliche Forschung an den japanischen Universitäten." *ZfbF* 5 (1953): 42–47.

Yamazaki, Hiroaki. "Development of Large Enterprises in Japan – An Analysis of Top Fifty Enterprises in the Profit Ranking Table (1929–1984)." A paper given at the Anglo-Japanese Conference, Business History Unit, London School of Economics, Aug. 20, 1986.

Zeidler, Klaus. *Anforderungen an kaufmännische Führungskräfte: Ergebnis einer Rollenanalyse.* Frankfurt: Akademische Verlagsgesellschaft Frankfurt, 1972.

Zimmermann, H. J. "Trends and New Approaches in European Operational

Research." *Journal of the Operational Research Society* 33 (1982): 597–603.

Zisswiller, R. "Finance Courses at the Graduate Level in Different European Institutions." E.I.A.S.M., no number, n.d.

Zur-Muehlen, Max von. *Business Education and Faculty at Canadian Universities*. Ottawa: Information Canada, 1971

Zysman, John. *Political Strategies for Industrial Order: State, Market, and Industry in France*. Berkeley and Los Angeles: University of California Press, 1977.

Periodicals

Academy of Management Journal
Academy of Management Review
Administrative Science Quarterly
The American Economic Review
Annales de sciences économiques appliquées
Annales des mines
Der Arbeitgeber
Die Betriebswirtschaft
BFuP = Betriebswirtschaftliche Forschung und Praxis
British Journal of Industrial Relations
The British Journal of Sociology
Bulletin des Ponts et Chaussées et des Mines
The Business Graduate
Business History Review
Cahiers, CEFI Technologie et formation des ingénieurs
DUZ = Deutsche-Universitäts-Zeitung
Econométrica
Economica
The Economic Journal – The Journal of the Royal Economic Society
Economie et humanisme
The Economist
Educational Studies in Mathematics
Energy World
L'Enseignement du contrôle de gestion
Enseignement et gestion
European Business
European Journal of Engineering Education
FAZ = Frankfurter-Allgemeine-Zeitung
Harvard Business Review
Herald Tribune
Hommes et commerce
Hommes et techniques
Human Relations
Industrial Relations: A Journal of Economy and Society
Information, Bildung, Wissenschaft
Interfaces
Journal of Applied Psychology
The Journal of Business

Journal of Cross-Cultural Psychology
Journal of Economic Literature
Journal of General Management
The Journal of Industrial Economics
Journal of International Business Studies
Journal of Management Studies
Journal of Occupational Behavior
JORS = Journal of the Operational Research Society
Journal of the Royal Statistical Society
Der Leitende Angestellte
Lloyds Bank Review
Le Management
Management Today
Metroéconomica
Le Monde
Le Monde de l'éducation
New Society
Nordisk Tidsskrift for Økonomie
Nouvelle Revue de l'économie contemporaine
OMEGA
ORQ = Operational Research Quarterly
Organizational Behavior and Human Performance
Organization Studies
Oxford Economic Papers NS
Quarterly Journal of Economics
Revue d'économie contemporaine
Revue d'économie politique
Revue de l'enseignement supérieur
Revue de statistique appliquée
Revue française de gestion
Revue française de l'énergie
Revue française de recherche opérationnelle
Revue française de sociologie
Revue génerale de l'électricité
Revue génerale des chemins de fer
Sloan Management Review
Social Research
Social Science Information
The Sociological Review
Sociologie du travail
Sociology
The Sunday Times
Technikgeschichte
THES = Times Higher Educational Supplement
Der Volkswirt. Wirtschafts-und Finanz-Zeitung
Die Welt
Die Wirtschaftsprüfung
Wirtschaftswoche
ZfB = Zeitschrift für Betriebswirtschaft
ZfbF = Zeitschrift für betriebswirtschaftliche Forschung

ZfhF = Zeitschrift für handelswissenschaftliche Forschung
ZfOR = Zeitschrift für Operations Research
ZVDDI = Zeitschrift des Verbandes deutscher Diplom-Ingenieure
ZVDDK = Zeitschrift des Verbandes deutscher Diplom-Kaufleute
ZVDI = Zeitschrift des Verbandes deutscher Ingenieure

Index